Sheila Davis

THE CRAFT OF LYRIC WRITING

Writer's Digest Books

Cincinnati, Ohio

To my husband,
whose literary standards have shaped my own.

Second printing October 1985

Library of Congress Cataloging in Publication Data
Davis, Sheila
     The craft of lyric writing.

     Bibliography: p.
     Includes index.
     1. Music, Popular (Songs, etc.)—Writing and publishing.
I. Title.
MT67.D25   1984   784.5'0028   84-22080
ISBN 0-89879-149-9

Book design by Joan Ann Jacobus.

*"True ease in writing comes from art, not chance,
as those move easiest who have learned to dance."*
Alexander Pope

Contents

Preface

In the mid-seventies, when The Songwriters Guild decided to offer its first songwriting "pop shops" in New York, I chaired the panel of professionals who evaluated the demonstration (demo) tapes submitted by aspiring songwriters. The screening sessions were eye-opening—or, more accurately, ear-opening—experiences. As we listened to each song, evaluating its musical structure, subject matter, and lyric development, one fact became dramatically clear to me: the majority of applicants had only a slight understanding of the requirements of a professional lyric. Those sessions left me wondering what could be done to raise the writing level of the apprentice to that of the professional.

Saul Bellow once defined a writer as "a reader moved to emulation." To paraphrase Bellow, a songwriter is a song lover moved to emulation. The pop "chart" hits of my youth were written by the likes of Rodgers and Hart, George and Ira Gershwin, Johnny Mercer, Dorothy Fields, and Cole Porter. They were my creative mentors; theirs were the musical structures, the whistleable tunes, the perfectly rhymed lyrics which I unconsciously emulated.

The creative efforts of many aspiring lyricists and composers today have been shaped for the most part by music more notable for its incessant beat than for its memorable melodies and by lyrics that are often unclear—when audible. Small wonder, then, that the songs of the nonprofessional often reflect an unfamiliarity with basic musical forms and writing principles which songwriters of my generation assimilated from exposure to what is generally acknowledged to be the best of American popular music—the classics.

In 1979, as special projects director for the Guild, I created a new songwriting service: The Critique Session. The objective was to give members an opportunity to uncover, through professional analysis, any flaw in a song's construction before it became finalized in a costly demo. In preparing to conduct the sessions, I wrote a two-page *Lyric Writing Guideline* highlighting the critical points where most new writers tend to go wrong. Those early Feedback Sessions, as they were first called, generated strong interest in a lyric-writing course. After a good deal of thought, I worked out a ten-week syllabus and in January 1980 began to teach the craft of lyric writing.

The emphasis was on structure. Both perennial favorites (what we call "standards") and current hits were played and analyzed in detail, and weekly writing assignments were given. Student lyrics underwent close scrutiny for universality, clarity, development of theme, singability, and viability in the contemporary marketplace. At the end of that first course, class members, excited by the discovery of writing *principles* and eager to know more, wanted to continue. Thus, Beyond the Basics was created—an ongoing "advanced" class where we all continue to explore the fine points of lyric writing.

Since that first course, I have critiqued considerably more than five thousand lyrics written by hundreds of students. In the process of defining principles and codifying theory, I have learned more about the craft of lyric writing than I ever dreamed there was to know. Enough to fill a book.

Acknowledgments

Teaching, I have happily discovered firsthand, is a great learning experience. It has been neither through my personal songwriting successes (and failures) nor through the study of the best-crafted songs that I have learned most about what makes a song work or not work. Rather it has been through my efforts to help focus the writing of neophytes.

Without my students, there would be no *Craft of Lyric Writing*. Their generosity in permitting me to expose to the world their flawed early efforts helped immeasurably in presenting the theory of lyric writing offered in this book. I am very grateful to them all.

I especially want to thank those who kindly lent me their books, records, and cassettes for study, or volunteered to do independent research: Charles Cook, Eda Galeno, Eben Keyes, Marc Miller, Jim Morgan, Kirk Olsen, Larry Paulette, June Rachelson-Ospa, Carolyn Sloan, John Stanley, Jim Stingley, Joe Weinman, and Barry Wittenstein. A special word of appreciation to Dorothy Berman, whose request for a class on the theory of humor was the inspiration for the chapter, "From Pun to Funny."

A bow also to Frankie MacCormick, a walking encyclopedia of songwriting esoterica; the efficient staffs of the Index Departments of both ASCAP and BMI, who supplied copyright facts; NARAS for historical data; and the Songwriters Guild for making available their Ask-a-Pro cassette library.

I am indebted to all the songwriting professionals who gave so generously of their time in personal, phone, or mail interviews, candidly responding to my questions about their creative process: John Blackburn, Dewayne Blackwell, Irving Caesar, Steve Dorff, John Hartford, Burton Lane, Fran Landesman, Barry Mann, Amanda McBroom, Ewan MacColl, Trevor Nunn, Marty Panzer, Mitchell Parish, Carole Bayer Sager, Cynthia Weil, and Billy Edd Wheeler. A special bow to Michael Feinstein, who acted as my surrogate in an "interview" with Ira Gershwin.

A big bouquet to those music publishers who granted permission to reprint, in their entirety, more than two dozen lyrics of our finest wordsmiths, past and present. Finally, my deep appreciation to all editorial guiding hands: Judson Jerome for his wise counsel in things poetic; Dan Ricigliano, who lent his expertise in musical matters; editor Nancy Dibble for her invaluable suggestions; and editor-in-chief Carol Cartaino, whose initial interest and sustained enthusiasm supported the project every step of the way.

To all, my gratitude for helping make *The Craft of Lyric Writing* a reality.

Sheila Davis
New York, October 1984

Introduction

I've heard it said that lyric writing cannot be taught. I have discovered otherwise. More accurately, it is talent that cannot be taught. And insight that cannot be taught. And emotional honesty. But the craft and technique of lyric writing assuredly can be taught.

Sustained success in any form of creative writing—whether fiction, playwriting, screenwriting, or lyric writing—depends upon an understanding of specific principles and theories that are teachable—and learnable. A gifted writer, fortified with a foundation of the craft and armed with a commitment to excellence, can then exploit that talent to its utmost.

The art of shaping words *for* music, or *to* music, cuts across many other disciplines. The best lyricists, whether they're aware of it or not, are using elements of phonetics, linguistics, grammar, semantics, metrics, rhyme, rhythm, poetics, phonology, communications, sociology—and even the psychology of verbal behavior. A synthesis of theories from these fields forms the lyric writing principles outlined in this book.

The sole concern in the coming chapters will be learning to write well. So instead of guidelines on "genre" writing—that is, country, R&B, rock, or gospel—the emphasis will be on songwriting techniques that apply to whatever genre you choose.

You'll find no formula for writing a hit song because there is no formula—any more than there is one for writing a hit play or a hit novel. Let's make an important distinction: a number-one record is not necessarily a number-one *song;* sales figures are unreliable barometers of quality. The objective here is to point the way to writing songs that can stand on their own—independent of synthesizer wizardry or superstar charisma. The assumption is that a well-written song not only has a good chance of becoming a hit, but also of becoming a standard.

Helpful hints on how to make demos and meet publishers or advice on how to get your act together will be left to those books (listed in the appendix) that deal with the marketing aspects of songwriting.

The focus of *The Craft of Lyric Writing* is on pop, film, and theater because these are the fields that attract most aspiring songwriters. But there are many other alleys off Tin Pan where gifted wordsmiths have created successful careers—sometimes without ever having a single recording, much less a hit: radio and TV commercial jingles, industrial shows, the children's field, opera librettos, special material for revues and cabaret acts, regional theater, sacred choral music, and the vast educational market. Detailed discussion of these specialties is beyond the scope of this book, but keep in mind that they exist; and rest assured that for whatever purpose you want to write words to be sung—whether it be to motivate a General Motors salesman or teach a three-year-old the alphabet—the same principles apply.

I have watched new writers start at square one, slowly develop an understanding of lyric-writing theory, and, with a relentless practice of its techniques, make the leap from amateur to professional. I am confident that, given talent, tenacity, and sustained self-belief, you can do the same.

"*Lyric writing is like talking to the world.*"
Carolyn Leigh

part one

UNDERSTANDING SOME BASICS BEFORE YOU BEGIN

chapter 1

Striking the Common Chord

"A good song embodies the feelings of the [people], and a songwriter is not much more than a mirror which reflects those feelings. If I can manage to put into words and music the feeling of the kid from Podunk and the one from the Bowery . . . then I'll have something."
Irving Berlin

Popular songs wield a lot of power. They can make us laugh, get us to dance, and move us to tears. Songs can inspire us to pick ourselves up when we're down and to reach for the impossible dream. They tell us when times are a-changin', mirror our sexual mores, and reveal our values.

Songs speak for us.

Our most enduring songs—those that have spoken for millions through the decades—are more than mere background music. They are significant threads in the tapestry of our lives—the words we sang in school assembly with linked hands, "No Man Is an Island," and whispered at the prom, "Save the Last Dance for Me"; songs that celebrated our vows, "We've Only Just Begun," and even eulogized our heroes, "Abraham, Martin, and John."

Every truly successful song expresses a universally understood meaning. We can all relate to the blues of "Rainy Days and Mondays" or the elation of "I've Got the World on a String." We have all felt the agitation of "Goin' Out of My Head" or shrugged philosophically "Que Será, Será—whatever will be, will be."

What exactly is "universal"? Webster's definition puts it neatly for the lyricist: It is a meaning shared by, or comprehended by all.

Songs embody experiences common to everyone: the adventure of first love, the frustration of misunderstanding, the anguish of jealousy, the wistfulness of goodbye. A singer does not offer a sermon we must heed, or a code we must decipher, but rather a universal truth we already know: "Harper Valley P.T.A." dramatizes the maxim "people in glass houses shouldn't throw stones"; "She's Not Really Cheatin', (She's Just Gettin' Even)" illustrates what's sauce for the goose is sauce for the gander; the materialist values of "Mr. Businessman" remind us that it is easier for a camel to go through the eye of a needle than for a rich man to enter the kingdom of heaven. Such songs vivify, and thereby reaffirm, the fundamental tenets of our common experience.

We Identify with the Singer

Lyrics that resonate with universally felt emotions foster strong identification between the performer and the audience. A song is successful when an audience responds with a recognition that says: "Me, too . . . I've felt that . . . I've seen what you've seen . . . I know what you mean." That is what our applause says. The performer is singing not so much *to* us as *for* us.

The *New York Times* critic Robert Palmer underscored that premise in his review of a Tom Petty concert as he examined the reason for the audience's enthusiastic reception: "*. . . [Petty] has a knack for writing songs that express, in a straight-forward manner, his listeners' most basic attitudes*—dissatisfaction with job and hometown, a deep-seated need to believe that love really can conquer all." [italics mine.] When we sing along, fusing ourselves with the singer, it is because the lyric reflects something fundamental we think, or feel, or believe. That is what motivates us to buy the record or sheet music: we want to play the song over and over again—to make it part of our lives. Often, we memorize the words. And when a song title or lyric line fits the situation, it slips quite naturally into our conversation: "Laughing on the Outside (Crying On the Inside)" . . . "It Ain't Necessarily So" . . . "California, Here I Come."

A Psychologist Theorizes

Songs can put us in touch with our feelings. Have you ever found a particular song unaccountably spinning round in your brain? Psychologist Theodor Reik in *Haunting Melody* advanced the theory that when a tune comes into our minds for no apparent reason, it is because the words to that musical phrase express what we are thinking or feeling at that moment. For example, a woman unnerved by a chance encounter with a former lover realizes—after they've said goodbye—that she's mentally humming "Just When I Thought I Was Over You." Seeing him unexpectedly triggered a wave of emotion; she wasn't as "over him" as she believed. That unconscious thought connected itself to a familiar melody—one whose lyric expressed her emotion.

The Singer Is the Song

Before a song can find an audience, it must first find a singer who relates to the lyric's point of view.

On one of her Tonight Show appearances, Diana Ross discussed with Johnny Carson how she went about picking her material. The superstar said that the words of her songs tended to reflect her state of mind. She referred in particular to two of her major chart successes, "Upside Down" and "It's My Turn." The former was selected at a time of emotional crossroads, and the lyric echoed the singer's own inner turbulence. "It's My Turn" was recorded as she was making big changes in her career and putting her talent on the line as a film producer. Diana Ross affirmed my theory that a song must speak for a singer before it can speak for us.

In a *New York Times* interview discussing the selection of standards for her album *What's New?* Linda Ronstadt reechoed the concept that the singer, in effect, becomes the song: "All the tunes I choose have to be stories about things that have happened to me or to people around me." The classics Ronstadt chose for *What's New?* and its follow-up album *Lush Life* reflect the most basic human emotions: each lyric embodies some aspect of love—its lack ("Someone to Watch Over Me"); its expectation ("When I Fall in Love"); its joy ("I've Got a Crush on You"); its frustration ("I Don't Stand a Ghost of a Chance"); its cruelty ("Mean to Me"); its demise ("When Your Lover Has Gone"); and its eternal attraction ("Falling in Love Again"). These lyrics, all written decades ago, still speak for us today.

Singers are constantly on the search for songs that reflect common denominator emotions—those that they have personally felt, and which they believe will create intense audience identification. Kenny Rogers put it this way: "I look for lyrics that every woman wants to hear and every man would like to say . . . giving people the words that they can't find to describe their feelings." Kenny Rogers's description of the kind of lyric he seeks sounds like a formula for writing a standard.

What Makes A Standard A Standard?

A standard is a song that maintains its popularity years after its initial success because the lyric's sentiment exerts a timeless appeal.

In a survey "based on performances, sheet music and record sales" *Variety,* the entertainment trade paper, once chose "The Golden 100" most popular songs of all time. An analysis of the themes of those 100 titles showed that about 85% were love songs (as you might have guessed)—positive ones such as "I'm In the Mood for Love," "You Made Me Love You," "All the Things You Are"; and sad ones like "Stormy Weather," "All Of Me," and "I'll Be Seeing You"; the remainder could be classified as seasonal, "White Christmas," "Easter Parade"; patriotic, "God Bless America"; or inspirational, "You'll Never Walk Alone." Those are the biggies, the blockbuster golden oldies—many of which are still generating new recordings after fifty years.

It may seem too obvious to state, but each of these songs became a standard because its lyric reflects a universal emotion: it spoke for us.

WRAPUP

The song-selecting philosophy of artists like Diana Ross, Linda Ronstadt, and Kenny Rogers can serve as an important guideline for all aspiring songwriters if they remember the viewpoint of these superstars: a desire to sing about something they have either personally experienced or which they believe their audience will want to hear.

The relevance to every lyricist of the singer-song fusion cannot be overstressed. It is the very heart of successful songwriting. First, strike a common chord.

chapter 2

A Lyric Is Not a Poem

"Since most of [my] lyrics . . . were arrived at by fitting words mosaically to music already composed, any resemblance to actual poetry, living or dead, is highly improbable." Ira Gershwin

Professional songwriters refer to the words of a song as the "lyric," not as the "poem." Nonprofessionals often use the words *poem* and *lyric* interchangeably as if they were synonyms. Because a poem and a lyric share the features of words, and meter, and rhyme, the two are sometimes confused—by untrained ears.

At the first session of each of my Basics Courses, I always ask the group: How many of you write poetry? Consistently about one third of the students raise tentative hands. But before I even ask, I know the answer, because I've read over the "lyrics" submitted by each applicant: there is always a poem or two masquerading as a lyric.

Anyone with aspirations to be a *pop* songwriter needs to understand that a lyric is not a poem, and why. I stress *pop* song because there is a separate genre which is an exception: the art song. Typically, an art song *is* a poem set to music, having subtle and interdependent vocal and piano parts. It is not created for a mass audience; it is intended to be sung primarily in recital. Such classical composers as Schumann, Mahler, and Elgar have repeatedly turned to poetry for their "texts." Poems have also been the inspiration for vocal works with orchestral accompaniment; for example, "Sabbath Morning at Sea" by Elizabeth Barrett Browning is part of Elgar's renowned song cycle, "Five Sea Pieces," recorded by soprano Janet Baker. The poems of Shakespeare, Goethe, and Baudelaire, as well as those of contemporary poets, continue to be set to music. Recently classical composer Ned Rorem turned to the work of American poet Robert Hillyer for his text.

Function and Form

Let's examine the ways in which a lyric and a poem differ. For one thing, a completed poem is self-sufficient; it is ready for its audience. The poet's sole goal now is getting the work into print. Because a poem is designed to be *read*, its length can vary from one short stanza to several pages. It can be complex in its language, laced with foreign words and classical allusions, even ambiguous in its meaning. Readers have infinite time to stop, reread, and mull over.

A finished lyric, however, is an unfinished product; it is half a potential song. Let's assume the writer started with a strong idea which has been well crafted into a workable song form. The lyric still has three more goals to achieve: It has to please a composer who will want to write a melody for it; it has to appeal to a professional singer who will want to perform it; and it has to entertain an audience who will enjoy listening all the way through.

Above all, its meaning should be instantly clear. Unlike a poem which exists on paper, a song exists in time, as the motor of its melody propels the words forward. The listener, unlike the reader, gets no footnotes and must understand the lyric as it's being performed. One confusing line or inaudible word will derail the listener's attention. Unlike a poem, whose language can be as abstract as a cubist painting, a lyric should be as direct as a highway sign. Most important, a lyric is designed to be sung. Its writer, therefore, must be instinctively musical and must choose words that roll off the tongue and soar on high notes. Every word should sing.

Content and Style

Lyricists and poets mine the same quarry of age-old human emotions. There are, after all, no new emotions, only fresh ways of treating them. Poems written by Oliver Wendell Holmes in the 1880s reflect the same romantic themes as the lyrics written by Rupert Holmes in the 1980s—although they, of course, differ in style. In the poem "Voiceless," the poet Holmes laments the unspeakable sadness of the unexpressed emotion: "Alas for those that never sing/But die with all their music in them." Lovely—but not a lyric. In Rupert Holmes's words to "Speechless," one inarticulate lover complains:

I can sing your song
I can sigh in the night
This is true—
But, oh, pretty darlin'
I'm SPEECHLESS at the sight of you

There's a stylistic contrast! The poet's treatment of the subject is abstract and philosophical. The lyricist makes it personal and conversational—two qualities that are essential in contemporary songs.

Paul Simon turned a classic poem into a pop song, and we can see the differences in detail. The poet Edwin Arlington Robinson (1869-1935) told the ironic tale of Richard Cory, a wealthy aristocrat. In 1966 singer/songwriter Paul Simon found the poem contemporary enough to adapt. Read the original and then the lyric, and see if you can pinpoint the changes in form and style made by Simon.

RICHARD CORY
Edwin Arlington Robinson

Whenever Richard Cory went down town,
We people on the pavement looked at him:
He was a gentleman from sole to crown,
Clean favored, and imperially slim.

And he was always quietly arrayed,
And he was always human when he talked;
But still he fluttered pulses when he said,
"Good morning," and he glittered when he walked.

And he was rich—yes, richer than a king—
And admirably schooled in every grace;
In fine, we thought that he was everything
To make us wish that we were in his place.

So on we worked, and waited for the light,
And went without the meat, and cursed the bread;
And Richard Cory, one calm summer night,
Went home and put a bullet through his head.

RICHARD CORY
Paul Simon

They say that RICHARD CORY owns one half of this
   whole town
With political connections to spread his wealth
   around,
Born into society a banker's only child
He had ev'rything a man could want: Power, grace,
   and style.

But I work in his factory and I curse the life I'm livin'
And I curse my poverty—and I wish that I could be,
Oh, I wish that I could be—
Oh, I wish that I could be RICHARD CORY.

The papers print his picture almost ev'rywhere he
   goes
RICHARD CORY at the op'ra—RICHARD CORY
   at a show
And the rumor of his parties and the orgies on his
   yacht!
Oh, he surely must be happy with ev'rything he's got.

But I work in his factory and I curse the life I'm livin'
And I curse my poverty—and I wish that I could be,
Oh, I wish that I could be—
Oh, I wish that I could be RICHARD CORY.

He freely gave to charity, he had the common touch
And they were grateful for his patronage and they
    thanked him very much
So my mind was filled with wonder when the evening
    headlines read
"RICHARD CORY went home last night and put a
    bullet through his head."

The ironic theme is as timeless as it is universal. Can you think of an axiom that "Richard Cory" illustrates? Actually, there are at least three: "Money doesn't buy happiness"; "You can't tell a book by its cover"; and "The other man's grass is always greener."

Changing the Structure

Let's see what Simon did. He took four stanzas of iambic pentameter (the intricacies of meter will be covered in Chapters 18 and 19) and reshaped them into a verse/chorus pop structure. He divided the story into three verses that unfold the plot in stages, and he followed the first two with a chorus that summarizes the singer's feelings. With his recurring chorus, Simon met the need of the listener to hear the familiar—something most poems don't offer.

The first verse provides four important facts: *who* (Richard Cory), *what* (is rich), *when* (now), and *where* (this town). The second verse supplies more details about the man's character and lifestyle. The third surprises us with a twist ending. The chorus contrasts the singer's workaday world with Cory's millionaire-playboy existence.

Language Style

The poem employs the editorial "we" and is set in the past, placing an emotional distance between the narrator and the audience. In his lyric Simon creates audience identification with the singer by personalizing: "*We* worked" changes to "*I* work." The events are happening now so the listener is more involved. Where the poem generalizes ("richer than a king"), the lyric particularizes ("a banker's only child . . . orgies on his yacht"). The language style becomes conversational: "the papers print his picture almost ev'rywhere he goes." Contractions also help to loosen up the formality of the poem—*I'm, ev'rything, livin'*. Simon, then, by switching to the first person and the present tense, by adopting a conversational style and then molding the whole thing into the verse/chorus form, has transformed a poem into a lyric.

A Caveat

Before you grab your poetry anthology off the shelf and decide to rework some W.H. Auden, whoa! Don't touch anything written after 1908, because under current law it has copyright protection. If you'd like to try your hand at modernizing the classics—and it's not a bad way to develop your craft—pick a poem that's in the public domain (PD). Public domain simply means that the work is no longer protected by copyright and therefore belongs to the public to appropriate or adapt.

A Footnote on "Poetic"

During the sixties we heard a lot about the "poetry" of rock. Writers like Joni Mitchell, Peter Townshend, and especially Bob Dylan were dubbed "poets." Critics delighted in analyzing the multilayered symbolism, the imagery, the oblique metaphors prevalent in the lyrics of the post-Tin Pan Alley school. Many lyricists openly acknowledged their stylistic debt to Dylan Thomas and T.S. Eliot. But the bottom line still is, poetic or not, those lyrics were conceived as lyrics designed to be sung. The term "poetic" was given as an accolade for the *quality* of the writing, not as a *definition* of it.

The lyrics and music of Jerry Herman have twice received Broadway's highest award, the Tony—in 1964 for *Hello Dolly!* and in 1984 for *La Cage Aux Folles.* At a Dramatists Guild seminar held in New York in the fall of 1983 Herman summed up his views on the subject of the poem versus the lyric: ". . .Lyric writing and poetry are two totally different things. I write both music and lyrics, and I don't think of lyrics as an independent art form. I think of them as being connected to the melody. That's part of the reason I would have to say, I don't write poetry, I write lyrics."

WRAPUP

As already noted, the professional term for a song's words—the one used by songwriters, publishers, and producers alike—is a lyric. Only two kinds of people refer to it as a poem: amateurs and song sharks. Song sharks are shady operators who bilk unsophisticated amateurs out of hundreds of thousands of dollars annually by charging a fee to set music to their "poems" and to "record" them.

If you ever run across small ads in the back pages of music magazines that use such come-ons as: "*Poems* wanted—by song studio" or "*Poems* needed for songs and records" or "Hear your *poem* sung," you are forewarned. Legitimate publishers and record companies never advertise for lyrics. And they certainly don't charge for them. They *pay* for them!

chapter 3
The Features of a Winning Lyric

"The idea makes the song . . . the idea, and the enterprise and courage to present that idea in fresh, beautiful, eloquent words."
Dorothy Fields

1. AN IDENTIFIABLE IDEA

The majority of popular songs express one moment's feeling—a single emotion like desire ("Can't Take My Eyes Off You"), or surprise ("I Can't Believe That You're In Love With Me"), or regret ("Didn't We"). Some make a simple statement (or ask a simple question): "Don't Fence Me In," "All I Want For Christmas Is My Two Front Teeth," or "What's Love Got To Do With It?" Those "ideas" are self-evident because the title tells it all. Lyrics with plots may be thought to say something more complex; but well-written story songs also embody a simple idea that can be summarized in a few words. For example, "Same Old Lang Syne" (p. 157) tells of a Christmas Eve encounter of two former lovers in a grocery store; that's the story. The *idea* the lyric conveys can be said to be "it's sad that nothing lasts forever," or, put another way, "everything changes."

A song's identifiable idea should, of course, strike a common chord—be understood by all.

Where do good lyric ideas come from? Everywhere. Anywhere. Soak up the sights and sounds and attitudes around you. Billy Joel said, "I listen to people talk about what's going on in their lives—family, friends, relationships—and I pick up on it." You can turn the day's events into songs the way a prism turns sunlight into rainbows. You just have to be "angled" right.

Carry a notebook so when you overhear an intriguing remark on a crowded bus or supermarket line, it won't be lost forever. Don't count on remembering it when you get home. Keep a pad and pencil in every room, for that sudden idea, or in case a line springs from a book you're reading or a phone conversation.

Some Sources for Lyric Ideas

NEWSPAPERS can generate ideas for song plots. One of Lennon and McCartney's most highly regarded lyrics was triggered by a news article. Paul reflected on the genesis of "She's Leaving Home": "There was a *Daily Mirror* story about this girl who left home and her father said: 'We gave her everything. I don't know why she left home.' But he didn't give her what she wanted."

At some point in every course I assign students to adapt a news story or article containing a strong universal theme or dramatic situation: a high school reunion, weekend fathers, the singles scene, career versus children, and so on. Each lyricist chooses his own perspective so the results are always astounding in their variety.

THE SOCIAL/ECONOMIC CLIMATE provides a rich idea source. Socially concerned writers have been moved, for example, by the plight of the unemployed. Yip Harburg in 1932 wrote the classic "Brother, Can You Spare a Dime?" Commenting to author Max Wilk on the period, he said, "You couldn't walk along the street without crying, without seeing people standing in bread lines, so miserable. Brokers and people who'd been wealthy, begging, 'Can you spare a dime?' " When collaborator Jay Gorney played him a melody (that had been inspired by a Hungarian lullaby), Harburg remembered the phrase that had been haunting him and matched the extra two notes with the word *brother* at the beginning of the line. Harburg admitted giving great thought to the treatment of the lyric. He carefully avoided making his railroad builder "petty, or small, or complaining," but rather "bewildered that this country with its dream could do this to him." Fifty years later Billy Joel particularized the economic conditions of Pennsylvania coal miners in 1982 with his chart success, "Allentown." Joel, like Harburg, portrayed his miner as strong ("it's hard to keep a good man down") and similarly bewildered: ". . . and still waiting . . . for the promises our teacher gave if we worked hard."

The women's movement spawned the chart topper "I Am Woman," and the Grammy winning "I Will Survive," which almost became a new anthem. The escalating divorce rate is reflected in such successes as "Jones vs. Jones," "Hard Time for Lovers," and "What's Forever For?"

CURRENT EVENTS that evoke broad public emotional reaction—Woodstock, the moon walk, assassinations of our heroes—always trigger song treatments. The Copyright Office of the Library of Congress confirms that shortly after momentous headlines, its mailroom is inundated with sacks of cassettes from aspiring writers seeking copyright protection. "The Last Time I Saw Paris" and "The Death of Emmett Till" are the responses of deeply affected professional writers. A headline song must naturally be released while the event is still fresh. "Ride, Sally Ride" was on the radio before our first female astronaut left for the stratosphere. The self-contained writer/performers signed to labels have a clear edge in getting out such a record. It's close to impossible for an unknown writer to break into the profession with a current-event song—get it recorded, released, and distributed to stores through professional channels before the idea is out of date. I remember a novice songwriter who spent two thousand dollars to record his musical tribute to John Wayne, convinced he had written a hit; the song as well as its rendition lacked professionalism and was no competition for the half-dozen records already released by major labels on the subject (at no cost to their writers). As a general guideline, it's more productive to concentrate on broader themes that won't become obsolete overnight.

FADS AND FOIBLES frequently translate into novelty hits. Songs about hula hoops, CBs, the Hustle, or junk food can make it to the charts, but as with current events, the record has to get out in a hurry, and there is usually only one—like "PacMan Fever"—per trendy subject. For the beginning writer the same caveat applies: Avoid the highly topical unless you have a direct pipeline to a recording artist or record producer.

FILMS AND TV SITCOMS can give you ideas for a lyric's emotional situation. "I get a lot of really good inspiration from movies," admitted hit writer Bob Seger. He's not alone. Hugh Prestwood—wondering why Dorothy, after discovering the land of Oz, chose to go back to Kansas—turned his speculations into a song, "Dorothy," that has already charmed its way into records by Judy Collins, Amanda McBroom, and Jackie DeShannon. Carole Bayer Sager told me: "I saw the movie *ET* and I was so inspired that I just had to write a song"; "Heartlight" was the result.

The team of Kenny Ascher and Paul Williams, two film buffs, has found movies to be juicy sources of lyric ideas. In collaborating sessions they would come up with concepts based on the dialogue or emotional conflict of a character in a particular scene. You can add to your plot inventory without leaving your living room by watching sitcoms, soaps, and film shows.

BOOKS provide a rich source of lyric ideas. In a talk with aspiring songwriters at a Songwriters Guild seminar, veteran lyricist and Grammy winner Norman Gimbel gave this advice: "I think reading good literature is a great source for a lyric writer. It gives you relationships of people juxtaposed to one another. It is the heat of the human condition. You can get great ideas that way. Use anything that feeds your head with words and thoughts." He certainly takes his own advice. The idea for "Killing Me Softly With His Song," written with Charles Fox, came from a scene in a novel Gimbel had read in which a character—listening to a jazz pianist—commented, "He's killing me softly with his blues." The line impressed Gimbel, who put it into his notebook; seven years later he transformed the bar into a concert hall, the pianist into a singer/guitarist, and the one affected into a young woman . . . and the line into a standard.

REAL PEOPLE, past or present, have been set to music and "vinylized." Singer/songwriter Don McLean painted a striking picture of van Gogh in "Vincent." The subject might seem too esoteric, yet the song has garnered recordings by other artists, including Jane Olivor. "Willy, Mickey, and the Duke"—a musical tribute to the baseball biggies Mays, Mantle, and Snider—generates air play every year during the season. Ex-

Eagle Don Henley, writer of the 1982 rock smash, "Dirty Laundry," himself became the subject of a song by singer/writer T-Bone Burnett, who put a lyric, "Don Henley," to the traditional folk ballad, "John Henry." Composer/artists have a definite advantage in getting a cut on a "portrait" song. Nevertheless, if you are burning with desire to "lyricize" Virginia Woolf, or Galileo, or Katharine Hepburn, do it, by all means, but—and it's a big but—with the understanding that a lyric without built-in broad appeal might get rejected by publishers. Being a recording artist would be a definite help, or failing that, knowing one who feels as strongly about the subject as you do. One more thought: Living celebrities who zealously guard their right to privacy might exert pressure to ban even a flattering song; to be safe, stick to people who are in no position to sue.

YOUR OWN LIFE is unquestionably the richest and strongest idea source of all. "My inspiration, whatever that may be," Cole Porter said, "doesn't come out of the air; it comes from people and places." You are unique. No one else on earth sees with your eyes or feels with your heart; no one else has your precise point of view, set of values, or emotional makeup. Amanda ("The Rose") McBroom told me that a vivid dream about her mother was the inspiration for the stunning three-minute drama, "Portrait," which expresses the universal conflict in every mother/daughter relationship. Carol Hall wrote "Jenny Rebecca" as a warm welcome-to-the-world for a friend's daughter. Her eye was not on the top-40, but the song is now a classic, with recordings by stellar performers in three different fields—Barbra Streisand in pop, Mabel Mercer in cabaret, and Frederica Von Stade in concert. Marty Panzer, expressing a personal desire for fatherhood, wrote the lyric, "I Want a Son." With a musical setting by Steve Dorff, the song has traveled around the world in a Kenny Rogers platinum album.

Irving Berlin confessed that his wistful "When I Lost You" came from his "own personal experience . . . when my wife died." Alan Jay Lerner tells in his memoir of when he was a shy ten-year-old suffering from a crush on the "prettiest and most popular" girl in his dancing class, and how he would place himself every Saturday on a bench opposite her building on Fifth Avenue hoping to see her come in or out. Years later, for *My Fair Lady,* he drew on his remembered longing and wrote the touching ballad, "On the Street Where You Live."

Using your own life is not limited to personal experiences; it includes *imagining* how a particular emotional situation would feel or a specific place would look; Harry Chapin never drove a cab, but he wrote convincingly about an episode in a "Taxi," and Yip Harburg had never seen "April in Paris," yet he could picture "holiday tables under the trees."

Using your own life means taking those fragments you've collected—from books, poems, fragments of conversation or snippets of soap opera dialogue—and converting them into lyrics expressing something that you want to say to the world.

Using your own life also means using *your own* thoughts, attitudes, and beliefs, as opposed to someone else's. There is an inherent danger in writing lyrics with secondhand emotions (ones that hold no significance for you personally) in the belief that they're just what some publisher, producer, or artist is looking for. Ironically, such songs are usually rejected because they're synthetic—they lack real feeling.

A word of caution. It is often remarked, "You can write a song about anything these days." That's *almost* true, but not quite. There are some ideas that are too insignificant, or negative, or autobiographical, or controversial, or suggestive. Certainly, unlikely subjects have been treated in recorded songs: Harry Chapin's "Dogtown" (on bestiality), Smokey Robinson's "Dynamite" (an ode to oral sex), and Michael Jackson's disavowal of paternity in "Billie Jean." There is, however, an important distinction to remember: lyrics on what we might term X-rated themes are invariably written, played, arranged, sung, and produced solely by the artists themselves (as with the three songs just mentioned). Singer/songwriters can escape the traditional filtering process of writer-to-publisher-to-producer-to-singer. The nonperforming writer cannot evade it. Even if your lyric makes it to the recording stage, the record could be stopped dead by a radio station that refuses to offend its listeners (or advertisers). Unless you're an artist too, it just makes good sense to stay with universally acceptable themes, at least until you've achieved some recognition.

Keep a notebook handy. Then reach out to everything "that feeds your head with words and thoughts." Listen, look, and wonder. Speculate: "What is she doing out with him? What's their story?" You'll soon get the self-generating-idea habit. Your chances of coming up with good ideas are greater when you are seeking them than when you aren't. "It's not an inspiration business," said Jule Styne. "Only amateurs have to be inspired."

As you collect concepts for songs, pretest them: try to reduce the substance of what you want to express to a one-sentence paraphrase. If you can, you know you've got an idea worth working on.

2. A MEMORABLE TITLE

"I always try to reach for a distinctive title." Leo Robin

"First, there is the title (that) hits like a bullet; when a title occurs, I have begun." Johnny Mercer

Johnny Mercer began with a title and often ended up with a standard: "Hooray for Hollywood," "You Must Have Been a Beautiful Baby," "Day In, Day Out," "Fools Rush In," "Blues in the Night," "One for My Baby," "How Little We Know," "Autumn Leaves," "Satin Doll," "Days of Wine and Roses"—one page couldn't list the hundreds of his hits.

When I asked Ira Gershwin whether his lyric ideas had been generated by snatches of conversation, a newspaper headline, or a popular expression, his response was, "Half of my titles came from those sources."

Ron Miller, who has topped the charts with "I've Never Been to Me" and "Touch Me In the Morning," said: "I always, absolutely, unequivocally get a title first. I may spend days finding the right title; once I find it, I may write the lyric in twenty minutes." Many successful writers have made "title first" their main modus operandi; it is a skill worth acquiring. Your notebook should reserve a big section for that sudden fresh title that will spark a new lyric.

It's important to realize that every week, many publishers receive from 50 to 100 similar-looking, undistinguished envelopes from unknown songwriters. Frequently, inside each envelope is a cassette demo labeled with such unimaginative titles as "You and I," "I Miss You," or "Baby, Baby." They would hardly make a publisher rush to turn on the cassette player. Fresh and distinctive titles, on the other hand, such as the hits "Sunglasses At Night" and "The Warrior," would immediately stand out from the crowd and provoke interest. That's what you want your title to do for your song.

Some Sources for Titles

ANTONYMS. Words of opposite meaning, known formally as *antonyms*, can lay the foundation for memorable titles. Contrasts, such as black/white, cold/hot, and up/down are both easy for the listener to grasp and enjoyable to hear. Country writers are especially adept at playing with opposites. A typical week's country chart might list such successes as "Somewhere Between Right and Wrong," "Nights Out at the Day's End," "You're So Good When You're Bad," "The Last Thing I Needed the First Thing This Morning," "Making a Living's Been Killing Me." Antonyms can break through writer's block: make a list of all the opposites you can think of, and then try to turn them into titles as strong as the classics: "Full Moon and Empty Arms," "The Night We Called It a Day," "My Future Just Passed," "I Got It Bad (and That Ain't Good)."

ALLITERATION. Alliterative titles are effective because they hook the ear with repeated consonants. Oscar winners Hal David and Sammy Cahn have both racked up an impressive catalog of standards that illustrate the punching power of repetition. Among Cahn's hits are "High Hopes," "Teach Me Tonight," "Tender Trap," "Day by Day," "Time After Time," and "It's Been a Long, Long Time." Hal David scored with "The Look of Love," "Winter Warm," "Magic Moments," "Twenty-four Hours from Tulsa," "Blue on Blue," "Bell Bottom Blues," "A Message to Michael," "Saturday Sunshine," and "Windows of the World." "*Show* Me Tonight," lacks the clout of "*Teach* Me Tonight," and I wonder if "Message to *Andrew*" would ever have made it to the charts. Take a tip from winners, and underscore your titles with alliteration.

THE ATLAS, THE CALENDAR, AND THE RAINBOW. Words that require initial capitals—cities, states, days, months—instantly click in the mind. Titles with colors also make strong impressions. "Ruby Tuesday," for example, hits the mark three ways: with a color, a day, and an inner "oo" rhyme. "I Left My Heart in San Francisco," "Saturday Night Is the Loneliest Night of the Week," and "Purple Rain" all have that specificity that echoes in the memory. Lyricist John Blackburn told me that he and his collaborator, Karl Suessdorf, picked the title, "Moonlight in Vermont" (page 210) because they thought "a state song . . . if it is a hit, will last as long as the state." The team's theory proved to be a winner.

CONVERSATIONS. Nothing beats real life. A line of dialogue is a slice of reality and, used deftly, can lend authenticity to your lyrics. Ira Gershwin told me of a night on the town at a Greenwich Village club with his wife and her irrepressible friend Golly. They had hardly been seated at the table, when Golly impatiently exclaimed, "When do we dance?" Ira, ever on the alert for titles, made a mental note and soon turned the line into another Gershwin brothers success. Richard Rodgers tells in his autobiography, *Musical Stages,* of a Paris taxi ride with Larry Hart. The collaborators were escorting their dinner partners back to the hotel. Another cab barely missed hitting them, and as their taxi came to a screeching stop, one of the women cried, "Oh, my heart stood still." Hart immediately responded: "That would make a great title." Of course, it did. Johnny Mercer has told the story of his sidewalk encounter with a widely traveled old friend. When Johnny asked where the man was living at the moment, the (now famous) reply was, "Any place I hang my hat is home." A title struck, complete with alliteration, and years later he wedded it to a Harold Arlen melody. An ear less attuned would have missed a one-of-a-kind.

COLLOQUIALISMS. Familiar expressions make strong titles; for example, "now or never," "your place or mine," "sooner or later," and "signed, sealed and delivered." Although there may be dozens of versions of each such expression registered in the indexes of the three performing rights societies, ASCAP, BMI, and SESAC, you are free to write another treatment. *A title cannot be copyrighted,* so it's perfectly legal. For instance, the expression "break it to me gently" has brought chart success to four different writing teams in the last ten years. Still, it's a better idea to try to come up with one no one has done yet. *The Pocket Dictionary of American Slang* is a good source.

MAXIMS, ADAGES, AND EPIGRAMS. Those common observations, general truths, and witty, often paradoxical sayings, produce potent titles with built-in familiarity: "don't talk to strangers," "one day at a time," "sometimes you can't win," "easy come, easy go" have all been treated lyrically. Pick a fresh one and, with a strong treatment tied to an equally strong melody, maybe you'll create a classic like Carolyn Leigh's "When in Rome (Do as the Romans Do)" or George David Weiss's "Too Close for Comfort."

WORD SWITCHES. Give an old saw a new twist. Some successful examples are, "We've Got to *Start* Meeting Like This," "Hurts So

Good," "Two *Hearts* Are Better than One," "The Pages of a *Look,*" and "You Could've Heard a *Heart Break.*" Experiment with "love" as a word substitute; it works wonders: "The High Cost of *Loving,*" "If the *Love* Fits, Wear It," "You're Gonna *Love* Yourself in the Morning," or "Better *Love* Next Time." Johnny Mercer (who used every device in the book) revamped a cliché into "Can't Teach *My* Old *Heart* New Tricks."

FILMS. Johnny Mercer jotted down an expression of Henry Fonda's—"Jeepers Creepers"—which years later fit perfectly as the title of a Harry Warren tune he was working on. Mae West's memorable cinematic one-liner, "Peel Me a Grape" was picked up by David Frishberg and immortalized in a much-admired and performed cabaret song.

BOOKS. Franklin Roosevelt Underwood turned the bestselling paperback title, "Real Men Don't Eat Quiche" into special material for jazz singer Suzanna McCorkle. It's lucky for songwriters that book titles can't be copyrighted so you are free to check your bookstores and library shelves: "A Walk in the Spring Rain," "That Goodbye Look," "Gone with the Wind," and "I Never Promised You a Rose Garden" all were novels before they were songs—and became songs before they were films.

POETRY. Poetry anthologies are a great source for titles. "Always True to You (in My Fashion)" is by Cole Porter via Ernest Dowson, the poet who also provided Johnny Mercer with the title of his Oscar winner, "The Days of Wine and Roses." Sammy Cahn's "Be My Love" came from Christopher Marlowe. Noel Coward found "Sigh No More" in Shakespeare, and Ecclesiastes was the source for Pete Seeger's "Turn, Turn, Turn." G.K. Chesterton's refrain "I think I will not hang myself today" from "A Ballade of Suicide" was the inspiration for "I Don't Think I'll Fall in Love Today" by Ira Gershwin. It's a good idea to do your "borrowings" only from public domain works and to keep them down to a few words.

One-word Titles

Any week of the year, the *Billboard* Hot 100 survey lists eight to ten one-word winners, showing that less is often more memorable. The November 13, 1982, chart tallied a whopping twelve! The first four were from the ever-popular source, female names: "Valerie," "Gloria," "Mickey," "Athena," "Heartlight," "Muscles," "Maneater," "Nobody," "Pressure," "Gypsy," "Africa," and "Shakin'." From Berlin's "Always" to the Dean Pitchford/Michael Gore success "Never" (from the film *Footloose*), the pros have sought out powerful single words that say it all. Composer/producer Giorgio Moroder featured one-word titles in his score for the 1983 film success *Flashdance;* in addition to the Grammy-winning title hit, the soundtrack album included "Romeo," "Maniac," "Imagination," and "Manhunt." There is no other specific title technique I know of that applies to such a large proportion of hit songs. Armed with the statistics that *10 percent of all contemporary successful records have one-word titles,* it may be worth setting up a new category in your notebook.

Although there is no songwriting rule that limits the number of words in a title, it is generally believed that the shorter, the better—with a maximum of five or six words. But titles that have required two lines on a record label certainly exist; for example, "How Ya Gonna Keep 'Em Down on the Farm After They've Seen Paree," "If I Said You Had a Beautiful Body (Would You Hold It Against Me?)," and "Does the Spearmint Lose Its Flavor on the Bedpost Over Night." Sometimes more is more.

Which Comes First?

"Title first" was the basic collaborative process for Alan Jay Lerner and Frederick Loewe on the scores of *My Fair Lady* and *Gigi*; the title triggered a melody in the composer, and the melody evoked the words from the lyricist. If you think about all the glorious songs from those productions and consider the output of hundreds of evergreens from the Gershwins, who also used this technique, you'll realize the effectiveness of the method. This process works as well for pop as for theatre and film songs; Cynthia Weil scores again and again on today's charts by discovering the title in her collaborator's preexisting melodies and then writing the lyric to the tune: "Somewhere Down the Road," "Come What May," "Holding Out for Love" (with music by Tom Snow), and "Just Once" (with husband Barry Mann) are solid gold examples.

Write Your Title

Whether your preferred process is that of Tim Hardin and Tom Paxton, who write the words first, or whether like Billy Joel, Randy Newman, and Paul Simon, you start with the music, the objective is the same: write your title. With characteristic wit and style, Ira Gershwin put it succinctly:

> *A title*
> *Is vital;*
> *Once you've it,*
> *Prove it.*

You prove it by making sure it's what your lyric is all about. It's the name of the product—what a listener asks for in the record store. If it's a forgettable one, not strongly and clearly placed in the lyric or not repeated enough throughout the lyric, you may lose the sale. Even though major artists rely on video clips to promote records, the nonperforming songwriter still must design a song for the radio—a song with a title distinct enough to compete with the sounds of conversation, a vacuum cleaner, a fire truck, and all the other distractions that come between your lyric and your target. A time-honored solution is to choose what publishers and producers term a "hook" or "hooky" title—a memorable word combination that cuts through ringing telephones, crying babies, and jet roar to grab the ears of your noncaptive audience.

Until the day the Watchman replaces the Walkman (or song videos replace records), your best strategy is to sell your *listener* with a strong song title.

Exceptions That Prove the Rule

Although it makes good sense to follow time-tested guidelines which prescribe that the title must be an integral part of the lyric, a few songs ignoring the unwritten laws have become monster hits and triple-A rated ASCAP standards. The full titles to "Canadian Sunset" and to "Weekend in New England," for example, can't be found in the lyrics. In "Stardust" and "The Rose," a subtle one-time mention is all we get. It takes something special, however—a major artist like Hoagy Carmichael or Bette Midler, or inclusion in a film or Broadway musical—to thrust such songs into the limelight. Then their merits will keep them there. Generally, pop music and subtlety make poor bedfellows; it's safer to find a memorable title and repeat it.

3. A STRONG START

"It is the first line that gives the inspiration and then it's like riding a bull. Either you just stick with it, or you don't. If you believe what you are doing is important, then you will stick with it no matter what." Bob Dylan

If a news article doesn't make you keep reading, you turn the page; if your song doesn't excite a publisher immediately, he turns off the cassette player. "The song's got to grab hold in the first thirty or forty seconds," according to Irwin Schuster, senior vice-president of the Chappell Music Company, one of the world's largest publishing houses. Schuster says that the average producer he plays a song for won't wait two minutes for it to "happen," he'll simply stop the tape. Multiply Schuster's statement by hundreds of publishers and producers and you'll know what your song demo faces as it joins all the envelopes pouring into music business offices in New York, Nashville, and Hollywood.

Start strong. In a three-minute song there isn't a second to waste on rambling words. Your lyric must quickly do two things: make contact with your listener, and then make him want to hear more. Like good newspaper copy, a well-constructed lyric tells us the *who* and *what* right at the top in as few words as possible. Listeners, like readers, have short attention spans. Hook them, and hold them.

Dorothy Fields, who rates high on every top-ten list of America's lyricists, knew how to start strong and end stronger. Never one to waste a word or be indirect, her opening lines thrust you into the heart of the action: "Grab your coat and get your hat" ("On the Sunny Side of the Street"), "I Can't Give You Anything But Love," "I'm in the Mood for Love." It's worth mentioning that although these lyrics (to Jimmy McHugh melodies) were written over five decades ago, they are still getting new recordings because their appeal is timeless as well as universal.

Successful songs grab the listener's attention by a variety of time-proven first-line devices:

THE QUESTION. "What good is sitting alone in your room?" ("Cabaret": Kander/Ebb); "Do you know the way to San Jose?": (Bacharach/David); "Is this the little girl I carried?" ("Sunrise, Sunset": Harnick/Bock); "How many roads must a man walk down?" ("Blowin' in the Wind": Dylan).

THE GREETING. "Well, hello there, good old friend of mine" ("Come in from the Rain": Sager/Manchester); "Hey there, Georgy Girl": (Dale/Springfield); "Hello, young lovers, whoever you are": (Rodgers/Hammerstein); "Hey there, lonely boy": (Carr/Shuman).

THE SUGGESTION OR REQUEST. "If you're going to San Francisco, be sure to wear flowers in your hair" (Phillips); "Don't go changing to try and please me" ("Just the Way You Are": Joel); "Say it loud, I'm black and I'm proud" (Brown); "Take out the papers and the trash" ("Yakety Yak": Leiber/Stoller).

THE PROVOCATIVE STATEMENT. "I've been alive forever, and I wrote the very first song" ("I Write the Songs": Johnston); "I rode my bicycle past your window last night" ("Brand New Key": Melanie); "My momma done tol' me when I was in knee pants" ("Blues in the Night": Mercer/Arlen); "Maybe I hang around here a little more than I should" ("I Honestly Love You": Allen/Barry).

THE TIME FRAME. "It's quarter to three" ("One For My Baby, And One More for the Road": Arlen/Mercer); "It's nine o'clock on a Saturday" ("Piano Man": Joel); "It was the third of June " ("Ode to Billy Joe": Gentry); "Wednesday morning at five o'clock" ("She's Leaving Home": Lennon/McCartney).

THE SITUATION. "All my bags are packed, I'm ready to go" ("Leaving on a Jet Plane": Denver); "We had the right love at the wrong time" ("Somewhere Down the Road": Weil/Snow); "Isn't This a Lovely Day (to be caught in the rain?)": (Berlin); "My child arrived just the other day" ("Cat's in the Cradle": S. and H. Chapin).

THE SETTING. "Dancing in the Dark" (Dietz/Schwartz); "On a train bound for nowhere" ("The Gambler": Schlitz); "Sittin' in the morning sun" ("Sittin' on the Dock of the Bay": Cropper/Redding); "It was raining hard in Frisco" ("Taxi": Chapin); "Met my old lover in the grocery store" ("Same Old Lang Syne": Fogelberg).

THE VISUAL IMAGE. "Over by the window there's a pack of cigarettes" ("Him": Holmes); "The autumn leaves fall past my window": (Mercer/Kosma); "Starry, starry night" ("Vincent": McLean); "Varnished weeds in window jars" ("Tin Angel": Mitchell).

THE OCCUPATION. "I am a lineman for the county" ("Wichita Lineman": Webb); "Behind the bar I see some crazy things" ("You Could've Heard a Heart Break": Rossi); "I make my livin' off the evenin' news" ("Dirty Laundry": Henley/Kortchmar); "When you're truckin' down the highway in an eighteen-wheeler rig" ("Look for a Home Cookin' Sign": Miller).

Practice these first-line techniques. With every new lyric you write, run down the list and see which device will strengthen your start. Wherever possible, include pronouns in your opening line—*you, me, I, my, I'm, your, we,*—so your audience immediately knows who is thinking or feeling or performing the action. When you can pull your listener into the song with an opening line, you will have mastered a vital technique of good craftsmanship.

4. A PAYOFF

"I feel that building a whole song to the end, you have to draw some conclusion for the person listening to it, and if you don't, there's no reason to write it in the first place." Jim Webb

If you attended a play and the second and third acts were essentially repeats of the first, you would want your money back. A well-constructed play develops through exposition of details and rising action to a climax and a conclusion. A well-constructed lyric—on a much smaller scale, of course—does the same. It goes somewhere.

A good example is "The First Time Ever I Saw Your Face" (page 128). In both its construction and content, the song is classically simple, musically as well as lyrically. It makes one affecting statement: I've loved you from the moment I laid eyes on you. If you read it reversing the order of verses one and three, the lyric doesn't work. The emotional progression is out of sequence: *first we see, then we hear, then we feel, then we know.* "Till the end of time" is clearly the conclusion. That's the wrapup—the payoff.

Payoff Techniques

All well-written songs make the audience feel they've experienced something. A lyricist's objective is to evoke an emotional response from the listener, whether it's a smile, a laugh, or stunned silence.

Here are some time-tested techniques to create your payoff:

TENSION. Many wistful ballads, like "Smoke Gets in Your Eyes" and "Blame It on My Youth," embody the clash between expectation and fulfillment. We create drama by engendering, sustaining, increasing, and resolving a state of tension. The principle applies equally to lyric writing. First you establish the singer's or singee's present emotional state, amplify the circumstances, reflect on the situation, and then draw a conclusion. In "Alfie," a lyric of rare simplicity and emotional power, Hal David illustrates the technique masterfully. Opening with the memorable question, "What's it all about, Alfie?" and contrasting the philosophic outlook of the singer and singee, David builds to the climactic line, "I believe in love, Alfie." The lyric continues to grow in intensity and concludes with an emotional wallop: that without love, "You're nothing, Alfie." You keep the listener involved when you gradually reveal information and arrange ideas in ascending order of forcefulness: state the least important facts first and save the most important for last.

THE CONVERSATIONAL DEBATE. The clash of incompatible tastes is the basis of the 1937 classic "Let's Call the Whole Thing Off" (Gershwins) as well as a 1981 update of the same conflict, "What Are We Doin' in Love?" (Goodrum). Opposing wills underpin the conversational debates in such songs as "Barcelona" (Sondheim) from the Broadway show *Company,* in "Anything You Can Do I Can Do Better" (Berlin) from *Annie Get Your Gun,* and in the Oscar-winning standard, "Baby, It's Cold Outside" (Loesser).

Most argumentative duets, such as the three just mentioned, have been generated by the conflict of a dramatic situation, either in a Broadway show or a film musical. Pop duets usually reflect a harmonious attitude as in "Reunited" (Perren/Fekaris), "Endless Love" (Richie), and "Up Where We Belong" (Jennings/Sainte-Marie/Nitzsche). The device of the conversational debate has been virtually untapped by the nontheatrical songwriter. Now that the video explosion has expanded the musical marketplace, creating new opportunities for extended song forms, it's likely that inventive lyric writers will explore the potential of this classic dramatic device. The conversational debate provides an ideal scaffolding for a mini video musical.

THE QUESTION PLOT. As Madison Avenue admen have long known, a question is an effective attention-getting device. Many successful songs like "Why Did I Choose You?" (Martin/Leonard) and "What Is This Thing Called Love?" (Porter) feature questions as titles, but these are rhetorical questions—musings not seeking a reply. A question *plot,* on the other hand, presents an enigma in the first verse which is not solved until the end of the song.

The 1925 classic "Who" (Harbach/Hammerstein/Kern) posed the

question in the opening line, "Who stole my heart away?" The answer didn't arrive until the song's concluding four words: "no one but you." "Who" exemplifies the most elementary of question plot songs. A more sophisticated example is "Guess Who I Saw Today" (Boyd/Grand) from the revue *New Faces of 1952.* In the much-recorded standard, a wife—after fixing her husband a martini upon his late arrival from the office—asks him the title question. She then describes her shopping break in a dimly lit French café where she had noticed a couple in an obvious liaison. The suspense is not broken until the last line, when she finally answers her own question: "Guess who I saw today . . . I saw—you." The objective in a question plot is to sustain suspense by withholding the answer until the very end of the song.

CONFLICT. Conflict—the opposing action of incompatible forces, internally or externally—is essential to drama and a mainstay of lyric writing. In the mid-fifties The Coasters exemplified the generation gap with "Yakety Yak (don't talk back!)" In 1966 "Society's Child" catapulted teenage Janis Ian into national prominence with the story of a parent-child conflict caused by an interracial romance. Lyrics that dramatize the singer's mixed feelings—especially regarding a romantic relationship—connect strongly with an audience. The agony of ambivalence turned the otherwise plotless "Feelings" (Albert) into an overnight standard. The extramarital double-bind has led to such chart toppers as "Torn Between Two Lovers" (Yarrow/Jarrell) and "Me and Mrs. Jones" (Gilbert/Huff/Gamble). One reason that sad love songs seem to outnumber happy ones (on top-40 play lists) is that happiness lacks conflict. The ending of a relationship generates more dramatic juice: it's much easier to find a new slant on "You done me wrong" than to find a fresh way to say "I love you."

THE TURNAROUND. Ira Gershwin was a master of the small surprise. In the lyric "They All Laughed," a pair of unlikely lovers cause consternation among friends who doubt the relationship will last; in a duet, the couple recalls the similar scorn visited upon other adventurers: Fulton, Columbus, and Marconi. The windup is, "but ho, ho, ho, who's got the last laugh now?" The little conjunction, *but,* is often the big link to the turnaround. Irving Berlin used it in "I Got *Lost* in His Arms": the lady in question ultimately announced her delight at being swept away in the line, "but look what I *found.*" In "This Is the *End* of a Beautiful Friendship," the song's resolution engenders listener satisfaction with, "but just the *beginning* of love." The final line in a turnaround is usually a simple reversal of the title.

THE TWIST. A twist really jolts us with the unexpected. Fran Landesman's "In Bed with a Book" tells of an avid reader who devours everything from Dickens to Mailer. The last line reveals her more passionate interest: "I love to curl up in bed with a good book—or the chap who wrote it." The twist at the end of "The Naughty Lady of Shady Lane" (Bennet/Tepper) reveals that we've been had: the flirtatious, unpredictable female described turns out to be not a hooker, as we had been led to believe, but "only nine days old." Back in the forties cabaret singer Dorothy Shay told the saga of a woman who was in love with a married man and determined at all costs to keep him by her side. The audience was taken totally by surprise to hear her announcement: "Some things are bound to be/I'm in love with a married man/Who is married to me."

In writing both the twist and the turnaround, it's useful to start from your closing line and work up.

THE SUSPENSE STORY. Suspense requires a slow build to a strong payoff. In "Coward of the County" (page 122), the line, "something always told me they were reading Tommy wrong" subtly foreshadows the irony of the title and begins a story that builds steadily to a dramatic climax. The restrained and skillfully written lyric maintains tension through a hint—a wait—a fulfillment. You create suspense by controlled design.

Coming Full Circle

Most lyrics are linear; they develop from the given to the unknown and build to the payoff through the various ways just described. A circular lyric returns at its end to a significant word or line which has been used near the outset, thereby underscoring the theme by repeating it. In "Same Old Lang Syne" (page 157) Dan Fogelberg set a snowy Christmas Eve scene for an encounter of two former lovers; after an intimate autobiographical exchange, they wave wistfully goodbye as the snow turns into rain.

In the opening line of "Desperado" (Frey/Henley), the singer accuses the singee of emotionally "riding fences." In the lyric's concluding line, the singer warns him to come down from his fences "before it's too late." Other examples of the circular technique echo in "You and Me (We Wanted It All)" (Sager/Allen), "Out Here on My Own" (L. and M. Gore), and "In the Ghetto" (M. Davis).

Study the best of the past—songs by lyricists such as Irving Berlin, Yip Harburg, Dorothy Fields, and Ira Gershwin. Analyze what method they used to develop a song to a payoff; all their time-proven methods still apply. Experiment with the devices just outlined. Every time you try a new technique and make it your own, you add one more building block to a solid foundation of craft.

5. AN APPROPRIATE FORM

"Lack of form . . . is the great failing with beginning songwriters. Either they aren't concerned with it, or they just don't understand it." Jim Webb

When we listen to a song, we are continuously sorting out in our minds what we are currently hearing, what we have already heard, and what we have been led to expect next. As a song streams past us, the mind's eye as well as the ear seeks a clear design. An audience can more easily assimilate the meaning of a lyric when it's able to "see" the structure effortlessly. Successful songwriters appear to understand this phenomenon, consciously or unconsciously.

Finding the Form

After you have the beginnings of a lyric—an identifiable idea, a memorable title, and a strong opening line—the next step is to put them into a form that will create the result you're after. The lyricist's situation is a little like that of a novice chef with a bowl of melted chocolate, eggs, flour, and sugar. Now what? For both the chef and the lyricist, a clear understanding of the function of form is necessary. In the case of the cook—well, a soufflé won't result if the raw materials are poured onto a cookie sheet; and a pie pan can't be expected to produce a layer cake. To produce the product you have in mind, you must put the ingredients into the ideal form.

What kind of song do you have in mind? Do you want to express a philosophical idea that's on the poetic side, like "Blowin' in the Wind"? Do you want to write a ballad with a last-line turnaround like "Falling in Love with Love" ("but love fell out with me")? Do you want to move your listeners onto their feet the way "Breakdance" does? The emotional response your lyric evokes will be determined, to a significant degree, by the form you select: the AAA, the AABA, and the verse/chorus are of course, music forms; there are no precise lyric structures, as such.

Poets have it easier than lyricists; they have fixed forms to work within—such as haiku, the limerick, the sonnet, or the villanelle—forms that are defined by specific syllable counts, or rhyme patterns, or numbers of lines. Lyricists who create without the framework of a melody have to work more or less from instinct, from absorbing, over years of listening, the basic patterns of songs. Therefore it's no surprise that many non-composing lyricists prefer to put words to existing music, because it eliminates the dilemma of structure.

Writing "From Scratch"

When a lyricist writes words to a collaborator's tune, the composer has already laid out the pattern, with a particular rhythm, an implied title placement, and a rhyme scheme. Most professional lyricists, however, know how to write "from scratch" as well as to design an inherently musical lyric without the scaffolding of a melody. It's a simple matter of understanding how the musical forms work. It is evident from my classes that many novice writers believe that the only form for a song is the verse/chorus. This misconception is like an aspiring architect thinking that the sole design for a house is the split-level.

In the following chapters, we will examine the AAA, the AABA, the verse/chorus, and the blues forms in detail, with definitions, lyric examples, and diagrams to help you understand how they work.

WRAPUP

As you analyze the standards—songs that are sung, played, and recorded long after their initial popularity—you'll discover that they share five common characteristics:

1. An identifiable and universal idea
2. A memorable title
3. A strong start
4. A payoff
5. An appropriate form

When your first draft possesses each of these features, you can be sure you're on the way to a successful lyric.

"An important principle I've always believed in is: Content dictates form." Stephen Sondheim

part two

MASTERING THE SONG FORMS

chapter 4

Putting Songwriting Terms Into Perspective

". . . our vocabulary changes [as] the times change." Bill Gaither

We are now in the age of techno-pop with a new, fast-growing vocabulary. It has become virtually impossible to discuss songs today without mentioning the "groove"—a particular rhythmic "feel" that underpins almost every hit record. And "synth" and "synth sound" are popular shorthand terms for a synthesized beat (or groove).

Computer wizardry has moved into the songwriting process. Not long ago, a songwriter could build a career with a pencil, a pad, and an upright piano. Today's pop composers and lyricists often rely on an awesome array of electronic gadgetry to shape songs into the hit formats demanded by the pop marketplace: a multi-track cassette recorder, a drum machine, and a polyphonic synthesizer are commonplace in the home demo studios of budding songwriters. These exciting electronic tools can "layer" sounds in ways never possible before, and their potential for amplifying artistic expression is enormous. Digital magic can unquestionably enhance the presentation of well-conceived musical ideas; it cannot, however, substitute for an understanding of song structure.

In order to take full advantage of the new technology, you need to understand the classic song forms and the terms for their various parts.

Because a popular song unites rhymed and metered words with a melody, a songwriter's terms come from both poetics and music. Over the last century and a half our popular music has evolved in content, rhythm, and form. As the shape of songs changed, so too did the terms by which we identify their various parts: *verse, chorus, refrain,* and *bridge,* for example, which stood for one thing in songs written in the thirties and forties, refer to something quite different today.

The Verse and the Chorus—Then

Let's consider three well-known standards: "Anything Goes" (Cole Porter), "As Time Goes By" (Herman Hupfeld), and "Over the Rainbow" (Harburg/Arlen). Each of these songs has a short introductory section called the *verse,* whose main purpose is to set up the lyric's situation. From the twenties to the fifties, songs generally had verses, especially those written for Hollywood and Broadway. The second section of the song was called the *chorus* or *refrain*—terms that were used interchangeably.

After a song's film or theater debut, the verse was often omitted in performances and recordings. Astute publishers must have realized that the way to increase sheet music and record sales was to stress the chorus, the heart of the song. It became common for performers to sing the chorus one and a half times, helping to fix the song's title in the listener's memory. "You're the Top," "As Time Goes By," and "Over the Rainbow," as we know them today, are actually the chorus sections of verse/chorus songs.

Today's Verse/Chorus Song

Most contemporary songs are considerably longer and wordier than those written forty or fifty years ago. Today's "verse/chorus"—our most popular song form since the mid-sixties—is a different musical structure entirely. Generally, it has no separate introductory section. A current verse/chorus hit is an integrated format consisting of usually two or three verses which alternate with a second musical section called the *chorus*. The chorus contains both the song's title and main message, and it often repeats (and repeats) at the end of the record.

The Hook

The repeated title section of the song is called the *hook,* the part of the song that grabs the listener's attention and tends to remain in the mind after the song is over. The term *hook* can also refer to any memorable melodic figure, which, more often than not, contains the song's title.

Although the term *hook* was not in fashion when songwriters such as Irving Berlin, Cole Porter, and Richard Rodgers were turning out their hits, they all managed to write songs that have continued to hook audiences for three generations. What *hook* translates to, in nonjargon language, is simply an identifiable idea linked to a memorable title—the first two "features of a winning lyric" outlined in Chapter 3.

The AABA Form

The chorus part of "Anything Goes," "As Time Goes By," and "Over the Rainbow" can also serve to illustrate the classic song form, the AABA. Melodically this form divides into four parts: the first is generally an 8-bar phrase (A) which immediately repeats (A); it is followed by a contrasting melody called a *bridge* or *release* (B), which then returns to a repeat of the first section (A). The A sections contain the dominant melodic theme and, therefore, the song's title (hook). The AABA is a seamless whole from first verse to the song's end. In contrast, the stop-start quality of the verse/chorus song seems to take a deep breath prior to the chorus and then say, "Here comes the point of the song."

The important thing to know is that the AABA form is alive and well today. It continues to serve as the framework for contemporary songs in every field—pop, country, film, and theater.

The Bridge

The bridge of an AABA is essential to that form, being its contrasting part. The term *bridge* today can also apply to a third and optional section of a verse/chorus song which makes a new musical and lyrical statement; it often acts as an interlude between the second verse and the final chorus. A verse/chorus song can exist without a bridge; the AABA cannot. In our contemporary record formats of three to four minutes, an instrumental break (without words) may also be termed a musical bridge. Both kinds of bridges are common features of today's songs.

The AAA Form

The last of the three main song forms is the simplest—the AAA. Music theorists call it the "one-part song form" to indicate that its music consists of only one section which repeats with little or no variation. Historians of American popular music often refer to the AAA as "the strophic form." Strophic derives from *strophe,* a Greek word meaning stanza or verse. This musical form evolved as early composers turned for their texts to psalms or poems, which they set to a melody that repeated with each successive verse.

The terms "strophic form" and "one-part song form," though correct, sound too formal for a songwriter's vocabulary. Since I've never heard any pop lyricist or composer use those expressions, I've chosen the simpler *AAA*, another common term for the form. I want to note, however, that the AAA is not limited to three verses (the number is virtually infinite), but three seems to be the most frequently used number.

A Word on the ABAB

Some songwriting books refer to today's verse/chorus form as the ABAB. They identify a verse as the A, and a chorus, which is the contrasting musical sections, as the B. In the interests of clarity, consistency, and historical accuracy, I will refer to the verse/chorus song solely as the verse/chorus song. Here's the reason: there is an older ABAB form, a structure popular from the twenties right into the sixties, in which many of our most famous standards were written—songs like "Swanee," "Sometimes I'm Happy," and "Fly Me to the Moon." Its B section is in no way a chorus, lyrically or musically.

The Refrain

As already noted, lyricists and composers of those early AABA songs used the word *refrain* interchangeably with *chorus.*

A *refrain,* in poetic terms, traditionally refers to a phrase (or a line or two), usually at the *end* of a verse, that recurs in successive verses.

Edward Lear, for example, in his classic poem, "Calico Pie," frames the close of each verse with the poignant lament: "They never came back/they never came back/they never came back to me." I will use the term *refrain* throughout the book to mean that repeated line (often ironic) that outlines the final line or two of the verses of so many AAA songs.

Format = Form

The word *format* has recently wedged its way into the vocabulary of music publishers, producers, and songwriters. For decades the term, used by both radio and television staffers, referred to the layout of a program—a comedy format, a game show format, and so on. Currently, music stations employ *format* to describe the kind of music they play, such as "easy-listening format" or "top-40 format."

Music producers today with a string of gold and platinum records are said to have found "winning formats." Music publishers ask songwriters to bring them "hit formats." Clearly, the term—a substitute for the old word *form*—has arrived. You'll, therefore, be reading in the coming chapters about "the AABA format" or the "verse/chorus/bridge format."

WRAPUP

Now that you've had an overview of such songwriting terms as *verse, chorus, refrain,* and *bridge*—what they meant in the thirties and what they mean today—you're ready for the next four chapters, which will discuss in detail the main songwriting forms.

chapter 5

The AAA Form

"Your form depends upon your purpose. . . ." Norman Gimbel

The earliest songs sung in colonial America, before we had home-grown music, were hits from London's pleasure gardens and comic operas, written primarily in the simple AAA form. After the passage of the country's initial copyright act in 1790, our pioneering music publishers began to extend their imports to include popular Irish ballads by Thomas Moore, Scottish songs of Robert Burns and Sir Walter Scott, and the works of important European composers living in England. Most of these songs were a series of verses set to the same simple melody. Thus it was inevitable that our first native-born songwriters would adopt that format as a blueprint for success.

Folk singers have traditionally leaned toward the simplicity of the one-part song form. When Pete Seeger, for example, wanted to prick the American conscience with his question, "Where Have All the Flowers Gone?" or to adapt Ecclesiastes in "Turn, Turn, Turn," or to exhort the underdog to affirm "We Shall Overcome," he repeatedly picked the AAA form to deliver his messages.

Graphed, the AAA form looks like this:

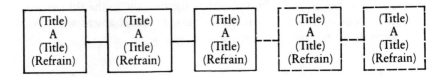

There is no chorus and no bridge. Musically speaking, when you've heard the first verse (frequently sixteen bars) you've basically heard it all. Within verses, however, a note or two is often added or subtracted here and there to accommodate changes in the song's words, and sometimes a lyric phrase is repeated at the end of a verse for emphasis. Musicians identify these slight melodic variations A A' A", which is read as A, A prime, A double prime.

TITLE PLACEMENT

There are no rigid rules about placement of titles, just as there are none about any other aspect of lyric writing. There are only sensible guidelines. As is indicated by the parentheses in the diagram, the title in the AAA conventionally appears in either the top line or the last line of each verse.

Repeating your title in the identical spot in successive verses not only contributes to the unity of your lyric, but improves the chance that the lyric will make a dent on the listener's memory. In "Scarborough Fair," "Puff the Magic Dragon," and "Try to Remember," the opening line contains the title; and in such AAA classics as "My Cup Runneth Over," "Gentle on My Mind," and "I Walk the Line," the title concludes each verse.

Two eighties chart hits, "Yesterday's Songs" and "Tryin' to Love Two Women," each featured an opening line title, *plus* a closing refrain. Your title placement depends upon your purpose. Some lyrics evolve in a mysterious fashion with a will of their own, and their titles may appear only once, as in "The Rose."

THE VERSE: HOW LONG AND HOW MANY?

A verse is composed of a series of lines arranged in a recurring pattern of meter and rhyme; the word *verse* has generally replaced *stanza* in popular song parlance, but either is correct. Music is also metered, being built on a series of grouped beats set off by vertical lines into measures or "bars." Because music is mathematical and built generally on 4-bar phrases, it is common to find verses made up of four or eight lines. A composer however, may stretch two lines of lyric over four bars of music.

The number of lines in a verse is probably determined less by musical convention than by the human mind's ability to process information. In a renowned paper on the subject, "The Magical Number Seven, Plus or Minus Two," psychologist George A. Miller contends that the human memory can span no more than nine items at a time. Our zip codes, telephone and credit card numbers—arranged in clusters of three or four digits—attest to the acceptance of Miller's theory. It simply makes good sense, then, to help your listener comprehend your lyric by dividing it into easy-to-follow eight-line (or fewer) sections.

The number of verses in an AAA lyric is restricted only by the needs of your story (and the attention span of the audience). One of our most popular early songs, "The Minstrel's Return'd from the War" by John Hill Hewitt (1825), said all that was needed in three verses, but our first great international hit, "Jim Crow," a minstrel song performed in blackface by its composer, T.D. Rice (1832), required twenty-one. Gordon Lightfoot's "The Wreck of the Edmund Fitzgerald" took twenty-eight eight-bar phrases to tell its story. Toni Tennille made only two verses of lyric work in "Do That to Me One More Time": an instrumental break and a repeat of the first verse stretched two verses into a hit record.

The verses in an AAA structure work similarly to the panels on a pictorial folding screen which might depict, for example, the four seasons or the seven deadly sins. Each section makes a complete statement but has been conceived to work sequentially as one element in a bigger design. Because of the independent quality of its verses, the form is well suited to a lyric that features a jump either in time frame, in geography, or in both. That's one of the reasons "By the Time I Get to Phoenix" works: the form is ideal.

BY THE TIME I GET TO PHOENIX

A: *BY THE TIME I GET TO PHOENIX*
She'll be risin',
She'll find the note I left hangin' on her door.
She'll laugh when she reads the part
That says I'm leavin'
'Cause I've left that girl
So many times before.

A: *BY THE TIME I MAKE ALBUQUERQUE*
She'll be workin',
She'll prob'ly stop at lunch and give me a call, but
She'll just hear that phone
Keep on ringin'
Off the wall
That's all.

A: *BY THE TIME I MAKE OKLAHOMA*
She'll be sleepin'
She'll turn softly and call my name out low. And
She'll cry just to think
I'd really leave her
Tho time and time
I've tried to tell her so,
   She just didn't know
   I would really go.

In "By the Time I Get to Phoenix" Jim Webb has created a unique split-screen effect where we follow the singer driving eastward from Arizona to Oklahoma, and simultaneously we watch his ex-lover going through the motions of her day.

The words repeated in each verse's opening line—"By the time I
_____"—underline the start of successive sections. This technique, also used in "The First Time Ever I Saw Your Face," makes it easy for the listener to perceive the shape of the form and consequently to follow the story. Both "Phoenix" and "First Time Ever" exercise a common option: to pick the opening line, the first in a series of variations, for the song's title.

Consistently in the second line of every verse Webb emphasizes the moving clock: "*She'll be risin' . . . she'll be workin' . . . she'll be* sleepin'. . . ." The device of restating words at the start of subsequent lines helps give the listener his bearings with the echo of familiar sounds. Such repetitive techniques tend to diminish the need to match sounds (to rhyme) at the *end* of a line. End rhyme in "Phoenix" makes an appearance only once in every sixteen bars of music.

As the song unfolds, we see her ". . . find . . . read . . . laugh . . . stop . . . hear . . . turn . . . call . . . cry . . ." and we realize, about the time that she does, that he's never coming back. The lyric dramatizes how sensory progression works: first we see, then we hear, then we feel, then we know. This is a fine example of stating ideas in both chronological and emotional order.

THE EXTENSION. In the concluding line of "Phoenix," we hear the irony so common to this form: "She just didn't know/I would really go." Because this line appears only once, at the song's conclusion, it is not a refrain, which, by definition, recurs at each verse's end. Rather, it is a one-time *extension* of the last A which serves to delay reaching the final note of the song and to add emphasis to the conclusion. In "Phoenix" the extension lengthens the final verse's lyric by two lines and its music by four bars. Musical extensions, sometimes called codas, are common to all three forms. I will use the term to apply to any lyrical addition at the end of a verse or chorus which automatically requires an extension of the music.

THE IRONIC REFRAIN. In many of the best-known AAA lyrics, irony is central to the theme, with a repeated refrain punctuating the end of each stanza. The caustic, "He was her man, but he was doing her wrong" closes each of the thirteen verses of the century-old "Frankie and Johnny." A refrain may echo exactly each time or may vary, according to the needs of the story. In "Frankie and Johnny" we hear these modifications: "He was her man, but he was doing her wrong/He was my man, but he's a-doing me wrong/He was your man, but he's a-doing you wrong."

In the hands of lyricists with something meaningful to say, the AAA delivers a potent punch. It was a popular form in the sixties and framed many of that decade's memorable songs. Certain themes (often social statements) seem to work best in an uninterrupted sequence of verses. Without the detour of a bridge or the interruption of a chorus, the AAA often holds the listener's attention with the periodic recurrence of the lyric's point—a refrain, which sometimes contains the song's title:

> *"And the big fool said to push on." ("Waist Deep in the Big Muddy": Seeger)*

> *"Oh, when will they ever learn?" ("Where Have All the Flowers Gone?": Seeger)*

> *"They're all made out of ticky tacky, and they all look just the same." ("Little Boxes": Reynolds)*

> *"The answer, my friend, is blowin' in the wind, the answer is blowin' in the wind." ("Blowin' in the Wind": Dylan)*

Time and again Bob Dylan found that the AAA form offered the most natural shape for reechoing his lyrical ironies: "The Times They Are A-Changin' "; "All I Really Want to Do (is baby be friends with you)"; "Stuck Inside of Mobile with the Memphis Blues Again"; "I'm a long time a-comin', an' I'll be a Long Time Gone."

It is these ironic statements (traditionally at the *end* of the verses) that characterize the emotional "feel" of the AAA. The writers who instinctively choose this form know that their key statement belongs at the *close* of a verse rather than at the top of a chorus. It's a matter of subtlety. The refrain, coming where it does, understates the irony.

Nashville writers keep the AAA form on the charts with refrains that embody such popular themes as the troubled cheatin' heart; a typical example is the 1983 hit, "What She Don't Know Won't Hurt Her (but it's destroying me)" (Lindsey/Rowell).

Vignettes and Portraits

Joni Mitchell, like Bob Dylan, found the symmetry of the AAA form ideal for voicing her views on life. One of her most popular singles, "Big Yellow Taxi," restates (at the end of each verse) the price of progress: "They paved paradise and put up a parking lot." "For Free" paints a picture of a sidewalk clarinetist whose music-making brings him satisfaction without the drawbacks of celebrity. The wry refrains of "Rainy Night House" and "A Case of You" reflect some personal "passages" of its main characters.

The autonomous nature of its verses makes the AAA particularly suited to portraiture. In "Ladies of the Canyon" Mitchell musicalized one aspect of the sixties by creating a cast of three flower children—Trina, Annie, and Estrella—whose bohemian lifestyles enlivened the California valleys. Her quasi-autobiographic "Cactus Tree" tells of a lady who is adept at dodging commitment; three verses profile successively a sailor, a mountain climber, and a businessman who seek the lady's hand. A fourth continues the list of suitors whom she eludes, and ends with the ironic comment that the lady has a heart that is both as full, and as hollow, as a cactus tree.

A THEATER SONG GETS GEOMETRIC

Sheldon Harnick's witty lyric, "The Ballad of the Shape of Things," written for *The Littlest Revue* (1956), proves that the AAA is as much at home in the theater as in pop, a fact demonstrated earlier by Cole Porter in "Miss Otis Regrets" and "Friendship." "The Ballad of the Shape of Things" also confirms that a title—when it summarizes the song's substance—need not even make an appearance.

Completely round is the steering wheel
That leads to compound fractures.
Completely round is the golden fruit
That hangs in the orange tree.
Yes, the circle shape is quite renowned,
And sad to say, it can be found
In the dirty low-down runaround
My true love gave to me,
Yes, my true love gave to me.

A: *Completely square is the velvet box*
He said my ring would be in.
Completely square is the envelope
He wrote farewell to me in.
Completely square is the handkerchief
I flourish constantly.
As it dries my eyes of the tears I've shed.
And blows my nose 'til it turns bright red.
For a perfect square is my true love's head
He will not marry me.
No, he will not marry me.

A: *Rectangular is the hotel door*
My true love tried to sneak through.
Rectangular is the transom
Over which I had to peek though.
Rectangular is the hotel room
I entered angrily.
Now, rectangular is the wooden box
Where lies my love 'neath the grazing flocks
They said he died of the chicken pox
In part I must agree;
One chick too many had he.

A: *Triangular is the piece of pie*
I eat to ease my sorrow.
Triangular is the hatchet blade
I plan to hide tomorrow.
Triangular the relationship
That now has ceased to be.
And the self-same shape is a garment thin,
That fastens on with a safety pin
To a prize I had no wish to win;
It's a lasting memory
That my true love gave to me.

As Jim Webb chose geographic places to map "By the Time I Get to Phoenix," Sheldon Harnick picked geometric figures to silhouette "The Ballad of the Shape of Things." Such thematic devices orient the audience to the song's structure, and the listener—reassured of his bearings—can simply relax and enjoy the story.

Harnick used the AAA for all it's worth, restating the circle, square, rectangle, and triangle motifs three times each in their respective verses. Every verse resonates with repeated consonants, lubricating the motor of memory: "perfect pearl," "sad to say," "dirty low-down," "lies my love," "piece of pie," "self-same shape," "wish to win." His consistent *e* rhyme closing couplet of each verse acts to outline the form and helps us follow his story.

Certainly, one of the delights of "Shape of Things" is its obliqueness: Harnick *describes* familiar objects instead of naming them. With a combination of subtlety and symbol, we hear "wooden box" instead of a blunt "coffin"; "garment thin/that fastens on with a safety pin" for "diaper" and "prize I had no wish to win" in place of the obvious, "baby." Had he called a coffin a coffin, the lyric would have lost some of its grace.

As a footnote on our changing times, I find that when I play Blossom Dearie's delightful recording of ". . . Shape of Things" in class, many of the younger students wear a bewildered expression at the song's end, while older ones are laughing. Harnick's subtle reference to a triangular-shaped (fabric) diaper was lost on those brought up in the age of disposable Pampers.

The meter and rhyme scheme make additional contributions to the listener's pleasure: long lines alternate with short ones; multisyllable words jostle monosyllables; and the always fresh rhymes ping in a wide variety of sound mates, with one three-line matched rhyme in each verse, leading to a laugh.

Part of the fun, of course, is the tongue-in-cheek use of "my *true* love," irony again underpinning the AAA. In "The Ballad of the Shape of Things" Sheldon Harnick's sophisticated design and consummate craftsmanship exploit this simple form to the ultimate.

BENDING THE SHAPE

When a professional completely masters a classic form, there may come an itch to bend it. If a structure, in its pure state, simply won't work for a particular lyric (and the other two forms don't seem able to do the job), then it's time to experiment. Don Henley expanded the basic AAA in his 1983 top-40 "Dirty Laundry." It looked like this:

Henley wrote a succession of seven verses, with the title, "Dirty Laundry," wrapping up each one. The story was told *within* the verses and worked without any additional section. But Henley, a producer/artist as well as a songwriter, obviously felt that an exciting rock record required more musical variety than the pure AAA form could deliver, so he added an ironic refrain *outside* the verse: "Kick 'em when they're up/Kick 'em when they're down." It gave the arranger an extra repeated hook to play off. The restated line is a refrain, not a chorus. A chorus embodies the title and summarizes the song, and if it were removed, a song would collapse. The seven verses of "Dirty Laundry" packed an emotional wallop without the refrain. Yet, there is no question that the added irony and the added melody made for a stronger commercial product. As is indicated by the diagram, a third musical section—an extended instrumental break midway through the song—served to increase the entertainment value for rock record buyers.

In the summer of 1983 Jackson Browne climbed the charts with another AAA, "Lawyers in Love." Browne, like Henley, augumented his (three) verses of lyric with a long instrumental break. Also, the nonsense syllables "ooo sha la la" played against the semi-snide social statement of the verses. Browne, an old hand with the AAA from his seventies folksy soft-rock period, broke open the form and added the synthesizer sound of the eighties to make a compelling record.

Breaking New Ground

Jim Morgan's lyric, "Higher Than She's Ever Been Before," takes the AAA to a new place. Like Don Henley and Browne, Morgan expanded the structure: he used his refrain, sometimes doubled in length, to move his story forward.

HIGHER THAN SHE'S EVER BEEN BEFORE

Verse: *Pretty Patty Peterson from Paterson New Jersey*
Is climbing on a Greyhound with a suitcase in her hand
'Cause the scene at home is awful, so she's leaving it forever
She's almost broke but knows that she can make it on her own
Her plans are kind of hazy but she'd like to be a model
'Cause a lot of people say she looks a little bit like Brooke
And she's got a year of high school and the greatest expectations
And she's HIGHER THAN SHE'S EVER BEEN BEFORE

Refrain: *And she soars*
And she sighs
And her troubles melt beneath her as she flies

Verse: *Pretty Patty Peterson has reached her destination*
A terminal, a city, and she doesn't know a soul
Till a guy named Hawk approaches and he says "Hey how 'ya doin'?
N' you're really lookin' good n' hey I'll bet you're new in town."
And he listens to her story and he's really understanding
N' he says he knows a guy he thinks can get her into flicks
So they go to Hawk's apartment where they do a little powder
With some other girls who live there and then they do some more
And she's HIGHER THAN SHE'S EVER BEEN BEFORE

Refrain: *And she soars*
And she sighs
And her troubles melt beneath her as she flies
And she floats
When she's high
And the weeks pass euphoriously by

Verse: *Pretty Patty Peterson has got a little habit*
So Patty and the Hawk have formed a kind of partnership
Where he fulfills her needs as long as she fulfills her quota
Which she's presently fulfilling on the Minnesota Strip
She puts makeup on her bruises (The Hawk can be persuasive)
But as long as she delivers he's as sweet as he can be
And today he's upped her quota and he's also upped her dosage
'Cause every day it takes a little more
To get HIGHER THAN SHE'S EVER BEEN BEFORE

Verse: *Patty's feeling low and so she's having an injection*
(Part) *It's done, and she releases the belt around her arm*
And suddenly she's climbing past the point of no returning

Refrain: *And she's sick*
And she's sore
And she cannot seem to get up off the floor
And she screams
And she cries
And her life is passing right before her dilated eyes

Verse: *Pretty Patty Peterson was laid to rest this morning*
(Part) *In Potters Field as "eight three seven K eleven four"*
And if God is great and good and really truly understanding
Then she's HIGHER THAN SHE'S EVER BEEN BEFORE

Verse: *Pretty Debbie Darlington from Arlington, Virginia*
Is climbing on a Greyhound with a suitcase in her hand
And so is Jill from Maine
And so is Cindy from Milwaukee

And likewise Mike from Michigan
And Kim from Baltimore
And they're green as grass; they don't know what's in store
And they're HIGHER THAN THEY'VE EVER BEEN BE-
  FORE.

This lyric has clearly been shaped by a writer in control of his craft. We are led into the drama casually with the light touch of alliteration. Our attention is hooked, and it never wavers. The deemphasis on end rhyme is not accidental, but by design. Morgan sensed that the traditional ping/pong, ping/pong would be detrimental to the seriousness of his theme, so he used the adhesiveness of matched vowel sounds (broke/knows/own) interlaced with matched ending consonants (broke/Brooke, thinks/flicks) and subtle alliteration (Hawk/he/hey/how) and inner rhyme, to bind the lines into cohesive verses. Full end rhyme was unnecessary. The listener's ear, satisfied by rhyme substitutes, focuses on the sense of the story rather than its sound.

Like all fine writers, Jim Morgan has fun with words—such as "euphoriously," a synthesis of *euphoric* and *gloriously*. He also makes words do double duty; for example, the dual meaning of *terminal* goes by us unnoticed, until, in retrospect, we realize what the word foreshadowed.

Hawk is another instance of a word that resonates with implications. We are told obliquely, not bluntly, that the character is a pimp; the name triggers our awareness of the word's double definition: "predator," and "offering for sale." The lyric is exemplary at showing, instead of telling. Never do we hear directly that he beat her up, but rather that "she puts makeup on her bruises" and he "can be persuasive."

The Outside Refrain

"Higher Than She's Ever Been Before," like so many AAA songs of the sixties, makes a meaningful statement. Morgan, however, had more to say than could be contained within the classic AAA structure. What to do? More verses would not have met the needs of his drama; he clearly required another recurring section. But a one-time bridge wouldn't have worked. Neither would a chorus, and besides, the song's title was set into the last line of the verses. What, then? A refrain—outside the verses. A refrain with short lines to offset the long ones of the verses. A refrain whose re-echoed *i* rhyme scheme helps bind together three sections of uneven length. A refrain outlined with the repeated opening phrase "and she . . . and she . . . and she . . ." And just as our ear would have been tired of the sameness, Morgan shifts to: "and *her* life is passing right before her dilated eyes." That line is also notable for other reasons. Had he chosen to match the rhythmic length of the other two refrain last lines, he might have written, "right before her eyes." That would have worked fine. It says all we need to know. But the line was made more potent by the addition of another foot to the meter, with the word "*dilated*." The extending word (which in itself means "extended") emphasizes the climactic line by augmenting it—and while the word is bringing us a sharper picture of the action, its first syllable subtly tells us she is dying.

The refrain contains another instance of wordplay with the homonym *soar/sore*. Also, the title is multilayered in meaning, pyramiding from her joyful sense of freedom, to a drug euphoria, to her redemption.

The story comes full circle as another busload of innocents hits the wicked city—potential new pawns of street games. The lyric takes the runaway-girl plot of "She's Leaving Home" (on page 115) to its ultimate, making a strong statement about the climate of the eighties. With its closing hint of androgyny (Kim), "Higher Than She's Ever Been Before" speaks for its time.

WHERE'S THE PAYOFF?

Each of the three AAA examples in this chapter employs one or more of the payoff techniques outlined in Chapter 3. In "By the Time I Get to Phoenix," Jim Webb draws the ironic conclusion, "she just didn't know I would really go." "The Ballad of the Shape of Things" builds to the surprise of the unexpected pregnancy. In "Higher Than She's Ever Been Before," Jim Morgan uses two techniques: with rising action the song climaxes in Patty's death; then through an echo of the opening line ("Pretty Debbie Darlington"), he makes a larger statement about contemporary society—that Patty's tragedy is likely to be repeated. In the AAA the payoff obviously must come in the last verse, where some kind of comment is given or conclusion drawn.

WRAPUP

Acquiring craftsmanship is a two-part process: first developing an understanding of what constitutes good writing, and then putting those principles into practice. For your independent study, get copies of some of the more than thirty AAA lyrics mentioned in this chapter and analyze what makes them work. A good source is *Great Songs of the Sixties* (published by the New York Times Quadrangle Books), which contains twelve AAAs.

Think about a suitable theme—one with multiple characters, or changing locales, or shifting time segments. Or maybe you'll come up with a unique concept such as Sheldon Harnick's geometric figures. First try a lyric in the classic AAA structure, and when you feel you've mastered that, then experiment with variations.

chapter 6
The Verse/Chorus Form

"Always make the verse as interesting as the chorus." Sheldon Harnick

"If there's anything I've learned over all these years, it's that you've got to let the listener know when you've hit your chorus."
Barry Manilow

When the family gathered around the player piano for a sing-along in a mid-nineteenth-century parlor, the sheet music reflected America's eclectic tastes: there were songs by Schubert and Mendelssohn, Bellini arias (outfitted with new "pop" lyrics), along with ballads by Stephen Foster. The form was still predominantly the AAA.

By the time of the Civil War the verse/chorus structure had made an appearance. Each side of the battle boasted its own anthems—in the North, "Kingdom Coming" by Henry Clay Work, and in the South, Dan D. Emmett's "Dixie" were notable examples. Soldiers learned the words from songsters—pocket editions of lyrics with themes ranging from army life and political corruption to romantic golden oldies like "Oh! Susanna."

Then as now, the verse/chorus form proved the power of repetition: an account of a Chicago Court House Square rally in 1862 documents the first public rendition of the legendary "The Battle Cry of Freedom"; the crowd of a thousand, already stirred by emotional rhetoric, found it easy to join in the singing of the rousing short chorus as it rolled around again and again.

> *Yes, we'll rally round the flag, boys*
> *We'll rally once again*
> *Shouting the Battle Cry of Freedom*

Many songs from that era—among them "John Brown's Body," "Grandfather's Clock," and "Marching Through Georgia"—still rouse us today because of the power of the sing-along chorus.

THE VERSE/CHORUS GOES "SOLID GOLD"

Thirty years after the *a capella* introduction in Chicago of "The Battle Cry of Freedom," the performance of another verse/chorus ballad, "After the Ball," brought a San Francisco theater audience to its feet for five minutes of sustained applause. "After the Ball," became America's first million (sheet music) seller. In his autobiography, Charles K. Harris related that he had witnessed a lovers' quarrel at a dance, triggering the idea for the song, which he finished, words and music, "in one hour's time."

AFTER THE BALL

Verse: *A little maiden climbed an old man's knee*
         Begged for a story—"Do uncle please,
         Why are you single; why live alone?
         Have you no babies; have you no home?"
         I had a sweetheart, years, years ago;
         Where she is now pet, you will soon know.
         List to the story, I'll tell it all,
         I believed her faithless AFTER THE BALL.

Chorus: *AFTER THE BALL is over, after the break of morn—*
         After the dancers' leaving, after the stars are gone,
         Many a heart is aching, if you could read them all;
         Many the hopes that have vanished AFTER THE BALL.

Verse: *Bright lights were flashing in the grand ballroom,*
         Softly the music, playing sweet tunes,
         There came my sweetheart, my love, my own—
         "I wish some water; leave me alone."
         When I returned dear, there stood a man,
         Kissing my sweetheart as lovers can.
         Down fell the glass pet, broken, that's all,
         Just as my heart was AFTER THE BALL.

Chorus: *AFTER THE BALL is over, after the break of morn—*
         After the dancers' leaving, after the stars are gone,
         Many a heart is aching, if you could read them all;
         Many the hopes that have vanished AFTER THE BALL.

Verse: *Long years have passed child, I've never wed,*
         True to my lost love, though she is dead.
         She tried to tell me, tried to explain;
         I would not listen, pleadings were vain,
         One day a letter came from that man,
         He was her brother—the letter ran.
         That's why I'm lonely, no home at all;
         I broke her heart pet, AFTER THE BALL.

Chorus: *AFTER THE BALL is over, after the break of morn—*
         After the dancers' leaving, after the stars are gone;
         Many a heart is aching, if you could read them all;
         Many the hopes that have vanished AFTER THE BALL.

His verse/chorus lyric is a linear story told in three 64-bar verses; each is followed by a 32-bar chorus which both summarizes the action and comments upon it. Harris, one of the most successful songwriters of his time, clearly knew how to emphasize a title: with nine title mentions, a listener, hearing the song through only once, would know what to request at the sheet music counter.

HOW IT WORKS

Graphed, the basic verse/chorus structure looks like this:

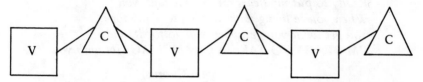

A triangle represents the chorus, not only to differentiate it from the verse, but also to underscore a principle: A chorus embodies both the musical peak and the lyrical point of the song. Unlike a refrain, which is the *concluding* musical phrase of an AAA song's verse, the chorus starts a new and separate musical statement.

The dominant characteristic of the verse/chorus song is assertiveness—unlike the unassuming quality of the AAA form, where no one section stands out from another. A chorus, by its very nature, calls attention to itself. As it interjects its points between the story line of the verses, it seems to shout: Hey, listen to me, I have something to say. The structure is ideal if you want periodically to restate an emphatic capsulized message. That's why Norman Gimbel and Charles Fox choose it for "Ready to Take a Chance Again," their Grammy-nominated theme for the film *Foul Play.* The song sums up in its chorus the emotions of the picture's leading lady, a divorcée, who is willing to make a new commitment. The message, however, is a timeless one that speaks for everyone who has ever fallen in love twice.

READY TO TAKE A CHANCE AGAIN

Verse: *You remind me I live in a shell*
Safe from the past
I'm doing okay,
But not very well;
No jokes, no surprises
No crisis arises
My life goes along as it should
It's all very nice
But not very good, but

Chorus: *I'M READY TO TAKE A CHANCE AGAIN*
          Ready to put my love on the line with you
          When you're living with nothing to show for it
          You get what you get when you go for it, and
          I'M READY TO TAKE A CHANCE AGAIN with you.

Half   *When he (she) left me in all my despair*
Verse: *I just held on*
         My hopes were all gone
         And I found you there, and

Chorus: *I'M READY TO TAKE A CHANCE AGAIN*
          Ready to put my heart on the line with you
          When you're living with nothing to show for it
          You get what you get when you go for it, and
          I'M READY TO TAKE A CHANCE AGAIN with you.

(Repeat Chorus)

The opening verse, with an admirable economy of words, captures the feelings of someone joylessly going through the motions of being alive. The words are a perfect marriage with the minor mode of the verses' music, which then brightens into the major as the melody climbs up to hit "chance again" and reaches still higher to affirm "on the line." Gimbel required only a half-verse to complete the story, which brings the soaring twelve-bar chorus back even sooner to restate its affirmative message.

Some other songs in the basic one verse/one chorus alternating pattern well worth your study are: "Nobody Does It Better," "Don't Cry Out Loud," and "Material Girl."

TITLE PLACEMENT

There is no question that the strongest place to put your title is in the first line of the chorus. An audience waiting through a verse (and often, two) is eager to get where your song is going. Listeners experience a strong sense of satisfaction upon identifying the title. They unconsciously say to themselves: Now I understand what this song is talking about. A title placed squarely in the opening line italicizes the chorus and, by emphasizing the song's structure, makes the lyric's meaning easier to perceive.

Hiding your title away somewhere in the middle of the chorus or delaying it until the last line puts a severe strain on your audience's attention span. You run the risk of their tuning out. Listeners don't want to have to work hard to decipher the message. It's part of a writer's craft to make it easy for them. Many a verse/chorus hit of the 1890s and 1900s is still familiar to us today because its instantly recognizable chorus features a top-line title; for example, "The Bowery," (1892), "My Wild Irish Rose" (1899), "Meet Me in St. Louis, Louis" (1904), and "My Gal Sal" (1905).

Putting the name of your product where it can be easily heard, and repeating it so that it will be remembered, is a sound lyric-writing precept. But it's not an ironclad rule. Every song has a life of its own, and well-conceived exceptions will deservedly find their audience. It didn't do Stephen Foster's "Old Folks at Home" any harm to save its title for the chorus's final words; the song's message got across. Some other examples of last-line-in-the-chorus titles that were worth their "wait" in gold records were "Escape," "What's Forever For?" "Separate Ways," and "She's Not Really Cheatin' (she's just gettin' even)." It's worth restating, however, that these successes are exceptions to a guiding principle: Marry your title to the opening musical phrase of the chorus.

Title Framing

If your title frames the chorus at the top and bottom as does "After the Ball," so much the better. Framing is a strong device which provides not only clarity and memorability, but even more important, a kind of emotional closure.

EXAMPLES:

_____ (TITLE) _____	"Love Will Turn You Around"
_____	"Some Mem'ries Just Won't Die"
_____	"Reunited"
_____	"What Are We Doin' in Love?"
_____	"Rhythm of the Night"
_____ (TITLE) _____	"Hang on Through the Holidays"

Another fortifying technique is reemphasizing the title at midpoint: twice is good, and three times is even better.

_____ (TITLE) _____	"Glory Days"
_____	"Somewhere Down the Road"
_____	"Every Woman in the World to Me"
_____ (TITLE) _____	"More than Just the Two of Us"
_____	"Up Where We Belong"
_____	"Kiss Me in the Rain"
_____ (TITLE) _____	"Stranger in My House"

Sometimes a chorus consists solely of an incessantly repeated title: it is often referred to as a hook chorus:

Lies, lies, lies, yeah
Lies, lies, lies, yeah
Lies, lies, lies, yeah.

I'm a One-Man Woman
I'm a One-Man Woman
I'm a One-Man Woman

I'll Tumble 4 Ya
I'll Tumble 4 Ya
I'll Tumble 4 Ya

Previewing the Title

Over a hundred years ago Charles K. Harris demonstrated a lyric device in "After the Ball" which has helped sell songs ever since: previewing the title in the last line of the verse. Of course, you don't simply staple it on to the end of a verse for effect; it must evolve from the lyric in a natural fashion and feel inevitable, as if no other line could possibly be there.

Some successful lyrics you can study that employ the technique are: "Straight from the Heart," "I Write the Songs," "I'll Never Love This Way Again," "She's Playing Hard to Forget," "Fool in Love with You," and "You Can't Be a Beacon if Your Light Don't Shine."

One cautionary word: Be careful that your rhyme scheme doesn't grow too predictable or too monotonous by your using the title in both verse and chorus.

Reserving the Title

Previewing in the verse's final line is a plus in that it emphasizes the title. However, using all or even some of the words of the title haphazardly anywhere else in the verses ultimately dilutes its power to both surprise and please a listener. Let's say your title is "Missing You," with a simple repetitive chorus:

Missing you
I'm missing you
That's all I do, night and day.
You're in each sound I hear
Each sight I see
Each word I say.

Because the language of the chorus is general, the verse should show specific examples of how, when, and where the singer does the missing—reserving the word itself—as well as the rest of the words in the chorus—exclusively for the chorus. For example, the verse could start:

Walking alone through the park today
I pretended you were by my side . . .

That's "missing you" without using the words. The principle is especially important with abstract titles: "Missing You," "All Over Again," or " A Dream Away," lacking concrete pictures, need all the help they can get to stand out.

This guideline does not apply to a character's name, such as "Richard Cory." If it has been sprinkled in the verses, the preview of it will serve to underscore the name's "titleness" when the chorus hits.

A Title Exception: "The Gambler"

Successful exceptions to the rule are usually exceptional songs. Don Schlitz's "The Gambler," the 1978 Grammy winner for Best Country Song, is an exceptional lyric in every sense of the word. For one thing, the singee dies during the song. And not many choruses make an impression on millions of record buyers without any assistance from the song's title.

The semantic richness of the chorus—the final advice of a poker player—is both universal and timeless: success in life, as in poker, has a lot to do with how we play our cards. The title untraditionally appears in the verses, popping up in different spots: in the third line of the first verse, the first line of the fourth verse, and the sixth line of the fifth verse!

THE GAMBLER

Verse: *On a warm summer's evening*
On a train bound for nowhere
I met up with a GAMBLER;
We were both too tired to sleep,
So we took turns a-staring
Out the window at the darkness
Till boredom overtook us and
He began to speak.

Verse: *He said: son, I've made a life*
Out of readin' people's faces
Knowing what the cards were
By the way they held their eyes.
So if you don't mind my sayin',
I can see you're out of aces,
For a taste of your whiskey
I'll give you some advice.

Verse: *So I handed him my bottle*
And he drank down my last swallow
Then he bummed a cigarette
And asked me for a light.
And the night got deathly quiet
And his face lost all expression,
He said, "If you're gonna play the game, boy,
You gotta learn to play it right.

Chorus: *You gotta know when to hold 'em*
Know when to fold 'em
Know when to walk away
And know when to run,
You never count your money
When you're sittin' at the table
There'll be time enough for countin'
When the dealing's done.

Verse: *Every GAMBLER knows*
That the secret to surviving
Is knowing what to throw away
And knowing what to keep
Cause every hand's a winner
And every hand's a loser
And the best that you can hope for
Is to die in your sleep."

Verse: *And when he finished speaking*
He turned back toward the window
Crushed out his cigarette
And faded off to sleep
And somewhere in the darkness
The GAMBLER, he broke even,
But in his final words
I found an ace that I could keep:

Chorus: *You gotta know when to hold 'em*
Know when to fold 'em
Know when to walk away,
And know when to run,
You never count your money
When you're sittin' at the table
There'll be time enough for countin'
When the dealing's done.

(repeat chorus)

Words and music by Don Schlitz. © 1978 Writers' Night Music. Used with permission.

Graphed it looks like this:

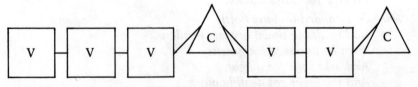

   "The Gambler" reaffirms that time-honored strategies for title placements are not hard and fast "musts." A true craftsman who knows the "rules" earns the right to break them.

THE VERSE: HOW MANY? HOW LONG?

Questions arise in every Basics Course about the structure of verses. What is the best length? How many is too many? There are no pat answers such as: write an eight-bar verse followed by a four-bar hook chorus, and *voilá,* a platinum record! No one can legislate creativity, or would want to. A good rule of thumb is the communication theory of "seven, plus or minus two" discussed on page 35. The concept, of course, holds true for a verse in any song form. For that matter, it applies to a chorus and a bridge. Your objective is a taut lyric. Six to eight lines of lyric (corresponding to six to eight bars of music) is a common number. Although ten to twelve are not unheard of, it is extremely difficult to maintain dramatic tension in a verse that long; the words and music had both better be fascinating to hold a listener's attention before the title strikes. Two tight stanzas are always preferable to one flabby one.

A good verse-writing guideline comes from a popular music publishing expression: "Don't bore us, get to the chorus." It means don't keep your listeners waiting too long to learn where your song is heading, or they'll tune out before it gets there. Admittedly, on occasion, several verses may be needed to say what has to be said. In "The Gambler" it took Don Schlitz three verses to establish his story sufficiently before he could introduce the first chorus. We weren't bored because he told us something new in each line, slowly moving his plot forward. There were no padded words, and no lines restating a fact we had already learned. Every word works to create the setting, the character, and the atmosphere.

Length and number of verses can vary. If your lyric is written before the music—whether it's going to be a country story song or a synth-pop dance tune—the content and style of your idea will dictate the length and shape of its sections. When the music comes first, as it did in "Somewhere Down the Road" and "Just Once," the composer takes the responsibility for creating well-proportioned parts.

Lyricists who believe that "anything is good enough in the verse if you have a good hook"—take heed. That false assumption is based on the premise that nobody listens to the words of the verse anyway. 'Tain't so. Although the eleven-year-old owner of the record "Maniac" may be unable to synopsize the song's plot, you'd better believe that the ears of the professional who picked the song for the film *Flashdance* (record producer Phil Ramone) scrutinized every word.

The demo-screening philosophy of another Grammy-winning producer, Jay Graydon, typifies the demands of today's publishers and producers: "If the verse is stinko, I'll take the tape off; if the verse is okay, I'll wait to hear the chorus." Remember to treat your verses with the same care you give the chorus.

THE CHORUS: ITS CONTENT AND SIZE

Veteran hit lyricist Sammy Cahn said: ". . . all verses, if you really think about it, merely add up to, 'and that's why I say . . .' " It's a sure-fire technique to smoke out a faulty chorus. Conversely, a well-developed chorus always passes the screening process: That's why I say:

"... *After the Ball Is Over.* ..."
"... *I'm Ready to Take a Chance Again.* ..."
"... *Touch Me in the Morning.* ..."
"... *There's a Stranger in My House.* ..."

Even when the title doesn't appear in the chorus, as in "Fifty Ways to Leave Your Lover" and "The Gambler," the "that's why I say" test proves equally effective with "quote" choruses: And that's why I say: "Slip out the back, Jack . . ." Or, and that's why I say: "You gotta know when to hold 'em." In essence, that's the mechanism of the structure: the title is a synopsis of the chorus, which is both an outcome of the verses and a summation of the song.

Can the Chorus Content Change?

It may seem that the words of all choruses repeat without variation each time they come around. Many do, such as "Richard Cory," "The Gambler," and "I Will Survive." Almost as often, though, the content of the chorus changes to accommodate the needs of the story; you can look ahead to "I'm Gonna Hire a Wino" in Chapter 9 and "Coward of the County" in Chapter 11. In these and other complex plots, the lyricist may need to utilize the chorus as well as the verses to advance the action of the story. You can make the verse/chorus structure produce a beginning-to-end dramatic tension: simply continue to unreel the emotional action within the choruses. I applied the technique in "She Knows" (page 57). When variations are necessary, it's important that you maintain the inherent recognizability of the chorus by restating the title in the expected places.

When you read over the verse/chorus examples in the book, you'll see that the length of a chorus is fairly elastic. The ideal shape is simply whatever feels proportionately right. Knowing how much is "right" is a knack you'll develop from a lot of practice. As you analyze successful songs on your own (which is the best way to internalize a sense of structure), you'll discover a common chorus-to-verse ratio pattern: the chorus, more often than not, is identical in length, half as long, or twice as long as the verse.

VARIATIONS ON A FORM

There is no simple blueprint for the one perfectly shaped verse/chorus song any more than there is for the one perfectly shaped house. In each case, both function and personal style create the structure. "The Gambler" demonstrates that some songs require three introductory verses. Other ideas may demand a double chorus—two back-to-back four- or eight-bar phrases that are musically identical (or nearly identical) but with lyrical content changes, such as "Escape (the Piña Colada Song)."

The trend is toward augmenting the simple verse/chorus format. Since the early seventies the fundamental verse/chorus structure diagrammed on page 47 has been dressed up with accessories. More often than not, current pop, rock, dance, and even country-crossover hits contain a climb or a bridge, or both.

The Climb

A climb has long been a part of the songwriter's art, but until fairly recently it didn't wear a name tag. It was simply that occasional (unlabeled) section that appeared between the end of the verse and the start of the chorus. Independent publisher/producers like Vince Castellano have discovered the climb's potential as an extra audience-hooking device; Castellano suggests to staff writers that they include one in the design of their verse/chorus songs.

At its simplest, a climb is a couplet (two rhymed lines in the same meter) which pull away from the verse both verbally and musically, and reach up toward the chorus. A climb functions as aural foreplay, to extend and increase the song's emotional tension by delaying the arrival of its climactic section.

Building a climb into a verse/chorus gives your song a fresh contour; it can, of course, stretch beyond a couplet to accommodate your lyrical or musical purpose. Here is vintage Rupert Holmes, a song whose structure has a mind of its own; "Nearsighted" says what it needs to say in one verse, one climb, and two and a half choruses:

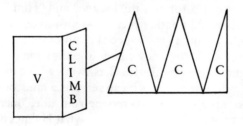

NEARSIGHTED

Verse
8 bars:

If you take these glasses from my face
I think that you will find
I'm undeniably, certifiably
Just this shade of blind.
But I don't envy those of you
With 20-20 vision
Who see the world for all it's worth
With crystal-clear precision.

Climb
4 bars:
There's more to see than can be seen
More said than what is heard;
The day is brighter, softer, lighter
When it's slightly blurred.

Chorus
16 bars:
NEARSIGHTED. It's another lovely day.
NEARSIGHTED. So I stumble on my way.
I don't judge a friend or lover
By a first or second look,
Nor a book just by its cover—
Hell, I can't even see the book.
NEARSIGHTED. Loving life is such a breeze.
NEARSIGHTED. Cause I see just what I please.
And it pleases me to see you
I won't change my point of view.
NEARSIGHTED, all I need to see is you.

Half
Chorus
8 bars:
Though I'm slightly out of focus,
I can see my dreams come true
Clearsighted, NEARSIGHTED
NEARSIGHTED, all I need to see is you.

"Nearsighted," with its wry charm, has made a life for itself outside its original album, "Partners in Crime," as a favorite with sophisticated supper-club audiences. Rupert Holmes, who topped the charts with fundamental verse/chorus formats in "Escape" and "Him," proves again that when you understand a basic structure—its assets and liabilities—you can then reinvent it to suit a lyric's special requirements. (It's also worth noting that Holmes certainly knows how to parlay the one-word title!)

"Nearsighted" exemplifies Ira Gershwin's advice to "prove" your title, and like all well-written lyrics it can serve as a minicourse in writing principles. For example, consider "reserving your title," mentioned a few pages back. See how well the concept works: what Holmes did was show the effects of nearsightedness in the verse, strike an attitude about it in the climb, and identify the condition by name in the chorus. Imagine, if we had heard the word *nearsighted* in the verse or the climb, how uninterested we would be when the chorus finally struck.

Holmes keeps the tension line of the story pulled tight. Not until the second half of the (double) chorus do we learn of a love interest—"and it pleases me to see you . . ." What the song achieves is a fresh way to say I love you without *saying* "I love you"—an accomplishment that raises the rating of a lyric many notches above the ordinary.

Mastering the climb will help you add vitality to your verse/chorus lyrics. Study these additional examples: "Come What May" and "Here I

Am" recorded by Air Supply; "I Made It Through the Rain" recorded by Barry Manilow; "Heartbreaker" recorded by Dionne Warwick; and "If Ever You're in My Arms Again" recorded by Peabo Bryson.

The Bridge—What It's For and Where to Put It

How can you tell when your verse/chorus song should have a bridge? You learn to sense it. Sometimes the need is obvious: for example, when a plot requires a little more information yet not enough to warrant a whole new verse. A two-line bridge can make the perfect link in the chain of events. Or maybe the tune is too four-square; a fresh musical section would offset the predictability of the verse/chorus, verse/chorus pattern. Or perhaps—although you feel you've already said all you need to say, the song is simply over too fast to make a satisfying record. A bridge can be the ideal musical "stretcher" to which you can easily add a new thought.

As a climb functions to build tension, a bridge works to provide contrast in lyrical content, meter, and melody. The listener has been concentrating through several verses (and at least one chorus) to follow the story line; a short musical transition can be a welcome relief from sameness and make the return of the final chorus more satisfying. Although the bridge, more often than not, is musically "new," it doesn't have to be. You may find that half a verse (either the first half or the last) can be just the transition you need. The half-verse device worked well for "Somewhere Down the Road" (Snow/Weil) and "Him" (Holmes).

Lyrically speaking, your bridge doesn't justify its existence if it merely restates a fact we've already been told. Ideally, a bridge adds dimension to a lyric by expanding the content of the verse or chorus, or by giving new insight into the singer's feelings.

To enrich your understanding of the function of bridges, analyze the current hits. Here are some past successes together with the artists who recorded them: "Stranger in my House"(Ronnie Milsap), "Our Love Is on the Faultline" (Crystal Gayle), "Up Where We Belong" (Joe Cocker and Jennifer Warnes), "I Write the Songs" (Barry Manilow), and "Just Once" (James Ingram). In one of my own songs, "She Knows," a bridge was the only place to make a key statement.

SHE KNOWS

Verse: *Tell me how she got suspicious*
When we've both been so discreet?
You get home in time for dinner,
Phone me only from the street.
Were you singing in the shower?
Did you leave some telltale sign?
Well, I guess a wife has subtle ways
To read between the lines . . . so now

Chorus: *SHE KNOWS, SHE KNOWS*
I always knew one day you'd say
SHE KNOWS, SHE KNOWS
The words still take my breath away,
I hear a love song coming to a close
Now that we know—SHE KNOWS.

Verse: *You say she's going crazy*
Wond'ring who and where and when,
That ev'ry time you leave the house
Her eyes fill up again.
You are torn between a promise
And a castle built on sand—
Well, I see the answer on your face
And in your trembling hand—
You are thinking that

Chorus: *SHE KNOWS, SHE KNOWS*
I'm more than just a sometime fling.
She feels, SHE KNOWS,
And her knowing changes everything.
A dream world is ending—
Two words, and pouff, it goes—
Why'd you tell me SHE KNOWS?

Bridge: *Well, I'm not gonna cry.*
I say hooray for what's been.
So come kiss me goodbye
While my eyes are still dry
Before it all sinks in—
That she fin'ly

Chorus: *KNOWS*
Now you'll go back—and she'll forgive
And so it goes—
You'll both work out some way to live.
And I will remember
You love me so much, it shows—
Funny, that's how————SHE KNOWS.

© 1983 Solar Systems Music. Used with permission.

DEVELOPING YOUR STORY

As a check that you haven't restated a fact or feeling that the listener already knows, it's helpful to write a prose synopsis for each stanza. Here's one for "She Knows":

First
Verse: *Singer learns from her lover that his wife has sensed their relationship.*

First
Chorus: *Shows her stunned reaction to his announcement and senses it's all over.*

Second
Verse: *She plays back his feelings to him and interprets his nervousness.*

Second
Chorus: *She lets us know it was a long-term affair; resents his telling her.*

Bridge: *Decides to make it easy on him to say goodbye by saying it first, thereby avoiding a soap opera scene.*

Final
Chorus: *Realizes the irony: his loving her was what gave him away.*

Making such a synopsis is a reliable safeguard against repeating yourself. The mere process of analyzing the thought expressed in each stanza, even if you don't write it down, will help weed out twice-stated ideas and propel your story forward.

WHERE'S THE PAYOFF?

A point made in Chapter 3 bears repeating: well-constructed lyrics, like good plays, are built upon exposition, rising action, and conclusion. They look, in effect, like this:

Where the payoff comes in a song is not fixed but is as individual as the song itself; however, the lyric should maintain its dramatic tension as long as possible before it peaks. A poorly written lyric can feel like this:

The plot line peaks too soon, so from that point the song goes downhill emotionally.

Superimposing the development line over some variations of the verse/chorus structure, we can see the possibilities for payoff place inherent in the form:

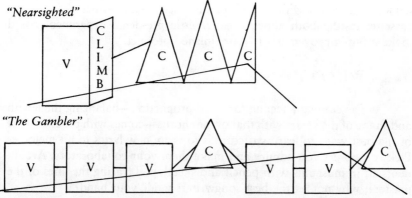

"Nearsighted"

"The Gambler"

"She Knows"

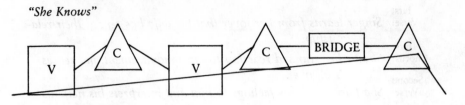

"Nearsighted" makes its wrapup in the final half-chorus: "I can see my dreams come true . . . all I need is you." In "The Gambler" it's the last verse that contains the summation: ". . . in his final words I found an ace that I could keep." That line leads right into the chorus, which now—because the gambler is dead—resounds with more weight. "She Knows" maintains its tension until the last word, when the singer realizes that her lover *showed* his love, which answers her opening-line question, "Tell me how she got suspicious."

For a refresher on how to build your lyric to a satisfactory conclusion, turn back to the Payoff section of Chapter 3. You'll also find more methods to develop second verses and bridges in the next chapter, on the AABA form; the techniques for writing successful AABA bridges work equally well in the verse/chorus form. If you suffer from chronic second-act trouble and seek immediate relief, jump ahead to Chapter 7.

WHICH COMES FIRST, VERSE OR CHORUS?

One important demo decision worthy of some advance thought is whether to introduce the song with the verse or with the chorus. Your choice will be based upon the effect you're trying to create. Starting off with the chorus is unquestionably an attention-getting device: the listener immediately knows the title and pretty much the gist of the song. If, however, it's important that your story start low key and build slowly toward the surprise of the chorus, then you'll want to open with the verse.

Although verses more often open a song than not, many successes have hooked the listener by leading with the chorus, hits such as: "Touch Me in the Morning," "Do You Know Where You're Going To?" "Nobody Does It Better," and "Sleeping Single in a Double Bed." Before the costly demo, try a dry run with a simple piano-voice or guitar-voice treatment on cassette, testing both approaches. A little pre-demo experiment could make a big improvement in your finished product.

WRAPUP

Developing a feeling for good proportion—balancing the length and shape of the verses with that of the chorus—comes with practice. One of the best ways to learn structure is to write new lyrics to hit melodies. Pick composers you admire and make them your collaborators. Art students sit in museums with pencil and sketch pad tracing the lines of the masters; why not let the best songwriters guide your hand?

chapter 7

The AABA Form

"The AABA structure—with its four 8-bar blocks—is at the root of all Western art music, folk music, and theatre music." Lehman Engel

Until the early years of the twentieth century the average verse/chorus song was weighted down with six or seven verses, each about ten lines long. By the 1920s both the number of verses and their length had been greatly reduced. By the mid-thirties even the one- or two-verse introduction had become an optional feature. What slowly evolved was a 32-bar chorus composed of four sections of equal length; within that tight structure a number of musical patterns emerged—the ABAB, ABAC, AABC, and the most enduring of them all, the AABA.

The introductory verse, which was still being written occasionally during the forties, had a lyric content of pure fluff and was dispensable to the song's plot. The reason for its existence, other than as a musical convention of the day, was to give the stage or screen star more to perform by way of a charming setup for the chorus. Such AABA standards as "Blue Moon," "Just One of Those Things," and "Memories of You" have verses that are little known and not missed—except, perhaps, to collectors of trivia.

In essence, the AABA "chorus" was and is the song. During the decades from 1910 to 1950 America's greatest musical innovators—Irving Berlin, Jerome Kern, George Gershwin, Richard Rodgers, Arthur Schwartz, Cole Porter, Vernon Duke, Vincent Youmans, and Harold Arlen—created melodies in the AABA form for which the adjectives "charming," "gorgeous," "soaring," and "eloquent" have often been applied. The music of the AAA and the verse/chorus forms rarely achieve such accolades. When we hear the lament: ". . . they don't write 'em like that any more!" the *that* usually means an AABA song written (music first) by one of the aforementioned illustrious composers during the period known as "the golden years of Tin Pan Alley."

Though there is no right or wrong way to create a beautiful song, it is significant that so many of our standards were conceived first as melodies. Lyrics were generally fitted to the tune, resulting in such songs as "Smoke Gets in Your Eyes," "Without a Song," "More Than You Know," "April in Paris," and "The Way You Look Tonight." When a composer pours out a tune he *has* to write because the music is welling up inside him, as opposed to having to accommodate a lyrical meter he finds less than inspiring, a superior melody inevitably results.

Aspiring contemporary songwriters eager to develop their craft to the utmost might find it significant that the AABA form still thrives today, not only in Hollywood and on Broadway, but also on the top-40 and country charts. In a marketplace dominated by the synthesized hook-chorus song, it can be easy to overlook the subtleties of the AABA.

HOW IT WORKS

The chief reason so many beautiful melodies have been written in AABA is simple: the form flows. In contrast to the stop-start quality of both the AAA and the verse/chorus, the AABA expresses one moment's feeling in a fluid statement. The AAA musical setting, with its segmented repetitions, can never hope to equal an AABA in complexity or emotional development, and relatively few verse/chorus tunes can compete in originality and elegance with the best of AABAs.

The AABA structure allows no 4-bar interlude between verse to slow its momentum, and no italicized chorus to overstate a melodic or lyric phrase. Each section moves seamlessly into the next, building to a conclusion that leaves an audience emotionally satisfied.

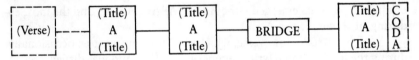

The earliest AABAs were built on an 8-bar phrase followed by an identical 8-bar phrase, contrasted with an 8-bar bridge or *release* of new music that returns to the first phrase, with or without a slight extension (coda) to mark the end of the song. Ever since Cole Porter expanded the classic 32-bar song to 48 measures in 1932 with "Night and Day," no one keeps strict count of the number of bars. The A sections contain the form's dominant melodic phrase and therefore contain the song's title as well as the substance of lyric idea.

"Sunny Side of the Street" rates high on the list of all-time AABA standards. The timeless melody is by Jimmy McHugh and the ageless words by Dorothy Fields. Here it is, complete with its little-known verse:

ON THE SUNNY SIDE OF THE STREET

Verse: *Walked with no one,*
And talked with no one, and
I had nothing but shadows
Then one morning you passed
And I brightened at last.
Now I greet the day
And complete the day
With the sun in my heart
All my worry blew away
When you taught me how to say:

Chorus: *Grab your coat and get your hat*
A: *Leave your worry on the doorstep*
Just direct your feet
To THE SUNNY SIDE OF THE STREET.

A: *Can't you hear a pitter pat*
And that happy tune is your step
Life can be so sweet
ON THE SUNNY SIDE OF THE STREET.

B: *I used to walk in the shade*
With those blues on parade
But I'm not afraid
This rover, crossed over.

A: *If I never have a cent*
I'll be rich as Rockefeller
Gold dust at my feet
ON THE SUNNY SIDE OF THE STREET.

Like all fine craftsmen, Dorothy Fields makes lyric writing sound finger-snapping easy. Sensing the best spot for the tune's title, she made sure her listener would know it on one hearing by popping it into place, three times. Traditionally, the bridge is a place for musical and lyrical contrast: this one plays against the sunshine of the A sections with a flashback to gloomier days. Fields could have let her lyric get preachy, but instead she told, in a fresh way, how finding someone special made her feel happy. With total simplicity and directness, Dorothy Fields matched the lilt of Jimmy McHugh's tune and created a song of rare timelessness: after fifty years it's still getting new records.

TITLE PLACEMENT

Traditionally, there are two title spots in the AABA: in either the first line or the last line of the verse. Skilled lyricists intuitively pinpoint the music's most identifiable phrase, drop in the title, and work from there, forward or backward. Some first-line-title songs for your study from both "then" and now are: "Don't Blame Me," "Just One of Those Things," "When Sunny Gets Blue," "On A Clear Day (You Can See Forever)," "Born Free," "Time in a Bottle," "Everybody's Talkin'," "Raindrops Keep Falling on My Head," "Yesterday," "What Now My Love," "Yesterday's Songs," and "She's Got a Way."
Some last-line titles include recent successes from film, theater, pop, and country fields as well as golden oldies: "As Time Goes By," "Little Girl Blue," "He Ain't Heavy, He's My Brother," "Until It's Time For You To Go," "Just the Way You Are," "Come in From the Rain," "My Way," "What I Did for Love," "One Hundred Ways," and "Don't It Make My Brown Eyes Blue."

The Music Life and How to Succeed in It, a songwriting guide published in 1935, offered this advice on AABA title placement: "The title should be repeated at least twice—once at the beginning and once at the end [of the song]. Many . . . songwriters make the mistake of mentioning the title only at the beginning. This is almost as bad a mistake as neglecting to repeat the melody theme." The advice still holds. Two mentions are good, but three (as in "On the Sunny Side of the Street") make a stronger impression.

Title Exceptions

As always, there are exceptions to the rule. The title to "Evergreen," for example, makes its first appearance tucked away in the middle of the second A and reappears once more as the song's final word. Dan Fogelberg's "Longer" opens the song and reechoes in the next line, but never shows up again. "Evergreen," a movie theme, was co-written (with Paul Williams) by the movie's star Barbra Streisand, and "Longer" was penned and recorded by a writer/performer. These songs obviously didn't make the charts through the customary process of being signed by a publisher, who then had to find an artist to record them. The songs were written by the artists themselves for specific projects—a film and an album. It is safe to say that most publishers, on the lookout for clear-cut commercial formats, would have "passed" on both these songs—good as they are—had they come in over the transom. Over the last decade it has been hard to sell a ballad. Without their guaranteed records, "Evergreen" and "Longer" would have been considered "work songs," meaning that getting them recorded would have required a long-term commitment. No publisher can be blamed for preferring songs that sound like something teenagers will want to dance to—something with a beat and a repeating chorus. But the bottom line is: when well-written AABA ballads get the required exposure, the public responds and makes them long-run winners. "Evergreen" has been recorded by more than a dozen other artists since its initial record—and has become a new standard.

To be on the safe side, make your title, through repetition, immediately recognizable to your listener upon one hearing. Be aware of the risk inherent in writing a song whose title is hard to locate or to remember. If, however, you've written about an idea that's important to you, and you're sure it can't be expressed any other way, don't compromise the lyric's integrity. "Stardust," the Mitchell Parish/Hoagy Carmichael classic, is resounding proof that an exceptional lyric can create an impact without the customarily repeated title. If you truly have said something worth listening to, your song will find its audience. It just may take a little longer.

BRIDGE DEVELOPMENT DEVICES

Traditionally, the bridge takes the listener to a new musical place which sounds inevitable both in its arrival and its return to the final A. The accompanying words should also give the listener a fresh aspect of the story. Bridges develop best through some kind of rhetorical contrast: *contrast* is the operative word in the following techniques:

Change the Pronouns

If every section of a lyric were dominated by the same pronoun, whether *you* or *I* or *she* or *they,* the listener would soon nod off. All good writers have a built-in boredom detector and can intuit when to switch personal pronouns. In describing the tall, tan, and lovely "Girl from Ipanema," (Gimbel/Jobim) the verses emphasize *she,* and when the bridge hits, we (unconsciously) sigh with relief at hearing the welcome, ". . . oh, but *I* . . ." The first two As in "Send in the Clowns" (Sondheim) employ the plural pronoun *we* (less personal) as well as the indefinite *one;* part of the emotional impact of the song's climactic bridge results from the first appearance of the intimate *I,* as it brings the singer's candid confession of poor timing.

Introduce the Opposite

The bridge of "If You Go Away" (McKuen/Brel) shows the results of rhetorically flipping the coin. Just as the title's (repeated) use is about to overtax the listener's enjoyment of the familiar—"if you go away . . . if you go away . . . if you go away . . .," a contrast in verbs breaks the monotony: ". . . but if you stay. . . ."

"When Sunny Gets Blue" (Segal/Fisher) achieves a beautifully balanced lyric with a cheery bridge over wistful verses. In contrast to the opening sections, which paint a portrait of a loveless lady in the doldrums, the bridge brightens the picture by recalling her smile.

The bridge of "Ol' Man River" (Hammerstein/Kern) features a double contrast: the focus switches from *them* and *he* to *you* and *me* and counterpoints the back-breaking "sweat and strain" of the laborers along the river bank against the sedate Mississippi "just rollin' along."

Particularize

When the subject matter of the verses is treated mostly in general statements, the song requires seasoning with specifics. There are three ways to do it: you can illustrate with examples, elaborate with details, or expand with close analysis. For instance, the verses of "Ac-cent-tchu-ate the Positive" (Mercer/Arlen) exhort the audience to do what the title suggests. Had the bridge repeated the nonspecific language of the verses, the listener would have felt more preached to than entertained. Fortunately, the message was leavened with lighthearted examples of how Jonah and Noah kept their chins up.

After its verses proclaim that love is "What the World Needs Now" (Bacharach/David), the bridge not only counters with what we *don't* need, but also particularizes natural resources: mountains, meadows, cornfields, rivers, and so on.

In the A sections of "The Surrey with the Fringe on Top" (Rodgers/Hammerstein) we get an overview of the outside of a slick rig; in the bridge we get a full-color closeup of the buggy's "yeller" wheels, brown upholstery, and genuine leather dashboard.

"When I Need You" (Sager/Hammond) is a lyric that asks the lover to stay true while they're apart—a pretty general idea. The bridge fills in the particulars: that the singer is a performer who's on the road a lot. That fact increases our understanding of why he asks the lover to "hold out" as he does, until they're together again.

Using the technique of close analysis, the lyricist switches from a long-distance to a close-up lens. In many ballads, such as "Come in from the Rain" (Sager/Manchester), "Time in a Bottle" (Croce), and "You and Me, We Wanted It All" (Sager/Allen), the bridge takes a penetrating look at a relationship, and gives us the very heart of the song—an insight that resonates with a universal and often poignant truth.

Personalize

The bridge of "The Impossible Dream" (Darion/Leigh) stems a cascade of impersonal infinitives—*to dream, to fight, to bear, to run, to try*—with the personal, "This is *my* quest . . ."

After the introductory verses of "The Last Time I Saw Paris" (Hammerstein/Kern) describe how the city looked in the spring (*its* heart, *its* trees), the bridge, in contrast, focuses on the singer's reactions and feelings about the city (*I* dodged . . . *my* heart). It is through personalization that such songs achieve their emotional connection to the listener.

Draw a Conclusion

Some verses overflow with specificity. By bridge time the listener needs both a rest from examples and something more: the reason for their existence. In "They Can't Take That Away from Me" (the Gershwins), the last thing we would want to hear in the bridge is more details, however charming. We get just what we want: a statement that the singer will "always keep the mem'ry of" all those particulars.

The bridge of "Smoke Gets in Your Eyes" (Harbach/Kern) provides double contrast: first it shifts the emphasis of the pronouns from *they* to *I*, and then it reveals the ironic situation that *they* were right—the "true love" has gone and the singer is alone.

Flashback

A flashback is a scene inserted into a story, novel, film, or play which interrupts the chronology of events and tells something that happened previously. The device is common in lyrics, comparing the way things are with how they used to be.

In the bridge of "Do You Know Where You're Going To?" (Masser/Goffin), the theme from *Mahogany,* the relentless *questions* posed in the verses (do you know, do you like, do you get, etc.) are balanced by a *statement* flashing back to the earlier happiness of the estranged lovers.

Another movie song, "With You I'm Born Again" (Connors/Shire), is the mirror image of *Mahogany's* theme: the verses celebrate new and (presumably) eternal love; the bridge reflects on the loneliness of the lovers before they met.

Flashforward

The flashforward looks at the future as it hopefully will be, conditionally could be, or regretfully won't be. In the verses of "Over the Rainbow" (Harburg/Arlen) Dorothy's dreams of a magic land are still of a general nature; in the bridge she personalizes them ". . . someday I'll . . ." moving to the specific in a preview of her arrival in Oz.

Entrances to the Bridge

Sometimes it's hard to find the right road to the bridge. If your creative motor has stalled, try to look at your story from another angle. Here are some time-tested phrases that may trigger an approach: so now I . . . but once we . . . I guess you . . . remember when we'd . . . I can tell that . . . I wish you'd . . . maybe if . . . if only. . . . The whole trick is to stay focused on your subject from the beginning to end.

STRETCHING THE FORM

Prior to the sixties it took lyricists a scant fifty to seventy words to fill out the lean 32-bar frame of the AABA song. Contemporary composers seem to have exchanged those half- and whole-note melodies for patterns of eighth and sixteenth notes such as in "Rainy Days and Mondays." Multinote measures are one of the distinguishing characteristics of today's songs, whose lyrics now average between 135 and 175 words.

In addition to adding notes and words, something else has been happening to the shape of the AABA; the structure itself has stretched to accommodate the three- to four-minute record format. Many current AABA songs look like this:

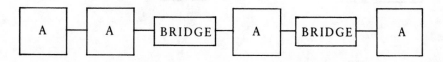

Of course, the introductory verse has long since been dropped. The classic 32-bar chorus ended at the third A. The contemporary AABA prolongs the song's climax by reprising the bridge, where the lyric's story frequently continues to develop with new words. This extended AABA, usually 40 or more bars, now ends with a fourth A section whose lyric content might be all new, partly new, or a repeat or composite of a previous verse. Here is how the extended AABA lyric works in some contemporary successes:

"Do You Know Where You're Going To?" (Recorded by Diana Ross)

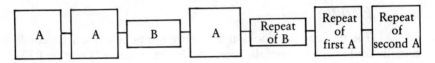

"When I Need You" (Recorded by Leo Sayer)

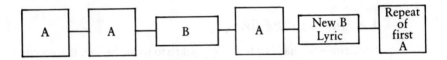

"Out Here on My Own" (Recorded by Irene Cara)

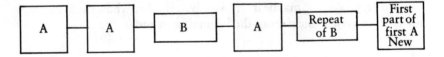

"She's Got a Way" (Recorded by Billy Joel)

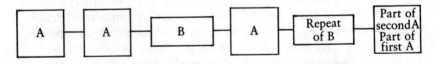

"Memory" (Recorded by Barbra Streisand, Barry Manilow, Judy Collins)

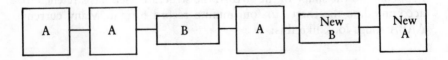

LEAPING FROM THE STAGE
TO THE CHARTS

The London and Broadway hit musical *Cats,* inspired by poems in T.S. Eliot's *Old Possum's Book of Practical Cats,* adds another AABA ballad to the illustrious roster of theater songs. Early in the show's New York run, "Memory" hit the pop charts twice with versions by superstars Barbra Streisand and Barry Manilow. Not since "Send in the Clowns" grabbed the Grammy in 1975 has a song from a Broadway show generated so many recordings, both vocal and instrumental, and entrenched itself in the repertoire of club singers.

The melody of "Memory"—with its Puccini-like sweep—is one of Andrew Lloyd Webber's most memorable. The lyric is a true hybrid, in which Trevor Nunn deftly worked some words from T.S. Eliot poems into his own design. Trevor Nunn, the director of *Cats,* told me in a letter about the song's genesis:

> Andrew wrote the tune in response to my urging that Grizabella needed to have a climactic and emotional utterance during which something of her increasing loneliness would be revealed, and ending with an appeal. The difficulty was to get the lyricist to lose his or her own authentic voice and assume Eliot's without resorting to imitation; and at the same time making a song that would be essentially detachable. I was not the natural choice for lyricist . . . [but] others were approached and sadly discarded.
>
> I resorted to early Eliot poems for the tone of voice I was after, but I tried to quote as little as possible, and to make the lyric tie in with what was emerging as the theme and plot of the show.

The scene is a London city dump; the time, midnight; the event, the annual all-night revel of catdom during which the elder statesman, Old Deuteronomy, will bestow upon one chosen cat a new life. Grizabella, a once glamorous feline, sings of days gone by when she was beautiful. Now, loveless and past her prime, she tries to believe that tomorrow will be a better day. The song brings down the first-act curtain with her plea to Deuteronomy, "Touch me." At the end of the second act Grizabella becomes the one "touched." Her reprise of "Memory" signals her rebirth and triumphant ascent into the "heaviside layer."

The lyric is set in the expanded AABA format with a second bridge and concluding fourth A. Italicized words are from T.S. Eliot.

MEMORY

A: *Midnight*
Not a sound from the pavement,
Has the *moon lost her* MEMORY?
She is smiling alone.
In the *lamp*light
The *withered leaves* collect at my *feet*
And the wind begins to moan.

A: MEMORY
All alone in the moonlight
I can smile at the old days
I was beautiful then;
I remember
The time I knew what happiness was:
Let the MEMORY live again.

B: Ev'ry *streetlamp*
Seems to *beat*
A *fatalistic* warning;
Someone *mutters*
And the *streetlamp gutters*
And soon it will be *morning.*

A: *Daylight*
I must wait for the sunrise
I must think of a new life
And I mustn't give in
When the dawn comes
Tonight will be a MEMORY too,
And a new day will begin.

B: *Burnt out ends*
Of smoky days,
The *stale* cold *smell* of *morning,*
The *streetlamp* dies
Another night is over
Another day is dawning,

A: *Touch me,*
It's so easy to leave me
All alone with my MEMORY
Of my days in the sun,
If you touch me
You'll understand what happiness is,
Look, a new day has begun.

In three of Eliot's early poems, Trevor Nunn found the ideal "tone of voice" he was after, along with key scene-setting words and phrases. For example, the lyric's time-spanning pattern—from midnight to daylight—is modeled after the poem "Rhapsody on a Windy Night," which opens at "twelve o'clock" and proceeds through its six stanzas to "four o'clock." In addition to providing "streetlamp," "midnight," "fatalistic," and the "mutter/gutter" rhyme, "Rhapsody" contributed the line, "the moon has lost her memory," which Nunn inverted into a question. "Prelude I" was the source of "burnt out ends of smoky days" and "withered leaves." From "Prelude II" he found scattered words to fuse into the lyric's line "the stale cold smell of morning."

Trevor Nunn accomplished his goal "to quote as little as possible" and to create a song that both served the plot and was "essentially detachable." The atmosphere and the tone of "Memory" are decidedly Eliot, the poet—and properly so—but it is Nunn's instinctive songwriting ability that makes the lyric so recordable. Every word falls perfectly on the music, which is one of the reasons performers find it a pleasure to sing. Its vowels cascade in a glissando of tones, sliding down from the higher pitched opening -i- of *midnight* to the doleful -o- of *moan*. If you read the lyric aloud, you'll hear how the words make their own music. Word repetitions outline the form: *I must* wait/*I must* think; *another* night/*another* day. Alliteration propels the action: *m*idnight/*p*ave*m*ent/*m*oon/*m*e*m*ory/*m*oan.

The A sections are marked by a unique pattern: they seesaw between the exterior setting and an interior monologue (the thoughts of the singer), as the clock hands turn. The first A section sets the almost eerie street scene, which dissolves into a flashback of the singer's youth; the bridge—particularizing with details—returns to the street where "someone mutters" and the lamp burns down as night moves toward sunrise.

The AABA structure does not lend itself to time movement in the sense of hours or days *literally* changing during the lyric. Specific time movements, whether implied or expressed, tend to disrupt the seamless flow of the "one moment's feeling" inherent in the form. In "Memory" the time change works pretty well. The theater audience, of course, sees the dawn slowly lighting the sky as the song unfolds; the radio and record listener can hear the announced shifts: "Midnight . . daylight . . . morning." I would think Nunn faced a tough choice, however, regarding title placement: the opening dotted quarter-note figure—dum dum—is clearly the title spot for a song to be called "mem'ry." Thus it was not want of skill that dropped the title "Memory" into four unorthodox places, but rather expediency: the time frame had to be set—then reset.

Some of the song's fans still request of musicians: "Please play that song called 'Midnight,' or 'Moonlight,' or 'Mem'ries'—you know, the one from *Cats*." Sidestepping the traditional title placement has an obvious drawback. In "Memory," the plot requirements took precedence.

In this extended AABA the second bridge and final A section continue to move the action forward: the bridge declares "Another night is over/Another day is dawning." The song climaxes with the last A's "(If you) touch me/You'll understand what [my] happiness is" which echoes back to "I remember the time I knew what happiness was." We've come full circle with hope for tomorrow.

It's ironic that Eliot's belief that "true poetry can communicate before it is understood" applies so well to "Memory." Many lovers of the song, swept up in the emotion generated by the combined words and music, are confused about the lyric's story. Because they haven't seen *Cats*, they don't know what is implied by a "fatalistic warning," or why time moves from midnight to sunrise, or more important, to whom "touch me" is addressed. The song's success, like that of "Send in the Clowns, " is an anomaly which seems to defy the principle of clarity. Several recording artists of "Send in the Clowns" have publicly admitted not understanding the lyric, which, in the context of the scene in *A Little Night Music* for which it was written, is poignantly clear.

The main, if not sole, concern of the theater lyricist is to write the most appropriate words for a given character in a given situation. If the song then goes on to find a wider audience outside the show—wonderful; that's a welcome dividend. But if the lyric isn't totally understood by the nontheater-going record buyer, that is no reflection on the lyricist's lack of skill; a theater song is not designed for the radio listener. What the fans of "Memory" have responded to is the perfectly clear philosophy of the lyric: an acceptance of the past and an anticipation of a brighter tomorrow—in short, a resounding affirmation of life.

The AABA Expands

Gordon (Sting) Sumner—the main creative force behind the most acclaimed group of 1983, the Police—is a classically trained composer and keyboard artist whose musical tastes range from Gershwin's *Porgy and Bess* to the jazz orchestrations of Miles Davis. During what he terms "creative troughs," Sumner hones his craft with challenging musical exercises; for example, he orchestrated Ralph Vaughn Williams's Sixth Symphony for an Oberheim synthesizer! That project required him to master many technical complexities, such as matching diverse rhythms of different instruments—the bass in 4/4 time and the oboes in 12/8. After the feat of literally performing a symphony solo, his innovation with the AABA song form was a mere bagatelle.

In "Every Breath You Take," the number-one single of the Police's multimillion-selling album "Synchronicity," Sumner took the AABA to a new place: he added a C section.

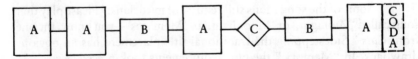

In an interview in *Musician Magazine* Sting, as Sumner is professionally known, said that "Every Breath You Take" wrote itself in ten minutes; while vacationing in Jamaica, he woke up in the middle of the night, went straight to the piano, and the song "just came out." How effortlessly the unconscious works its apparent magic—on an informed intellect.

It's interesting that Sting, who had programmed himself with Gershwin songs, repeated a lyric-writing choice that Ira Gershwin made decades ago in "I Got Rhythm." Just as Gershwin had elected to bypass what would normally be the title phrase, "who could ask for anything more," so did Sting ignore his own obvious title line at the end of each A section, "I'll be watching you." Instead, he picked the lyric's opening phrase.

"Every Breath You Take" vividly illustrates that the verse/chorus structure is not the sole path to the top of the charts. Its lyric appears in Chapter 19 with an analysis of how the song's meter contributes to its meaning.

THE ABAB/ABAC FORMS

Back when Berlin, Kern, Gershwin, Porter, and Rodgers were composing their AABA standards, they were also turning out an equal number in the ABAB form. Like the AABA, the ABAB and its variant, the ABAC, were generally 32 bars, but instead of three As spanned by a bridge, these structures consisted of two 16-bar sections joined together rather like Siamese twins: identical ones in the case of the ABAB, and fraternal ones in the ABAC. Here is how they look, along with some of their best-known songs:

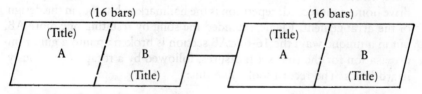

" 'Til the Clouds Roll By"   "I Could Write a Book"
"Swanee"   "Sometimes I'm Happy"
"Fly Me to the Moon"   "But Not for Me"
"Odds and Ends of a Beautiful Love Affair"

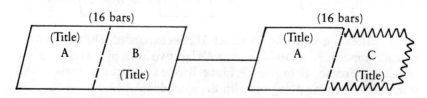

"A Pretty Girl Is Like a Melody"   "Moon River"
"April Showers"   "Tea for Two"
"White Christmas"   "Call Me Irresponsible"
"Poor Butterfly"   "What Kind of Fool Am I"
"Too Young"   "Days of Wine and Roses"

The C section is graphed to show that the C bears some musical similarity to the B section. Often it begins with the same phrase, but then it finds somewhere new to go.

Over the past twenty years the verse/chorus form, especially in top-40 rock songs, has overshadowed these structures and relegated their use mainly to theater and film songs. Henry Mancini, for example, found the ABAC's seamless quality ideal for his movie themes, "Days of Wine and Roses" and "Moon River"; their combined successes earned him a mantel full of gold and platinum trophies.

Updating the ABAB

Because of the closed-ended nature of the ABAB and ABAC, with no repeatable hook refrain or chorus—both structures have been considered outmoded for the pop marketplace. It therefore took Lionel Richie, a self-contained writer/recording artist whose songs don't have to pass through the publisher/producer screening, to break new ground with an old form. In the spring of 1984 he brought the ABAB back to the charts with "Hello."

Here's how Richie modified the classic form to make it comply with today's longer record formats: First he stretched the time between the twin AB sections by inserting a 4-bar instrumental; that alone made it feel more contemporary. The end of the second AB is, in effect, the end of the song, musically and lyrically. However, those 32 bars are still too spare to drive home a hit record; repetition is the hallmark of hits. So, in the design of the arrangement, Richie extended the song by restating one more AB, but in a unique way: the 16-bar AB section is broken up into a guitar improvisation for the first six measures, followed by a recap of previously heard lyrics. The record looks like this:

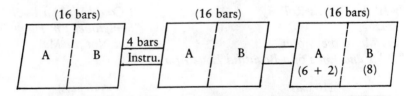

The song is still the classic ABAB, but expanded. The third AB is a lyrical composite: a recap of the first A's last two lines, plus a repeat of the words in the second B. In essence, Lionel Richie's "stretching" of the ABAB is parallel to what's going on with the extended AABA.

Where Does the Title Go?

In "Hello," Richie was unconventional with his title placement. The closing line of each AB section was "I love you," sounding, as it hit the traditional title spot, like the natural title. My guess would be that he picked the title "Hello"—the first word in the seventh line of the 16-bar

AB—because it has a fresher and more memorable ring to it. His giant hits "Still," "Easy," "Lady," and "Truly" make it apparent that Lionel Richie knows the power of one-word titles. It also proves once again that a writer with a record contract has more leeway to ignore the "rules."

The two logical title spots in the ABAB and ABAC remain either the opening or the closing line of each AB or AC section. You unify the song by "marrying" the title, which is the synopsis of your lyric idea, to the main musical phrase, as in "Sometimes I'm Happy" and "What Kind of Fool Am I?"; when we hear only the melody of those songs, we usually recall the words.

You Can't Keep a Good Form Down

In this increasingly acoustic age, it is heartening to know that an ABAC song can break through the blare of repeated rock choruses to make its subtle message heard. "When October Goes"—an ABAC lyric written by the late Johnny Mercer and set to music and sung by Barry Manilow in the mid-eighties—went gold. It would appear that a classic form is forever contemporary. Let Johnny Mercer's posthumous standard encourage you to experiment with the ABAC—a form that clearly can still beat a path to the charts.

WRAPUP

The AABA, with or without variations, obviously works, as "One Hundred Ways," "The Girl Is Mine," and "Stuck On You" attest. Study songs written in the form—both old and new. You'll find three more AABA classics in Chapter 17: "Moonlight in Vermont," "I Got Rhythm," and "Mountain Greenery."

To get the feel of the form, practice writing new lyrics to AABA melodies. Experiment using top-line titles and last-line titles in the basic, extended, and augmented versions. Practice until you've assimilated the shape. As you listen to the radio or records, try mentally to diagram a song as it streams by. It's an excellent exercise for learning structure.

Everything evolves from form. When you master song structure, you will have built a foundation for writing successful lyrics.

chapter 8

A Bit of the Blues

"The blues come from nothingness, from want, from desire."
W.C. Handy

"Blues is truth. Blues are not wrote: the blues are lived."
Brownie McGhee

"The blues is a feeling and when it hits you, it's the real news."
Huddie (Leadbelly) Ledbetter

Before there was jazz, before there was soul, before there was rock and
roll, there was the blues:

> *My moder's dead, my fader, 'crost de sea,*
> *My moder's dead, my fader, 'crost de sea,*
> *Ain't got nobody to feel an' care for me.*

And this even more desperate plaint:

> *Gwine to de river, take a rope an' a rock,*
> *Gwine to de river, take a rope an' a rock,*
> *Gwine to tie rope roun' my neck, an' jump right over de*
> *dock.*

The blues began as an Afro-American work song which originated
with the newly freed Southern slaves, largely unskilled laborers. The lyrics
concerned the singer's miseries—economic, sexual, and political. Unlike
spirituals, which are choral in nature, the blues are a one-man (or one-
woman) affair.

> *Gwine lay my head right on de railroad track*
> *Gwine lay my head right on de railroad track*
> *'Cause my baby, she won't take me back.*

"Sorrow-songs" were often sung out-of-doors, the improvised
complaints of exploited workers in cotton fields and "the sunless depths"
of mines. These melancholy moanings were also the "trial and tribulation
music," as Mahalia Jackson put it (in *Time* magazine), "of the men on the
railroad track layin' crossties; everytime they hit the hammer, it was with a
sad feelin', but with a beat. Or it was the sound made by the men sellin' wa-
termelons and vegetables on a wagon drawn by a mule, hollerin' 'water-
mellllon!' with a cry in their voices." Other lyrics told of double-crossing
women, deserting men, whiskey, morphine, and chain gangs:

> *Don' want no man puttin' sugar in my tea,*
> *Don' want no man puttin' sugar in my tea,*
> *'Cause I'm evil, 'fraid he might poison me.*

Dey tell me Joe Turner's come an' gone—O, Lawdy!
Tell me Joe Turner's come an' gone—O, Lawdy!
Got my man—an'—gone, Come wid this fo-ty links of
chain—O, Lawd!

"Joe Turner" is considered to be the prototype of all blues. "Turn-er" was in actuality a man named Joe Turney, brother of the governor of Tennessee, Pete Turney (1892-1896); he periodically came to Memphis to lead the latest batch of convicts to the Nashville penitentiary, where he was the "long chain man." His name, mispronounced in the legendary song, was intoned with terror. The music of the classic "Joe Turner" was sung all over the South as the underpinning for a variety of lyrics on differing complaints.

The Shape of the Blues

Lyrically the blues is a three-line phrase, the second being a repetition of the first (reinforcing the misery), and the third being an answer or "holler." The three lines of verse translate musically to three 4-bar phrases, AAB—creating the classic 12-bar blues; the structure repeats for as long as the singer has a story to tell. Melodically the A and B phrases are quite similar, thereby emphasizing the complaint through both lyrical and melodic repetition.

The harmony, as rudimentary as the primitive imagery of the "field hollers," limited itself to the basic I, IV, and V chords of the scale. In the key of C, for instance, the I, IV, and V would be the C chord, the F chord, and the G chord.

A	I	I	I	I
A	IV	IV	I	I
B	V	V (IV)	I	I

The Blue Note

It was the blacks' vocal treatment of the third note in the scale—the *mi* of *do, re, mi*—which led to the term "blue note"; their slurring, swooping, and sliding around the third creates that melancholy mood of blues, its very heart and soul. The blue note is that vocal sound which floats between the major and minor. The more such notes—often adding the seventh and fifth notes of the scale—the "meaner" the blues. That blue note sound continues to characterize much jazz, soul, and rock music.

A Little Booze'll Chase the Blues

While the themes of blues lyrics often centered on mortality, even suicidal tendencies were often tempered by comic overtones. "The Railroad Blues" is characteristically self-mocking. Author and composer Kay Swift (writer of the classics "Can't We Be Friends?" and "Fine and Dandy") told me she learned "The Railroad Blues" in 1916 from "two Southern women when I was a teenager at a summer camp in the Adirondacks."

THE RAILROAD BLUES

I got THE RAILROAD BLUES,
I got THE RAILROAD BLUES
But I ain't got the railroad fare
I got THE RAILROAD BLUES,
But I ain't got the railroad fare
If my shoes hold out, I surely will get there.

I was standin' on the corner
I was standin' on the corner
Wid my shoes an' stockin's in my han'
I was standin' on the corner
Lookin' for a woman who ain't got no man.

If the river was booze
If the river was booze
An' the sea was claret wine,
If the river was booze
An' the sea was claret wine,
I'd get drunk, an' stay drunk all the time.

If I should die
If I should die
If I should die in Tennessee
If I should go an' die
In Tennessee,
Ship my bones, ship 'em C.O.D.

If I should die
If I should die
If I should die in Arkansas
If I should go an' die
In Arkansas,
Ship my bones, ship 'em to my mother-in-law.

If she don't want 'em
If she don't want 'em
Just throw 'em in the sea.
If she don't want 'em,
Throw 'em in the sea
So the fishes an' crabs'll've a mighty good time on me.

The Blues Hits Tin Pan Alley

In 1914 W.C. Handy brought the blues to Tin Pan Alley and forever changed the sound of American music. Handy, a black cornetist and arranger and the bandleader of the Mahara's Minstrels, first encountered the blues when he witnessed the enthusiastic response given to a band performing New Orleans blues and ragtime in Cleveland, Mississippi. He sensed that "this had the stuff people wanted." He had an acute ear for words as well as music, like this melodic lament of a drunken woman he overheard: "My man's got a heart like a rock cast in the sea." He stored away such colorful one-liners for future use.

In 1909 Handy composed his first blues, a campaign song for a Memphis mayoralty candidate, "Mr. Crump." The song was credited with helping to elect Crump, and it continued to be sung by blacks in Memphis long after the election. In 1912 he renamed it "The Memphis Blues," published it himself, and later sold it outright to a New York music publishing firm. His next composition, however, "The St. Louis Blues," was rejected by every New York publisher. It wasn't until Handy moved his publishing operation to New York that the song began to be performed by such major singers of the day as Sophie Tucker and Gilda Gray. The blues had now come to stay. Its impact on the white musical establishment was immediate. By 1917 "whitewashed" blues began emanating from the cubicles of every top songwriting team in Tin Pan Alley. Some early titles included: "I've Got the Army Blues" (Gilbert), "The Alcoholic Blues" (Laska/Von Tilzer), "Left All Alone Again Blues" (Kern/Caldwell), "Schoolhouse Blues" (Berlin), and "The Yankee Doodle Blues" (Caesar/Desylva/Gershwin).

In 1920 Mamie Smith became the first black singer to record a blues song, "Crazy Blues." The record, an instant hit, formed the cornerstone of what was to become a thriving, if small, segment of the recording industry called "race records," geared exclusively for black audiences.

It wasn't until the late forties with the urbanization of black folk music that the term was changed to "rhythm and blues"—R&B, for short. The driving rhythms and strongly punctuated beat of those early urban blues, Dixieland, and boogie-woogie dance records have been gathering momentum, and they throb today in our synthesized technopop R&B hits.

A Semanticist Looks at Blues Lyrics

The blues is more than a 12-bar music form; it is an attitude toward life.

Back in 1954 the eminent semanticist S.I. Hayakawa took a penetrating look at American lyrics "in order to discover their underlying assumptions, orientations, and implied attitudes." In a paper addressed to the Second Conference on General Semantics and later published by the International Society for General Semantics in its review, *Et cetera*, Hayakawa compared the lyrics of popular songs with those of blues songs. In the article "Popular Songs vs. the Facts of Life," he contended that pop lyrics are generally full of unrealistic fantasy—longings for a "dream-girl or dream-man" who, if found, would magically solve life's problems. In contrast, the lyrics of blues songs exhibit a "tough-mindedness . . . and a willingness, to accept change and acknowledge the facts of life . . . that is rarely manifest in pop songs."

Hayakawa held that "the ideals of love, as depicted in popular songs, are usually impossible ideals." It was his opinion that the life-goes-on-and-I'll-be-all-right philosophy manifest in blues lyrics provide society with more realistic "equipment for living" than the romantic demands made on life reflected in most pop lyrics.

That's a provocative observation. Considering the far-reaching influence of popular music—especially on the country's youth—what responsibility, if any, do lyricists have to provide society with more realistic "equipment for living"?

WRAPUP

Since Hayakawa's analysis of pop lyrics over thirty years ago, the blues—via R&B, gospel, and soul songs—have been changing both the rhythm and the rhetoric of popular music. But contemporary pop lyrics still would seem to have a long way to go to match the emotional resilience and folk wisdom reflected in "classic" blues.

The songs of the great blues singer Bessie Smith recorded in the twenties and thirties have been reissued by Columbia Records on double albums: "Empress," "Empty Bed Blues," "Nobody's Blues But Mine," and "The World's Great Blues Songs." Discovering Bessie Smith will not only bridge the gap between the "Railroad Blues" and contemporary R&B, but will also provide fine examples of what Hayakawa meant by lyrics that reflect a mature acceptance of "the inevitability of change in a changing world."

"Obviously all the principles of writing apply to lyrics."
Stephen Sondheim

part three

PERFECTING
YOUR TECHNIQUE

chapter 9

Picking Your Treatment and Choosing a Point of View

"A song can be written a thousand different ways." Norman Gimbel

If you attended a formal church wedding where the bridegroom wore a black tailcoat over green jogging pants, what would you think? Is he putting you on? Is he making a statement about marriage? Did the tailor ruin the trousers? You wouldn't know what you were expected to feel. Amusement? Sympathy? Outrage? You would be bewildered by the inconsistency of his outfit in such a setting.

Similarly, a lyric that presents a mixed message confuses us and therefore falls flat. We don't know how to react. A song that moves an audience to wipe their eyes, or roar with laughter, or rise to their feet exerts its impact by maintaining a definite and consistent style, point of view, and emotional tone throughout. In order to achieve a unified lyric, the writer must have a sure sense of the effect he or she is after: Do you want your listeners to be amused? Touched? Inspired? First *you* must know; then if you do the job well, there's a good chance an audience will react the way you want them to.

CLARIFY THE MODE

A lyricist and a novelist have something in common: they can both treat their subject matter in a variety of ways, or *modes*. I am borrowing the term from literature where fiction is categorized by a range of modes—the historical novel, romantic novel, naturalistic novel, and so on. Songs too can be set in different modes. If we consider the possibilities as a spectrum between the extremes of history and fantasy, we see how the writer's slant on the subject determines the mode. On one end, lyrics can depict the black-and-white of events that have actually happened, such as in "The Star-Spangled Banner." (All "historic" songs, however, needn't be treated seriously.) At the other end of the spectrum is the rainbow of pure imagination reflected in "Lucy in the Sky with Diamonds." It might be helpful to think of your lyric treatment options like this:

HISTORY	REALISM	ROMANCE	FABULATION	FANTASY
The way I believe it was	*The way I see it is*	*The way I feel about it*	*The way I think it could happen (though it's improbable)*	*The way I imagined it (though it's impossible)*
Star-Spangled Banner	Dirty Laundry	Sad Songs (Say So Much)	Up, Up and Away	Lucy in the Sky with Diamonds
Comin' In On a Wing and a Prayer	In the Ghetto	Ebony and Ivory	I'm Going to Hire a Wino	Rudolph the Red-Nosed Reindeer
The Ballad of Ira Hayes	Jack and Diane	The Impossible Dream	A Boy Named Sue	Puff the Magic Dragon
Oxford Town	She Works Hard for the Money	Everything Is Beautiful	Miss Otis Regrets	Yellow Submarine
The Burning of Atlanta	Sniper	Up Where We Belong	Jailhouse Rock	Run, Run, Run
Ballad of Emmett Till	Positively 4th Street	Autumn in New York	In the Year 2525	Magical Mystery Tour
Battle Hymn of Lt. Calley	Allentown	Little Green Apples	Marvelous Party	Ferdinand the Bull
Ballad of Davy Crockett	Better Sit Down, Kids	I'm All Smiles	Mad Dogs and Englishmen	Alligator Wine
The Battle of New Orleans	Dreams of the Every-day Housewife	Oh What a Beautiful Mornin'!	When the Idle Poor Become the Idle Rich	Santa Claus is Comin' to Town
Tom Dooley	The Windows of the World	Can't Help Falling in Love	Hello Mudder, Hello Faddah!	Love Potion #9

Songs in the historic mode that depict actual events or real people mushroom during periods of economic instability or in wartime. Social upheaval seems to bring out the latent sociologist in a lyricist. The forties and the sixties were both decades that spawned more serious social commentary than the seventies' "me-generation." Lyrics written in the historic mode may represent a small percentage of our musical heritage, but they constitute an important chronicle of our past.

A romantic outlook on life has traditionally dominated pop music. The main theme is love: lost, strayed, or stolen—or magically materializing out of a blue moon or a London fog. In fact, a belief in magic and miracles permeates the romantic mode in which lyrics resound with a conviction that no mountain is too high to climb or to move, and no dream too far-fetched to come true. Songs set in the realistic mode have a more feet-on-the ground way of looking at life and give us a stronger sense of the way things are, compared with the romanticist's focus on personal feeling. Of course, the realistic mode can be fictionalized. For example, Harry Chapin created "Sniper" and peopled his epic with a cast of imagined characters; the effect was stunningly realistic, making us believe that's the way it really was.

Fabulation, in a lyric as in fiction, can be defined as a story that violates normal probabilities. Fabulation allows a writer to play with an idea that falls somewhere between the possible of the romantic and the incredible of the fantastic. The ideas portrayed in this mode are highly unlikely, but they balance enough truth with their improbability to let us pretend they could happen. Accepting Jim Webb's invitation to an "Up, Up and Away" balloon ride isn't as easily done as going for a spin in a "Little Red Corvette," but we'd like to think we could be asked.

It's not too likely that a warden would throw a party for the inmates, but that's what we believed in Lieber and Stoller's "Jailhouse Rock." Noel Coward was a fabulist par excellence, peopling his lyrics with an antic array of glitterati cavorting on the Riviera ("Marvelous Party") or living it up in Bangkok and Rangoon ("Mad Dogs and Englishmen"). His witty "world weary" songs about improbable people delighted theatergoers decades ago and charm us still on records.

Fantasy is fun. Because real life is often too heavy to handle, a touch of whimsy is always welcome. When we're clearly asked to "willingly suspend disbelief," as Coleridge put it, we're only too eager to respond. Who wouldn't want to party on the "Yellow Submarine" for an escapist weekend? And it's cheering to believe in "Puff the Magic Dragon" or that "Santa Claus is Comin' to Town." The fantasy mode, statistically, may be the least chosen by lyricists, but a fantasy song that becomes a perennial favorite, such as "Rudolph the Red-Nosed Reindeer," can earn its creators an equally fantastic income.

Many potentially workable ideas don't make it to vinyl because the lyricist loses sight of his or her chosen mode. Whatever your treatment option, be definite and be consistent. Here's a student lyric that shuttles be-

tween realism, romance, fabulation, and fantasy and can't decide what it
wants to be.

KNOCKED HIM OUT

I went downtown just to look around,
Had a dollar and a quarter in my pocket.
I met a girl, a friend of a friend,
She had too much money in her wallet.

She looked just like a Playboy queen,
She said, "Your life has just begun;
Here's $25,000.
Let's go have some fun!" What?!!!

KNOCKED HIM OUT
KNOCKED HIM OUT
KNOCKED HIM OUT
She KNOCKED HIM OUT of his mind.

We rented a big red limousine,
She said, "Come on let's fly."
The car became a Phantom jet,
We soared up in the sky.

We flew around the world,
Took some photos of the view,
She smiled and passed the wine and said,
"I'm real glad I met you." What?!!!!

KNOCKED HIM OUT
KNOCKED HIM OUT
KNOCKED HIM OUT
She KNOCKED HIM OUT of his mind.

We flew off to Hawaii,
Had a swim with Stacy Keach,
We dined on steak and lobster,
Took a penthouse by the beach.

We laughed and talked till midnight,
Saw a movie on TV
Halfway through the show she said,
"Why not take all of me?" !!!! What?!!!

KNOCKED HIM OUT
KNOCKED HIM OUT
KNOCKED HIM OUT
KNOCKED HIM OUT of his mind.

Given: A Playboy bunny is wandering around with $25,000 ready to splurge on a 24-hour spree with a friend of a friend. That is, to say the least, improbable. But not impossible. So we're starting out with fabulation. At this point we have to be willing to accept the premise as realistic, with that "suspension of disbelief." Okay, let's say such a bonanza could happen to someone. But when the red limo turns into a plane—whoa! That's *Chitty Chitty Bang Bang* fantasy. Now we're thrown off kilter because what started out as an unlikely plot has suddenly turned into an impossible one. The global highjinks then end disappointingly when the final verse brings us abruptly back to a ho-hum world with the couple staring into a TV screen. What have we got here? A modal mishmash. Although the columns on page 83 are meant to be general guidelines and not rigid positions, it is nonetheless true that all successful lyrics immediately announce their mode to the listener and develop within it. Consistency is the operative word.

SELECT THE POINT OF VIEW

The point of view is the voice through whom the story reaches the listener. The same three voices that operate in novels, plays, and poetry work in lyrics as well: first person, second person, and third person.

First Person

The first person is the singer who employs *I* or *we* and who addresses *you* in the singular, with the focus on the *I*. The majority of popular lyrics are written in the first person. It is the active participant, the most intimate voice, and it creates the strongest listener identification: "I Didn't Know What Time It Was," "You Are the Sunshine of My Life," "We Kiss in a Shadow." Because songs speak for us, we respond more to a lyric that says "*I* need," "*we* dance," "*my* life," "*our* house." Every lyric idea, of course, isn't ideally suited to the first-person voice; for example, the messages of "Johnny Can't Read" and "Jack and Diane" work best from the view of the observer. In many cases, however, "personalizing" a statement transforms a bland treatment into an exciting one.

A student lyric, "Weekend Father," contained a potent idea: a divorced father's fear that, in time, the diminished contact with his son would damage their relationship. In the initial treatment the point of view was that of an unidentified onlooker: ". . . *he's* a weekend father." The rewrite changed the perspective of the voice to the first person and multiplied the impact of the song: "*I'm* a weekend father. . . ."

BEWARE OF THE "KINKY I." Lyricists must be vigilant, however, in their use of the personal *I*. First, determine that your idea embodies a universally felt emotion and that the story is about recognizable characters in situations an audience will readily comprehend. Most important, be sure that the singer is likable. When you choose the first person, you are asking a singer to merge with the viewpoint expressed—to become, in effect, the "I." It would be helpful to lyricists if there were a sign on every typewriter: "Each lyric I write asks professional performers to sing my ideas to the world as if they were their own." Offbeat subjects or lyrics reflecting idiosyncratic attitudes are poor candidates for first-person songs. Such themes are best treated in the third person. In that way, the singer becomes an observer and is not fused with a character who may be unsympathetic (more on the third-person vantage point later).

WATCH OUT FOR "MINDREADING." Writing from the first person plural vantage point of "we" has one tricky aspect: be careful not to play mindreader. A lyric that makes one person (of the couple) assert that both will always feel this or remember that is synthetic and, as a result, without genuine feeling. It is unrealistic for anyone to presume that another person will cherish a shared moment the same way. In real life no one would make such a presumption; it seems odd that lyric writers do this frequently.

"And We Were Lovers," is a moving ballad because the singer—looking back upon the great affair—swears "*I* will remember till the day I die that we were lovers," not "*we* will remember . . ." We can *hope* the other will remember, but we can't affirm it. The ironic charm of Alan Jay Lerner's "I Remember It Well" touches us because it points up the singularity of people: two reminiscing former lovers discover that their individual recollections of an evening together are totally different.

A lot of breakup songs that have passed through my classes suffer from the mindreader syndrome: "we're" both feeling this emotion or "we're" both thinking this thought. They make claims for two heads or hearts instead of one. It's more realistic to say: *you've* been doing that, so *I've* been acting like this, and we're not getting anywhere—spelling out how the actions and *re*actions of each have led them to let a good thing go wrong. The *we* works better when you show the differences in the two people. Don't treat your characters as if they were clones of each other. When a lyric rings true, the audience responds; "You've Lost That Lovin' Feelin' " has been a hit over and over again for twenty years because it's real—and singular. It's one person observing the changes in another. Try to make your lyrics reflect the thoughts and emotions of one real human being, without clairvoyant powers. Very often in real life we experience feelings of disappointment and frustration because someone is unable to guess what we want for Christmas, or to sense when we want to make love. Gordon Lightfoot said it like it is: "If You Could Read My Mind."

Note: Our-love-is-here-to-stay songs such as "Endless Love" and "We've Only Just Begun" don't come under the mindreading caution. In those lyrics, rather like a wedding vow, one singer is looking forward to (in effect, pledging) a lifetime of love with the singee; that's not mindreading.

DUETS. Duets come in two basic styles; the attitude of both singers is in harmony, or it is in conflict. The majority of duets reflect a shared emotion—for example, "Let's Call the Whole Thing Off," "Reunited," "What Are We Doin' in Love," and "We've Got Tonight." In such songs both singers are feeling the same thing at the same time—let's break up, let's make up, let's make love, and so on—so they can sing in unison or harmonize, interchanging lines easily. Actually, these lyrics work even when sung by only one singer, but they are, of course, more effective when sung by two.

The less commonly heard duet finds two characters at opposite emotional poles, with one trying to change the other's mind: "Baby, It's Cold Outside," "Barcelona," "Anything You Can Do, I Can Do Better," and "You're Just in Love." These four songs were composed by theater writers and are lyrically and musically more sophisticated than the usual pop songs. Conceived as sung dialogue (at times almost an argument) with their lines often overlapping in contrapuntal melodies, they of course work only with two singers.

A duet such as "Barcelona" from *Company* is so dependent upon the theatrical situation that it cannot be performed outside the show without an explanatory setup: the song is sung in the bed of an airline stewardess on the morning after a one-night stand. Those important facts are not given in the lyric, and knowing them is essential to the listener's understanding of the song. On the other hand, "You're Just in Love" and the 1949 Oscar winner, "Baby, It's Cold Outside," were both big hits because they reflect instantly understood situations that require no introduction.

Second Person

Second person is the one sung to and is reserved primarily for advice giving, encouragement, or entreaty. The second person can be either the communal *you* found in inspirational or philosophical lyrics such as "Climb Every Mountain," "Pick Yourself Up," and "Ac-cent-tchu-ate the Positive," or a specific *you* as in "Maneater" and "Tell Her About It." Gospel songs are usually written in the second person's nonspecific *you*.

A song aimed at the communal *you* must ring with a meaning that is both clear and universal. The following student lyric seeks broad listener identification by its choice of voice:

HOME

HOME is the question you finally answer
HOME is the hollow you finally fill
Simple and clear as the rain on the rooftop
Gentle and strong as the sun on the sill.

HOME is the habit you've never quite broken
HOME is the hearth where you warm your soul.
When everything 'round you is coming to pieces
HOME is the place where your heart can feel whole.

HOME is a mansion that echoes with memories
HOME is a room with a simple chair
HOME is together and home is alone
HOME is the place that you'll know when you're
*   there*
HOME is the place that you'll know when you're
*   there.*

© 1981. Used with permission.

A song that presumes to speak for millions by defining the word *home* had better stick to indisputable truths. When a lyric addresses the world through the second person and says, in effect, "This is what home means to you, isn't it?" it faces the danger that the reply will be "*No,* it isn't." The essential weakness in the lyric lies in its ambiguous treatment of the very word it claims to define; it's unclear whether a childhood home is meant ("the habit you've never quite broken") or a newlywed home ("the hollow you *finally* fill"). Such diffused (and even contradictory) single-line definitions lack the ability to evoke broad listener identification. Because home may have been where one was supported or undercut, cherished or ignored, the connotations of the word are highly individual. A writer's personal truth is not automatically a universal truth.

TALKING TO THE SINGEE. *The singee* is my term for the one sung to or about. In second-person lyrics that address a specific singee like "Desperado" and "Tell Her About It," the writer must always establish the singer-singee connection. In both these lyrics it's clear that the singer is a friend of the person sung to, and in each case the singer is offering friendly advice.

Sometimes the tone of a singer-to-singee lyric is more critical than friendly. In "You're So Vain," for instance, the singer (a former lover of the mirror-checking man in the apricot scarf) is telling him off, rather than counseling. A recorded "angry tone" song like Carly Simon's "You're So Vain" and Billy Joel's "Big Shot" is almost always the product of a writer/ performer's psychohistory—they are singing their own feelings. The lyricist (who in these cases is also the singer) didn't try to get another performer to do the scolding for him or her—which is exactly what a nonperforming lyricist of an "angry" song must do.

If you're feeling hostile toward a particular person in your life, a lyric isn't the ideal place to work it off. Unless you're a recording artist, you'll have to get a publisher willing to look for a singer to identify with your anger. That's pretty unlikely. But if you are determined to *write* it out (rather than jog it off, or throw darts) try to create a character with whom an audience can at least say, "I know someone like that. . . ." Bear in mind, however, that successful angry lyrics, even in second person, are a rarity.

A footnote on anger: A lyric expressing outrage at economic injustice, such as "Take This Job and Shove It" is likely to find many sympathetic ears: this is frustration pinpointing the ills of society, not anger singling out the flaws of an individual.

Third Person

Third person uses *he, she, they,* and often includes the collective or editorial *we.* The voice is that of the storyteller as in "Ode to Billy Joe" and "The Gambler" or the social commentator in "Who Will Answer" and "They Call It Making Love."

Third person is the best way to handle subject matter that could put an artist in an unsympathetic light. Instead of having to merge with a character who has been cheating, for example, or who is a loser, a singer in a third-person treatment becomes an onlooker, comfortably telling the audience about someone who has "Lyin' Eyes," or who is a real "Nowhere Man." A Sheena Easton hit, "Modern Girl," puts the singer in the role of a narrator who tells us about a woman spending a night with a man and how after morning showers and coffee, they go separate ways to their respective jobs. In the chorus Sheena comments from her observer's view: "*she's* a modern girl" who is doing the best she can in these times of uncommitted relationships—not, "*I'm* a modern girl." In the second verse the girl turns down a date with the fellow she had spent the previous night with because she preferred to stay home and watch TV. Callous? Indifferent? Self-centered? Maybe. But Sheena Easton isn't required to be the object of our possible criticism. She's safe; she's an onlooker, and we accept her observation of a trend in comtemporary sexual mores. The writers were able to make a statement about our times that could most successfully be made from a narrator's point of view.

A third-person treatment allows more flexibility in your subject matter because it's not asking a performer to *be* the character, but rather to tell about him or her. Seeing a weary tray-toting waitress gave Donna Summer the idea for "She Works Hard for the Money." Had lyricist Summer put the concept into first person, the song wouldn't have got to first base, much less receive a Grammy nomination. We empathized with the story of a hard-working woman; we would have been turned off hearing the woman complain about her own tough life.

MAINTAIN YOUR VIEWPOINT

Maintaining a consistent viewpoint is a basic principle of good writing. If your lyric starts out speaking from the third person, the audience will be befuddled to suddenly hear *you* instead of *him* in a subsequent section, as in this student lyric:

LOVE YOU OR LEAVE YOU
(an excerpt)

Verse: *He* sips a glass of brandy in his chair
He always gives her a loving stare

He's changed since the day they first met
But all the good times are hard to forget.
Chorus: Should *she* LOVE *YOU* OR LEAVE *YOU*
Should she go, should she stay
Does she want *you*
Does she need *you*
She don't know if she should go.

© 1981. Used with permission.

The first verse establishes the voice of the narrator observing the actions and attitude of the "he" in relation to a "her." We are then jarred by the chorus's "should she love *you* or leave *you*." Such an abrupt shift in viewpoint from third person to second person renders the lyric unusable.

There are two ways to solve the duality: one would be to keep the opening verse as is but change the title to "Love *Him* or *Leave* Him." That unifies the viewpoint. Such a choice, however, would create another kind of problem: the missing singer-singee connection. What is the relationship of the singer to the couple and why are they being sung about? If there *is* no relationship, then the singer should be an objective observer of society, making some comment on the human condition, as in "Eleanor Rigby."

A better choice would be to put the lyric into first person, like this:

You sip a glass of brandy in your chair
You always give me a loving stare
You've changed since the day we first met
But *I* find the good times hard to forget.

Should *I* LOVE YOU OR LEAVE YOU
Should *I* go, should *I* stay,
Do *I* want you
Do *I* need you
I don't know if *I* should go.

I have found that a mixed-pronoun problem seems to be the result of a writer's ambivalence: a strong desire to deal lyrically with an emotional subject that conflicts with a need to disavow its autobiographical nature. Subject matter that involves raw feeling often requires more psychic distance before a lyricist can handle it successfully.

Some Exceptions to the Rule

Although the principle of unity dictates that lyrics should maintain uniformity of pronouns and verbs, exceptions, of course, exist. In his tribute to Vietnam war heroes, "Goodnight Saigon," Billy Joel made a deliberate and effective break in the collective "we" perspective of his narrator. A "ghost" crew member of a downed helicopter seems to be thinking aloud, almost as if he were addressing the American conscience, as he recalls the camaraderie of a crew that promised they would all go down together. In a momentary aside he says, "Remember Charlie?" as if he were suddenly talking to his buddies. It was an inspired touch which personalized what might otherwise have been a heavyhanded message. It worked because it came at the *top* of a verse, not somewhere in the middle. It was clear.

A shifting viewpoint can also work when it alternates consistently from section to section; for example, verses in third person, and choruses in first. Suppose, for example, you want to comment on the high divorce rate; you could create three vignette verses about different couples breaking up and then shift into a personal statement chorus, something like: "I keep wondering why nobody stays together anymore."

Exceptions to the general rule work when they are purposefully designed to achieve a desired effect. Such a case is Sheldon Harnick's lyrical dialogue between Tevye and Golde from *Fiddler on the Roof*. Golde is irritated and a bit embarrassed by Tevye's relentless question, "Do You Love Me?" In response to him she lists the chores she has performed "for *you*" for twenty-five years, but postpones her answer by posing a question of her own: "Why talk about love right now?" When he persists, she throws up her hands in weariness and addresses heaven: "Do I love *him*?" and highlights the moments they have shared for a quarter century, rhetorically asking the Almighty, "If that's not love, what is?" The shift from "Do I love *you*?" to "Do I love *him*?" is not inconsistency, but an effective technique to give the audience insight into the character and set up her ultimate response: when Tevye finally wears her down, she admits—in a beautifully understated line—"I suppose I do."

In *Sunday in the Park with George*, the Broadway musical inspired by Georges Seurat's painting "A Sunday Afternoon on the Island of La Grande Jatte," Stephen Sondheim creates a moving theatrical moment by substituting the third person for the first. In the song "Lesson #8," George is looking at a children's grammar book, a kind of French Dick-and-Jane reader, only the children are named Charles and Marie. George begins to read at random some of the first-grade phrases like "Marie tosses the ball . . . Charles misses the ball . . ." He slowly segues into singing about himself and his recently deceased grandmother Marie in the same stylized short sentences: "George misses Marie . . . George misses a lot . . ." Being self-analytical through the third person works in a theater song because we know who is singing. In a pop song, without a "seeable" character, such a device would be difficult (if not impossible) to employ.

CHOOSE THE GENDER

If you can write a song that either male or female can credibly sing, you have doubled your chances of getting a record. There are one-gender songs, such as "Happiness Is a Thing Called Joe" and "Sweet Sue," that have become classics, but a song with such a built-in limitation cannot hope to rack up the number of individual cover records that continue to be generated by unisex songs like "Body and Soul" and "I'm in the Mood for Love."

If you should get an idea like "I'm a Woman," which demands a female vocalist (unless it's in a transvestite show), then by all means write it that way. Don't compromise what you believe to be a unique (though limiting) lyric concept, for commercial considerations; you won't get a stronger shot at a record with a weaker lyric. On the other hand, if an idea can accommodate him/her and he/she switches in pronouns without watering down its special quality, make the changes. (See "Ready to Take a Chance Again" on page 48.)

Occasionally a lyric that was originally written for a specific gender can, with minimal alterations, fit the opposite sex. "Memory" is clearly for a female, yet Barry Manilow and Johnny Mathis recorded it by changing the line, "*I* was beautiful then," to "*life* was beautiful then."

The best of all possible worlds is a lyric designed as a potential duet which also works independently, sung either by a male or female vocalist, such as "To Me" or "Up Where We Belong."

UNIFY YOUR LANGUAGE STYLE

The leading language style of lyrics is conversational, a term that admittedly is imprecise because the question remains, whose conversation? Language styles range from the "absobloominlutely" cockneyisms Alan Jay Lerner chose for Eliza Doolittle in *My Fair Lady* to the well-bred accent of Desirée, the stage actress in *A Little Night Music* who sings "Send in the Clowns."

Theater writers tailor words to their characters; so do pop writers—in a less clear-cut way. The "character" may be simply the lyricist making a philosophical point, as in "Both Sides Now" or may be a vividly drawn lusty female proclaiming "I'm a Woman." A song's diction—poetic or street wise—must be internally consistent with that character. In "Both Sides Now" Joni Mitchell selected imagery from a uniformly metaphoric word palette—*angel hair, feather canyons,* and *ice cream castles.* We would have been jarred by the inclusion of mundane articles like *shirts* and *socks* and *lard*—words that sound just right when we hear Peggy Lee sing Leiber and Stoller's "I'm a Woman." Aptness is all. Oscar Hammerstein's choice of "*ford* every stream," over *cross* every stream in "Climb Every Mountain" reflects his unerring ear for phonetic nuance. *Ford* is the superior word because it is consistent with the inspirational aspect of the message, the majestic quality of the music, and the dignified character of the nun singing it.

Split-Level Language

Successful lyrics have a consistent language style, whether it's "Play That Funky Music" or "How Great Thou Art." Here's a student lyric that can't make up its mind whether it's hip or tender:

LET ME PRETEND

Wake up and smell the coffee brewing
Act as if you've got all day to spend
Reach out and pull me down beside you
Later you may disappear
But for now LET ME PRETEND.

Lie still and hold me in the shadows
Make me think today will never end
Lean back and share the Sunday paper
But for now LET ME PRETEND.

Don't give me a half-hearted valentine
What I want is your best shot
Open up and give me half a chance
And I'll give you all I've got

You get up and dash to meet a friend
You smile and say you'll call tomorrow
I may never hear from you again
But for now LET ME PRETEND.

© 1981. Used with permission.

The singer has the post-coital blues—anticipating the imminent departure of her Saturday night sleepover guest. The scene is clear with its references to coffee brewing and the Sunday paper. But "lean back," "shadows," "valentine" and "let me pretend" are romantic ballad words at war with the uptempo dance-oriented "tough" language of "best shot" and "give you all I've got." A split-level language style as well as inconsistencies in viewpoint and tone (which this lyric also has) reflect the writer's lack of focus. It's important to understand your characters—not only what they're feeling, but also the way in which they'd be likely to express it.

MAINTAIN THE EMOTIONAL TONE

Consistency as a trait, may be, as Emerson asserts, "the hobgoblin of little minds," but in lyric writing it's a prerequisite to success. The *tone* of a lyric reflects how the writer feels about the subject—from outrage to irony. It is the lyricist's job to set and maintain the emotional tone, whatever it may be. Only when the tone is consistent can an audience know what they are supposed to feel.

A student lyric, "Our Last Night," lacks believability because the writer changed his attitude about the lyric's situation halfway through the song. The most striking inconsistency is one of tone: the serious note on which the lyric begins vanishes by the final chorus. The writer conceived the lyric for a young male singer:

OUR LAST NIGHT

Verse: *From the start your parents said that I was all wrong*
They think that our affair has gone on much too long
Your friends could never see what you saw in me
They say that I'm no good and now you agree

Chorus: *Tonight's OUR LAST NIGHT*
So turn on the light
I want to see our love
Shining clear and bright
I want to smell your hair
Want to see your eyes
I want to feel your soul
Want to taste your sighs
I want to hear your heart beating, "it's all right"
Tonight's OUR LAST NIGHT
And OUR LAST NIGHT is gonna last . . . forever.

Verse: *We were too much in love or so the saying goes*
The gods must have laughed at us, God only knows
Seems that our fairy tale wasn't quite in rhyme
We played at "let's pretend" once upon a time

(CHORUS)

Bridge: *Kiss me kiss me kiss me kiss me*
It's your sweet kissing that I'll be missing
Touch me touch me touch me touch me
Violate and taint me, Simonize and fingerpaint me
Hold me hold me hold me hold me
Your warm caress is what finesse is
Love me love me love me love me
Oh baby, how I prize you, I've gotta memorize you

(CHORUS)

The playful bridge sounds as though it had been stapled on from some other song; its waggish wordplay and interior rhymes contradict the earnestness of the opening verse. But the lyric falls apart even before that: we are asked to believe that the singee, who has apparently told her boyfriend she now thinks he's "no good" (and therefore she is breaking off the relationship), is ready to start making love. That's hard to believe. If, however, the writer had stayed with his opening-line thought that (as in "Society's Child") the *parents* were breaking up the relationship, then we would accept that both the singer and singee would be eager for one passionate "last night." When a lyricist devises a song plot from imagination rather than from personal reality, the success of the lyric depends upon the author's insight into human behavior and his ability to keep the characters' actions and speech internally consistent.

Let's stay on the-end-of-a-romance as a theme, since nothing seems to start a songwriter's creative juices flowing faster than misery. Breakup songs can be treated in a broad range of emotional perspectives. For example:

Wistful	"The Shadow of Your Smile"
Philosophical	"It Was Almost Like a Song"
Overwhelmed	"The End of a Love Affair"
Breezy	"Just One of Those Things"
Grateful	"I Wouldn't Have Missed It for the World"
Spiteful	"Cry Me a River"
Supplicatory	"Touch Me in the Morning"
Jealous	"Don't It Make My Brown Eyes Blue"
Remorseful	"Workin' My Way Back to You"
Gloating	"Who's Sorry Now"
Analytical	"If He Walked into My Life"

That list barely makes a dent in the possibilities. The guideline for tone—for every facet of lyric writing—is be definite and be consistent.

A FABULATION SUCCESS

Dewayne Blackwell sat down at two o'clock one morning after performing in a night club, and "before the sun came up" he knocked out his 1983 country hit, "I'm Gonna Hire a Wino to Decorate Our Home." When he found the mode, the language style, and the tone he wanted, he stayed with it all the way. "I'm Gonna Hire a Wino to Decorate Our Home" is a consistent blend of barroom imagery, down-home dialect, and tongue-in-cheek playfulness. The inventive and totally unified lyric added up to fabulated fun and a real Grammy nomination.

I'M GONNA HIRE A WINO
TO DECORATE OUR HOME

Verse: *I came crawlin' home last night*
Like many nights before
I finally made it to my feet
As she opened up the door
And she said, "You're not gonna do this anymore."
She said:

Chorus: *I'M GONNA HIRE A WINO TO DECORATE OUR*
HOME
So you'll feel more at ease here
And you won't need to roam
We'll take out the dining room table
Put a bar along that wall
And a neon sign will point the way
To our bathroom down the hall.

Verse: *She said: Just bring those Friday paychecks*
And I'll cash 'em all right here
'N I'll keep on tap for all your friends
Their favorite kind of beer
And for you I'll always keep in stock
Those soft aluminum cans
And when you're feelin' macho
You can crush 'em like a man.

Verse: *She said: We'll rip out all the carpet*
And put sawdust on the floor
Serve hard boiled eggs 'n pretzels
And I won't cook no more
There'll be Monday night football
On TV above the bar
And a pay phone in the hallway
When your friends can't find their car.

(repeat chorus)

Verse: *She said: You'll get friendly service*
And for added atmosphere
I'll slip on something sexy
And cut it clear to here
Then you can slap my bottom
Everytime you tell a joke
Just as long as you keep on tippin'
Well, I'll laugh until you're broke.

Verse: *She said: Instead of a family quarrel*
We'll have a barroom brawl
When the Hamm's bear says it's closin' time
You won't have far to crawl
And when you run out of money
Then you'll have me to thank
You can sleep it off the next morning
While I'm puttin' it in the bank.
She said:

Chorus: *I'M GONNA HIRE A WINO TO DECORATE OUR
           HOME*
           So you'll feel more at ease here
           And you won't need to roam
           Then when you and your friends get off from work
           And you have a powerful thirst
           Well, there won't be any reason why
           You can't stop off here first.

The idea came from a chance remark of Dewayne's one evening during the intermission of his singer-songwriter gig at a club in a small town northeast of Sacramento. He told me, "I was sitting down with a group of people who came in to see me regularly. It was almost quitting time and they asked if I'd like to go out to have a late breakfast. I made some crack that my wife would be hiring a wino to decorate our home if I didn't get home. As soon as it came out of my mouth, I knew it was a hit. I said, 'You guys come back next week and I'll sing that one for you.' " But Blackwell had to wait two years before the "hit" he knew he'd written became a reality in the record by David Frisell.

"Wino" is the kind of lyric that has earned for country writers their well-deserved reputation for craftsmanship. The lyric is never vague or abstract, but full of strong verbs like *crawl, rip, crush,* and *slap* and concrete images: *neon sign, sawdust, aluminum cans, pay phone, hard-boiled eggs,* and *pretzels.* You can almost smell the beer.

Blackwell achieves his unified blue-collar language style by dropping his g's and using contractions: *feelin', pullin', closin', gonna, I'm, you'll, it's, I'll.* The playful tone never wavers in this account of a wife's highly improbable monologue. He developed his idea to the limit and entertained us with every consistent word. It may have been Dewayne Blackwell's desire to write a song that he could perform himself that set this lyric into a narrative, rather than making it a woman's first-person song. I think it just as likely, though, that his choice of viewpoint was simply good instinct; he knew it would make for a more successful song.

WRAPUP

Test every idea against each of the three viewpoints, and pick the one with which you can create the most effective lyric. Then if you focus on your chosen mode, point of view, language style, and tone—and keep consistent—your lyric will make a strong impression upon its audience.

chapter 10

Getting from the Personal to the Universal

> *"Some people write for themselves and some people write for other people; each deserves the audience he asks for."* Paul Leka

Successful lyricists are good communicators. They know how to talk to the world, as Carolyn Leigh put it. They have developed the technique to take personal observations, ideas, and experiences, and turn them into lyrics that make millions of people say, "I know just what you mean."

The professed goal of Carole Bayer Sager, one of the country's most successful lyric writers, is to communicate. She told me, "I've never been interested in writing for a select group of 50 people. I'm interested in getting my songs to the widest audience . . . that is how you affect people so that they can enjoy or feel or whatever it is the song is trying to achieve; and the more people that hear it, the better."

Your prime objective as a lyricist is to write songs that will speak for others as well as for yourself.

DEVELOPING AN IDEA WITH UNIVERSAL APPEAL

Some writers have a knack for coming up with titles that sound like hits. A title, however, isn't a developed idea; it's only a starting place. Let's say, for example, that you thought of the title "Born Winner." Sounds promising: we've all known or heard about someone who appears to be extraordinarily lucky in life. The title now must acquire a point of view, an emotional attitude, a story line that comes to a payoff of some kind and, of course, an appropriate form.

Let's look at a student lyric written before the writer learned how to turn an intriguing title into a fully developed idea.

BORN WINNER

Verse: *He gets up ev'ry mornin'*
Always feelin' fine.
His shower's always hot
And his trains are all on time

He's never late for work
And his work's the best you'll find
HE'S A BORN WINNER.

Verse: *He can eat like crazy*
And never gain a pound.
He always gets the girls
You know he's been around;
He's a good-lookin' man
Who keeps on gettin' down
HE'S A BORN WINNER.

Chorus: *HE'S A BORN WINNER*
A BORN WINNER
All his life he's always won.
HE'S A BORN WINNER
A BORN WINNER
Always wins with everyone.
Winning isn't everything
But he wins everything
HE'S A BORN WINNER—number one

Verse: *When he plays the game*
He always plays to win.
Even if he lost, you know,
He takes it on the chin.
He knows where he's goin'
'Cause he knows where he's been.
HE'S A BORN WINNER.

Chorus: *HE'S A BORN WINNER*
A BORN WINNER
What he touches turns to gold
HE'S A BORN WINNER
A BORN WINNER
I'll bet he even broke the mold.
Winning isn't everything, but he wins everything
Every time he's winnin', it's only the beginnin'
HE'S A BORN WINNER
HE'S A BORN WINNER.

A provocative title and a scene-setting start. Then what happens? Nothing. The reaction of the class after hearing it read was a unanimous "so?" The writer defined neither his relationship to the "born winner" nor his attitude toward him, so we feel nothing. Does the singer admire him? Envy him? Resent him for being a "have" because he is a "have not"? Where is the conclusion? The lyric is merely a recitation of ways in which someone appears to be very lucky. The writer of "Born Winner" neglected to take a stand on his subject. The lyric lacks an attitude we can identify with, in contrast to Rod Stewart's recording of "Some Guys Have All the Luck."

Can "Born Winner" be saved? Definitely. But it must first acquire two things: an emotional attitude, and the singer-singee connection. In order to relate to a song, a listener must be able to identify the emotion being expressed—regret, envy, lust, loneliness—and also must understand who is singing to whom, and why.

Make the Singer-Singee Connection

When Hall and Oates sang about a "Maneater," they were clearly tipping off a friend about a particular carnivorous female; the lyric manifests a definite attitude—a warning. When Carly Simon detailed the egocentric characteristics of the wearer of the orange ascot in "You're So Vain," she let us know he was her former lover—and her disdain was unmistakable. To stay interested, a listener must understand why the singer is telling us about a particular person, or persons. For instance, in "Richard Cory," (page 8) we learn that the singer works for the singee; the song illustrates a universal truth: that money can't buy happiness. *When you link the singer with the singee, you connect the listener to the song.* Let's plot a rewrite.

Since the second verse is merely a paraphrase of the first, (with no new information), we'll throw it out and move up the third verse to replace it. Now we've got room to develop a real story line. There are plenty of potential plots. Here's one approach: what if, for example, the singer (maybe the next-door neighbor) had been having a long-term affair with the wife of the singee? Now *that's* a connection, and one that creates a potent ironic situation—that he's not such a winner on the home front. The lyric could now begin to work because it would reflect a universal truth: appearances are often deceptive.

In its first draft, the emotional profile and development of "Born Winner" looks like this: (START) ————— (FINISH). Nothing happens. A well-constructed lyric goes somewhere and looks more like this:

Now that we've established a relationship between the singer and the singee and outlined a scenario with an ironic attitude, the lyric can be worked out in any number of ways to reach an effective conclusion.

Learning to Filter Your Experience

Professional songwriters know how to translate personal experiences into songs that will be appreciated by a wide audience. It all comes down to understanding that a lyric needs to strike the common chord.

Rick Nelson's hit "Garden Party" was based upon a concert of his in New York's Madison Square Garden at which old fans greeted his new image with less than enthusiasm. Nelson's disappointment and frustration weren't simply dumped whole into a lyric; he sorted out the *meaning* of his painful experience and distilled its essence, reaffirming a universal truth: the important thing is to satisfy yourself, not to please others.

Many beginning writers merely hold a mirror up to their lives in the belief that any personal event—because it "really happened to me"—is, ipso facto, appropriate song material. This is a dangerous assumption.

Occasionally a student will read an intensely dramatic lyric of obvious personal significance: the torment of life with an alcoholic mate, the awesome death of an infant sibling, or a long-suppressed bitterness toward a divorced parent. Their experiences were fashioned into lyrics just as they actually happened—rather like a rhymed "Dear Diary" entry. These new writers have not yet learned how to turn raw autobiography into a song with a meaning common to all. The lyrics were *private* rather than universal. Fellow students were unable to say, "I've felt what you've felt"; instead, we all felt embarassed, as though we had unwittingly overheard a therapy session.

THE STEP-BY-STEP PROCESS

This does not for a minute mean that a subject such as divorce—or for that matter, drug abuse, prostitution, homosexuality, or incest—is unsuitable for lyrics. On the contrary, all these themes have been treated in a manner that made them recordable. The key word is *treated.* How do you go about *treating* personal experiences (or touchy subjects) successfully in a lyric? How do you begin with an autobiographical event and end with a lyric to which millions will respond? I offer this approach, which has often proven effective for workshop students:

From PERSONAL to GENERAL to PARTICULAR = UNIVERSAL.

I'll elaborate. First, try to reduce your *personal* experience to a simple *general* thought or emotion which an audience will immediately understand. Next, find a set of *particular* circumstances that illustrate that general statement. If all goes well in your treatment, the resulting lyric will reflect an idea that is *universal,* so that any listener will be able to say, "I know what you mean." For example, maybe you finally worked up the nerve to tell off a boss who had acted unfairly or abrasively, or perhaps you summoned up the courage to call a beautiful girl or a handsome man you feared might reject you. Those two unrelated experiences share one common feeling: daring to take a chance—willing to be sorry, rather than safe. That's one possible interpretation of those events; there could be several. The important thing is to learn the technique of extracting from your experiences some clear meaning that can be summed up in one simple phrase. The final step requires inventing a new set of circumstances, a story line that dramatizes that meaning which you have distilled from your autobiographical event.

Let's examine the process in action, with a student's first draft. The writer, a male, candidly told the class that his breakup with a married lover generated this lyric. He said he had written it as a woman's song.

NINE OUT OF TEN

Verse: *Had lunch with my old friend Judy today*
Had so much inside me I needed to say
I told her how I was falling deeper for Lou—
That by Christmas his divorce was sure to come thru.
Judy gave me her hanky as I started to cry,
She ordered more vodka, then started to sigh:
She said, "I know exactly what you're going thru,
And I gotta speak out, friend, cause I've been there too."
Then she said,

Chorus: *NINE OUT OF TEN of those married men*
Never leave their wives (uh-uh) for the other woman.
I'll say it again
NINE OUT OF TEN
Never leave their wives (uh-uh) for the other woman.

Verse: *I hugged her goodbye and told her I'd phone*
And the sting of her words followed me home.
I bought myself a paper, and a bottle of wine—
To try and get her words off my mind.
I flipped to Ann Landers and what did I see
But a letter from someone signed "Waiting patiently!"
Her story was mine in ev'ry way
And I hurried to read what she had to say.
Ann said,

Chorus: *NINE OUT OF TEN of those married men*
Never leave their wives (uh-uh) for the other woman.
I'll say it again
NINE OUT OF TEN
Never leave their wives (uh-uh) for the other woman.

Verse: *Well, needless to say, her prediction was right,*
Lou broke it off Thanksgiving night.
So here's some advice to you ladies out there
Who bet with your heart when you have an affair,
I've learned

104 The Craft of Lyric Writing

Chorus: *NINE OUT OF TEN of those married men*
Never leave their wives (uh-uh) for the other woman.
I'll say it again
NINE OUT OF TEN
Never leave their wives (uh-uh) for the other woman.
Are you listenin', my friends, I said,
NINE OUT OF TEN
NINE OUT OF TEN
NINE OUT OF TEN (repeat and fade)

©1984 by Larry Paulette. Used with permission.

This is a good first draft, although there was a general feeling in the class that the final verse was a bit preachy. A little revising will eliminate that criticism. When the lyric is polished and teamed with a compelling tune, "Nine Out of Ten," with its memorable title, will be competitive in the marketplace. It's what pop (as opposed to theater) lyric writing is all about: a simple story that strikes a common chord. Taking his personal experience, the lyricist reduced it to one universally acknowledged truth—that most married men don't leave their wives for the other woman. He then invented a fictitious set of circumstances to illustrate his point. It's interesting that in the treatment process, the lyricist chose to recast the jilted lover as a woman—exactly what Jim Webb did in "By the Time I Get to Phoenix." Webb, in discussing the song in a newspaper interview, said: "I Wrote 'By the Time I Get to Phoenix' for a girl I was in love with who didn't love me." [The song (on page 36) tells of a man leaving a woman.] "That's the way I wanted it to be," said Webb. "I never said the song was the gospel truth." In fact, successful songwriting is not usually gospel truth, but rather a reshaping of experience.

HOW TO AVOID DEAD ENDS ON THE ROAD TO THE UNIVERSAL

Don't Tell a Private Story

A class was given an assignment to write a lyric on the parent/child theme. In preparation, the students were played songs that treated the subject successfully—"My Pa," "I Want a Son," and "Ships (That Pass in the Night)." The student writer of "Sunday Rain" failed to take the vital steps from personal to general to particular, and consequently missed the universal connection.

SUNDAY RAIN
(Excerpts)

Verse: *I remember waiting*
With my nose pressed against the glass

For your rosy roundish figure
To set foot upon the grass
But when I saw you coming
I always turned away
And tucked my feelings deep inside
They were hidden yesterday

Verse: We always sat together
Playing mother-daughter games
You'd make your move to touch me
I'd tease and call you names
And if you tried to kiss me
I withdrew my cheek
We never found each other
In our game of hide and seek.

Chorus: SUNDAY RAIN, SUNDAY RAIN
Always seemed to fall
Raindrops stained my windowpane
On Sundays when you'd call.

Verse: O mama, sweet mama why'd you have to go
I never understood, I grew angry, did you know.
In my world of day dreams
I'd forget the pain locked in my head
And I spent nights with strangers
Pretending that making love was love instead
I look through many windows
Trying to catch a ray of sun
But the ghost of the abandoned child
Still shadowed me at twenty-one.

The lyric possesses genuine feeling—an admirable quality which sometimes compensates for a multitude of flaws—but in this case, it's not enough to counteract the lyric's *private* content. What might she have done to turn her personal experience into a lyrical statement to which we can all relate? Well, she could have decided to show that parent/child relationships are subject to communication problems—the idea embodied in Ian Hunter's "Ships (That Pass in the Night)." Or she might have chosen to illustrate the painful effects of divorce on a small child, a subject portrayed in a country hit for Tammy Wynette, "D-I-V-O-R-C-E." By neglecting to discover in her personal experience a commonly understood meaning, the writer of "Sunday Rain" speaks only for herself, and thereby excludes the listener. That makes it private instead of universal.

Here's an excerpt from another student lyric which falls in the private story category:

When you were thirty and I was three
This world was so amazing to me
I'd sit and giggle on your knee
And ask you why things were
And you'd tell me stories of an actor's life
How you made 'em laugh, or hold their breath
You always put my mind at ease
When you were thirty and I was three.

© 1983. Used with permission.

This grown daughter's wistful reflection upon her childhood closeness to her father is touching, but it's not a lyric. Nowhere in the remaining verses did the writer provide the listener with something to share; we were emotionally shut out. The writer again took autobiographic matter without transmuting it in some fashion so that it could work as a song. No conclusion was drawn about parent/child relationships in general, that could have made the lyric common to all.

Writing about individuals an audience doesn't readily recognize, in situations they don't understand, is a dead end on your road to the universal. Although you can certainly use your life, rich in its uniqueness, you must first identify the universal element in your experience which will permit millions to say, "I know what you mean."

Build in the Situation

From time to time in class a lyric is read that elicits the reaction: "It sounds like a theater song." What does that comment mean? It frequently indicates that the song is dependent on a "script" which is not implicit in the lyric but exists only in the head of the writer. The audience is therefore in the dark about the *situation* in which the song takes place. Here's an illustration:

YOU'RE A STAR

Verse
(A):
You've got charisma to spare
Got charm and flair
Your sex appeal is way above par,
With a dazzle that can't be bought
Can't be learned or taught,
YOU'RE A STAR!

Verse
(A):
I've seen you walk in a room
And pow! kaboom
The glitterati stop where they are
You don't seem to know it yet,
But I'm ready to bet
YOU'RE A STAR!

Bridge *There's a page in* Who's Who
 (B):   *You were bound to fill,*
        And without any doubt
        You can and you will.

Verse   *And when those bravos are hurled*
 (A):   *And all the world*
        Appreciates the wonder you are,
        Save a seat in your limousine
        For the first who'd seen
        YOU'RE A STAR.

© 1981. Used with permission.

On the positive side, the lyric is well written; it has charm, and it develops to an effective conclusion. But, it doesn't *work* as a pop song. The reason is not simply that terms like *glitterati* and *charisma* are too sophisticated for the pop market—although that's a point worth noting: they are. But it doesn't work for a more fundamental reason: the audience has no idea who is singing to whom, or why. *The lyric is not characteristic of all.* We can't recognize the singer or the person being sung to. This is a theatrical-situation song without a theatrical situation.

What the lyricist did is invent two fictitious characters: it sounds as though the singer is a friend of an aspiring actress and he is buoying her confidence with a "you're-gonna-make-it" pep talk. The audience unfortunately hasn't been let in on the plot in the author's head. But—let's suppose we are watching an old Mickey Rooney/Judy Garland movie. Judy has tearfully turned to her good friend for some positive reinforcement after being rejected for the lead in the Rotary Club revue. He delivers the ego buildup she needs by singing her "You're a Star." Now does the lyric work? Sure it does, because we can see the circumstances that make the song valid—who is singing to whom, and why. Although attaining the universal requires particularizing the general, this lyric particularizes to a fault. "You're a Star" is a case of *over*particularizing—creating characters and a situation too uncommon to be characteristic of all. As a consequence, the lyric lacks listener empathy. Though it reflects a universally recognized emotion (one that could be characterized as "I believe in you"), we cannot all sing along with "You're a star." The situation is too singular.

Pop lyrics must be designed to stand alone, with their "circumstances" built in. Since a lyricist can't run around reciting preambles or handing out footnotes, make sure your lyric leaves nothing unexplained.

Avoid Overparticularizing the Singee

It's important to create a singee we can recognize. In "Nine Out of Ten," the singer had lunch with the singee, Judy. In that lyric Judy was characterized by the writer merely as a friend without further personality profile. That simple identification makes the story more universally acceptable; she could be anyone's friend.

Here's a singee we all can't recognize:

THE EGO TRIP

Verse: *I hear you're back from Hollywood with a seamless tan*
And you've gotten to be a celebrity of sorts.
You're the hostesses' delight
And quite the ladies' man—
The life of the party
On private tennis courts.

Chorus: *Well, THE EGO TRIP you're traveling on*
Is turning me off real strong
So I'm writing you out of my future
And turning you into a song.

Verse: *I always knew you had a need to be center stage,*
When you looked in my eyes you only saw your own,
And before I finished a story
I could hear you turn the page,
And even when you kissed me
You were off somewhere alone . . .

Chorus: *Well, THE EGO TRIP you're traveling on*
You don't need me along
So I'm writing you out of my future
And turning you into a song.

© 1980. Used with permission

On the whole, "The Ego Trip" is well crafted; there are some fresh rhymes (*sorts/courts*) and an occasional original turn of phrase such as "seamless tan" to characterize nude bathing. But, the singee is overparticularized. The first question is, what recording artist will identify with this writer's clearly autobiographic annoyance with one specific person? The lyricist neglected to take those necessary steps from the personal to the universal. We can probably all identify with the feeling that someone we know, or know about, is on an ego trip—that's universal enough; but it's the *treatment* of the subject matter that has made the lyric a poor contender for a pop record.

You may well ask, what about "You're So Vain," a hit song with a similar critical attitude toward the singee? The fundamental, and very important, difference between "Vain" and "Ego" is that the former was written and sung by the same person (Carly Simon), who had a recording contract with a major label. The writer of "Ego," on the other hand, is a non-performing lyricist. Carly Simon, or any other self-contained writer/recording artist, simply has more latitude in the autobiographical area. As a general guideline, it's a wise policy to make both your singer and singee recognizable so a listener can say, "I know who you mean," rather than the overparticularized actress of "You're a Star" or the self-centered singee of "Ego Trip," with whom the average listener cannot identify.

Beware of Making the Singer Sound Quirky

I remember a lyric presented in class that was solely concerned with a chronic inability to dress appropriately for the weather; it recounted a series of episodes such as being drenched in a backless dress and freezing at the beach in a bikini. The writer, neglecting to give some reason for the absent-mindedness, such as being in love, merely characterizes the singer as not too bright. We can all relate to forgetting an umbrella on occasion, or underpacking for a vacation trip, but a lyric must build in some universal truth to elicit a broad audience response.

Here are two excerpts from student lyrics reflecting attitudes that are idiosyncratic rather than universal. Before a song can be heard by millions, it must first find a singer who will say, "That's just how I feel." I believe these offbeat viewpoints may have a hard time finding performers:

> *My last fling was a drinker,*
> *The one before had an urge to bet,*
> *All I want is a standard woman,*
> *Damaged goods is all I get.*
> © Used with permission.

> *My mother gave me fairy tales*
> *No view of what is real*
> *She spoke of love and happiness*
> *Not the torment that I feel.*
> © Used with permission.

How many singers will record a lyric that rests on the idea that former lovers were "damaged goods"? How many singers would believe they'd have a hit song by complaining about the way their mothers brought them up?

Each of these lyrics reflects a highly individualized viewpoint. Like "You're a Star," these songs could work within a context, if a character in a dramatic situation were explaining how he or she got that way. Unfortunately, that was not their authors' objective; the writers had conceived their lyrics to be competitive in the recording marketplace. The ideas, however, are simply too narrow to appeal to a broad audience.

Always Put Your Singer
In an Attractive Light

In addition to lacking universality, two of the ideas just presented contain another critical flaw: they put the singer in an unfavorable light. The woman who never seemed to know how to dress for the weather would make any performer sound a bit foolish; the man who is apparently attracted to alcoholics, chronic gamblers and in the full lyric, a thief, sounds like a poor judge of character.

Always put your singer in an attractive light. Avoid making the singer sound selfish, egocentric, unethical, weak-willed, judgmental, or the like. It's vital to understand that a singer *merges* with the lyric. On the TV magazine show *Entertainment Tonight,* Tina Turner expressed what happens to her when she performs: "When you sing the words to a song, you become that story." *Lyricists who are not self-contained artists must keep in mind that they are writing words to put in the mouth of a professional singer—with all that implies.* In other words, when you use the word "I" in a lyric, make sure you give the singer statements that will make him or her appeal to millions.

WRAPUP

As you listen to both standards and current hits, be analytical. Pinpoint the lyrics' universally shared meaning. In your own writing, when you've finished a first draft (but before you try out the lyric on anyone for feedback), give it this test: Is my idea big enough to bear the weight of being set to music, self-sufficient enough to require no further explanation, and universal enough to arouse the interest of a top recording artist? You should be able to answer "yes" to each. Then ask yourself, "For whom does my lyric speak?" If you can honestly reply, "For millions," you already possess an important key to success.

chapter 11

Focusing on the Time, the Place, and the Plot

"I find it useful to write at the top of the page a couple of sentences of what the song is to be about—no matter how flimsy."
Stephen Sondheim

DEFINE THE TIME FRAME— REAL OR IMAGINARY

The time frame of a lyric reflects the singer's attitude toward the event or feeling expressed; the song can be set in the present, the past, or the imagined or hoped-for future.

The time frame you choose dictates your verbs. The present tense has the greatest impact on the listener: "I watch you pack your bag, and feel too numb to speak." Written in the past tense, the lyric takes on a remoteness: "I remember the day you said goodbye, I cried the whole night long." The future, by putting the greatest distance between the singer and the action, automatically reduces the impact of the song upon the listener: "Maybe someday I will walk away and close the door behind me." Three different effects. Drama is always now. Narrative is always then. "She's Leaving Home" (page 115) is drama, now. "Coward of the County" (page 122) is narrative, then. In rare instances, they can be united, as in "Sniper" (page 160).

Just as the majority of popular songs are written from one unchanging point of view, so are they commonly conceived to present one moment's feeling. The *when* is unspecified, imagined time, rather than real time. Even a lyric with a flashback ("You Light Up My Life") or one with references to morning, noon, and night ("I Say a Little Prayer") or to seasons of the year ("If Ever I Would Leave You") is not *set* in these periods; the writer has merely underscored the emotion of the moment by comparing the current situation to the way things either once were or may be.

A story song, on the other hand, like "Coward of the County," with a specific chronology of events, or a quasi-documentary like "Piano Man" are set in real time. Billy Joel put us right into the local bar where the "Piano Man" plays by announcing, "It's nine o'clock on a Saturday. . . ." Time then stands still as we are introduced to the weekend regulars in their home away from home.

Whether your song simply expresses one moment's feeling like "Don't Give Up On Us" or tells a story that spans three generations like "Cat's in the Cradle," your objective is to be clear. You can't hope your listener will guess the time frame. It is the lyricist's job to tell it.

If you establish a particular part of the day as the song's time frame—breakfast, twilight, midnight, or whenever—*keep the action there throughout the entire song unless you clearly specify otherwise*. For example, "Touch Me in the Morning" is obviously sung at night by a woman asking her lover to stay until morning. Although she looks back upon the beginning of the relationship as well as ahead to the morning's final goodbye, the song's emotional moment never moves.

When the clock hands turn during the action of your story, the listener can only know if you show it. As the chapters on song forms pointed out, both the AAA and verse/chorus lend themselves to changing time zones because of the stop/start quality of their structures: it is the transitional bar of music which so often comes between verses or between verse and chorus that creates a kind of emotional separation from section to section and permits that passage of time. Conversely, the AABA, with its beginning-to-end seamless melody, feels much more like one unvarying moment's statement.

In a verse/chorus lyric, a student did a good job of showing us the movements of two lovers on the night they called it a day:

First verse: *"The clock on the bar says 6:30 I've ordered us two double ryes."*

Third verse: *"The clock on your wall says 11:00 We drown in each other's embrace."*

Fifth verse: *"My watch on your table says 7:00 I get up and dress in the gloom."*

© 1983, Eben Keyes II. Used with permission.

The more precisely you pinpoint the period of events, the more easily the listener can follow your plot.

Even "Thought" Lyrics Need a Time Frame

In the lyric just quoted, *real* time passed during the evening of the song, and naturally the listener had to be told. It is equally important in songs where the singer is merely *thinking,* that you decide exactly when the thinking is taking place. For example, a student got derailed from the time track she had started on: "This morning when you said goodbye. . . ." That opening line clearly sets the moment of the lover's leaving and tells the listener that the song is taking place later the same day. That's fine; we're all set to hear more. But in the second verse we're told: "Each morning when I wake, tomorrow's still today." How's that again? Now the writer has confused us by saying, in effect, that the lover has been gone for some time and the singer is still suffering with the same intensity as the day he said goodbye. Such plot discrepancies occur because a writer has given no thought to *when* the singer is doing the thinking. Consequently, the song lacks unity—it's missing that one moment's feeling. Had this student written a guideline at the top of her paper: "It's evening, and the singer is thinking back to this morning when her lover left her," she would have stayed within the one-day setting she originally conceived.

The breakup theme frequently gives writers clarity trouble because the feelings expressed in such songs are more often *thought* than spoken; an interior monologue lacks the stabilizing anchor that a specific time frame and setting would supply. As an aid to clarity, set yourself an imaginary clock for the action of each song, even when that action is only thought. For example, you could mentally place your "action" at 2 A.M. as the singer lies sleepless with the radio on remembering the singee. The bed and the radio don't have to be stated in the lyric, but if the where and when of a song's emotional moment is vivid in your mind, chances are it will be vivid in your writing.

SET THE SCENE

Johnny Mercer made "One for My Baby (and One More for the Road)" something more than another drowning-my-sorrow-in-drink song by creating a three-dimensional scene in a bar at closing time, with Joe, the bartender, to whom the singer could pour out his heart.

When you present a real-life backdrop for your song, as Mercer did, you lift the lyric out of the standard bland into the colorful particular: the cheering bus of "Tie a Yellow Ribbon," and the disco floor of "Last Dance" contributed immeasurably to the success of those songs by bringing the audience directly into the scene.

Specificity makes for memorability, and nothing could be more specific than an actual place in which to put your characters and your action. Scene setting has the same advantages as clock setting, as well as the same inherent dangers. Here's a student first draft with a lot of potential but a small problem.

I CAN'T MAKE LOVE TO YOU

A: *When we met in the hotel bar last night*
Laughing the night away
I got lost in the light of your eyes so bright
A pretty city Saturday
You asked me if I'd spend the night
I wonder if you knew
I wanted you before I said
I CAN'T MAKE LOVE TO YOU.

A: *I'm sorry I don't want another round,*
It's already half-past two,
So let me go my way alone,
Before I'm kissing you.

> *I know it won't work, I've been here before,*
> *And ended up cryin' the blues*
> *Please understand, you're a very nice man,*
> *But, I CAN'T MAKE LOVE TO YOU.*
>
> B: *I'm in the market for a steady man*
> *Who lives in the neighborhood.*
> *You'll have to get on a plane when I call*
> *And that wouldn't be any good.*
>
> A: *I'm usually not as cold as I seem*
> *You, with your eyes so sincere,*
> *If we get it on till you leave at dawn*
> *Then I'll be left with my tears.*
> *I do understand you're passing through*
> *With a casual point of view, but*
> *Love's not as simple as "be here now,"*
> *I CAN'T MAKE LOVE TO YOU.*

© 1982. Used with permission.

Can you tell what isn't working? First let's give credit for all the positive accomplishments. The structure is in a perfect AABA form. The strong plot can be synopsized in one sentence: a woman who wants a full-time relationship passes up a tempting one-night stand with an appealing out-of-towner. The language style is consistently conversational. The title is provocative and memorable. So far so good. Then what's wrong?

The first A section is set in what appears to be the morning after an encounter in a bar, and the singer is remembering last night. The second A, without warning, plops us in the present at the hotel bar in what sounds like a dialogue over drinks. The listener is now trying to determine if the song is a flashback to the previous night (taking place in the singer's head), or is happening now in a bar. The trouble is it's half and half.

There are two obvious rewrite options that could unify the lyric: have the singer be with him in the bar for the whole song, or have the singer think about him the next day for the whole song. Making the story happen *now* is, of course, more immediate than having it *remembered*. One way to start would be to shift the first verse into present tense and move the action back to the bar: ". . . meeting you in the bar tonight . . . I could get lost (or, I'm afraid I'll get lost) in the light of your eyes . . . now, you ask if I'll spend the night. . . ." An even more effective opening would be to lead off the song with the second verse: "I'm sorry, I don't want another round" is a hook opening line which pulls us right into the story.

The first draft of this lyric dramatizes, by unintentional comparison, the forcefulness of the present tense over the past, when a singer *lives* the moment in a particular place rather than recalls it.

An example of doing it right is "How Am I Supposed to Live Without You," a hit for Laura Branigan. The writers conceived the song, not as vague introspection, but as a face-to-face conversation, making the singer confront her lover to check out what's what. The result: a lyric that produces a strong impact upon the listener because it's viewed from the first person, set in the present tense, and rooted in a believable real-life scene.

KEEP YOUR EYE ON THE CLOCK

The more sharply you perceive the *when* and *where* of your action—however minimal your plot—the more successful your lyric will be. What a songwriter needs is "Cinderella eyes": one on the clock and one on the door. If you can see the scene, then you can show it. Your listener must *hear: when* a character moves from a boardroom to a bedroom; *where* the night has turned into morning; and *who* is talking to whom. The lyricist has to find a way to make it clear. Successful writers do it with apparent ease.

In 1967 Lennon and McCartney held up a disquieting mirror to family life in their tale of a runaway girl. With stunning simplicity "She's Leaving Home" covers a time span of two days.

SHE'S LEAVING HOME

Verse: *Wednesday morning at five o'clock*
As the day begins,
Silently closing her bedroom door,
Leaving the note that she hoped would say more,
She goes downstairs to the kitchen
Clutching her handkerchief
Quietly turning the backdoor key
Stepping outside she is free.

Chorus: *SHE (We gave her most of our lives)*
IS LEAVING (Sacrificed most of our lives)
HOME (We gave her everything money could buy)
SHE'S LEAVING HOME after living alone
For so many years. ('bye 'bye)

Verse: *Father snores as his wife*
Gets into her dressing gown
Picks up the letter that's lying there
Standing alone at the top of the stairs
She breaks down and cries to her husband,
"Daddy, our baby's gone.
Why would she treat us so thoughtlessly?
How could she do this to me?"

Chorus: *SHE (We never thought of ourselves)*
IS LEAVING (Never a thought for ourselves)
HOME (We struggled hard all our lives to get by)
SHE'S LEAVING HOME after living alone
For so many years. ('bye 'bye)

Half *Friday morning at nine o'clock*
Verse: *She is far away,*
Waiting to keep the appointment she made
Meeting a man from the motor trade.

Chorus: *SHE (What did we do that was wrong?)*
IS HAVING (We didn't know it was wrong)
FUN (Fun is the one thing that money can't buy)
Something inside that was always denied
For so many years.
SHE'S LEAVING HOME. ('bye 'bye)

The first verse tells us the *when* and *where* and that the *who* is female—enough facts to keep us listening. By the end of the first chorus
we've surmised that the "she" is the daughter, and this fact is confirmed by
the first word of the second verse. We've been held in suspense as the story
unfolds, but were never confused.

Directness and clarity frame the action: "Wednesday morning at
five o'clock, the day begins . . . Friday morning at nine o'clock, she is far
away. . . ." In between, a mini movie takes place. We follow the daughter's stealthy predawn escape to freedom, down the back stairs and out the
back door on her way to a secret rendezvous with her lover. We see the
mother in her dressing gown reading the note, and we hear the (parentheti-
cal) parental cries of confusion and heartbreak counterpointed against the
harmonized commentary of the narrator. The writers' insight into the irony of parent-child alienation echoes in the memory: "She's leaving home
after living alone for so many years."

The music to which Lennon and McCartney fused their words is a
mazurka which renowned composer/author Ned Rorem pronounced
"equal in . . . melodic distinction to those of Chopin." The Beatles, whose
melodies have tapped such diverse music as Indian ragas and symphonic
forms, utilized the string quartet eloquently for the song's instrumental
backing. In "She's Leaving Home" every element dovetails into an integrated whole. Lennon and McCartney's statement on the generation gap is
both universal and timeless. Because they obviously had a sharply focused
picture of the story's action, they were able to vivify it for us.

DISCRIMINATE BETWEEN AN INTERIOR MONOLOGUE AND DIALOGUE

French novelist Paul Bourget originated the term "interior monologue" to designate the flow of a character's innermost thoughts. In a pop
song the singer, more often than not, is simply thinking, as in "Feelings."
Some lyrics can be perceived two ways: For example, "You Don't Bring
Me Flowers" could be taken as daydreaming, with no one present—an interior monologue; it can also be perceived as one side of a conversation;
that's why it worked as a duet with Barbra Streisand and Neil Diamond.

Songs that request something of the singee such as "Don't Walk
Away" or "Do That to Me One More Time" are obviously part of a dialogue. There are other lyric situations, however, where two people are together in a scene, and the singer is thinking the whole song, not addressing
the singee. The important thing is to decide which kind of lyric you want to
write, an interior monologue or one half of a dialogue. A clear lyric requires clear thinking. The simple trick is to keep your mind on the time, the
place, and the plot. With practice the technique will soon become second
nature.

The student writer of "Agnes" had not yet learned to stay focused;
the verse, bridge, and chorus sound as though they had been taped together from three separate songs.

AGNES

Verse:
(Talking
to singee)

Oh baby won't you tell me
Where you run to at night
I feel like such a fool
When I turn out the lights
Baby I love you
Won't you tell me what's wrong
I know we've lost some magic
Now I'll try to be strong.

Bridge:
(Thinking)

Sometimes I get to feeling
That I'm all by myself
That mine is the only hurting heart
But a world full of lovers
Is a world full of pain
And a world full of people
All feeling the same.

Chorus:
(Addressing
nonspecific
you)

There's a star in the sky
For every broken heart
There's a flicker of light, I know
So don't wonder why

> *There's a million stars above*
> *There's a million broken hearts below.*

Verse:
(Talking to singee)

> *Oh baby I go crazy*
> *When I look in your eyes*
> *I see a burning ember*
> *Where there used to be fire*
> *Baby have I lost you*
> *Have you drifted away*
> *Temptation got you running*
> *I can't beg you to stay.*

Bridge:
(Thinking)

> *Sometimes I get to thinking*
> *When I'm all by myself*
> *That fate took its worst out on me*
> *But crying alone*
> *Is crying in vain*
> *In a world full of people*
> *All feeling the same.*

Chorus:
(Addressing nonspecific you)

> *There's a star in the sky*
> *For every broken heart*
> *There's a flicker of light, I know*
> *So don't wonder why*
> *There's a million stars above*
> *There's a million broken hearts below.*

© 1983. Used with permission.

In the first verse the singer appears to be *talking* to the singee. At least we're making a reasonable assumption that *baby* is with him when we hear a line like "Won't you tell me what's wrong?" But in the "bridge"—poorly used here, more like an extension of the verse—the viewpoint changes, and the singer becomes reflective; we now get the impression he is alone. In the chorus, which continues to be ruminative, it seems that he is no longer talking to "baby" but is addressing the nonspecific you. There is an implied "you people" in the line, "Don't (you people) wonder why. . . . The language style also shuttles between conversational in the verses and poetic in the chorus. As a result of the disparity of its parts, the lyric lacks cohesion.

One way to pull this lyric together is to continue the conversation with the singee, which the writer dropped. Had he maintained the momentum of the dialogue, the verse could have culminated in a chorus expressing an idea like: "I can't go on like this much longer" or "I think you got someone on the side" or "Feels like there's cheatin' in the air tonight"—some personal statement that would have developed the hint dropped in the first verse—that baby's been playing around.

The present chorus, impersonal and philosophical, could make a good summation statement for another kind of lyric—for example, a set of new vignette verses which dramatize different broken-heart stories. Making that rewrite choice, the song would then reflect, in a consistent manner, a camera-eye view of a world where love doesn't seem to last.

This is a schizophrenic first draft which, with a good rewrite, could turn into *two* well-adjusted songs.

KEEP YOUR MIND ON YOUR PLOT

There is nothing more important than keeping your mind on what your song is about and what your characters are like—how they think and feel. This writer's understanding of her own character was murky:

I'M NOT GONNA LET LOVE SLIP AWAY
(an excerpt)

Verse: *Love was just a little game to me*
Just something I played at in the night
I'd get my kicks, and then let it go
With the morning light.
Love was something I let fall through my fingers
So many times before
Love was something I told myself
I wasn't gonna let in the door
Till you came into my life
And shone your sweet love light
And I knew—yeah, I knew,
I wasn't gonna let love get away, no.

Chorus: *I'M NOT GONNA LET LOVE SLIP AWAY*
This time I'm gonna hold on
I'M NOT GONNA LET LOVE SLIP AWAY
Slip away, slip away out of my arms.

© 1983. Used with permission.

The situational setup in the opening verse leads us to understand that the singer used to be a playboy and that prior to meeting the singee he had never wanted to make a commitment. But the chorus says that the singer wanted former involvements to last—and implies that he wasn't good at holding on to a relationship. The thought embodied in the title is incompatible with the circumstances described in the verse.

To make the lyric work, there are two rewrite possibilities: either retain the verse (well, most of it) and come up with a title that implies that "this time, for the first and last time, I want love to stay," or revise the verse to fit the chorus by changing the situation to reflect someone who never knew how to hold onto what he wanted. The line "Love was something I let fall through my fingers" is the only one in the verse harmonious with the title; it is at odds with the point of view expressed in all the other lines of the verse. This fledgling lyricist, instead of concentrating on what made her character tick, was merely stringing words together.

PUTTING THINGS IN THE RIGHT ORDER

For a lyric to be effective, its components must be presented in proper order, like the courses on a menu: if the cherries jubilee were served before the steak, a dinner guest would certainly be confused. Similarly, if each section of your lyric doesn't arrive in a logical sequence, your listener will also be confused. Every line should flow smoothly into the next, and each verse, chorus, and bridge should be the natural consequence of the preceding section. No detail in the lyric should be given more importance than it deserves, and all parts should cohere into a unified whole. It's a matter of proportion.

A poorly proportioned lyric can have two kinds of problems: either the facts are out of emotional or chronological order, or a minor element of the plot is overemphasized. "I Feel Like Takin' Up with You" has both problems:

I FEEL LIKE TAKIN' UP WITH YOU

A: *Been on my own*
    For such a long long time
    Feelin' stronger . . . I'll be fine
    Breakin' up has made me blue
    I FEEL LIKE TAKIN' UP WITH YOU.

A: *I've been around*
    I don't need illusions
    Now that I've found you
    There won't be confusion
    I've been needin' someone new
    I FEEL LIKE TAKIN' UP WITH YOU.

B: *Last one was a knockout*
    It's done . . . he just dropped out
    Lord what a beautiful man
    Said he had to hurry
    Told me not to worry
    I was dutiful . . . you understand

A: *Maybe you have the inclination*
    Baby, here's your invitation

> *If you need some down-home lovin' too*
> *I FEEL LIKE TAKIN' UP WITH YOU.*

B: *Last time he showed up*
   What a blast, what a blowup
   Said he was leavin'
   I didn't believe him, then he
   Made knockdown, drag-out love to me.

A: *Well, then was then and*
   Now is now
   Make me forget him, show me how
   You know just the thing to do, 'cause baby,
   I FEEL LIKE TAKIN' UP WITH YOU.

"I Feel Like Takin' Up with You" suggests that the singer is making a romantic overture to someone she has just (or recently) met. She's on the rebound from what appears to be a number of sad affairs, and she's asking a new man to help her forget the "last one." (Hardly a flattering invitation, but that's the plot we're given.)

In the first A section of this AABA lyric, we hear "feelin' stronger" before we are told what the singer is recovering from. *Then* comes "breakin' up has made me blue." That's backwards. In order to follow a lyric, the listener needs to hear the events presented in a logical sequence. Here's a way to fix it: without regard to the original scansion, let's edit out the extra "long" and "on my own," and state the facts as they happened:

> *I've been down*
> *For such a long time*
> *Breakin' up had made me blue,*
> *But I'm much stronger now, and*
> *I FEEL LIKE TAKIN' UP WITH YOU.*

That's an easy-to-follow opening; but in the second A we hear a *non sequitur:* "Now that I've found you, there won't be confusion." Where does the idea of *confusion* come from? The rhyme illusions/confusion is the clue: the writer let an easy rhyme falsify his meaning. The line sounds like a last-verse summation of *some* song, but not *this* song. It contradicts the casual (and apparently short-term) request for "some down-home lovin' . . . you know just the thing to do."

The first bridge over troubled verses describes how the singer was taken in by "a beautiful man," and the second points out how she loved his good lovemaking in spite of his bad treatment. (The lyric also puts the singer in an unflattering light—a separate problem which was covered in Chapter 10.)

The fault under scrutiny here is one of order and proportion: there's too much emphasis on the past. Where are some comments about "you," the supposed subject of the song? What's the new man got that attracts her? Why does she want to take up with him? *He* is the appropriate subject for the bridge, not the former lover. Overstating an unimportant aspect of a plot throws a lyric out of perspective. The writer lost sight of the song's title: "I Feel Like Takin' Up with *You*" (italics mine).

PROS PUT IT ALL TOGETHER

To tell a story that spans decades with a cast of six characters requires, to say the least, keeping focused. "Coward of the County," Kenny Rogers's number one country crossover hit, is a story about Tom (the son of a criminal), his wife Becky, and the Gatlin boys. Tommy's guardian uncle narrates the tale with a chorus that reechoes the deathbed advice of the father.

Billy Edd Wheeler, co-writer of "Coward" with Roger Bowling, told me that the lyric was the fusion of Roger's desire to write a song about "a promise" and Billy Edd's idea to tell a story about "somebody who comes from behind—an underdog." Roger triggered the lyric with the opening line: "Everyone considered him the coward of the county." Billy Edd loved it: "That got us to thinking about why he was a coward, but we still didn't know where the song was going. We rewrote it two or three times over a period of several months, and it kept getting better each time. At one time we had the turning point of the story that Tommy goes into a church and prays, and his uncle gets behind the pulpit where Tommy couldn't see him and speaks: 'It's all right, son, sometimes you have to fight to be a man.' But that seemed awfully hokey, and Roger solved it by having him pick his daddy's picture up off the mantel and talk to the photograph. We went through so many versions, it's hard to remember all we did have in there. I think Roger was a genius at setting songs up and staying on the subject."

Staying on the subject is a good guideline to help you plot a clear and well-developed lyric. The recorded version of "Coward" shows none of the painstaking patchwork of rewriting. Each section flows seamlessly into the next.

COWARD OF THE COUNTY

Verse: *Everyone considered him the COWARD OF THE COUNTY,*
He'd never stood one single time to prove the county wrong.
His momma named him Tommy, but folks just called him yellow,
But something always told me they were reading Tommy wrong.

Verse: *He was only ten years old when his daddy died in prison*
I looked after Tommy 'cause he was my brother's son,
I still recall the final words my brother said to Tommy,
"Son my life is over, but yours has just begun—

Chorus: *Promise me son not to do the things I've done,*
Walk away from trouble if you can.
It won't mean you're weak if you turn the other cheek
I hope you're old enough to understand
Son, you don't have to fight to be a man."

Verse: *There's someone for everyone and Tommy's love was Becky.*
In her arms he didn't have to prove he was a man,
One day while he was working, the Gatlin boys came calling
They took turns at Becky, there was three of them.

Verse: *Tommy opened up the door and saw Becky crying.*
The torn dress, the shattered look was more than he could
stand
He reached above the fireplace and took down his daddy's
picture
As his tears fell on his daddy's face he heard these words
again

Chorus: *"Promise me son not to do the things I've done,*
Walk away from trouble if you can.
It won't mean you're weak if you turn the other cheek
I hope you're old enough to understand
Son, you don't have to fight to be a man."

Verse: *The Gatlin boys just laughed at him when he walked into the*
barroom
One of them got up and met him half way 'cross the floor,
When Tom turned around they said, "Hey, look old yellow's
leaving,"
But you could've heard a pin drop when he stopped and
locked the door.

Verse: *Twenty years of crawling was bottled up inside him,*
He didn't hold nothin' back—he let 'em have it all.
When Tommy left the barroom not a Gatlin was standin'
He said, "This one's for Becky," as he watched the last one
fall.

Chorus: *"I promised you, dad, not to do the things you've done,*
I walk away from trouble when I can,
Now please don't think I'm weak, I couldn't turn the other
cheek
And papa, I sure hope you understand,
Sometimes you gotta fight when you're a man."

Everyone considered him the COWARD OF THE COUNTY.

The provocative opening hints that the tale will have a twist, and we are not disappointed. Summarizing the verses, we find that each tells us something new and moves the plot forward. The writers briefly sketch in Tommy's background and make the requisite link between the singer and the singee—uncle and nephew. Characters enter, scenes change, and time moves on. No one element of the story is overemphasized.

The writers integrated a number of complex matters: The lyric spans a period from Tom's youth to adulthood; the chorus works first as the words of the dying father, second as the words Tommy speaks to his father's photograph, and finally as the thoughts Tommy addresses to his father's memory; the setting moves from Tommy's living room to a barroom, and all the while spoken dialogue cuts in and out of the narrator's voice. The writers, by maintaining a sharp focus on time, place, and action, wove all three into a unified whole.

WRAPUP

After you know the *who* of your plot, then ask yourself: *Where* is my story happening? *When* is it taking place? Is the singer alone and *thinking* the events of the song in an interior monologue like "One Less Bell to Answer"? Or is the singer *with* the "you" in question and speaking, in what could be called a one-sided dialogue, as in "The Shadow of Your Smile"? As you write, keep the scene in front of your eyes. If you change the *when* and *where*, lead the listener through the moves clearly. Be certain you've stuck to your idea. Then make sure you present your facts in ascending order of magnitude, as in Irving Berlin's memorable conclusion of "Always"—where the singer vows to love, not for just an *hour*, or a *day*, or a *year*, but *always*.

A good trick to ensure that the details of your story arrive in the right order is to ask yourself: "And then what?" Try it before each phrase of "Coward of the County." You'll get a logical next line every time. It works with all well-crafted lyrics.

chapter 12

Making It Simple, Clear, Concise, and Direct

"It is easy to be simple and bad; being simple and good is very difficult." Hal David

"Never have a line you have to explain." Sammy Cahn

A lyricist must tell a complete story in usually less than one hundred words (not counting repeated choruses). There is no room in such a tight structure for words that don't pull their own weight.

Statesmen, clergymen, slogan makers, and successful writers in every field practice the virtues of simplicity and directness. They choose words that are instantly understood, words that grab attention, hold interest, and stir emotions. We long remember the short phrase that conveys a strong idea:

> *In God we trust.*
> *Home is where the heart is.*
> *Give me liberty, or give me death.*

Each of these lines is pared to the bone. Each is memorable. But what if, instead of "Give me liberty, or give me death" Patrick Henry had said: "Being executed is preferable to existing without freedom"? Would those nineteen syllables have echoed down the centuries? I doubt it. Short words are stronger than long ones. The active voice, "give me death," is stronger than the passive, "being executed." Pronouns are also important; when the individual *me* disappeared, so did the emotional impact.

Simplicity is a concept that beginning lyricists often misunderstand. Simple does not mean simplistic; nor does it connote dullness. It is uncomplicated and readily understood, like a Rembrandt etching, or Lincoln's Gettysburg Address. No wonder that the adjectives "striking," "elegant," and "classic" are often coupled with the word "simplicity."

For the lyricist, simplicity translates to: keep to one idea and eliminate subplots. A lyric is a miniature, not a mural. Many novice writers tend to overwrite: they complicate with unnecessary characters, clutter with irrelevant details, and pad with superfluous words. In class it is not unusual to hear a first draft with enough plot material for two or three lyrics.

One idea per song is enough. When a hard-to-follow lyric is read, I ask a fellow student to restate the story in one simple sentence. If the listener requires several to paraphrase it, the writer slowly begins to realize that some major pruning is in order. *It is impossible to communicate in a lyric what you cannot express in one simple sentence.*

A complex lyric is one that is difficult to follow. Complexity is exactly what you want to avoid. Here is a first draft, one of the early works of a new professional before he understood the importance of simplicity.

THE ONLY MUSIC

*I have always written love songs
That I play on my guitar;
Last year I played a lot of tunes
For friends or in a bar.*

*I did a hundred love songs,
But they didn't mean a thing,
'Cause I'd lost THE ONLY MUSIC
That made me want to sing.*

*When my woman up and left me,
Then my world turned cold and grey,
So when I played my songs of love,
My heart was far away.*

*Their words had no more meaning
Than a far-off doorbell's ring,
Since I'd lost THE ONLY MUSIC
That I knew I could sing.*

*Then I heard you play piano
In a dim and quiet room,
Your dark hair falling on the keys
Was filled with bright perfume*

*Then love songs flowed within me
Like deep water from a spring,
For you played THE ONLY MUSIC
That made me want to sing.*

*I went home and wrote my love songs
'Till the sun filled up the sky;
I wrote them and I changed them,
I sang and rearranged them,
Until my voice went dry.*

*So tonight I'll come and find you,
And my love songs I will bring;
You'll listen as I say them,
Together we will play them,
Together we will sing.*

Then if you should want my love songs,
And then if you should want me,
I'll write a love song for ourselves
In a sweet and simple key.

As we play our song together,
For my love to you I'll bring,
For you'll be THE ONLY MUSIC
That makes me want to sing.

© 1982. Used with permission.

In an effort to develop his plot, the writer extended at the beginning and end instead of intensifying within. Too much ground is covered without any clear time frame—that is, until the eighth verse when, without any preparation, the word "tonight" jumps out at us. The lyric would be vastly simplified by cutting the first woman from the plot and starting the song with his finding someone new.

To further fog our perception of the events, the title, "The Only Music" suffers from three semantic shifts; the first two times we hear it, *music* is used figuratively, representing the joy of life that left with the first love; the third use is literal, where *music* refers to the songs played by the dark-haired lady; the last reference swings back to figurative—this time reflecting an elation engendered by the prospects of a new romance *plus* his renewed creativity. Such shifting puts a severe strain on the listener. The title of a well-conceived lyric reflects the essence of the song, whether it's "I'm Just Wild About Harry" or "She Believes in Me." "The Only Music" refers to totally different things and people at different stages of the lyric: a symptom of plot complexity. In contrast, remember how the title "Higher Than She's Ever Been Before" worked (page 41). The title represented three stages in Patty Peterson's life, and escalated in meaning with each appearance in the lyric.

The impact of "The Only Music" is also diffused by the variety of feelings it reflects—sad, discouraged, inspired, eager, hopeful. We don't know how to react, and so we feel nothing. Make your lyric emit one clear-cut emotion and make that one emotion build.

HOW SIMPLE SIMPLE CAN BE

In the last chapter we examined "She's Leaving Home" and "Coward of the County," two lyrics with changing time frames and multiple characters. In spite of their movielike plots, each lyric can still be boiled down to one short sentence—showing that an intricate plot and a serious subject can be written simply and clearly.

Except for story songs, pop songs are basically plotless. They express a single attitude or emotion: I'm confused, I'm lonely, I'm jealous,

I'm lucky, I love you.

A lyricist's objective is to express one thought in a fresh way. Ewan MacColl's "The First Time Ever I Saw Your Face," for example, merely shows "I've loved you from the first moment I laid eyes on you." That's all it says. That's as much as any song needs to say.

THE FIRST TIME EVER I SAW YOUR FACE

A: *THE FIRST TIME EVER I SAW YOUR FACE*
I thought the sun rose in your eyes
And the moon and stars
Were the gifts you gave
To the dark and the end of the skies.

A: *And THE FIRST TIME EVER I kissed your mouth*
I felt the earth move in my hand
Like the trembling heart
Of a captive bird
That was there at my command, my love.

A: *And THE FIRST TIME EVER I lay with you*
I felt your heart so close to mine
And I knew our joy
Would fill the earth
And last till the end of time, my love
THE FIRST TIME EVER I SAW YOUR FACE
YOUR FACE, YOUR FACE, YOUR FACE.

Every thought is framed with pronouns: *I saw . . . your face . . . I thought . . . you gave . . . I kissed . . . I felt . . . my hand . . . I lay . . . your heart . . . our joy.* As the relationship progresses from the look, to the kiss, to the consummation, the emotion develops from awe to passion to commitment. The AAA form, with its successive musical restatements, serves ideally to reaffirm the singer's claim of love.

Since he lives in London, Ewan MacColl answered my question, "Which came first, the words or the music?" in a letter: "I had the tune fairly well worked out before I began the lyric. The song came complete [in] not more than half an hour. I didn't do any rewriting at all." It well may be that working from a melody, as he did, brought out the best in MacColl, the lyricist. His consistent (poetic) style and marked preference for one-syllable words combined to create a lyric of rare feeling.

TECHNIQUES OF COMPRESSION

Writing words to music is a great training ground for lyricists. The tyranny of a musical structure demands clear thinking and often elicits a writer's best efforts. Conversely, lyricists who must write, or who choose to write, without the restraints of a melodic framework sometimes let words run away with them. It's common to see an entire first verse wasted in a weak setup. Sometimes a second verse merely repeats something we already know, only in different words. Or lines bulge with fillers—two or three wasted words where one could have done the job better. Generally, the leaner the lyric, the more impact it creates.

Delete Weak Starts

A lyric should begin at the first line of the first verse. That would seem to be a writing principle that goes without saying, but starting late is a common flaw in the work of new writers. These are the first two verses of a student lyric:

Too late, my little voice
Is reminding me
That things are not
What they appear to be
But OH BOY, OH BOY
I couldn't see.

What an actor you are
You could take a prize;
You whisper your love
As you hold me tight,
But OH BOY, OH BOY
It's all been lies.

© 1983. Used with permission.

The first verse of this AABA lyric is total flab; the song is one-quarter over and we've learned nothing. If the writer discarded its limp opening verse and started the song with the second one, the lyric could be off and running. We would then know immediately *who*, *what*, and *why*, and might be interested enough to listen to more.

Eliminate Padding

Some lyrics begin well but then get bogged down by paraphrasing. Repetition, the subject of the next chapter, is indispensable to successful writing. But redundancy—restating the same thought in different words—is padding. Writers often pad instead of develop. Here's a first draft in need of shaping up:

DESIGNER GIRL

Verse: *Guccis on her feet*
Jordache jeans look neat
Ralph Lauren is riding on her chest
Foster Grant'd her glasses
Her jacket is Bill Blass's
Leather boots by Frye to match the rest.

Chorus: *DESIGNER GIRL, DESIGNER GIRL*
She's someone else from head to toe
DESIGNER GIRL, DESIGNER GIRL
She never lets the real her show.

Verse: *Izod's crocodile*
Says her shirt's in style
Saint Laurent designs are just divine
Chanel's her favorite scent
Dior's magnificent
Her curves just can't be beat in Calvin Kleins.

Chorus: *DESIGNER GIRL, DESIGNER GIRL*
She's hard to read, she's hard to know
Ooh, DESIGNER GIRL
She never lets the real her show.

Verse: *You can't tell a book by its cover*
What counts is what you see inside
I don't know if I really love her
I wonder what she's trying to hide.

(repeat chorus)

© 1981. Used with permission.

This lyric doesn't qualify as an amusing "list" song such as "You're the Top." Showing us a woman whose own initials are not enough, the lyricist is using the opening verse as a setup. The second verse should tell us some *new* aspect about her we don't know—not more about her trendy wardrobe.

It cannot go without mention that the lyric's tone is judgmental and that the line "I don't know if I really love her" makes the singer less than sympathetic. It will take a major rewrite to make "Designer Girl" a potentially recordable lyric. After the second verse is deleted, however, there will be plenty of room to develop a fresh angle.

Take Up the Slack

A simpler kind of redundancy occurs when you use two words to say something fully said by one. For example: "*Unknown* stranger" is redundant; a stranger is someone we don't know. "*Small* boutique" is redundant; a boutique is a small shop. "*Public* persona" is a common verbal overkill; the persona is one's public façade. The most frequent verbal blunders are *very unique* and *very contemporary*. Unique means without equal: it's impossible to be "very without equal" or "very in the present." Good writing is concise. Delete words that don't do a job, that don't work to say exactly what you mean. The following random lines from student lyrics are larded with worthless words: *almost, really, too, very, just, quite,* and so on. Trimming the fat (in italics) would add impetus to the lines.

> We found out *almost much* too late
> It's a hope *that* we cannot *quite* explain
> *Just* something I played *at* in the night
> Her days are filled with *lots of* classes
> There's nothing *really very* wrong
> I don't have enough fingers to count the *endless* times
> Even though we're *very* far apart

Weed Out Modifiers

The main culprits of clutter are flabby adjectives and *-ly* adverbs. Make your nouns and verbs self-sufficient by trading two weak words for one strong one. For example:

CONDENSE A MODIFIED NOUN:	TO A STRONGER NOUN:
heavy rain	downpour
short letter	note
festive party	bash
surprise inheritance	windfall
small amount	pittance

CONDENSE A MODIFIED VERB:	TO A STRONG VERB:
drink noisily	slurp
walk slowly	amble
strike heavily	pound
speak haltingly	stammer
move nervously	fidget

Conciseness at Work

The only lyricist (to date) to win four Oscars and two Grammys is Johnny Mercer. Mercer, a songwriter's songwriter, was a master craftsman who made every word count. Reading through the hundreds of lyrics in his biography, *Our Huckleberry Friend*, you'll find no extraneous *just, nearly, much, and,* or *really*. He was without peer in writing words to music. "I *prefer* to have the music first," he said, "because I seem to catch the mood of the tune."

Some of the tunes he caught the mood of are: "Skylark," "You Were Never Lovelier," "I'm Old-Fashioned," "Come Rain or Come Shine," "That Old Black Magic," "Laura," "Midnight Sun," "Autumn Leaves," "Blues in the Night," and "Moon River."

MOON RIVER

MOON RIVER
Wider than a mile,
I'm crossin' you in style some day.

Old dreammaker
You heartbreaker,
Wherever you're goin'
I'm goin' your way.

Two drifters
Off to see the world,
There's such a lot of world to see

We're after the same
Rainbow's end
Waitin' 'round the bend,
My huckleberry friend,
MOON RIVER *and me.*

Written to Henry Mancini's wistful theme for the movie *Breakfast at Tiffany's*, "Moon River" earned both the 1961 Oscar and the 1962 Grammy awards. The words seem to catch the current of the water, sounding like small waves lapping: *wider, maker, breaker, you're goin'/I'm goin', see the world/world to see*. Not an extra word in sight.

"Huckleberry friend" is a word pairing of rare semantic richness: with a single adjective Mercer evokes wild berries growing along the water's edge, the blue of the river itself, and the adventurous drifter, Huckleberry Finn. With fifty-six well-chosen words he summed up the adventure of life. That's compression.

TECHNIQUES FOR CLARITY

Sticking to one idea, focusing sharply on the time and place, and using short, strong words all contribute to writing a clear lyric—but they don't guarantee it. In a structure as small as a lyric, every word—each *and* and *but*—weighs a lot and wields the power to confuse, if you let it. From your opening line, make every word say exactly what you mean. If your listeners must struggle to decipher your message, they will give up and tune out. Here are some ways to avoid potholes on the road to clarity.

INCLUDE PERSONAL PRONOUNS. Make sure your pronouns are in place: *you, me, I, we, my, our, mine,* and so on. These little words serve a big function. They tell us *who* is feeling or thinking, or doing *what,* as we saw in "First Time Ever" and "Moon River." Here are some vague opening lines suffering from the lack of pronouns.

"Empty arms that still long to hold/Dreams that refuse to be sold." Whose empty arms? Hold what? Whose dreams? No pronouns equals vagueness.

"Passing by/And refusing to look/At those who want to belong." Who is passing by? Look at what? Belong where? Twelve wasted words.

"The child inside/Sweet child, hasn't died/It lives there waiting for the days/A sad heart in pain/Needs the child again/To bring back those simple days." Twenty-nine words and we don't know what's going on. *What* child inside? Lives *where*? *Whose* sad heart? *Which* simple days? Every key personal pronoun that could have made the meaning as clear to the listener as it was to the writer is missing. What if he had said: "The child inside *me*, waiting for the day/*My* sad heart in pain/Needs *him* again/To bring back *my* simple (childhood) days." A lot clearer.

DETECT *ITOSIS. It* is a tricky word. When *it*s occur in colloquial expressions, they need no clarification: talk *it* over/if *it* takes forever/*it's* going to rain/*it's* a snap/*it's* a fact/*it* seems to me. Those *its* are immediately clear. Lyrics, however, often suffer from a widespread but not fatal malady I call *itosis.* The symptom is vagueness. The cure is simple: every *it* should be clarified.

At some point in grade school your teacher discussed the proper use of pronouns. In case you missed that grammar lesson, here's a recap of the rule: All personal pronouns—each *him, her, she,* and *they,* as well as the indefinite pronoun *it*—must refer to some previously stated word or phrase, which is called the *antecedent. Itosis* develops in two ways: when the *it* and the antecedent are separated by too many words, or when the antecedent is nonexistent. In each instance, the audience is distracted.

Here are examples of good usage: "New York's home, but *it* ain't mine no more" (Neil Diamond). No confusion. The pronoun follows three words after its antecedent. "You've lost that lovin' feelin', now *it's* gone, gone, gone" (Mann/Weil). That's clear—*it's* refers to lovin' feelin'. The meaning couldn't be misinterpreted.

Occasionally the word or phrase that clarifies *it* immediately *follows* the pronoun. (Guidelines usually have an exception.) An example is: "We wanted *it* all: passion without pain . . . " ("You and Me," Sager/Allen). That's clear too.

Here are some student examples of *itosis* caused by a nonexistent antecedent. "You've lost the race/'cause his freedom's in first place/you want advice/don't let him do *it* to you twice." Do what? Leave? Cheat? The listener shouldn't be made to guess.

"Was never my desire to make her mine/but loneliness captured me under its spell/I don't know which way *it* will go." What's *it?* The spell? The loneliness? The relationship?

A floating *it* causes more damage to meaning than the notorious dangling participle. Don't let your words lose their moorings. Anchor every *it* to an unmistakable word or phrase. That's a positive move toward clarity.

BEWARE OF HOMONYMS. Homonyms, words that sound the same but differ in their definitions, are fun for writers—of the *written* word. Lyricists, however, are heard, not seen. The ear must quickly perceive the meaning without visual aids. Here are two excerpts from a lyric illustrating how its writer fell into the homonym trap:

> *She wears the latest designer style*
> *The kind that will aid her wile.*

When the student read her lyric, the class was confused. Her voice dropped at the period on the word *wile,* thereby telling us the thought was over. But we didn't understand the thought. We presumed we had heard the word *while.* But what could "aid her while" mean? To compound the confusion, the word *wile*—a "ruse" or "trick"—is usually used in the plural; hearing it in the singular is part of the reason for the line's lack of clarity. Here's the other excerpt:

> *He's waiting as always, ready for her;*
> *In the time they have together*
> *the hours whir.*

It's the same problem. The line sounds as if the thought were unfinished as in . . . the hours *were* . . .(?). The easiest way to detect any aurally ambiguous words is to read your lyric aloud to someone, without giving the person a lyric sheet. Ask if any word or line is unclear; *then* hand out the lyric to verify if what was heard is what you read. You'll quickly discover if homonyms are confusing your audience.

GIVE YOUR LYRICS PUNCH

USE ACTIVE VERBS. Verbs in the active voice are more vivid than those in the passive. If your song has a phrase like, "the sky is lighted up by stars," make the stars do the job: "stars light up the sky." The idea in "the promises that *were made by* you and me," is said more effectively as "*we made* promises." Replace "our faith was destroyed by rumors" with "rumors destroyed our faith."

CHOOSE ONE-SYLLABLE WORDS. Short words are easier for the listener to understand and remember, and easier for the performer to sing. New writers often use fancy four-syllable words when a short word would deliver more impact. Directness has punch: "Tote 'dat barge, lift 'dat bale." Those six words from "Ol' Man River" are so quotable that they've become almost a cliché. An example of the effectiveness of one-syllable words is the close of "First Time Ever": "And I knew our joy/Would fill the earth/And last till the end of time. . . ."

There is a moment in Stephen Sondheim's musical *Sunday in the Park with George* when an artist explains to his lover/model why he can't give her the words she needs to hear—that his medium is paint and color and design, not words. In "We Do Not Belong Together" he sums up his relationship to his art and to her, "I am what I do . . . which you knew": eight eloquent monosyllables.

REPLACE ABSTRACTIONS. Beginning writers, especially those making the transition from poetry to pop, frequently fog their lyrics in abstractions: dreams, fears, hopes, pain. A listener quickly tires of groping through a misty landscape for something to hold on to. We want words that tell about people we can recognize who are feeling emotions we can identify with. Here are some lifeless outtakes from student lyrics which, if stated directly, would have had impact.

ABSTRACT	DIRECT
Lift the cloud, shine the light	Tell me what you're feeling
We've been stumbling too long in the shadows	It's time we make a decision
The world crept in on us	We've both changed

REDUCE NEGATIVE CONSTRUCTIONS. Every unnecessary negative statement diminishes the force of your thought—and wastes words. Practice putting ideas in a positive way. At busy Manhattan intersections stoplight signs caution pedestrians, "Cross at the green," not "Don't cross at the red." Look over your lyric. See if you can restate the *isn't*s, *don't*s, *aren't*s, and *not*s. For example:

INSTEAD OF:	TRY:
You're not calm	You're edgy
I can't remember	I forget
The fire isn't lighted	The fire is unlit
It can't be done	It's impossible
She wasn't careful	She was careless

This suggestion applies to tightening the body of the lyric, not to titles. Titles that give strong commands or that pose questions couched in the negative can be direct and forceful: "Don't Blame Me," "Don't Fence Me In," "Don't Sleep in the Subway," "Don't It Make My Brown Eyes Blue?" "Can't We Be Friends?"

MAKE STRAIGHTFORWARD STATEMENTS. A song has often been referred to as a three-minute movie. That's a good analogy. A movie contains all the information we need for its enjoyment, and so must the words of a song. Some novice writers, instead of writing a complete movie script, tend to write a soap-opera episode: that is, a lyric that presupposes that the audience is in on "the story so far. . . ."

In the first draft of "You Lost Your Touch" the writer was working from the premise that we already know who the "you" is in his life, where she has been, and what her relationship is to the singer. Lyrics don't come with voiceover announcements stating: "last week in our story. . . ." All the facts have to be there in clear, straightforward statements—unlike this first draft:

YOU LOST YOUR TOUCH
(an excerpt)

Verse: *You're back, you must be under attack,*
You think there's someone hot on your tracks,
You went somewhere to hole up and hide
You wasted time down South with the best,
Ran out of pills and luck with the rest,
I thought you had some sense on the side.

Chorus: *YOU LOST YOUR TOUCH*
Chasin' yourself this time
Afraid of what you'll find
YOU LOST YOUR TOUCH
You left your dreams behind.

All we can figure out is someone "came back" from "down South." Vague expressions like "with the rest" (who?), "with the best" (what?), and "left your dreams" (which ones—of love, success, wealth?) tell us nothing. The lyricist was so busy analyzing the singee, he had no room left to say how *he* felt. The critique given the student pointed up the lyric's main weakness: indirectness. In the rewrite, we learn the relationship between the singer and singee and understand exactly why he's through with her, because he tells us, directly.

Verse: *I loved you once, we started a home,*
You left me twice and flew off to Rome,
You found someone with money to burn.
I bought your act each time you came back

You smiled, I could not mount an attack
This time I think I've finally learned.

Chorus: *YOU LOST YOUR TOUCH*
Go back to him this time;
I've had enough.
I see right through your line
YOU LOST YOUR TOUCH
Now I can read your mind.

The vagueness is gone. The revision makes short, direct statements: *I loved, we started, you left, go back.* Now we can identify with the universal emotion: I've had enough. Now we can sing along.

PASS UP THE PASSIVE ATTITUDE. A passive lyric, like a limp handshake, makes a poor first impression. I'm not talking here about passive versus active verbs, but rather the attitude your lyric expresses. Publisher Norman Dolph of Four Moons Music, himself a lyricist, claims: "The mark of a neophyte song is its passive quality." Lyrics presented in class with even a tinge of passivity—from the perspective of either gender—consistently earn a collective "boo."

A song speaks for its time. "I Will Survive" expresses the contemporary view: down with namby-pamby, up with self-assertive. Lyrics that reflect a self-demeaning posture (especially a woman's) are out of sync with the eighties. Hit songs of decades ago may have exuded that "you-can-hurt-me-desert-me-beat-me-and-I'll-turn-the-other-cheek-and-take-it-forever" philosophy. But if written today, a lyric conveying that passé, doormat attitude will have a hard time finding someone to sing it. In fact, some pre-sexual-revolution lyrics are being revised in order to mirror the generally more assertive stance of contemporary women. As a case in point, Sheldon Harnick was asked to change the dated attitude reflected in "I'll Marry the Very Next Man," a song from his 1959 Pulitzer musical *Fiorello!* The original lyric, although playfully hyperbolic, made the singer appear masochistic: she merrily asserts she doesn't care how frequently her future husband might strike her—that she'd gladly fetch his pipe and slippers with her "arm in a sling." At the request of a student actress in a high school production (1984) of *Fiorello!*, Sheldon Harnick made the rewrite take a 180-degree turn: in the new version, the future wife of Fiorello La Guardia asserts that when he proposes, she will have him send her "tons of roses."

"I Will Survive" Does

Gloria Gaynor's 1979 Grammy-winning record, written and produced by the team of Dino Fekaris and Freddie Perren, has fulfilled its promise: it's a survivor. Unlike most fast-rising and equally fast-disappearing disco ballads, "I Will Survive" has gone on to garner records by a number of outstanding artists, including Roberta Flack, Gladys Knight, and Johnny Mathis. It speaks for males and females alike. Its message is clear, direct, and forceful.

I WILL SURVIVE

Verse: *At first I was afraid,*
I was petrified,
Kept thinkin' I could never live
Without you by my side.
But then I spent so many nights
Thinkin' how you did me wrong
And I grew strong
And I learned how to get along.

Verse: *And so you're back from outer space;*
I just walked in to find you here
With that sad look upon your face.
I should have changed that stupid lock,
I should have made you leave your key,
If I'd've known for just one second
You'd be back to bother me.

Chorus: *Go on now, go walk out the door;*
Just turn around now,
Cause you're not welcome anymore.
Weren't you the one who tried
To hurt me with goodbye?
Did you think I'd crumble?
Did you think I'd lay down and die?
Oh no, not I.
I WILL SURVIVE
For as long as I know how to love
I know I'll stay alive.
I've got all my life to live
I've got all my love to give and
I'LL SURVIVE. I WILL SURVIVE.

Verse: *It took all the strength I had*
Not to fall apart;
Kept tryin' to mend the pieces
Of my broken heart.
And I spent, oh so many nights
Just feelin' sorry for myself.
I used to cry,
But now I hold my head up high

Verse: *And you see me—somebody new*
         I'm not that chained up little person
         Still in love with you
         And so you felt like droppin' in
         And just expect me to be free,
         Well now, I'm savin' all my lovin'
         For someone who's lovin' me.

                    (repeat chorus)

The singer is assertive, honest, and likable. She admits her past vulnerability and is proud of her hard-won new strength. We admire her self-respect; she's determined to save her love for someone worthy of it. Every word commands our attention—short ones, strong ones, each said in a positive personal statement: *I grew strong . . . walk out the door . . . you're not welcome . . . I hold my head up high . . . I've got all my life to live. . . .* No passivity here, or murky metaphors, or abstractions—just straight talk—simple, direct, and clear.

WRAPUP

No one ever said simple was easy. Nevertheless, it's well worth all the effort to weed out unnecessary characters, like the first woman in "The Only Music," and to keep focused upon one idea. After your first draft give your lyric the title test: did you "prove it" by keeping your story simple?

For maximum impact, pare down your first drafts. Where you can, prune words like *but, well, so, then,* especially the worst offender, *just.* The better "clutter detective" you become, the more effective your writing will be.

Pick themes you can treat positively, where you feel comfortable saying *I* and making direct personal statements. Whenever you need some self-assertion therapy, take one daily dose of "I Will Survive" until your symptoms disappear.

chapter 13

Using the Power of Repetition

> *"The repetitive principle is at the very source of musical art and of poetry . . . ."* Leonard Bernstein
>
> *"Choose key words and play upon them."* Henry James

There's a story about a lighthouse keeper who became accustomed to hearing the clang of a bell every three minutes, day and night, as the beacon completed each round. One night when he was fast asleep, the bell mechanism failed to sound. He immediately bolted upright in bed and cried out: "What was that?" The lighthouse keeper felt dislocated because a fundamental rhythmic pattern of his life was interrupted.

A repeated pattern satisfies a basic human need for the recognition of the familiar. The mind demands the comfort of the known as well as the delights of the new. In fact, it can be said that all art consists of a balanced structuring of two elements: repetition and variation.

A painter repeats the colors and the curves and the angles of his design. A composer helps us follow his structure by restating some musical elements—a series of notes, or a rhythm, or a chord sequence. A lyricist can choose from a wide range of repetitive devices, from the subtle linking of vowel and consonant sounds to the full-scale restatement of an entire section of a song. Every well-conceived repetition not only provides gratification to the ear, but, by emphasizing and drawing together key words, lends organization and structure to the song. The chorus, the refrain, the return, and the title line are the strongest of all repetitive devices because they restate the biggest block of words.

REPETITION OF PHRASES AND FULL WORDS

The Chorus

In preceding chapters you've seen a number of examples of how the chorus of the verse/chorus song gives an audience that instant satisfaction of the familiar: "Richard Cory," "The Gambler," "She's Leaving Home," "Wino," and "Coward of the County." The verse/chorus song is considered the most commercial format for the simple reason that it allows for the replay of an entire section over and over. Sometimes upon hearing a song for the first time, we are able to sing along with the chorus by its second reprise: " . . . I'm ready to take a chance again/ready to put my heart on the line with you . . ." When we sing along, we make the song our own.

The Refrain

Chapter 5 showed how the AAA's one- or two-line refrain works to orient the listener to the design of the song. Bob Dylan's cryptic, "The answer, my friend, is blowin' in the wind" is a memorable refrain which frames each verse. The time-honored device builds in universal appeal through repetition and gives many AAA songs that everybody-join-in-and-sing quality which can make for standards: "Try to remember . . . then follow. . . . " (Jones/Schmidt).

The Return

The reappearance, for emphasis, of all or part of the opening verse at the end of the song is called a return. John Denver's "Annie's Song," Roger Miller's "King of the Road," and John Phillips's "California Dreamin' " are three AAA songs whose entire third verses are a full repeat of the first verse. Such a "recycling" creates a circularity to the story. The initial verse must, of course, contain ideas that can bear the weight of complete restatement, as in Thom Schuyler's "16th Avenue," in which the final verse is a return of the first.

Sometimes only a portion of the words is returned: "Out Here on My Own" (Lesley and Michael Gore), "She's Got A Way" (Billy Joel), "Somewhere Down the Road" (Weil/Mann) are songs that repeat one or more lines from the first verse in the final one and then add a new two-line wrapup. Reworking elements from early in the song into its finale helps to emphasize key words.

The Title Line

In the AABA form it's the song's title that serves as the primary source of needed repetition. When the lyricist uses this structure to the optimum, we hear the title repeat in the same place in at least two out of the three A verses, such as in the classics, "Body and Soul," "Oh, Lady Be Good," and "Try a Little Tenderness." More recent AABA hits, "Come In from the Rain," "She's Out of My Life," and "The Girl Is Mine," employ the same technique. The repeated title line simultaneously outlines the framework of the design and drives home the main point of the lyric.

Things that come in threes make memorable impressions, especially in lyrics. The triplet title invites the listener to sing along: "Do-Do-Do," "Let It Snow! Let It Snow! Let It Snow!" "Hold Me, Hold Me, Hold Me." Giant hits, every one. Three alliterated words effectively stamp themselves on the memory: "Bewitched (bothered and bewildered)," "Jingle, Jangle, Jingle," and "Baubles, Bangles, and Beads."

SUBTLE SOUND REPETITIONS

Some song ideas are not served well either by the summation of a chorus or by the repetitive commentary of a refrain. Nevertheless, the lyricist must still provide the listener with "soundposts of familiarity" to satisfy the ear. What if, like Joni Mitchell, you want to show how a lovelorn woman drifts through the changing seasons, waiting for the letter that never comes? In designing "Marcie," Mitchell found the ideal form for her linear story. "Marcie" would have been ruined by an intrusive chorus that stopped the action. The AABA, with its contrasting bridge, would also have been a poor choice. The composer/lyricist picked the AAA and augmented the structure in the second and third verses. In place of the more obvious kinds of repetition, Mitchell used a number of subtle repetitive devices that manage to hold our attention without interrupting the flow of the story. Treat yourself to reading "Marcie" aloud. Listen to the music her words make. Then read it again and see how many different sound patterns your ear can pick up.

MARCIE

MARCIE in a coat of flowers
Stops inside a candy store
Reds are sweet and greens are sour
Still no letter at her door
So she'll wash her flower curtains
Hang them in the wind to dry
Dust her table with his shirt and
Wave another day goodbye.

MARCIE's faucet needs a plumber
MARCIE's sorrow needs a man
Red is autumn green is summer
Greens are turning and the sand
All along the ocean beaches
Stares up empty at the sky
MARCIE buys a bag of peaches
Stops a postman passing by
    And summer goes
    Falls to the sidewalk like string and brown paper
    Winter blows
    Up from the river, there's no one to take her to
    the sea.

MARCIE dresses warm it's snowing
Takes a yellow cab uptown
Red is stop and green's for going
Sees a show and rides back down,
Down along the Hudson River
Past the shipyards in the cold
Still no letter's been delivered
Still the winter days unfold

Like magazines
Fading in dusty grey attics and cellars
Make a dream
Dream back to summer and hear how he tells her
Wait for me.

MARCIE *leaves and doesn't tell us*
Where or why she moved away
Red is angry, green is jealous
That was all she had to say
Someone thought they saw her Sunday
Window shopping in the rain
Someone heard she bought a one-way ticket
And went west again.

The most obvious repetition in the lyric is the word "Marcie" itself. Putting the name of the song at the opening of each verse, and consistently keeping it there, helps the listener follow the song's form as well as identify its title. Mitchell uses many other verbal echoes throughout "Marcie" which serve to emphasize structure or reinforce meaning.

ANAPHORA. A common literary device has the uncommon name of anaphora (a-NAF-ora). It is the repetition of a word (or like-sounding words) or a short phrase at the start of successive lines or verses. In the third verse of "Marcie" we find the device in the lines, "*Still* no let-ter's been delivered/*Still* the winter days unfold. . . . " Again in the last verse, the line starting "*Someone* thought. . . . " echoes in "*Someone* heard. . . . " You've seen other examples in "The First Time Ever I Saw Your Face," "The Ballad of the Shape of Things," "By the Time I Get to Phoenix," and "The Gambler," and you'll recognize anaphora again when you get to "I Got Rhythm" in Chapter 17. Anaphora, or start-of-line repe-tition, whichever you prefer, is a simple and forceful method for building in familiarity.

In the second verse the word *Marcie* starts two consecutive lines; in addition to being an instance of anaphora, the lines themselves are ex-amples of another rhetorical device, parallelism.

PARALLELISM. Parallelism is the presentation of similar or con-trasting ideas in a similar grammatical construction: "Marcie's faucet needs a plumber, Marcie's sorrow needs a man." Compare aloud the first two lines of each of the four verses; each is identical in meter, but listen to how much "weightier" the words in the second verse are than in any of the others. Linking the relationship of ideas heightens their meaning. Parallel-ism adds both cohesion and polish to a lyric, as we can see in her red and green color scheme. The use of red and green in "Marcie" is also an exam-ple of word motifs.

WORD MOTIFS. A motif is the repetition of a single word or group of words throughout a lyric, either expanding its significance or pointing up the theme. The motif of "Marcie" does both. Mitchell expertly paints reds and greens onto her canvas at the identical spot (the third line) in every verse, highlighting her design. With each appearance the colors take on new meanings—from confections, to leaves, to traffic signals, to emotions, growing in importance as they reappear.

Irving Berlin also used a color motif in a song for the 1938 Rogers and Astaire film *Carefree*. In "I Used to Be Color Blind" the singer, who has just fallen in love, sees nature's colors with a new intensity: the green in the grass, the gold in the moon, and the blue of the sky. At the song's end the focus is on the lover's coloring: the red cheek, the gold hair, and the blue eyes. By restating the blue and gold, Berlin personalizes the feelings of the singer and unifies his theme.

WORD ECHOES, or *anadiplosis,* as it's called by linguists, is the repetition of the last word in one line at the beginning of the next. ". . . and rides back *down/down* along the Hudson River . . ." and similarly, ". . . make a *dream/dream* back to summer." Richard Rodgers used echoes in the song "Look No Further" from *No Strings,* for which he wrote the lyric as well as the music.

SEQUENCE. Another literary device that contributes to the unity of "Marcie" is the sequence, a series of similar constructions that begin with the same kind of word—a verb, adverb, adjective, and so on. With four introductory one-syllable verbs we see Marcie "wash her flower curtains/hang them in the wind/dust her tables/wave another day . . ." Sequences bring coherence to a lyric as they emphasize the rhythm. The device is also used effectively in "We've Only Just Begun": "sharing horizons/ . . . watching the signs/ . . . talking it over/ . . . working together."

A sequence, in addition to being a literary term, is also a musical term: a melodic phrase that repeats at a higher or lower pitch. A lyricist's use of a word sequence is commonly the result of a sensitive ear matching the musical pattern, as in the just-quoted phrases from "We've Only Just Begun."

REPEATED PARTS OF WORDS

So far, we've noted only the repetition of full words, or a series of the same kinds of words, in grammatical structures. Much of the effect of "Marcie" comes from the more subtle chiming of paired *sounds*. In addition to end rhyme schemes—a major subject treated in Chapter 17— "Marcie" resounds with overlapping patterns of repeated vowels and consonants which contribute to the total meaning of the lyric.

Vowel Sounds

A vowel is the most prominent sound in a syllable. In English, the vowels are *A, E, I, O, U,* and sometimes *Y.* However, there are many more vowel *sounds* than there are vowels. For example, compare the sound that the *a* makes in these words: *gate, glare, gather, garden.* Phoneticians as far back as Demetrius (first century A.D.) have referred to "vowel music." We know that different vowel sounds when spoken in succession create a euphonious effect and thereby display their relationship to the musical scale. To illustrate: speak this sequence of words: *seat, sit, set, sat, soot, sought.* Hear the tones descending in pitch? The last line of the Rodgers and Hammerstein classic "You'll Never Walk Alone" is a fine example of a cascading vowel sound perfectly matched to a descending melody: "(you'll) ne-ver walk a-lone"—*eh, er, aw, ah, oh.* The sound a word makes is not always related to its spelling. For example, in "Marcie" we hear matching *o* sounds which come in a variety of spellings: *coat/goes/show/ postman.* Sound pairings are determined solely by the ear, not the eye.

ASSONANCE is the repetition of a particular vowel sound. Because it sings with the spirit of a rhyme, it has been called "vowel rhyme." In "Marcie" we hear these vowel clusters in the first verse: Mar*cie*/sw*ee*t/ gr*ee*ns; r*e*d/l*e*tter; fl*o*wer/s*ou*r; t*a*bles/w*a*ve/d*ay*. In the third verse: c*a*b/ b*a*ck/p*a*st/m*a*gazines/*a*ttic; f*a*ding/gr*ey*. In the fourth verse: Mar*cie*/l*ea*ves/ *a*ngry/gr*ee*n; *a*ll/th*ough*t/b*ough*t; j*ea*lous/w*e*st; Sund*ay*/r*ai*n.

I think it remarkable that in her palette of sound colors, blending 236 words, we never hear an *accented oo* sound throughout the song (the word *to* is unaccented). Whether consciously or unconsciously, Mitchell sensed that the warmth exuded by *oo* was incompatible with the bleak landscape she was painting. She achieved and maintained her atmosphere with broad strokes of *o, ee, aw,* and *a.* A gifted lyricist instinctively selects vowel colors that will produce the desired emotional effect. A narrow range of vowel sounds, for example, is more likely to describe a pensive, calmer state than a line with more extreme contrasts of sound. When you want to build a mood or create a setting, pick words not only for their explicit meanings but also for their emotive coloration.

Consonant Sounds

Consonants are the framework of the word and are classified according to the ways we articulate them—with the lips, tongue, and teeth. The related members of each group are *phonetic cognates,* a term coined by Sidney Lanier.

Dentals: *d, t, th* (as in *thin*), *TH* (as in *THis*)
Labials: *b, p, (m* is sometimes added)
Gutturals: *g, k, ng*
Labiodentals: *f, v*
Sibilants: *s, z, sh, zh, ch, j*
Nasals: *m, n, ng, nk*
Liquids: *l, r*

ALLITERATION is the repetition of accented consonant sounds in successive or neighboring words; it is also called "head rhyme." As children we were introduced to alliteration in the tongue-tying challenge of "Peter Piper picked a peck of pickled peppers." Clearly such consonantal overkill would be pointless in a pop lyric. However, it can be employed for high comic effect. W.S. Gilbert, lyrical partner of Sir Arthur Sullivan, is the king of "alliterationists" and an acknowledged bravura rhymer. Here is alliteration purposely carried to the *n*th degree:

> *It's a song of a merryman, moping mum,*
> *Whose soul was sad, and whose glance was glum*
> *Who sipped no sup, and who craved no crumb,*
> *As he sighed for the love of a ladye.*

W.S. Gilbert
From *Yeomen of the Guard*

Alliteration is a classic device for creating phonic patterns by lightly linking neighboring words. In "Marcie" Joni Mitchell interweaves alliteration and assonance for stunning effects. In the first verse, listen to the series of *s*'s that help the lines flow: ". . . stops inside a candy store/still . . .so . . . she . . . shirt . . ." They alternate with *w* repetitions of *wash* and *wind* and *wave*. All are intersected with vowel rhymes of *e*, *o*, and *a* sounds. There are more such sound patterns in verses two, three, and four.

Beyond simple alliteration, "Marcie" provides even more subtle variations called *concealed alliteration* or *consonantal clusters*. This is a linking of words whose initial consonants are related rather than identical; they are members of the same group of cognates such as the labials *b*, *p*, and *m*. Mitchell uses this device twice in "Marcie," ". . . buys a *b*ag of *p*eaches . . ." and then in "*p*ostman *p*assing *b*y." A less sensitive ear might have gone overboard with "*b*uys a *b*ox of *b*erries." Blunt. Three *b*s trivialize the thought. She also might have had the "*p*ostman *w*alking *b*y." Not nearly as effective without the connection of the second *p*. Concealed alliteration creates a phonetic variation on a theme.

Just when I thought I had noted every repetitive device Mitchell had employed, I made a discovery: a pronounced and sophisticated pattern of consonants I have not found in another lyric. My research into poetics—to identify her device—netted no label. So I have called it:

REVERSE ALLITERATION or *pairings of crossed consonants,* where the initial consonants of two or more consecutive words are repeated by a subsequent word group, *but in reverse order.* The following striking pairings of words are laced through the intricate tonal designs we've already noted: *coat of flowers/flower curtains* (*ctf/fct*); *back down/dream back* (*bd/db*); *green is summer/summer goes* (*gs/sg*); *bag of peaches/passing by* (*bp/pb*); *to dry/dust her table* (*td/dt*); *days unfold/fading in dusty* (*df/fd*); *like magazines/Marcie leaves* (*lm/ml*). Making this phonetic pattern was undoubtedly unconscious. Nonetheless, the existence of these seven pairs of "crossed consonants" undeniably reflects an ear seeking aural symmetry through varied repetition.

Joni Mitchell, one of our most literate lyricists, has used anaphora, parallelism, word motifs, echoes, sequences, assonance, and alliteration to weave a tapestry of colors, pictures, and emotions. Nowhere is alliteration overdone. Nowhere is meaning sacrificed for sound. Integrity, in
every sense of the word, is evident. The tonal architecture Joni Mitchell
achieves in "Marcie" is clearly the work of a writer who is a reader of literature and poetry. That's how a lyricist's ear is trained—by listening to the
way the finest writers achieve their effects.

ADDING THE RING OF THE FAMILIAR

In addition to the devices that abound in "Marcie," there are several more ways to inject memorability into your lyrics: through the ring of
the familiar.

EPISTROPHE. The repetition of the same word or words at the
end of successive lines or verses for rhetorical effect is called *epistrophe* (e-
PIS-tro-fee). It is the reverse of anaphora. Howard Dietz used the device effectively in the theater song "Triplets" from *Between the Devil* (with music
by Arthur Schwartz). He hammered home the triplets' special problems—
they looked *alike,* and dressed *alike,* and walked *alike,* and talked *alike.*

Irving Berlin's classic "All Alone" concludes with the lover affect-
ingly wondering where *she is,* and how *she is,* and if *she is* all alone too. In
"She's Got a Way," Billy Joel played with epistrophe by punctuating the
end of successive verses with three related words: *anyway, anywhere, everywhere.*

It's unnecessary, of course, to remember the term "epistrophe," or
even end-of-line repetition. The important thing is to *hear* how the device
can strengthen your writing.

AN ALLUSION is a direct or implied reference to a well-known
person or thing. Pop lyrics are often studded with the names of glittery
people and places: Garbo, Deitrich, Tiffany, Bogie, and Bacall, and the
ubiquitous Astaire. Bob Dylan made a feature of name dropping in his
1965 chronicle of society's woes, "Desolation Row." The landscape of his
lyric is dotted with over a dozen characters from history and literature:
Bette Davis, Romeo, Cinderella, Cain and Abel, the Hunchback of Notre
Dame, Einstein, Robin Hood, the Phantom of the Opera, Casanova, the
Titanic, Ezra Pound, and T.S. Eliot! A well-placed allusion can give instant
memorability to a lyric line: "I'll be rich as Rockefeller" ("On the Sunny
Side of the Street"); "Where have you gone, Joe Di Maggio?" ("Mrs. Robinson"). We remember, and we sing along. Of course, if your allusion is to
someone or something unknown to the listener, the desired effect fails.

A BORROWING is a word or phrase taken from another place.
It can be an expression from another language such as *ma belle* in the Beatles' "Michelle," or Superman's triumphant cry, "Up, up and awaaay,"

which gave Jim Webb a title with immediate familiarity. The slogan for the radio and TV public service campaign against drinking-while-driving, "The life you save may be your own," provided Joe Tex with the springboard for his 1978 hit, "The Love You Save Today (may very well be your own)."

Often a borrowing is from poetry or even older lyrics. The title of Arthur Hamilton's classic, "Cry Me a River," turned up as a line in the Bee Gees' late-seventies number one hit, "Emotion." For fun, in "Glass Onion" the Beatles recycled three of their own titles—"Strawberry Fields," "The Walrus," and "Lady Madonna."

Dan Fogelberg dropped Longfellow's "forest primeval" into "Longer." In "Who Will Answer" I altered Oliver Goldsmith's " 'Neath the spreading chestnut tree" to " 'neath the spreading mushroom tree" as an oblique reference to the atomic cloud. The 1930s labor song, "I dreamed I saw Joe Hill last night/alive as you or me" served as the matrix for Bob Dylan's "I dreamed I saw St. Augustine/alive as you or me." Michael Sembello's "Maniac" line, "when the dancer becomes the dance," echoes Yeats's "How can we know the dancer from the dance?"

A good rule of thumb is to limit your borrowings to short phrases from poems, plays, or novels in the public domain—those no longer protected by copyright and therefore available to use. It's also important to distinguish the legitimate borrowing of a few words from the illegitimate act of *plagiarism*—taking the ideas or words of another lyricist and passing them off as your own. If you are unsure whether a borrowing is fair use, your best safeguard is: When in doubt, don't.

SLANG AS A TOOL. When we use phrases in conversation such as "lay your cards on the table," "red-letter day," "a shot in the arm," or "cool it," we are talking in a kind of verbal shorthand. Our meaning is instantly clear because such slang expressions are a part of our collective vocabularies. By lacing a lyric with such colloquialisms, we help the listener understand the song.

"Sliding into slang," as Ira Gershwin alliteratively put it, can be a useful tool to build in the sound of the familiar. The expression must, of course, be universally understood; regionalisms are therefore poor choices. As a case in point, a lyric called "That's All She Wrote" was once read in class. The story was about neither a particular female nor writing of any kind, so we were all mystified by the line ending each verse. The lyricist (who came from a small town in upstate New York) explained that the phrase "that's all she wrote," was slang for "it's over." He had assumed it was universally known.

The use of trendy language is debatable. Expressions like "outasight," "go for it," and "Where's the beef?" have a limited life span, and therefore tend to date a lyric. For example, Paul Simon's "Fifty-ninth-street Bridge Song (Feelin' Groovy)" (1966) has become a charming relic of the sixties because its diction was timely rather than timeless. On the other hand, Simon's "Bridge Over Troubled Water" (1969) is as recordable today as it was the day he wrote it.

PUTTING THE TOOLS TO WORK

"There Is Nothin' Like a Dame" was a show-stopping number in the Rodgers and Hammerstein 1949 Pulitzer Prize musical *South Pacific*. The song was the amusing complaint of a group of wartime sailors, stationed on a remote island in the Pacific, who had long been denied the pleasure of female company. Hammerstein's lyric, even without music, is a treat for the ears. To fully appreciate the effects of the repetitive devices he works into the lyric, read it aloud:

THERE IS NOTHIN' LIKE A DAME

Verse: *We got sunlight on the sand,*
We got moonlight on the sea,
We got mangoes and bananas
You can pick right off a tree,
We got volleyball and ping-pong
And a lot of dandy games—
What ain't we got?
We ain't got dames!

Verse: *We get packages from home,*
We get movies, we get shows,
We get speeches from our skipper
And advice from Tokyo Rose,
We get letters doused wit' poifume,
We get dizzy from the smell—
What don't we get?
You know damn well!

Climb: *We have nothin' to put on a clean white suit for.*
What we need is what there ain't no substitute for.

Chorus: *THERE IS NOTHIN' LIKE A DAME—*
Nothin' in the world!
There is nothin' you can name
That is anythin' like a dame.

Verse: *We feel restless, we feel blue,*
We feel lonely, and in brief,
We feel every kind of feelin'
But the feelin' of relief.
We feel hungry as the wolf felt
When he met Red Riding Hood—
What don't we feel?
We don't feel good!

Climb: *Lots of things in life are beautiful, but, brother,*
There is one particular thing that is nothin' whatsoever in any
*   way, shape, or form like any other.*

Double   *THERE IS NOTHIN' LIKE A DAME—*
Chorus: *Nothin' in the world!*
         There is nothin' you can name
         That is anythin' like a dame.

         Nothin' else is built the same!
         Nothin' in the world
         Has a soft and wavy frame
         Like the silhouette of a dame.
         There is absolutely nothin' like the frame of a dame!

Verse: *So suppose a dame ain't bright*
         Or completely free from flaws,
         Or as faithful as a bird dog,
         Or as kind as Santa Claus—
         It's a waste of time to worry
         Over things that they have not;
         Be thankful for
         The things they got!

Chorus: *THERE IS NOTHIN' LIKE A DAME—*
         Nothin' in the world!
         There is nothin' you can name
         That is anythin' like a dame.

Climax *There are no books like a dame*
(C *And nothin' looks like a dame.*
Section): *There are no drinks like a dame*
         And nothin' thinks like a dame,
         Nothin' acts like a dame
         Or attracts like a dame.
         There ain't a thing that's wrong with any man here
         That can't be cured by puttin' him near
         A girly, womanly, female, feminine dame!

The lyric, which Hammerstein designed as a choreographed production number, is a long one: four verses, two climbs, four choruses (two singles and a double), and a climax. In spite of its length, the lyric maintains dramatic tension throughout its eleven (!) stanzas. Hammerstein's use of varying repetitive devices not only contributes to the lyric's cohesion, but to its charm.

    Anaphora outlines the verses: *we got/we get/we feel; epistrophe* frames the finale: *like a dame/like a dame/like a dame;* the *alliteration* of *s* and *n* sounds helps to link ideas in the first verse: *sunlight/sand/sea, sand/*

mangoes/bananas/dandy; allusions to Tokyo Rose, Red Riding Hood, and Santa Claus—along with other familiar concrete words like *volleyball* and *bird dog*—make strong impressions on the memory. *Parallel constructions* simultaneously underscore the rhythm and meaning: *sunlight on the sand/ moonlight on the sea; we get movies/we get shows; we feel restless/we feel blue.* The *word repetitions* in the line "we feel every kind of feelin' but the feelin' of relief" help engrave it in our minds, and restating "nothin' " throughout the chorus enables a listener to sing along after one hearing. A *question refrain* resounds at the same spot in the first three verses—*What ain't we got?/What don't we get?/What don't we feel?*—outlining the form as it builds the emotion.

Using *antithesis* (pairs of opposites), each climb contrasts "what they lack" against the verses' statement of "what they got." Finally the extended lines in both the second climb and the finale pyramid to an amusing peak through a kind of purposeful redundancy (known as *accumulatio*) in which each word in a series means essentially the same thing: "nothin' *whatsoever in any way, shape, or form. . . ."* and *"a girly, womanly, female, feminine. . . ."*

The hallmark of a well-written lyric is its ability to withstand scrutiny: Does every line tell us something we don't already know? Does each stanza move smoothly out of the preceding one and into the next? Do the ideas arrive in ascending order of importance and build to a satisfactory conclusion? In Oscar Hammerstein's hands, the answer is always "yes." "There Is Nothin' Like a Dame" belies the dictum that lyrics should never appear on the naked page without their musical clothes. This stunning lyric, merely recited, deserves applause.

WRAPUP

A lyric without repetitive elements would be as difficult to follow as a highway without road signs. Study "Marcie" and "There Is Nothin' Like a Dame." The more you understand how Joni Mitchell and Oscar Hammerstein achieved their effects, the firmer your grasp of craft will be. Your lyrics will also echo with that essential recognition of the familiar as you learn to apply the basic tools of repetition. Practice these techniques until they become instinctive. That's the real objective.

chapter 14

Being Specific

"The particular throbs with the life of the whole intuition, and the whole exists in the life of the particular." Benedetto Croce

When Rupert Holmes decided to write a lyric about relationships in the "nervous eighties" he was intrigued by the possibilities of a plot based on an ad in a personals column. What might happen, he wondered, if a restless woman, bored by her present mate, sought excitement with a stranger? What happened was a number one record. The surprise was that, although the song was aptly titled "Escape," the public went to the record stores requesting "The Piña Colada Song." For good reason. (The lyric appears on page 198).

"Piña colada" is a *concrete word* combination that names something specific. It also evokes a shape (of a bottle or glass, depending upon your experience), a fruity taste, and a frosty temperature. As a plus, it connotes fun and the potential of an exotic adventure. "Escape," on the other hand, is an *abstract word* and therefore incapable of projecting an image on the screen of memory. Although "Escape" was repeated four times by the chorus, it was outremembered by the multisensual piña colada.

"I Guess I'll Have to Change My Plan," introduced by Clifton Webb in the 1929 Broadway musical "The Little Show," posed the question: "Why did I buy those blue pajamas?" Over the years the song has acquired standard status as cabaret performers, from New York to London, comply with audience requests for "the blue pajama song." Concrete noses out abstract again.

"Fly Me to the Moon" is a jazz classic that composer Bart Howard originally called, "In Other Words." Though the public heard his title phrase outline the song's ABAB structure twice, it was the hooky opening request heard only once that it went to buy, and that ultimately became the song's legal title.

TECHNIQUES TO MAKE YOUR LYRICS MEMORABLE

Choose the Concrete Over the Abstract

When we experience a song for the first time, we are more likely to remember the concrete words, those that represent objects we could photograph—words like *piña colada, pajamas,* and *moon.* Abstract words—*escape, words, plans*—are shadowy and impersonal; because they cannot produce a picture for the mind's eye, they leave weak impressions in the memory. Lyrics composed solely of abstractions—about dreams, loneliness, emptiness, wanting, missing—need concretizing. Some specific "examples" will brighten an otherwise misty landscape.

What we remember about "They Can't Take That Away from Me" is the sharp outline of its particulars: the way she wore her *hat* and held her *knife*. Had Ira Gershwin generalized instead, with lines such as, "those *little things* you used to do," the lyric would be blurrier because we can't see *little things*.

Pick the Particular Over the General

Just as choosing concrete words over abstract ones makes for more memorable lyrics, using the *specific kind* rather than the *general category* creates clearer pictures. When Yip Harburg described "April in Paris," we visualize "chestnuts in blossom." As Sheena Easton's "Modern Girl" waits for her commuter train, we see her on the platform eating a tangerine. Particular equals sharp; general equals hazy: "Take Back Your *Mink*," rather than take back your *fur;* "In My Merry *Oldsmobile*," instead of my merry *automobile*.

In "There Is Nothin' Like a Dame," Oscar Hammerstein picked the particular every time: instead of entertainment—movies and ping pong; instead of fruit—mangoes and bananas. He gave us images that we not only can see and touch and taste, but can smell: letters doused wit' poifume.

The perennial popularity of the list song, from Rodgers and Hart's "The Lady Is a Tramp" to Paul Simon's "Fifty Ways to Leave Your Lover," attests to the power of the particular. Cole Porter, the unofficial king of the genre, guaranteed his Broadway audiences at least one sophisticated catalog of trendy events, exotic places, and elite names per musical: "You're the Top," "Cherry Pies Ought to Be You," "Friendship," "Farming," "I Get a Kick Out of You," "At Long Last Love," "Anything Goes," "Brush Up Your Shakespeare," "We Open in Venice," and "Let's Do It" are some of the best known.

In the contemporary list song "You're Moving Out Today" (Midler/Sager/Roberts), we are amused by the specific belongings being thrown after the disenfranchised lover: 45s/cassettes/a rubber duck/old tie-dyes/rubber hose/dirty books—all concrete items we could pack in a suitcase. In themselves they're fun, and they also tell us a great deal about the person being booted out, adding to our enjoyment.

REPLACE TAME VERBS. One positive way to make your words work is to pick verbs that particularize the action. Suppose, for example, you had started out a country lyric with the opening line: "He walked into the barroom. . . ." Not a bad beginning. In only five words we know the *who* and *where*. But you can say a great deal more without adding a word. Simply substitute a descriptive verb for the uninformative "walked." Depending on your story line, any one of the following verbs tells more than *walked:*

He ambled into the barroom	(without much on his mind)
He sauntered into the barroom	(in high spirits)
He stormed into the barroom	(in a rage)
He swaggered into the bar-room	(thinking he was terrific)
He stole into the barroom	(hoping to go unobserved)
He lunged into the barroom	(ready to kill)
He stumbled into the barroom	(possibly ill or wounded)
He staggered into the barroom	(probably drunk)

INTENSIFY WITH THEME WORDS. Good lyric writers unify their themes by using words associated with the theme. For example, in "Black Denim Trousers and Motorcycle Boots" Leiber and Stoller augmented their title idea with such expressions as *Highway 101, axle grease, rumble of his engine* and *screamin' diesel.* Ira Gershwin built to the payoff in his romantic lyric, "Our United State," by using related governmental words: *foreign entanglements, unconstitutional, a declaration of dependence, star-spangled happiness.* Highlighting your theme with related words serves to integrate your lyric and imbed it in the listener's memory.

USE SENSORY WORDS. A listener wants to see, hear, touch, smell, feel. Try to replace nonexpressive words with ones that will involve the senses:

Sight: inky, sallow, rosy, buttery
Sound: clamor, screech, snap, roar
Touch: cold, clammy, prickly, velvety
Taste: bubbly, salty, sour, sugary
Smell: smoky, woodsy, lemony, pine

Words that evoke color, texture, flavor, or aroma, and that appeal to several senses simultaneously, make the deepest grooves in the memory. Polysensate words like *mint, ivory, butterscotch, sandpaper, snow,* (and pina colada) help your lyrics make strong first impressions and long-lasting ones.

Evoke Through Imagery

Images are words that suggest physical sensation. The most common are visual ones which are often referred to as word pictures. "Marcie" is a memorable lyric mostly because of the vivid images Joni Mitchell creates: ". . . wash her flower curtains/hang them in the wind to dry . . . ." One of "Marcie's" best images evokes layers of meaning: ". . . dust her table with his shirt. . . ." Those six words simultaneously tell us: The man in her life is gone; they were intimate; she hasn't let go of the possibility of his returning; and she's angry.

Skillfully arranged images can produce a gamut of sensory experience. *Skillfully arranged* refers to the ability to create a series of word pictures which start at a distance and gradually come close enough to touch. Consider the fact that we are able to hear and see objects that are far off—mountain peaks and train whistles—but in order to touch and smell and taste an object, such as blueberries in a bowl, it must be at close range. A lyric, therefore, will mount to a climax through "a progression of images." In the very best kind of writing, the word pictures grow sharper in outline and more intense as the lyric develops.

Much of the effect of John Hartford's "Gentle on my Mind" (Chapter 19) is created by the skillful arrangement of its images. He touch-es all our senses as he subtly changes from a long-distance lens to a closeup of the singer in the final verse. We see this traveling man in a changing land-scape with its amber wheat fields and rusty junkyards, and we hear the faint sobs of some mother's daughter he had left behind. In the third stanza we get a glimpse of the man himself, still a vague figure in the distance walking along a railroad track. In the last verse, however, he comes so close that we could reach out and touch his stubbly beard and dirty hat. Finally, as we watch him drink some steaming soup, we feel what his "cupped hands 'round a tin can" are feeling. Hartford's images are so immediate, so tactile, we almost become the man. That's using imagery to its fullest.

LEARNING TO SHOW, NOT TELL

Particular words help project pictures; particular situations help prompt emotions. In order to communicate the emotion you feel to an au-dience, you need to find some kind of channel—"a set of objects, a situa-tion, or a chain of events." It's what T.S. Eliot called *the objective correla-tive*," something "particular which [will culminate] in a sensory experi-ence and immediately evoke the emotion."

Broadway and Hollywood songwriters get the "situation" handed to them when they are called upon to musicalize a scene or a character. Lyr-icists of theater and film songs, in depicting the outlook of an individual character in a specific situation, often create works of rare distinction like "Everything's Coming Up Roses," "Thanks for the Memory," "The Way You Look Tonight," and "What Are You Doing The Rest of Your Life?"

Pop songs, on the other hand, frequently lack the punch of the particular. Some lyrics appear less like the work of a writer with an idea to express than of a computer stringing together snippets of emotionless banalities: "Ever since the day we met/I knew we were made for each oth-er/I'll never be the same again/I'll love you long after forever"—generaliza-tions in search of a situation.

Composer Alec Wilder's research study of over seventeen thou-sand pieces of sheet music for his seminal book, *American Popular Song, The Great Innovators 1900-1950*, supported his "conviction that there are three levels of sophistication in the music of American popular songs: theatre songs, film songs, and Tin Pan Alley songs, reading downward in that order." Wilder's opinion is widely shared, for good reason. Theater and film songwriters, immersed as they are in characters playing out human dramas, deliver the stuff that real songs are made of—specificity.

Create a Situation

Lyricists lacking a scenario or libretto, with its juicy dialogue and emotional interplay on every page, admittedly have a greater creative challenge. They must learn to conjure up a mini script of their own, that "set of objects, situation, or chain of events" that will give a character a reason for the emotion and will motivate the feeling by creating the circumstances that produce it. When the writer does it well, we get a strongly felt, wonderfully particular I'm-hanging-on-to-my-dream lyric like "She Believes in Me," or an it's-all-over-between-us lyric like "I Will Survive."

As the leading character of "I Will Survive" (page 138) unlocks her front door to find her ex-lover has invaded the privacy of her home, she feels outraged; the lyricist has created a situation that provokes the emotion in the singer, and we in turn respond with empathy to her indignation. In "She Believes in Me" the audience is eavesdropping on a discouraged songwriter returning home late from another small-time gig. The listener feels the faith of his supportive wife and instantly identifies with the singer's continuing hope of success.

Find a Symbol

Very often a song that stirs an audience deeply has been built upon a circumstance that permits the lyricist to illustrate the emotion, rather than state it.

If a lyric announces "I'm so sad without you," or "I'm lonely alone in my bed," or "I'm going crazy with desire," what is there for the listener to *feel?* Nothing. A gifted lyricist doesn't *declare* the feeling, but *evokes* it. Mallarmé put it tersely: "To name is to destroy, to evoke is to create."

In addition to evoking emotion in your listener by creating a situation, you can also define an emotion through a symbol. When the singer in Rodgers and Hart's "It Never Entered My Mind" orders "orange juice for one," we know he's alone—not because he *told* us directly, but because he *showed* us. When Janis Ian said "In the Winter" she needed "extra blankets for the cold," we understood she had no bedmate to warm her. She *showed* us. In "The People that You Never Get to Love" (p. 200), Rupert Holmes's book store browser *showed* how shyness looks: "when you take a sudden interest in your shoes."

These everyday household items—orange juice, blankets, shoes—trigger instant recognition in the listener. As the words are sung, we feel the loneliness or the embarrassment because these significant objects possess the capacity to intensify our response. It is through the particular, not the general, that the universal is expressed—and felt. When your lyric creates a set of circumstances like a breakup, a reconciliation, or a chance encounter, and makes the audience do the feeling, through objective symbols, you're doing the job well.

Write a Story

Extending your situation into a chain of events produces a story song. That's taking the particular to the ultimate.

Story songs, at the very least, generously entertain us: the murder and mayhem of "Frankie and Johnny," the suspense and mystery of "Ode to Billy Joe." Sometimes they do more—they give us sing-along words of wisdom like the dying advice of "The Gambler" (page 51).

Once in a while a song comes along that creates the world in microcosm and invites us to participate in the drama as silent bystanders. Such a song is Dan Fogelberg's "Same Old Lang Syne." Its Christmas Eve setting doesn't deter disc jockeys from programming the record in mid-July. It is a song for all seasons.

SAME OLD LANG SYNE

Met my old lover in the grocery store
The snow was falling Christmas eve
I stole behind her in the frozen foods
And I touched her on the sleeve
She didn't recognize my face at first
But then her eyes flew open wide
She went to hug me and she spilled her purse
Then we laughed until we cried.

We took her groceries to the checkout stand
The food was totalled up and bagged
We stood there lost in our embarrassment
As the conversation dragged.
Went to have ourselves a drink or two
But couldn't find an open bar
We bought a six-pack at the liquor store
And we drank it in her car.

We drank a toast to innocence
We drank a toast to now
We tried to reach beyond the emptiness
But neither one knew how.

She said she married her an architect
He kept her warm and safe and dry
She would have liked to say she loved the man
But she didn't like to lie.
I said the years had been a friend to her
That her eyes were still as blue
But in those eyes I wasn't sure if I
Saw doubt or gratitude.

She said she saw me in the record store
And that I must be doing well
I said the audience was heavenly
But the travelling, it was hell.

We drank a toast to innocence
We drank a toast to now
We tried to reach beyond the emptiness
But neither one knew how.
We drank a toast to innocence
We drank a toast to time
And seeing in our eloquence
Another Old Lang Syne.

The beer was empty
And our tongues were tired
And running out of things to say
She gave a kiss to me as I got out
And I watched her drive away.
Just for a moment I was back in school
And felt that old familiar pain
And as I turned to make my way back home
The snow turned into rain . . .

The opening two lines manage to tell us who, what, when, and
where, in writing that is simple and direct. Lengthy though the lyric assuredly is, Fogelberg keeps us attentive by propelling his story forward. The
lyric is a model of unity; each stanza takes us clearly from supermarket to
liquor store, to car, and the final sidewalk farewell. But specificity is its
hallmark. For instance, the words, ". . . *stole* behind her . . . and I touched her on the *sleeve* . . ." give us a vivid mental picture not only of the action, but of the character of the singer—gentle, playful, and a bit restrained
in his greeting. (Fogelberg could never have created that effect had he
picked a nonparticularizing verb such as "I *went* behind her.") Then in
contrast, we see her spontaneous delight in "flew open wide" and with a
hug so enthusiastic that she "spilled" her purse. That's a picture!

With the specificity of bagged groceries and six-pack, we can envi-
sion the couple weighed down by packages as well as embarrassment.
When they reach her car, where they candidly profile their present lives to
each other, we learn about their tradeoffs: her choice of security over love,
his need for applause outweighing a desire for family life.

It's worth noting the small details—"the frozen foods," for example. Fogelberg might have said "cookie shelf" or "veg'tables," but those

words wouldn't have accomplished the specific job he wanted done—to subtly reinforce the chill of December's below-freezing weather. As the story moves into the coziness of the car, the flush of their intimate confidences is fueled by the beer, and the thermometer perceptibly rises: the snow turns into rain. The song's final word "rain" hangs on a melody note that merges into a fragment of the original "Old Lang Syne."

In "Same Old Lang Syne" Dan Fogelberg chose what Matthew Arnold termed "a fitting action." He then steeped himself in the feeling of its situation and thus was able to select those facts that would move his listeners in the way he desired. The lyric *shows* that all things must end; it never *states* it. The writer lets us draw our own conclusion.

Taking the Story Song to the Limit

Harry Chapin found the story song the ideal format to express his ideas. In a musical marketplace dominated by the simple-minded three-minute repetitive hook/chorus form, he broke through with extended linear stories often lasting four or five minutes. In Bruce Pollak's book *In Their Own Words* Chapin is quoted as saying that he didn't like to write "attitudinal" lyrics where the viewpoint of the writer is summed up by the title, such as in "You Are the Sunshine of My Life" or "Just the Way You Are." "What I try to do," he said, "is create the situation that created the attitude . . . physically create the atmosphere and let the listener *feel* it, rather than tell him how it affected me. It's a very cinematic technique. That's why my songs are so long."

His songs certainly are movielike: the winding rainy-night cab ride of "Taxi," whose driver and passenger rediscover each other after many years; the saga of "Mr. Tanner," the tailor from Dayton, Ohio, and his failed attempt to sing his way to fame in a New York concert hall; the aging has-been deejay of "W*O*L*D" who, in a final effort to put his life back together, phones the wife he had deserted years before, and finds she's remarried.

In his longest (9:50) and most ambitious song, "Sniper," Chapin dramatizes "what it's like to be frustrated—to at times feel like you really don't exist." His objective was to present the frenzied thoughts as well as the actions of a man demanding his one moment in the limelight. Chapin understood, however, that confusion cannot be rendered by confusion. He knew he needed a way to make the drama clear. At a Songwriters Guild Ask-a-Pro in New York, Harry Chapin discussed his approach to writing in general and "Sniper" in particular:

"I don't write traditional hooks, like 'baby don't get hooked on me.' I look for hooks in a different way; that insight, that sensitizing thing that reduces a very complex subject into something that is artistic, that is understandable—so that I don't communicate just with the intellectuals. The basic requirement for my songs is emotional honesty; in other words, that I understand the emotions about them. I've never been a sniper, but I understand what it's like to feel like you really don't exist. The point is, by your technique, by your effort, to find some way to make a leap from your own reality. Every song operates differently. What I was looking for in 'Sniper' was something that could reduce it. The key to 'Sniper' was realizing that what the guy actually was doing was having a conversation, that he was asking people if he was alive. He was speaking in the only language that America seems to understand at times, and that's violence, and yes, he got his answer in the same terms. When I got the idea of the conversation, everything broke out from there."

From the opening words, we can see the whole event played out both inside and outside the campus clock tower as well as within the sniper's mind. Even without benefit of the record's echo chamber effects to help define the multiple roles Chapin sings, the lyric is clear on the printed page. In its reproduction here, the voices from his past—a childhood acquaintance, his mother, a one-time date, his schoolteacher—are distinguished from the narrator's by italics. Bold print sets off the sniper's own anguished cries—past and present.

SNIPER

It is an early Monday morning, the sun is becoming bright on the land. No one is watching as he comes walking, two bulky suitcases hang from his hands. He heads towards the tower that stands in the campus, goes through the door and starts up the stairs. The sound of his footsteps, the sound of his breathing, the sound of the silence, for no one was there. *I didn't really know him. He was kinda strange. Always sort of sat there. He never seemed to change.* He reached the catwalk, he put down his burden. The four-sided clock began to chime. Seven a.m., the day is beginning, so much to do and so little time. He looks at the city where no one known him. He looks at the sky where no one looks down. He looks at his life and what it had shown him. He looks for his shadow. It cannot be found. *He was such a moody child. Very hard to touch. Even as a baby he never smiled too much. No no.* **"You bug me"** she said. **"You're ugly"** she said. **"Please hug me"** I said but she just sat there, with the same flat stare that she saves for me alone when I'm home. He laid out the rifles, he loaded his shotgun. He stacked up the cartridges along the wall. He knew he would need them for his conversation. If it went as he planned then he might use them all. He said: **"Listen you people, I've got a question. You won't pay attention but I'll ask anyhow. I've got a way that will get me an answer. I've been waiting to ask you 'til now. Right now! Am I? I am a lover who's never been kissed. Am I? I am a fighter who's not made a fist. Am I? If I'm alive then there's so much I've missed. How do I know I exist? Are you listening to me? Are you listening to me? Am I?"** The first words he spoke took the town by surprise. One got Mrs. Gibbons above her right eye. It blew her through the window, wedged her against the door. Reality pouring from her face, staining the floor. *He was kinda creepy. Sort of a dunce. Met him at a corner bar. I only dated the poor boy once. Just once. That was all.* Bill Wedon was questioned as he stepped from his car. Tom Scott ran across the street but he never got that far. The police were there in minutes, they set up barricades. But he spoke right over them, in a half mile circle in that dumbstruck city his pointed questions were sprayed. He knocked over Danny Tison as he ran towards the noise, and just about then the answers started coming, sweet, sweet joy! Thudding in the clockface, whining off the walls. Reaching up to where he sat, their answering calls. Thirty-seven people got his message so far. Yes he was reaching them, right where they are. They set up an assault team, they asked for volunteers. They had to go and get him, that much was clear. And the word spread about him on radio and TV. In appropriately sober tones they asked: "WHO CAN HE BE!" *He was a very dull boy. Very taciturn. Not much of a joiner. He did not want to learn. No no.* **They're coming to get me. They don't want to let me stay in the bright light too long. It's getting on noon now, it's going to be soon now. But oh, what a wonderful song. Mama, won't you nurse me. Rain me down the sweet milk of your kindness. Mama, it's getting worse for me. Won't you please make me warm and mindless. Mama, yes you have cursed me. I never will forgive you for your blindness. I HATE YOU! The wires are all humming for me. And I can hear them coming for me. Soon they'll be here but there's nothing to fear. No, not anymore though they've blasted the door.** As the copter dropped the gas, he shouted: "Who cares!" They could hear him laughing as they started up the stairs. They stormed out of the doorway, blinking at the sun. With one final fusillade their answer had come . . . **"Am I—there is no way that you can hide me. Am I—though you have put your fire inside me. You've given me my answer can't you see. I was. I am. And now, I WILL BE."**

In a lyric of extraordinary length, no line, no word is ambiguous. Chapin scores direct hits on the ear with nouns and verbs we can see, and hear, and even smell: *suitcases, thudding, rifles, stormed, whining, cartridges, blasted, catwalk, sprayed, clockface, chime, stained, police, ran, knocked, copter, gas.* He fires off staccato rounds of repetitive phrases forecasting the barrage of lethal pellets to come: *the sound/the sound/the sound; he looked/he looked/he looked/he looked.*

He keeps figurative language to a minimum. The "conversation" is his metaphor for the sniper's one-sided dialogue of violence with a world of strangers. "Words" and "questions" are the well-aimed bullets reaching their targets. Powerfully clear.

Chapin literally kept his eyes on his own clock tower and let us know that the song is framed from "seven a.m." to "almost noon." The "Monday morning" identification added more specificity to our perception of the stillness of the campus scene.

The pronouns are in place, personalizing the agony of indifference, supplication, and rejection: " 'Please hug *me*' *I* said, but *she* just sat there, with the same flat stare that *she* saves for *me* alone when *I'm* home." Although the four characters whose echoing words taunt him are not labeled with neat name tags, Chapin makes it evident through skillful writing whose voice we're hearing. When it's important, he specifies, such as the victims: instead of calling them "the butcher, the baker," he identifies them as a newscaster would—Mrs. Gibbons, Bill Wedon, Tom Scott, Danny Tison—simple American names—which add to the documentary feeling of the lyric.

Using a parallel construction, Chapin underscored that the sniper lacked both the warmth of friendship and the solace of religion: "He looks at the city where no one had known him/He looks at the sky where no one looks down."

A guiding writing principle is: The leaner the lyric, the better. In "Sniper," however, it seems valid to use "qualifiers" for characterization. In four successive phrases, a childhood friend searches his memory for a picture of a youth who left no strong imprint: "I didn't *really* know him. He was *kinda* strange. Always *sort of* sat there. He never *seemed to* change." In this particular setting, that's not padding; on the contrary, it's purposeful writing.

"Sniper" grips us with the immediacy of a TV news remote. Without editorializing, Chapin presents the scene, and with insight and imagination he enriches the *who, what,* and *where* with a reasonable *why.* Afterward, we are made to think not just about this sniper and the social forces that shaped him, but by extension, about all the snipers, and hijackers, and political assassins who cry out for attention in the same violent language of our time. "Sniper" is a lyric of rare craftsmanship. Like the work of every fine writer, it reflects the ability of its author to see deeply, to think clearly, and to write simply.

WRAPUP

If being specific doesn't come easily to you, practice will help. The best exercise is to update the lyrics of such famous list songs as "I Can't Get Started," "Thanks for the Memory," or "These Foolish Things Remind Me of You." That will give you a title, a meter, and a rhyme pattern to start from. Filling in the blanks will get you to think in specific, concrete words. Look over all your own finished lyrics for places to particularize. Weed out meaningless modifiers: the most common offenders are *very, nice, great,* and *wonderful.* Replace each imprecise word with one that says exactly what you mean.

Find spots where you can turn a general term like *drink* into something particular like *milk* (or *rum*), or *makeup* into *lipstick,* or *that nice outfit* into *your blue dress.* The next time you get an urge to write an abstract lyric about broken dreams, or faith, or ambition, study the story songs of Harry Chapin, Tom T. Hall, or Bruce Springsteen. Then try to devise a situation, however slight, where you can show rather than tell the emotion and leave the feeling of it to your audience.

"One must be drenched in words, literally soaked in them,
to have the right ones form themselves into the proper
patterns at the right moment." Hart Crane

part four

SHARPENING
YOUR
TOOLS

chapter 15

Words and Wordplay

"Accurate selection of words is important to the expression of the feeling you're working for, as well as the visual imagery the line paints." Janis Ian

"The job of the lyric writer is to find the right word in the right place." Oscar Hammerstein

It takes the talent of a lyricist to turn a melody into a song the world can sing. In a famous music business story the lyric writer's contribution to a song was put into proper perspective: One evening when Mrs. Oscar Hammerstein and Mrs. Jerome Kern arrived together at a party, the hostess introduced them to another guest: "I'd like you to meet Mrs. Kern—her husband wrote 'Ol' Man River.' " Mrs. Hammerstein politely interjected, "No, *my* husband wrote 'Ol' Man River'; *her* husband wrote [humming] *dum dum dumda, da dum dum dumda.*" Though it's been said facetiously that you can't whistle a lyric, words are undeniably the substance of a song, the heart of what is being sung. Without words, the best that any beautiful tune can become is an instrumental.

First-rate lyricists, like all first-rate writers, take words seriously. They are fascinated by words—how they sound to the ear, feel in the mouth, and fit with the music. They weigh words for multiple meanings, and emotional color, and subtleties of sound.

VERBAL ACROBATICS

Making a word stand on its head, seesaw between literal and figurative, or do handsprings at your bidding is part of the fun of being a songwriter. Accomplished lyricists do all that and more: "What's good about goodbye?" (Leo Robin); "Living life in a living room" (Sondheim); "Uneasy in my easy chair" (Hart); "I'm a man of means by no means" (Roger Miller); "Yester-me, Yester-you, Yesterday" (Ron Miller); "A flat that would flatten the Taj Mahal," (Frank Loesser); "Almost can't be all most people ever know" (Robert Arthur); "How Can I Unlove You?" (Joe South).

Lyricists not only play with words, but when the occasion demands, they've been known to invent them. *Nonce* words—those created for the moment—have often been the result of the tyranny of rhyme and meter. That tyranny has been the mother of invention as resourceful lyricists purposefully mispronounced, or strained, or clipped in order to get that matching ping at the end of the line. Ira Gershwin, who was adept at the devices of shrinking or stretching words, produced such "nonces" as *emosh, disposish, effront'ry,* and *antiqueness.* Johnny Mercer renamed the Mason-Dixon Line, *Mason-Dixit.* In *Guys and Dolls* Frank Loesser took the liberty of mispronouncing *Barbasol* (which normally rhymes with *crawl*) to make it ping with *doll.* Carol Channing got another laugh line to play with when Leo Robin stretched "fools" into "foo*els*" to match with "jewels," and Larry Hart clipped Noel Coward to a nonce name, Noel *Cad.*

Cole Porter, in addition to coining *De-lovely,* telescoped the words *Tin Pan Alley* and *antithesis* in that song's verse to produce the portmanteau word, *tinpantithesis.* The term "portmanteau word" (a portmanteau is a large traveling bag) was coined by Lewis Carroll, whose *Alice in Wonderland* is strewn with such inventions. In "The Lady Is a Tramp" Larry Hart concocted *hobohemia* by piggybacking *hobo* and *bohemia.* A neologism, or newly minted word, popped up in the Grammy winner "Bette Davis Eyes" when Donna Weiss turned the noun *unease* into a verb in the line "she'll *unease* you." Cynthia Weil hatched "Heartquake" into a hit song title. W.S. Gilbert's verbifying of *butler—buttle—*even rates inclusion in the *Random House Dictionary.*

TAKING ARTFUL LIBERTIES. *Poetic license* is a deviation from fact or form, a liberty taken by a writer or an artist to achieve a particular effect. The Impressionist artist Edouard Manet, for example, in his famous painting "Boating," freely distorted reality for his own compositional ends: if the boom and the sail had actually been angled as he painted them, the mast would have been positioned *outside* the boat! Imagination and good instinct combined to create a vivid moment no camera could capture.

Liberties taken by lyricists sometimes extend beyond simply accommodating the restrictions of meter or rhyme. Maxwell Anderson in "September Song," for example, altered the facts by stating that wine (as if it were beer) is *brewed*—"the wine dwindles down to a vintage brew." Alan Jay Lerner knew perfectly well that one can crash only *through* the floor, not "through the ceiling," but he took the gamble in "Thank Heaven for Little Girls," and we accepted his inversion of gravity. True poetic license is the result of a flight of fancy rather than a failure of imagination.

WRITING ON TWO LEVELS. The term for saying more than one thing at the same time is *polysemy* (PA-li-SE-my)—having many meanings. Jim Webb has said, "I like writing two levels of understanding at the same time, if I can." He did just that with "the Wichita Lineman is still on the line," where the word *line* refers both to the singer's occupation and his emotions. Carole Bayer Sager's "Don't Cry Out Loud" contains a polysemantic use of *clown;* within the circus context of the lyric, the line "she took off with some clown" means both in the literal and in the slang sense. In my lyric "Going to Bethel," about the Woodstock weekend, the phrase "when we reached that sea of grass" suggested what the concertgoers were flying on, as well as lying on. Stephen Sondheim made the word *foundation* work two ways in "Putting It Together": " . . . first of all you need a good foundation" applied to both an artist's acquiring craft and getting grant money.

FIGURATIVE LANGUAGE

When we flavor our conversation with expressions like "You could have knocked me over with a feather," or "It was raining cats and dogs," we of course don't mean *literally* that we could have been felled by a feather or that animals were falling out of the sky. We are exaggerating for effect, by employing a device called a "figure of speech." Figurative language gives us the ability to convey more than what we mean, less than what we mean, the opposite of what we mean, or even something other than what we mean. Rhetoricians have defined over 200 different figures of speech. A familiarity with only a dozen or so will greatly enhance your facility for wordplay.

ANTITHESIS. Antithesis is a dramatic effect created by contrasting opposing ideas in parallel words or phrases. In "Gigi" Alan Jay Lerner memorably characterized the singer's bewilderment at noticing that a girl had magically turned into a woman overnight: had he been observing her *up too close, or back too far?* In "Send in the Clowns," Stephen Sondheim described two lovers on different wavelengths: one keeps *tearing around,* one *can't move.* Antithesis is readily grasped by the listener because of the sharp profile of its parts. Consequently, it makes for striking titles: "I'll Hold You in My Heart (till I can hold you in my arms)"; "(If loving you is wrong), I Don't Want to Be Right"; "Everytime You Cross My Mind, You Break My Heart."

OXYMORON. An oxymoron is a figure of speech which uses contradictory words for unusual effect—for example, *serious fun.* John Lennon synchronized sight and sound in the song "Tomorrow Never Knows": "*listen to the color of your dreams.*" Songs whose titles employ oxymorons include "Strong Weakness," "Sound of Silence," "Killing Me Softly with His Song," and "Marry Me a Little."

In "The Shadow of Your Smile" the word *shadow* represents *memory*. In the phrase "the *shadow* of your smile will *light* the dawn," Paul Francis Webster produced an oxymoron which is literally impossible, yet emotionally valid.

ZEUGMA. Zeugma (ZOOG-ma) is the use of a word to govern two or more words in such a way that it applies a different meaning to each. In the "Dear John" letter of farewell, Jim Morgan packs two ideas into one phrase: "my eyes are open wide and almost dry." By using the word *eyes* in both its literal and figurative sense, we learn that the departing lover knows what she's doing although she's having a tearful time doing it. More often than not, the zeugma uses a verb to yoke the two ideas, as in

Sheldon Harnick's ode to kleptomaniacal lovers "Me and Dorothea": they'll "steal a kiss, and then a towel." In "The Boston Beguine" Harnick scores twice with: "watch your heart . . . and . . . your purse," and "I was drunk with love and cheap muscatel." A lyric from class produced this example by Marc Miller, "the woman at the counter wears an apron and a scowl."

Such figures of speech not only add color and intensity to lyrics, but more important, they enable a writer to express complex thoughts or feelings that cannot be expressed in any other way. Through an understanding of metaphor and irony—the "twin bases" of poetic language— you will improve your ability to convey ideas that are beyond the power of literal language.

Metaphorical Language

METAPHOR. Whenever we compare two unlike objects, directly or indirectly, we are speaking metaphorically. The word *metaphor* stands for two things: it is both a particular figure of speech and a general category. As a figure, a metaphor is an implied comparison between dissimilar things. For example, *turnstile justice* is a striking metaphor widely used to characterize how the judicial system deals with prostitutes: they are arrested at night and freed in the morning—in, around, and out. In two words a metaphor conveys a complex idea which takes many more literal words to express. The term "metaphor," in its broad sense, encompasses a number of other figures of speech, such as *simile* and *personification*.

A metaphor compares indirectly, without *like* or *as*. In the word coupling *magazine husband,* for example, Bob Dylan's adjectival use of *magazine* suggests a mannequin of a man who is all looks and no substance. The meaning was evoked instead of stated. In the Beatles' "Lucy in the Sky with Diamonds," the striking phrase *kaleidoscope eyes* makes us imagine the distorted vision of the LSD tripper seeing the world as if through colored shards of glass. By using a metaphor, in "You Can't Be Too Strong," Graham Parker handled the touchy subject of abortion without calling a forceps a forceps; he alluded to it metaphorically as "talons of steel." Oblique but vividly clear.

Frank Loesser's masterwork *Guys and Dolls* contains a ballad, "If I Were a Bell," built entirely on enumerating the love-struck ways the singer would behave if she were a series of inanimate objects—a gate, bridge, duck, goose, salad, season, and of course, a bell. By using metaphorical wordplay, Loesser created a lyric with charm and freshness.

SIMILE. A simile (SIM-a-lee) is a comparison using *like, as,* or *than*. It is the most direct form of metaphor because both the literal and the figurative terms are named. In "Chelsea Morning," Joni Mitchell said, "the sun poured in like butterscotch." Oscar Hammerstein was a master of the fresh comparison; his original similes have embossed themselves upon our memories: ". . . restless as a willow in a windstorm;" ". . . tight-lipped as an oyster;" ". . . corny as Kansas in August."

When Jim Croce characterized "Bad, Bad Leroy Brown" as "meaner than a junkyard dog," he multiplied the dimensions of *mean*— snarling, vicious, less than human. The picture produced by the analogy strikes us with more impact than a whole truckload of nasty adjectives could deliver.

A distinguishing mark of a great writer, according to Plato, is the ability to perceive similarities in unlike things. A reliance on threadbare similes—black as night (or coal), hot as a poker, clear as crystal (or a bell), stiff as a ramrod, light as a feather—phrases deadened from overuse, proclaims, in effect: I have nothing new to say. Every lyricist with aspirations to originality should avoid such clichés and strive for fresh analogies.

APOSTROPHE. Paul Simon commanded our attention in the opening of "Sound of Silence" with the line "Hello darkness, my old friend." He was employing a figure of speech called *apostrophe* (a-POS-tro-fee) in which an absent person, or more commonly, an absent thing, is addressed as if it were present and will presumably answer. The Rodgers and Hart classic "Blue Moon" ("you saw me standing alone") and Johnny Mercer's lyrics "Skylark" ("tell me where my love can be") and, of course, "Moon River" are examples of songs built upon apostrophe.

PERSONIFICATION. When we give human qualities to inanimate objects or abstractions, we are personifying them. Because personification, which is closely related to apostrophe, is a figure we use in everyday speech, it is common in lyrics; for example, in "Marcie" (page 142), ". . . and the sand/all along the ocean beaches/*stares* up empty at the sky"; in Neil Diamond's "Cracklin' Rosie," "a dream that *asks no questions*"; and Ira Gershwin's "Love *Walked* In." A similar use of personification turns the singer into an object: ("I'm the train they call) The City of New Orleans." "I Write the Songs" is unusual, not so much because *music* is personified, but because the lyric is set entirely in the first person, thereby requiring the singer to proclaim to *be* the abstraction—"I am music."

SYNECDOCHE. A line in Seals and Crofts's "Summer Breeze"— "the smile *waiting* in the kitchen"—not only uses personification, characterizing an abstraction as human, it also employs another common subtype of metaphor, synecdoche (se-NEK-da-key)—using part to express the whole. The "*smile* waiting in the kitchen" stands, of course, for the *person* waiting in the kitchen. The Doors' depiction of the plasticized "Twentieth Century Fox" substitutes the woman's brains for the woman herself in the line, "since her *mind* left school." Christopher Cross employed the part for the whole memorably in his Grammy winner "Sailing" when he claimed "the *canvas* can do miracles."

METONYMY. Metonymy is a figure of speech we hear every day, especially from the media. Like synecdoche, which it resembles, metonymy (ma-TON-a-mee) substitutes one word for another word with which it is related or associated. We are substituting, for example, the place for the institution in such expressions as "The White House told the Kremlin" (the American government told the Russian government); or substituting the institution for those running it in "the subways increased their fares today" (actually the management of the transit system).

For those times when obliqueness is preferable to bluntness, metonymy does the trick; for example, marriage can be alluded to in lyrics without calling it by name: in "We've Only Just Begun," we're aware the singer just entered wedlock by the reference to *white lace and promises.* In Ira Gershwin's verse to "Someone to Watch Over Me," we're told, "I'd like to add his initial to my *monogram.*" The traveling man of John Hartford's "Gentle on My Mind" didn't want to be "shackled by . . . the *ink stains* that have dried upon some line"; and in "My Old Man" Joni Mitchell claims she needs no "*piece of paper from the city hall* keeping us tied and true."

In "Sniper" Harry Chapin used the figure twice: ". . . you have put your *fire* inside me . . ." and "*reality* pouring from her face . . ." preferable to the bluntness of "bullets" and "blood." Synecdoche and metonymy are subtypes of metaphor whose definitions tend to shade into each other; increasingly the term "metonymy" is being used to stand for both devices.

GUARDING AGAINST PURPLE PROSE. Metaphorical language is a rich ingredient that has the potential to enhance your lyrics. But, it comes labeled with a warning: always mix carefully, and never spread too thick or extend too far. Figures of speech and imagery in general require a delicate touch; too many different kinds of allusions, images, or comparisons bewilder the listener. There is such a thing as too much of a muchness. The guideline for metaphors is moderation. (More on the pitfall of mixed, multiple and overdone metaphors in Chapter 22.)

Extended Forms of Figurative Language

SYMBOLISM. A symbol, the richest form of figurative language, stands for or represents some other thing. A cross, for example, stands for Christianity; a crown for a kingdom. Abstruse poems laden with symbolism may require scholarly analysis for a total appreciation of their layers of meaning; lyrics, on the other hand, need to be instantaneously clear. Because a symbol presents only one half of the analogy, its use requires an audience to work, to be imaginative. To avoid the risk of being misunderstood, a writer must select symbols that are both recognizable and meaningful.

Bob Dylan's "A Hard Rain's A-Gonna Fall" is a symbolic lyric in which *rain* stands for more than a downpour, and thunder roars out a warning about our "sad forests" and "dead oceans." The repeated title line echoes impending nuclear disaster.

The rain in "Singin' in the Rain" is an *image* that means only what it says—rain, that's all. The rain in "Stormy Weather" is a *metaphor* that means something other than what it is apparently saying (that it keeps raining all the time); what the singer is really saying is she keeps crying all the time. "A Hard Rain's A-Gonna Fall" is a *symbol* that means both what it says and a lot more.

ALLEGORY. An allegory is a narrative that exists on two levels; below the surface meaning there lies a second meaning reached by means of symbolic figures of speech. The novels *Pilgrim's Progress, Animal Farm,* and the children's classic, *The Phantom Tollbooth* are allegories in which the characters embody ideas. Although allegorical songs are rare, the occasional one like "The Gambler" (page 51) doubles its impact because we enjoy the story on its own and can also appreciate it on a second level of meaning: it works as poker-playing advice and simultaneously suggests strategies for winning the game of life.

FABLE. Written in either verse or prose, a fable enforces a moral truth. It often features animal characters, but not always. "Coward of the County" (page 122), for example, can be considered a fable because it illustrates the axiom: Someday the worm will turn. Sandy Chapin's lyric "Cat's in the Cradle" exemplifies the biblical caveat "As you sow so shall you reap."

Avenues of Irony

Irony is any statement, situation, or plot that is characterized by some kind of incongruity: In a remark, the speaker intends the opposite of what is said; in a situation, its appearance belies the actuality; in a story, there is a discrepancy between the expectation and its fulfillment. Irony is an important device by which a lyricist can express a meaning contradictory to the one stated. Sarcasm, on the other hand (with which irony is often confused) is a potential pitfall. It is important to distinguish the two. Irony points up some kind of disparity, for example, between the way something is and the way it might have been, or used to be, or was expected to be.

Sarcasm, unlike irony, intends to hurt; it is usually a sneering or caustic remark that is, in fact, ironical because it says the opposite of what is meant: "Thanks a lot for the postcard" (when one wasn't sent), or "You're a big help" (when someone has made the situation worse), or "How do you like this lovely weather we've been having?" alluding to a solid week of rain. Sarcasm usually depends upon tone of voice to achieve its effect—one of the reasons it rarely works in pop songs. The only successful totally sarcastic lyric that comes to mind is, not surprisingly, a theater song, "Could I Leave You" from Stephen Sondheim's Tony Award-winning *Follies*. (More on the pitfall of sarcasm in Chapter 22.)

Ironic situations span a spectrum of moods. In "I Remember It Well" former lovers now in their golden years recollect the courtship days; each remembers *well,* but differently, and both are amused by the disparity of their recollections.

In "Free Again" Barbra Streisand discovers that instead of the feeling of exhilarating independence, she's got the post-breakup blues. The former lovers in "Looks Like We Made It" get a twinge of "that old feeling" during a brief encounter—in spite of each having made new romantic attachments. The singer in Ten CC's "I'm Not in Love" disavows his symptoms of love fever: that he didn't hang her picture to gaze at her, but only to cover a crack in the wall, and she shouldn't interpret his phone calls as a sign of interest. The way things appear, he protests, are not the way they really are. But he clearly protests too much.

It has been said that humility is the proper partner of irony, and one of the most successful ironic ballads would seem to validate the claim. When the actress of "Send in the Clowns" finally decides she wants the suitor she formerly rejected, her timing is off; it's too late. Her embarrassment for taking him for granted is touching, "sorry my dear . . . my fault, I fear." The irony is understated—a contributing factor to its poignancy. The choice between overstatement and understatement—two of the most frequently used kinds of verbal irony—depends upon the effect desired.

UNDERSTATEMENT. Understatement is a useful tool to underscore irony. When we represent something as less important than it actually is, we compel a greater esteem for it. In "You and Me (We Wanted It All)," what the couple had lost was the intimacy they once had—"*a little thing* called love." The listener reacts with more emotion when the writer treats significant things casually. Leo Robin illustrated that principle back in 1937 in the goodbye duet "Thanks for the Memory"—"no tears, no fuss, hooray for us."

Understatement (meiosis) as an evocative technique is characteristic of Stephen Sondheim's work. In the breakup song "It Wasn't Meant to Happen" from *Marry Me a Little,* the concluding three words are ". . . good try, goodbye." Low key and affecting. One of Sondheim's most compelling ballads, "Anyone Can Whistle," counterpoints the jaunty claims of the singer (to be able to read Greek and slay dragons) against her ingenuous request to be taught how to whistle. What makes the song touching is our ultimate realization that her inability to put her lips together and blow has been a metaphor for her inability to love. Treating a weighty subject in an offhand rather than heavy-handed manner is more likely to evoke a deep response in the listener.

LITOTES (LIT-o-tease), a particular kind of understatement, shows something is true by denying its opposite. We employ the figure in everyday speech when we want to understate something: "This is no small problem," or "He's not doing so well." In "Bette Davis Eyes" we learned about the character's perennially warm hands in the line, "her hands are never cold." Rupert Holmes used litotes to make the singer in "Escape (The Piña Colada Song)" attractively modest: assessing his personals ad, he commented, "I thought it wasn't half bad."

The use of restraint in a song's emotional subject matter is more common to theater songs than to pop songs. There are several reasons for this: the audience attending a Broadway musical—as compared with the listeners of the Hot-100 singles—is older, better educated, and sitting down. Radio's (and even MTV's) top-40 record audiences are moving targets, and mainly teenagers or younger. No wonder pop songs virtually demand sentiments that are boldly stated and relentlessly repeated, leaving little room for subtleties.

The book of a musical provides the lyricist with something the pop writer lacks: a given situation and a set of characters who are thinking and feeling specific things, many of which can be more effectively treated with understatement than exaggeration. The seated, attentive audience, having paid a lot of money to be entertained, is as ready to be treated to the subtlety of underplayed emotion as to the flamboyance of a can-can.

HYPERBOLE (hy-PER-ba-lee) is extravagant exaggeration. "Maniac," Michael Sembello's portrait of a dance-crazed woman ("she's a maniac on the floor"), overstated its way to the top of the charts. Michael Jackson's tongue-in-cheek "Muscles" deliberately exaggerated physical endowments for effect; we never for a moment believed Diana Ross's claim to want a man with "muscles all over his body," but we weren't meant to. Hyperbole suggests the impossible: "I'd walk a million miles for one of your smiles ("My Mammy")." That kind of sweeping declaration unquestionably makes an impression, as anything does that is blown up larger than life, but such exaggeration lacks the capability to evoke genuine feeling in the listener.

Lyricists sometimes choose to overstate an emotion in the belief they are dramatically conveying deep distress: "nothing can ease my *pain,*" or "there's an ache down deep in my *soul,*" or—(that frequently heard combination of buzz words)—"no one knows the *pain* I feel in my *soul.*" Insincere sentiments are incapable of touching an audience.

The principle is worth restating: It's more effective to treat heavy emotions with a light touch.

PARADOX. This figure of speech applies to any person or situation that appears to have inconsistent qualities. For purposes of lyric writing, we'll consider a paradox in its narrower definition as a statement used for shock value. A paradox, although seemingly self-contradictory, has some basis of truth. For example, Randy Goodrum used the incongruity in the idea "You don't have to like someone to love someone" as the basis for his hit, "What Are We Doin' in Love?"

George Harrison pointed out the odd reasonableness in the concept, "the farther one travels/the less one knows," and one of Stephen Sondheim's characters in *Marry Me a Little* observes in the title song that he wanted to be "passionate . . . but always in control."

In the Beatles' "She's Leaving Home" (page 115), the twist in the phrase "Fun is one thing that money can't buy" is a slyly subtle one. We have been so numbed by the cliché *money can't buy happiness* that we barely notice the truth of the fresh slant; the self-sacrificing parents had *bought* their daughter everything, but their chest-pounding martyrdom robbed her of any pleasure. "She's leaving home after living alone for so many years" is a paradoxical line. Because the insight has been understated, it is emotionally evocative.

SATIRE holds up human vices or follies to scorn or ridicule. It has been called the noblest form of humor. A satirist is inherently an idealist who attempts to expose the weaknesses or stupidities of human nature through the use of irony. Lyric writers with substantive ideas to express may find no welcome mat in the pop marketplace. During an Ask-a-Pro session at The Songwriters Guild in New York, Sheldon Harnick told aspiring theater writers about the cold shoulder his first successful show lyrics (from the 1955 *Shoestring Revue*) got at a major publishing house. "They said an incredible thing to me: 'There're too many ideas in your songs. Listen to the crap that's around, that's what we want.' It was another confirmation for me of the fact that I should do what I did best and not worry whether they're going to be hits. What attracted me to the theater were the kinds of things you could say—things that Yip Harburg was saying, and Marc Blitzstein."

Lyricists with a satirical bent consistently head for Broadway. *Finian's Rainbow*, with music by Burton Lane and lyrics by Harnick's mentor, E.Y. (Yip) Harburg, was a landmark musical of social significance which held racial prejudice up to ridicule. While he was at it, Harburg pointed up romantic hypocrisy in "When I'm Not Near the Girl I Love (I Love the Girl I'm Near)." Also, in "When the Idle Poor Become the Idle Rich" he amusingly exposed our tendency to criticize the poor for practices we tend to find charming in the wealthy.

Sheldon Harnick's own lyrical lampooning of political wheeling and dealing earned him the 1959 Pulitzer Prize for *Fiorello!* (music by Jerry Bock). The memorable "Politics and Poker," on the machinations of selecting a mayoral candidate, as well as "A Little Tin Box," in which graft was exposed in the courtroom sparring of prosecutor and defendants, are gems of insight and wit.

Occasionally a satirical song comes out of a show and gains popularity beyond the proscenium. An example is the Rodgers and Hart standard "The Lady Is a Tramp." Although the lyric gently mocks the high-gloss superficiality of upper-class mores (circa 1937), contemporary singers and audiences relate more to the song's affirmation of the simple life than to its outdated putdown of socialite slumming.

SENSE AND NONSENSE

Playwright, poet, and lyricist William Shakespeare knew a few things about figurative language and the uses of ironic understatement. He also enjoyed using nonsense words, especially in his theater songs.

It was a lover and his lass,
With a hey, and a ho, and a hey, nonino,
That o'er the green cornfield did pass
In the springtime, the only pretty ring time,
When birds do sing, hey ding a ding, ding!
Sweet lovers love the spring.

From *As You Like It*

Nonsense words have been an integral part of songs since man began to sing. Their emotional appeal is universal. Understanding how silly syllables wield their power over us has yet to be fully explored and is beyond the scope of this book.

Why, for example, did supposedly mature adults run to record stores to buy something called "Yaaka Hula Hickey Dula" (1916), "Diga Diga Do" (1928), "Ob-la-di, Ob-la-da" (1968), or "De Do Do Do, De Da Da Da" (1983)? It would take a staff of scholars with expertise cutting across the disciplines of linguistics, semantics, and psychology to answer that simple question in depth. But, we can at least identify some of the more obvious charms of nonsense words: They are eminently easy to sing and remember because of their repeated refrains of open vowels—"Fa la la la la" or "Na Na Hey Hey"—and like "Zip-A-Dee Doo Dah," they are usually playful and cheery.

Perhaps the appeal is more fundamental—simply a need for a bit of whimsy to offset grim headlines in the nightly news. Possibly pure nonsense speaks to the child in us. That could partially account for millions of grownups affecting baby talk in the refrain of "Three Little Fishies": "boop boop didum dadum wadum choo."

It would seem that if your instinct tells you to add a "doo wah" or a "hey hey" (as writers/producers Perren and Fekaris did in their number-one hit "Reunited"), it can't hurt your song any—and it just may help. Whatever the lure, the facts are clear; nonsense can be a winner.

TABOOS

A few decades ago "longshoremen's language" was restricted to longshoremen. "The ladies" were shielded from "the gentlemen's" postprandial cigar talk, and the raunchiest expletives overheard by children were the euphemisms "my gad" and "oh fudge." The words of our songs from back then reflected our living vocabularies, as they do today. In 1916 the closest we had come to lyrical profanity was "If I Knock the 'L' out of Kelly," and the word *mother,* as in "M-O-T-H-E-R, A Word that Means the World to Me," had yet to make its debut in a lyric as an adjective. Our threshold of permissible dinner-table profanity and vulgarity has plummeted since those innocent years, and our lyrics, of course, reflect the liberation.

All three of the country's broadcasting networks maintain a "continuity acceptance" department to monitor the language that goes out over the airwaves—including song lyrics—deleting those that could shock or offend public sensibilities. The recording industry, eager for airplay, keeps a watchful ear on its product.

Back in the forties and fifties the bleep button was busy. At the recording session of the original cast album of *South Pacific,* for example, the word *darn* was substituted for *damn* in the line "you know damn well" in "There Is Nothin' Like a Dame." By 1983, however, the line "He knows damn well" resounded from the radio in the song "Twilight Zone," without a ripple of protest.

The main unmentionables have traditionally been parts of the anatomy, excretion, sex, and death, in no particular order of censorability. In a 1962 presentation of the Rodgers and Hammerstein musical *Carousel* before the British Royal Family, "our hearts are warm, our bellies are full" was changed to "our hearts are warm, and we are full." Recently the words *bitch* and *whoring* wedged their way into hit lyrics, and the title "Take This Job and Shove It" climbed the charts.

Pockets of protest still exist, however. When the radio stations in Frankfurt, Germany, finally realized what "it" meant in "Nobody Does It Better," they yanked Carly Simon off the air—metonomically speaking. The South African Broadcasting Corp. (SABC) censored the "offensive" last line of Olivia Newton-John's "Physical": that there was nothing left to talk about unless it was "horizontally." The BBC banned the Police's "Roxanne" (about a prostitute). American broadcasters have also edited or completely pulled a number of songs whose lyrics they deemed "too explicit," including "Yum Yum," "Nasty Girl," "Ya Mama," and "Little Red Corvette." "Acapulco Gold" was crossed off radio play lists when deejays realized it referred to high-quality Mexican pot. The Voice of America gave an X rating to the 1983 Grammy winner "Sexual Healing." Bible Belt parents, outraged by a vulgarism picked up by their children from Joan Jett's rendition of the Stones' "Star Star," put pressure on the record label to remove the song; now the album sells in two versions—censored and uncensored.

Songs that contain the words *death, dying,* or *dead* (especially in the title) generally meet resistance in the marketplace. The stonewall that producer Milt Okun encountered when trying to release the first recording of "Blowin' in the Wind" (by the Chad Mitchell trio) is part of songwriting history. The reaction from record companies was unanimous: who wants to hear the word *death* in a song? When it comes to a serious treatment of mortality, it would seem that obliqueness is more acceptable than bluntness; "Honey," a number one record in 1968, alluded to death subtlely: "the angels came" and took the singee away.

A humorous treatment is a hearse of another color. When we know it's all in fun, songs can literally get away with murder; both Peggy Lee and Ella Fitzgerald made successful recordings of "Stone Cold Dead in the Market (I killed nobody but my husband)."

Although its lyric has nothing to do with death, "Killing Me Softly With His Song" met initially with total turndowns from record producers because of the word *killing*. Frustrated by rejection and spurred by belief in their song, writers Norman Gimbel and Charles Fox finally produced a record themselves, which ultimately led to the Grammy-winning version by Roberta Flack.

Self-contained writer/performers unquestionably have greater freedom to shock or offend. Billy Joel and Randy Newman, for example, can record—and have—words that the *New York Times* still finds unfit to print. And punk, funk, and rock groups who relish raunch can get air play on AOR (album-oriented radio) stations. Still, the nonperforming songwriter, whose songs must pass the editorial blue pencil of a publishing company screening committee, has to watch his or her *p*s and *q*s (and *f*s).

What words are *verboten?* As usual in lyric writing, there are no rigid rules. It would seem to be common sense, however, for a lyricist without a recording contract to avoid vulgarity and touchy subjects. Although I've heard the philosophy expressed that the best way to attract the attention of music business professionals is by writing something "outrageous" i.e., to be suggestive, or offbeat, I believe the soundest advice to the preprofessional is to treat universally appealing subjects with freshness and originality and to leave controversy to TV documentaries, and obscenity to graffiti.

WRAPUP

First-class lyricists are readers. The way to become "drenched in words" is to read great novels, plays, and poetry. The reading of good literature not only will give you an understanding of how the finest writers achieve their effects, it also will stoke the fires of creativity and increase your capacity for wordplay. To further enlarge your repertoire of words, invest in dictionaries—standard, reverse, synonym, slang, quotations, epigrams, et al.

Simplicity, directness, and clarity remain the hallmarks of fine writing; sandwiched in between your Webster's and your Roget's *Thesaurus* should be a slim paperback, *The Elements of Style* by William Strunk, Jr., and E.B. White. In fewer than 80 pages, you'll find the fundamentals of good usage that scaffold all first-class writing. The firmer your grasp of the basic requirements of style, the more successful will be your forays into figurative language.

chapter 16

From Pun to Funny

"We don't laugh at happiness, only at pain, discomfort, sorrow, catastrophe, or embarrassment." Lehman Engel

"Humor is about character, not cleverness." Stephen Sondheim

"Much humor . . . depends upon language that is very inappropriate to the subject at hand." S. I. Hayakawa

Attempts at humor evoke a range of reactions from an audience: a polite smile, a titter, a giggle, a chuckle, a guffaw, a belly laugh. Witty lyrics come in assorted sizes too, from the one-word pun to the full-blown comedy song.

The pun, a humorous member of the metaphor family, is a device that suggests dissimilar meanings for the same word or the same "sound." Cole Porter's "Don't Look at Me That Way" implies two definitions of the word *will* in the line, "My *will* is strong, but my *won't* is weak." Ira Gershwin wrapped up "But *Not* for Me" by punning with a homonym; after bemoaning his bad luck at love, the singer sadly concludes that most people's romantic plots end with a marriage knot, then restates the title but with a twist: "and there's no *knot* for me." The listener, without the aid of a lyric sheet, instantly gets the pun because it has been perfectly set up.

"Another *Sleepless* Night," the 1982 hit, didn't complain of insomnia, but rather celebrated lovemaking—thereby giving *sleepless* a new twist. In the country title, "She Got the Goldmine, I Got the Shaft," we easily get shaft's double definition: the vertical opening to a mine, and being victimized.

Puns are uncommon in lyrics, and when they do occur, they seem most often to be found in theater or country songs. The award-winning country team of Kye Fleming and Dennis Morgan parlayed their punning into a country crossover hit, "Nobody." When a suspicious wife asks her preoccupied husband who is on his mind, he replies, "Nobody." After receiving a phone call at home from "the other woman," the wife tells her husband, "Well, *nobody* called today," and that night, in a determined effort to save her marriage, she summons all her powers of seduction to prove she could make love to him "like *nobody* can." A humorous approach to infidelity found a broad audience (no pun intended).

Double entendre, literally double meaning, is an expression that can be interpreted two ways, one of which has a risqué connotation. When Johnny Mercer sang Johnny Burke's line, "She had the cutest *personality*," he was describing a particular curvaceous physical attribute rather than her sense of humor. When Laura Branigan told us about mama's "Squeeze Box," we knew it wasn't her accordion playing that kept papa awake all night. And Melanie's phallic implications of *his* "Brand New *Key*" (fitting her new roller skates) told us what kind of recreation she really had in mind. The singer of Stephen Sondheim's "Can That Boy Foxtrot" appears to be telling us about the terpsichorean talents of a boor who otherwise leaves her cold; through her suggestive reading of the title line and stretching of the initial consonant in *ff*ox, the audience realizes she's actually alluding to quite another activity.

SOME THEORIES

One man's laugh is another man's yawn. What people find funny and why is a subject that has filled volumes and continues to keep psychologists busy analyzing the ingredients of humor.

Aristotle contended that we laugh at a defect or physical ugliness that is neither painful nor destructive. But before we can laugh, we must be assured it is permissible—that, in effect, everything is "all right." A fundamental precondition for humor is a playful attitude, a readiness to share in the moment's nonsense. If, for example, we saw a man with a swollen jaw, we wouldn't laugh for fear that he might be suffering from a serious ailment. It would not be "all right" to laugh. If, on the other hand, we knew that the swelling was a temporary reaction to an abscessed tooth, and that it had blown up on the very night he had been planning an elaborate seduction dinner with a Playboy centerfold, we would find his temporary "deformity" ironic and funny.

Some theorists hold that laughter is always contemptuous or scornful and that it reflects a sense of triumph and superiority. The duet "Bosom Buddies" from *Mame* seems to bear out this theory. The duet features Mame and her best friend harmonically slugging it out. In between the protestations of unflagging friendship—comparing themselves to Amos and Andy and to Toklas and Stein—they thrust merciless verbal daggers. The audience, in obvious identification with the built-in ambivalences of friendship, cheers. The "scorn" theory seems to work here. Via a song, we get an opportunity to laugh at the foibles and faults of others. The lyric does the insulting for us, without our having to apologize later.

Literary theorist W.K. Wimsatt believed that the function of comedy is corrective: "society punishes by laughter the individual's deviation from the social norm." That premise is given weight by the long-run status of the musical version of *La Cage Aux Folles,* which centers around a homosexual "marriage." If Wimsatt is right, the heterosexual audience is paying for permission to laugh publicly at society's deviates (while being entertained). Jerry Herman, the musical's lyricist/composer, contends that "one of the underlying reasons for its success [is] the show treats Albin and George just as people in love." *La Cage Aux Folles* swept the 1984 Tony awards for best musical of the year; it could be said that the gay audience got the last laugh.

Noel Coward's revamping of Cole Porter's "Let's Do It" further illustrates the "corrective theory." In 1928 Porter wrote that birds and bees, and the Siamese, the Dutch and the Japs all do it: fall in love. The real fun for the listener, more than just enjoying the lyric's cleverness, was the implication of *it*. For that decade "Let's Do It" was considered quite risqué. Yet for all its tricky rhymes and puns ("sentimental centipede," "katydids do it," "*Letts* do it"), it didn't qualify as a true *comedy song*. That is, not until the 1960s, when Noel Coward's new lyrics went beyond cleverness into caricature. In his version, Coward one-upped Porter by replacing the fauna and faceless races with real celebrities. Then he characterized their libidinous activities (with or without partners), suggesting playfully that they had, if not *problems*, at least idiosyncrasies. In arch insults to glitterati past and present—Hemingway, Maugham, Poe, Louella Parsons, Liberace, Tennessee Williams, and others—Coward aimed his arrows at their erotic Achilles' heels. Just as *The Tonight Show*'s viewers, anonymous millions who lead unglamorous lives, snicker in delight as Joan Rivers pelts her famous targets with insults, listeners to Coward's celebrity-filled "Let's Do It" get a chance to look down at the upper crust. Recorded live at the Desert Inn in Las Vegas, the convulsions of Coward's audience would appear to reinforce theories that laughter is both scornful and "corrective." (Ever since Porter's death in 1964, legions of professional lyricists have parodied his list songs; but only the verses written by Noel Coward to "Let's Do It" have been granted a recording license by the Porter estate.)

Incongruity is Essential

The one factor on which theorists appear to agree is that the common denominator for comedy is incongruity. We don't laugh unless something is out of joint. For example, there is nothing humorous about a pig-tailed little girl skipping rope; that's a normal sight. However, seeing a fireman skip rope would make us stop and smile because his gender, age, and attire are inappropriate to the activity. Similarly the spectacle of three white-haired, black-robed judges skipping rope and singing "One, two, three O'Leary" would be even funnier; the greater the inconsistency or unsuitability in the circumstances, the greater the humor.

One of the mainstays of humor—after the pratfall—is the pie in the face. If a schoolboy belts a playmate with a lemon meringue, it's funny. If his bifocaled English teacher accidentally intercepts the pie, it's even funnier; the principle being that the greater the dignity of the victim, the greater the resulting amusement.

The frustrated puffy-faced lover, the judges on the jump rope, and the meringue-smeared professor embody an essential of humor: a disharmonious set of circumstances. A case in point is Lew Spence's song "God Only Knows." In the musical scene, Noah tells his wife that God has chosen him to build an ark. Knowing her husband as she does ("a leader, he's not!"), she berates God for making a poor choice to run His "floating zoo":

Well, nobody's perfect,
But look at who made the mistake!
Talk about working in mysterious ways—
This really takes the cake!

Talk about "the greater the dignity of the victim"! God scolding a mortal wouldn't rate a smile, but treating God like your next-door neighbor is pretty incongruous.

Much of the humor of comedy songs obtains from either inappropriate overstatement or ludicrous understatement: a weighty subject is treated lightly, and the trivial given solemnity. Again, it's incongruity shaping the language of funny songs.

For example, in Stephen Sondheim's caustic list of "The Little Things You Do Together" (that help a couple create a "perfect relationship"), among such items as swapping clothes and saving money, he casually tosses in "the children you destroy together." There's a heavy idea treated offhandedly with a "uh-huh, mm-hm" echo.

Alan Jay Lerner's ode to approaching senior citizenry, "Wait Till We're Sixty-five," is funny because it celebrates the opening of life's third act as though the curtain were just rising on its first. The legitimate, if minimal, up side of maturity—bus passes, discount movies, Medicare, and the possibility of year-round sunshine in "Tampa *Fla*" retirement—is playfully treated as if there were no down side. Underscored by the jauntiness of Burton Lane's melody, the idea works. The irony shines through the purposely overstated optimism. We are willing to go along with the joke.

Overstating for Laughs

"Overdoing it" is the entire theme of "I Get Carried Away" from the Broadway musical *On the Town* (music by Leonard Bernstein). In the lyric, written and performed by Betty Comden and Adolph Green, a sailor on leave browsing through the Museum of Natural History strikes up a duet with a fellow visitor after learning they share the trait of terminal impetuosity. Each outclaims the other in flights of excess: leaping from a concert seat to grab the baton from the conductor; ending a shopping spree by buying the store; getting angry enough at a movie villain to punch a hole in the screen; saying goodbye to a departing friend and hopping aboard the train.

In Alan Jay Lerner's "Come Back to Me" from the Lerner/Lane musical *On a Clear Day*, the fun is in the disparate word pairings. The singer is begging his lover to return any way she can: "in a trunk/on a drunk . . . wrapped in mink or saran." We are also amused by the juxtaposition of mock anger in "blast your hide" with the playful mispronunciation of "ruin" in "rack and *roon*."

THE PERSONAL COMEDY SONG

Because humor depends upon character and a situation, it is generally in the theater—musical comedies and revues—that most comedy songs originate.

The singer of a comedy song usually has a genuine problem, one that causes true anguish or frustration. The song is his or her complaint about it. Although the problem is always serious, the character's attitude toward it is consistently naive and frequently wry. The contrast between the straight facts and the bent viewpoint produces a fundamental incongruity which is the bedrock of humor and a prerequisite of laughter. The language of comedy is more ironic than metaphoric and either inappropriately overstated or understated.

Frank Loesser's "Adelaide's Lament" from *Guys and Dolls* is generally acknowledged to be the quintessential comedy song, and it abundantly fulfills the necessary conditions for humor. For fourteen years Adelaide's fiancé, professional gambler Nathan Detroit, has canceled a series of wedding dates in order to play high-stakes poker. Adelaide suffers perennial symptoms of an acute cold. Picking up a book on the causes of physical ailments, she discovers (as she reads aloud in her Brooklyn accent) that her relentless "sneezes and wheezes" result from the prolonged frustration of spinsterhood. That's a real problem.

Adelaide, a stereotypical "dumb blonde," clearly doesn't understand the medical terminology she struggles to pronounce: psychosomatic symptoms, upper respiratory tract, streptococci, chronic organic syndromes—giving the audience that edge of superiority which is believed by humor theorists to be a vital component of laughter. Enlightened as we are about the roots of asthma, migraines, and yes, even the common cold, we know Adelaide's conclusion is not farfetched. Because we also laugh when the ludicrous appears logical, "Adelaide's Lament" doubles our fun.

Jerry Herman hits the comedy target in *Mame* with "Gooch's Song." Talk about a problem! Virginal Miss Gooch, tired of her maidenhood and acting on the counseling of her swinging employer and role model, Mame Burnside, takes off to *live*. Unfortunately she overdoes it and arrives back at the Beekman Place duplex with a full maternity dress and an empty ring finger. Her complaint to her mentor—as she describes the amorous adventure which led to her present condition—is that Mame's instructions "left something out!" Miss Gooch's naive attitude toward a serious condition results in the requisite incongruity. We could also say that her pregnancy, used humorously here, would be that temporary "physical defect" that Aristotle cited; the scene was played "playfully," telling the audience that it was all right to laugh.

THE VISUAL SIDE

Gesture—working in tandem with words—can contribute greatly to the enjoyment of humor. In the case of standup comics, gesture alone can create the laugh. (Remember Jack Benny's limp wrists and rolling eyes.) The lyrics of true comedy songs work on their own, without enhancement. Nevertheless, the most skillful lyricists do more than write funny words. They provide a performer with lines that *play*—where meaning can be evoked, or intensified, or even altered by a shrug or a raised eyebrow. For example, in *Sunday in the Park with George,* George's disenchanted lover Dot blames his lack of attention for her turning to the baker, Louis. Hoping to make George jealous, she tells him about Louis's passion: "in bed . . . he *kneads* me." As her voice stresses the word, her fingers choreograph *kneading* dough; the audience laughs at the pun before the assist from the next line, "I mean like *dough*, George. . . ."

In *How to Succeed in Business Without Really Trying,* Frank Loesser created a unique visual treatment for the number, "I Believe in You." The song is sung by an egocentric, ambitious young businessman. The setting is the men's washroom of his company: plugging in his electric razor, he addresses his own image in the mirror while he shaves, in an amusing (and incongruous) statement of supreme self-confidence. Those who didn't see the show perceive "I Believe in You" as a love song addressed to a singee—and of course, it works perfectly from that viewpoint too.

Comedy is also served by costume. For example, the incongruity inherent in Sheldon Harnick's "The Boston Beguine" (the title itself is oxymoronic humor) was accentuated by the singer's dowdy outfit. On a bare stage, out comes Alice Ghostley in an oversized beige sweater and scuffy saddle shoes to passionately recall her one magical night of romance in "exotic" Boston: there in an Irish bar (called, incongruously, the Casbah) she "got drunk with love and cheap muscatel" and danced in a trance among the potted palms 'neath a voodoo moon. The music's overstated Latin rhythm mated to the lyric's prim New England setting produces a deliberate ill-suited pairing. Any listener to the cast album of *New Faces of 1952* would find "The Boston Beguine" a laughing matter, but for those lucky enough to have seen Alice Ghostley perform it, recalling the sight of that baggy sweater doubles the pleasure.

THE COMEDY PRODUCTION NUMBER

Murder, especially matricide, would seem to be an unlikely subject for a lyric. Its very inappropriateness is the reason it was able to be so happily sung and danced about in another memorable number from *New Faces of 1952.* Michael Brown's black comedy song "Lizzie Borden" was performed by the entire cast in a rousing production number which brought down the first act curtain:

LIZZIE BORDEN

Verse: *Yesterday in old Fall River*
Mister Andrew Borden died.
And they booked his daughter Lizzie
On a charge of homicide.

Some folks say, "She didn't do it."
Others say, "Of course, she did."
But they all agree Miss Lizzie B.
Was quite a problem kid.

Chorus: 'Cause you can't chop your poppa up in Massachusetts,
Not even if it's planned as a surprise.
No, you can't chop your poppa up in Massachusetts;
You know how neighbors love to criticize.

Verse: Now, she got him on the sofa.
Where he'd gone to take a snooze.
And I hope he went to heaven,
'Cause he wasn't wearing shoes.
Lizzie kind of rearranged him
With a hatchet, so they say.
And then she got her mother in
That same old-fashioned way.

Chorus: But you can't chop your momma up in Massachusetts,
Not even if you're tired of her cuisine.
No, you can't chop your momma up in Massachusetts,
If you do, you know there's bound to be a scene.

Verse: Oh, they really kept her hopping
On that August afternoon.
With both down and upstairs chopping
While she hummed a ragtime tune.
And her maw, when Lizzie whacked her,
Looked an awful lot like paw
Like somebody in a tractor
Had been backing over maw.

Chorus: Oh, you can't chop your poppa up in Massachusetts,
And then blame all the damage on the mice.
No, you can't chop your momma up in Massachusetts;
That kind of thing just isn't very nice.

Verse: Now, it wasn't done for pleasure
And it wasn't done for spite.
And it wasn't done because the
Lady wasn't very bright.
She had always done the slightest thing
That mom and poppa bid.
They said, "Lizzie, cut it out."
And that's exactly what she did.

Chorus: But you can't chop your poppa up in Massachusetts,
And then get dressed to go out for a walk.
No, you can't chop your poppa up in Massachusetts;
Massachusetts is a far cry from New York.

Why are we laughing? It's incongruous: a stage full of gaily costumed dancers doing high kicks as they sing about what fun Lizzie Borden had making mincemeat of her parents. Michael Brown playfully understated the enormity of the crime: "You know how neighbors love to criticize," "There's bound to be a scene," and "That kind of thing just isn't very nice." His language was appropriately offhand: *momma/poppa/chop/ whack/Miss B/problem kid/snooze,* and so on. He wrapped it all up with an ironic twist which, once again, reaffirms the requisite naiveté of the character: Lizzie was only being an obedient child. As if that payoff weren't enough, Michael Brown's final chorus pokes fun at New York City's crime rate.

WRAPUP

New York Times theater critic Walter Kerr has said that "Comedy . . . is the groan made gay." For your own enjoyment and analysis here are some other gay groans that will further substantiate the conditions for the solo comedy song—a problem, a complaint, and naiveté: "Why Can't a Woman Be More Like a Man? (Hymn to Him)" and "Just You Wait, 'enry 'iggins" from *My Fair Lady;* "Take Back Your Mink" from *Guys and Dolls;* "I Cain't Say No" from *Oklahoma!;* "A Puzzlement" and "Shall I Tell You What I Think of You" from *Anna and the King of Siam;* and "A Man's Home" by Sheldon Harnick from *Two's Company.*

I enthusiastically recommend the album "The Best of Allan Sherman" (Rhino Records, Los Angeles). Among the dozen gems of incongruity it contains are "Sarah Jackman" (set to the tune of "Frére Jacques"), "The Twelve Gifts of Christmas," and Sherman's 1963 chart hit, "Hello Muddah, Hello Fadduh! (A Letter from Camp)" that inspired the TV sitcom, *Camp Runamuck.* This album may well be the only one-hour course available on the art of the comedy song.

chapter 17
Rhyme and Other Sound Effects

"Tis not enough no harshness gives offense; The sound must seem an echo to the sense." Alexander Pope, *Essay on Criticism*

Rhyme, in the broadest sense, occurs when the same or similar sounds are placed so that they echo each other. In lyrics, as in poetry, the echo of rhyme is comforting to the ear. You have already seen in Chapter 13 how repetition of line beginnings (anaphora), accented consonants (alliteration), and vowels (assonance) exerts the power of adhesiveness: linked sounds help us remember the words, and thereby their meaning. Rhyme is the boldest sound linkage.

Hearing words chime in a discernible pattern, especially at the end of lines, is reassuring; we feel we have our bearings—like finding familiar signposts on a dark country road. As we listen to a lyric, we unconsciously compare the verbal pattern we have already heard to what we expect to hear, while simultaneously reacting to what we are actually hearing. Consistent and pronounced end-line sound mates attract and hold our attention and thus make the lyric easier to follow.

THE MAJOR ACCENTS OF RHYME

Rhyme is also known as *full rhyme, true rhyme,* and *complete rhyme.* The word *perfect* is implicit in the term "rhyme"; however, because perfect rhyme has been unfashionable in pop songs for over twenty years, I will identify the word *rhyme* with the adjectives *perfect, true,* or *full,* to distinguish it from those substitute sound mates which fall short of perfect rhyme.

A Definition: What is rhyme? Two or more words are said to rhyme when each contains the same final accented vowel and consonant sounds and a different consonant preceding that vowel, such as *shoe/true, barrel/apparel.* The word that sounds first is termed the rhyme agent, and the second of the pair, the rhyme mate.

Feet/greet/street are perfect rhymes; but *day/today* or *leave/believe* or *loud/allowed* are *identities* (also called identical rhymes or identicals). They sound flat because they have the *same* preceding consonant instead of a *different* one. Identities that try to pass themselves off as rhymes—whether in poetry or in lyrics—have traditionally been considered a flaw.

The spelling of a word is not a factor in rhyme, as you can see in the *shoe/true* pairing. Rhyme is solely a matter of sound. Homonyms, for example, sound the same but have different meanings—*him/hymn, soar/ sore, be/bee*—but they don't *rhyme* because they lack that contrast of differing preceding consonants. They can be useful to punning poets because readers can *see* their meaning. Homonyms can also be used by thoughtful lyricists who carefully, and aurally, set up the pun. Since homonyms are identities, not rhymes, they are generally better used in the middle of a line than at the end of it.

Eye rhymes are words that are spelled alike but pronounced differently: *great/threat; clear/pear; prove/love.* They should not be mistaken for true rhyme. (These three examples are actually a sound effect called *consonance*, which we'll get into later).

The most common rhymes are of one, two, and three syllables.

Masculine or *single* rhyme occurs with the matching of two or more one-syllable words: *wide/slide, mate/fate;* or with the last syllable of a longer word: *free/debris, late/anticipate. Feminine* or *double* rhyme occurs when the last two syllables of words agree: *ended/pretended/condescended/when did. Triple* (or *trisyllabic* rhyme) results when the last three syllables of words match in sound: *chasable/embraceable/irreplaceable/ trace a bul/*(let).

When a double or triple rhyme is made from more than one word, it is called a *mosaic* or *composite* rhyme: va*lise full/peaceful* (Berlin), *nocturne/clock turn* (Sondheim), *lot o'news/hypotenuse* (Gilbert), *wreck to me/*appen*dectomy* (Hart), Sir *Lancelot/romance a lot* (Mercer), *feminine/ lemon in/*(my tea) (Harnick).

W.S. Gilbert—Rhyme King and Mentor

It takes ingenuity to turn out double and triple mosaic rhymes. Practitioners of the art are usually inveterate readers of good poetry and the classics and are avid theatergoers. They also are frequently humorists. A talent for inventive wordplay leads them quite naturally toward writing for the stage and its more sophisticated audience.

The acknowledged rhyming virtuoso of all time is W.S. Gilbert, the lyric-writing half of Gilbert and Sullivan. In the late 1890s the team's English operettas, *The Mikado* and *H.M.S. Pinafore,* crossed the Atlantic to become American successes, with sheet music selling briskly alongside our pop hits of the day. Here's a sample from *The Sorcerer* (1877) as spouted by Mr. Wells, a dealer in magic and spells:

For he can prophesy   *Tetrapods tragical*
With a wink of his eye   *Bogies spectacular*
Peep with security   *Answers oracular*
Into futurity   *Facts astronomical*
Sum up your history   *Solemn or comical*
Clear up a mystery   *And if you want it, he*
Humour proclivity   *Makes a reduction*
For a nativity,   *in taking a quantity . . .*
With mirrors so magical   *Then if you plan it, he*

Changes organity
With an urbanity,
Full of Satanity
Vexes humanity

With an inanity
Total to vanity
Driving your foes
to the verge of insanity.

It would be several decades before Gilbert's urbane wit and rhyming wizardry would influence lyricists in America. P.G. Wodehouse (pronounced Woodhouse), one of the earliest collaborators of composer Jerome Kern, was among the first. His graceful and witty lyrics for *Oh Boy!* and *Leave It to Jane* in 1917 and *Sally* in 1921 showed the mark of his professional mentor. Ira Gershwin acknowledged both Gilbert and P.G. Wodehouse as his lyric-writing role models. Larry Hart studied the master at D'Oyly Carte matinees and pored over Gilbert's collected works, calling him the "greatest lyricist who ever turned a rhyme." Yip Harburg confessed that after Gershwin played him recordings of *Pinafore,* he was "starry-eyed for days" and that his "earliest education . . . was from Gilbert and Sullivan." Cole Porter cited the reason for his "going overboard" on tricky rhymes in his Yale days: "I was rhyme crazy due to the fact that I was Gilbert and Sullivan crazy; they had a big influence on my life."

Knowing as we do that all Gilbert's lyrics were written *before* Sullivan's music, our appreciation of his inventiveness doubles. He had no musical structure to inspire him or to provide the soundposts for rhyming. Gilbert created his own rhythmic structures and ingenious rhyming patterns. He worked words like clay: pulling, pinching, and reshaping to create fresh and surprising rhymes. In *H.M.S. Pinafore* we hear: "We're smart sober men/and quite devoid of fe-ar/In all the Royal N/None are so smart as we are." Legions of followers have copied Gilbert's methods to expand rhyme's potential.

Tricks of the Trade

LETTERING. Most of the 26 letters of our alphabet can be rhymed. Irving Berlin punned, "I'll see you in C-U-B-A." Mercer in his "G.I. Jive" made a feature of abbreviation with PVT., L.I.E.U.T., and M.P. who did K.P. on the Q.T. Sammy Cahn was able to fit a campaign lyric for John Kennedy to his "High Hopes" hit by spelling "K-E-*double* N-E-D-Y, Jack's the nation's favorite guy."

STRETCHING. A favorite technique of Ira Gershwin made short words fit a particular musical phrase: *Parties* expanded to *partiays* to match up with "shopping at Cartiers." Velvet became *vel-a-vit/tell of it,* and Garfield stretched to *Gar-a-field/far afield.* Cole Porter added a syllable to get: *puberty/Shuberty* and *flatterer/Cleopatterer.*

MISPRONOUNCING. Larry Hart reminded us that "English people don't say *clerk,* they say *clark,*" and he added that anybody who says it like that is a "jark!" In "Union Square," Gershwin replied to the question "The hell with whom?": "The hell with youm!" Sheldon Harnick teamed up *malfeasant/dezent*. In Hammerstein's hands *meadow* became *meader* to pair with *header*. In "Glow Worm" Mercer took a little license with *faster* to team up *vest-pocket Mazda/slow, or fazda*. Porter coupled *Milton Berle/Castor erl*, and in "Nobody's Chasing Me" he altered the title in one verse to match up with "Ich leibe Dich"—"Nobody's chasing mich." (When you employ the device, be sure to make your intended pronunciation clear in the spelling.)

INVENTING. Sometimes the right rhyme doesn't exist, so the ingenious create *nonce words* to meet momentary needs. When the Cowardly Lion in *The Wizard of Oz* needed an expletive to echo *rhinoceros*, Yip Harburg fused *impossible* and *preposterous* and made *imposerous!* The inimitable Gilbert coined *cottary* to describe Wedgwood china in the line "such a judge of blue and white/and other kinds of pottery/from early Oriental down to modern terra cottary." Such comic inventiveness is not to be confused with distorting an accent through ignorance or lack of skill—what I call "word warping." Because clever rhymes call attention to themselves, they are usually reserved for comedy songs.

Rodgers and Hart

Lorenz (Larry) Hart first teamed up with Richard Rodgers in 1918. Over a 24-year period they wrote a string of Broadway successes that produced some of America's most performed standards: "Blue Moon," "My Funny Valentine," "Lover," "The Lady Is a Tramp," "Mimi," "Bewitched," "My Heart Stood Still," "Manhattan," "Thou Swell," "My Romance," "There's a Small Hotel," "I Could Write a Book," and on and on.

Hart's lyrics were urbane, witty, and often touching. "Mountain Greenery," written for the second *Garrick Gaieties* in 1926, continues to rack up new recordings, especially among cabaret and jazz singers. The form is classic AABA with an introductory verse and several sets of "encore" verses in case applause demands "more!" In their usual collaborative process, Hart wrote the lyric *after* the melody. "Mountain Greenery" is a model of inventiveness in its variety of rhyme.

MOUNTAIN GREENERY

Verse: *On the first of May*
It is moving day.
Spring is here, so blow your job
Throw your job away.
Now's the time to trust
To your wanderlust.
In the city's dust you wait.
Must you wait?
Just you wait.

A: *In a MOUNTAIN GREENERY*
Where God paints the scenery,
Just two crazy people together.

A: *While you love your lover, let*
Blue skies be your coverlet;
When it rains, we'll laugh at the weather.

B: *And if you're good*
I'll search for wood,
So you can cook
While I stand looking.

A: *Beans could get no keener re-*
Ception in a beanery.
Bless our MOUNTAIN GREENERY home.

B: *It's quite all right*
To sing at night.
I'll sit and play
My ukulele.

A: *You can bet your life its tone*
Beats a Jascha Heifetz tone.
Bless our MOUNTAIN GREENERY home.

(ENCORES)

2nd
Verse: *Simple cooking means*
More than French cuisines
I've a banquet planned which is
Sandwiches and beans
Coffee's just as grand
With a little sand
Eat and you'll grow fatter, boy,
S'matter boy?
'Atta boy!

A: *How we love sequestering*
Where no pests are pestering
No dear mama holds us in tether.

B: *Mosquitos here*
Won't bite you, dear
I'll let them sting
Me on the finger.

A: *We could find no cleaner re-*
Treat from life's machinery
Than our MOUNTAIN GREENERY home.

A: *In a MOUNTAIN GREENERY*
Where God paints the scenery
With the world we haven't a quarrel.

A: *Here a girl can map her own*
Life without a chaperone.
It's so good it must be immoral.

B: *It's not amiss*
To sit and kiss,
For me and you
There are no blue laws.

A: *Life is more delectable*
When it's disrespectable,
Bless our MOUNTAIN GREENERY home.

In addition to the charm of the romantic let's-get-away-from-it-all theme, the lyric treats the ear to varying rhyme shapes, sounds, and placements. We hear a rich assortment of vowel colors in *a, au, us, e, oo, i, o, an, es, ing, own*. Hart never stays too long on one sound, which can grow monotonous. We also get all three rhyme lengths: single in *may/day, good/ wood;* double in *weather/together, quarrel/moral;* and triple in *greenery/ scenery, pestering/sequestering*—plus the memorable composites, *lover let/coverlet* and *life its tone/Heifetz tone.* We have to acknowledge that Rodgers's tune virtually demanded those length rhymes; the melody went DUM/DUM, and DUMda/DUMda, and DUMdada/DUMdada. Nevertheless, his collaborator met the assignment's challenge with originality.

Hart always filled in an internal rhyme (a rhyme in the middle of a line) when the music pointed the way. The verse end-rhyme scheme would have worked well without the inner dividend, "blow your job/throw your job," but it emphasized the jauntiness of the music. Then in the encore verse he outdid himself with the ingenious mosaic, "Planned which is/ sandwiches." Another writer might have ignored Rodgers' three-bar repeated melodic pattern at the end of the verse and not matched all three lines, but again, Hart filled in the musical blanks with, ". . . dust you wait/ must you wait/just you wait." Then he topped that with the inventive triplet (by clipping *what's the matter*), *"fatter, boy/s'matter boy/'atta boy."* The lyric also boasts the nonce word, *disrespectable*. Rodgers once remarked of his collaborator, "He really didn't know how *not* to be clever."

Hart, however, was not without his detractors. Lyricist Howard Dietz, for example, once said, "Larry Hart can rhyme anything—and does." He meant Hart overrhymed. Still, the members of Larry Hart's fan club far outnumber his critics.

In addition to the end-line strong beats of masculine, feminine, and triple end rhymes, Hart found spots in the melody to vary the flow of major accent rhyme. The next section discusses the main techniques.

MINOR ACCENT RHYME

BROKEN RHYME is a much admired artifice that breaks off the last word in a line to make its inner sound chime with the rhyming mate. Hart came up with *keener re-/beanery, cleaner re-/(ma)chinery.* Ira Gershwin gave us a smile with *butler/cutler/(y).* Stephen Sondheim achieved surprises with *blander/Ander/(sen)* and *(cha)teau/o-(verstuffed).* Lee Adams scored in "Put on a Happy Face" with one of my favorites, the subtle *(mask of) tragedy/glad ya de/(cided);* it sings so smoothly that it slips by virtually unnoticed.

TRAILING RHYME is a device in which a one-syllable rhyme agent is paired with either the first syllable of a two-syllable word or the first of two words, making a perfect rhyme plus a trailing syllable. In "Mountain Greenery" we find: *sting/finger, cook/looking, you/blue laws* and the unique *play/ukele(le).* In "Any Place I Hang My Hat Is Home" Johnny Mercer teamed *proves/moves me.* Dorothy Fields in "Don't Blame Me" linked *spell/hel(p it)* and *conceal/feel(ing).*

APOCOPATED RHYME is trailing rhyme in reverse. The two-syllable or two-word rhyme agent precedes its one-syllable rhyming mate, creating a cut-off (apocopated) effect: *answer/chance, clung to/sung, wid-er/pride.* Willie Nelson used it effectively in "Karma Coming Down" with *(under stand it/band).* Joni Mitchell in "A Case of You" was unusually innovative with the pairing of *darkness/bar.*

LIGHT OR WEAKENED RHYME contains one accented syllable paired with an unaccented one. The device, a favorite with Emily Dickinson (*bee/revery*) is common in songs. You've seen it in "She's Leaving Home" (page 115) with *thoughtlessly/me.* In Joni Mitchell's "Cactus Tree" we find *"memory/tree, eternity/free."* All these three-syllable words are sung as they are normally spoken, as they should be, with the accent on the first (or second) syllable: *THOUGHTlessly, MEMory, eTERnity,* not on the last syllable: *thoughtlessLY, memoRY, eterniTY.*

Many a beautiful melody has been marred by an inept lyricist who warped the pronunciation of a two- or three-syllable word to accommodate the musical accent. The ear winces at the sound of such offenders as *resCUE, yesterDAY,* and *harmoNY.*

The best lyricists always match word accents accurately to the music. When the desired word doesn't make a seamless fit with the tune, a craftsman instinctively chooses one-syllable word combinations. If, for example, the music goes daDUM, the word should go daDUM, not DUMda. Rather than twist *REScue* into *resCUE,* a more singable choice would be: *it's THROUGH/a CLUE/to YOU.* If the music goes DUMdaDUM, instead of warping *YESterday* into *YESterDAY,* try *ANy DAY/RIGHT aWAY/WON'T you STAY?;* and in place of *MEMoRY,* try *YOU and ME/ CAN'T you SEE/WE aGREE.*

CONTIGUOUS RHYME is an effect gained by the touching of two matched sounds within a line. Alan Jay Lerner butted *a* sounds in "the *late, great* me." Berlin's "They Say It's Wonderful" contains a contiguous rhyme in the line, "they tell me that love is *grand—and . . .*" Peter Townshend used it in "Squeeze Box": "I'm so *cold, hold* me." Other examples include "What's the *diff if* I live or die" (Cole Porter), "on a crowded ave*nue, you* are there" (Al Dubin), and "Some people of *one hun*dred and five" (Stephen Sondheim).

LINKED RHYME is an end-rhyme artifice common to early Welsh verse. It requires fusing the last syllable in one line to the first sound of the next. Here is a lyric example:

> You're a tax-free *bond*
> You're a Sammy *Cahn*
> *D*elight.

The rhyme is formed by fusing the *n* in *Cahn* to the *d* of *delight* to make a perfect ping with *bond*.

ECHO RHYME is a traditional poetic device, but rare in songwriting. It demands a playful attitude toward words. In echo rhyme, the final syllables in a line are followed by an echo of them, but with a change in meaning. Stephen Sondheim used the device in the "Echo Song" written for *A Funny Thing Happened on the Way to the Forum*. The singer asks a question and the gods' answer echoes it. Sondheim expands the technique so that sometimes the *first* part of a line is echoed instead of the last part. For example, the question, "Would he miss me?" is echoed as "Would he!" Other words are echoed by their homonyms—*forego/go!/ owe/Oh!* and *know/no!*

Echo rhyme is, of course, exempt from the injunction not to rhyme homonyms. To illustrate how it works, here are three verses excerpted from an uptempo dance song:

> *"You! You! You captured my attention*
> *Tension Tension Tension*
> *My fever, my fever is surprising,*
> *Rising! Rising!*
>
> *I'm look- I'm lookin' for somebody*
> *Body Body Body*
> *To give me, to give me satisfaction*
> *Action! Action!*
>
> *Feel passion! My passion is emerging*
> *Urging Urging Urging*
> *My, my interest, my interest is compounding*
> *Pounding! Pounding!*

INTERNAL RHYME, also called interior or inner rhyme, is that extra ping that chimes in midline. Internal rhyme abounded in Broadway scores by Cole Porter, Rodgers and Hart, and the Gershwins. It exudes urbanity, wit, and lightheartedness, and its prime practitioners were exponents of wordplay extraordinaire—punsters who took pride in their verbal facility. In "Mountain Greenery" we heard *blow your job/throw your job* between the end rhymes of *day* and *away.*

Songs, of course, mirror their times. Admittedly, lyricists writing in a pre-Hiroshima world had a little more to feel carefree about. The polish and panache of inner rhyme is uncommon in today's (pop-influenced) theater songs and virtually nonexistent in the top-40 marketplace. High-gloss lyrical chic in a rock and roll song would be as incongruous as a diamond stickpin on a tee shirt.

The point has already been made that it was the music that usually led an inventive wordsmith to the heights of imaginative wordplay. We know, for example, that such polished craftsmen as Ira Gershwin, Yip Harburg, Howard Dietz, and Larry Hart usually worked from a tune. The charming minor accent rhymes so common in their lyrics were the result of fitting melodies that took unexpected twists and turns.

When you are writing "dry" lyrics—without music—experiment by substituting these minor accent variations for the more common major accents of matched masculine and feminine rhyme. By breaking out of habitual patterns, you will create fresher lyrics. As a plus, it's likely that a varied rhyme pattern will evoke a more interesting melody from your collaborator.

To develop your rhyming muscles, practice resetting vintage Cole Porter, Arthur Schwartz, and George Gershwin. Pick some uptempo songs whose rhythmic patterns demand interior rhyme: "You're the Top," for example. When a master like Cole Porter leads the way, with a title as well as a blueprint of allusions to famous names and fancy places, his pattern isn't hard to follow. Here's a version of mine to give you the idea:

YOU'RE THE TOP

YOU'RE THE TOP
You're a hothouse orchid
I can't stop!
Cause you're plenty more, kid
You're a Barnum clown
You're a button-down from Brooks
You are Carson's timing
And Sondheim's rhyming
And Redford's looks.

You're the view
From the Versailles Garden
You come through
Like a midnight pardon
From the very start
When you made my heart flip flop
I've been glad to be the bottom when
YOU'RE THE TOP

The simplest way to train your ear to hear inner-rhyme designs is to collaborate with the best. Then, if you are presented with a melody that virtually cries out for that inner chime, you'll be better prepared to come through with flying verbal colors. Budding theater lyricists and special-material writers find it a short jump from recreating standards to creating originals.

THE TRANSITION PERIOD

During the golden years of Tin Pan Alley, perfect rhyme was in fashion. In fact, along with the 32-bar form, it was the norm. Before Cole Porter began expanding the tight structure, the lyricist had a potential of only fifty to seventy words to work with. Lyrics then, in the hands of our most polished writers—Gus Kahn, Irving Berlin, Irving Caesar, Mitchell Parish, Edward Eliscu, Otto Harbach, Dorothy Fields—sparkled with a wit, charm, and grace that few songs of later decades have displayed. While these craftsmen and a handful of other professionals rose to the challenge of the small form and polished their lyrical gems, hundreds of lesser talents ground out relentlessly rhymed clones.

Unimaginative writers took the easy way out and dropped in pre-dictable couplings: *met you/forget you, when we kissed/how I've missed, dreams come true/here with you, in my heart/never part* and the old triple-rhyme standby, *borrow/sorrow/tomorrow.* Knee-jerk rhyming. Ironically, many veteran writers who ascribe a higher artistic value to songs with perfect rhyme often thought nothing of reversing the natural order of words to achieve the relentless accuracy of full chimes. Songs of the period offered such inversions as: "upon the sands of time I'm walking," "you have never lovelier looked," and "my dreams you keep invading," phrases no human ever uttered. Small wonder, then, that the next generation of song-writers, emerging in the early sixties, found Tin Pan Alley "slickness" something to avoid rather than emulate.

The Rhymes They Are A'Changin'

The sixties were chaotic times: the crosscurrents of the women's movement, the civil rights movement, the drug subculture, the Vietnam War, and the ever-present threat of nuclear disaster created waves of social unrest. A new breed of singer/songwriter with serious ideas to express turned their backs on the "cadential jingle" of perfect rhyme and voted in favor of what they termed "naturalness" over perfection.

Admittedly, rhyme is limiting. And "perfection" can be sterile. Looking for a freshness that overused rhymes have lost, poets and lyricists have long sought substitutes for perfect rhyme. The alternatives wear a number of labels: near rhyme, approximate rhyme, slant rhyme, oblique rhyme, and false rhyme. There is nothing wrong with substituting a form of near rhyme to create a particular effect—as opposed to lacking the craft to rhyme perfectly. The use of near rhyme multiplies the possible end rhymes ten times.

ALTERNATIVES TO PERFECT RHYME

Consonance

Consonance (also called half rhyme, suspended rhyme, analyzed rhyme, and off rhyme) is the agreement of final consonant sounds, but with a differing preceding vowel sound, as in *soon/own;* the final *n* sounds agree, but *oo* and *ow* differ. Consonance was common in old English ballads, and many masters of English poetry preferred it to rhyme. In his love poems, Shakespeare used such examples of consonance as: *scant/want, fast/guest, pass/was, wrong/young.* John Milton was aware that end rhyme had a potential for producing a singsong effect that can trivialize the idea; because of the seriousness of the subject matter of *Paradise Lost,* he dismissed rhyme totally and substituted consonance and assonance.

Lyricists, too, have long felt the narrow confines of full rhyme; even the redoubtable W.S. Gilbert sought out consonance on occasion (and certainly not from want of skill). In *Thespis* (1871):

> *We know the fallacies*
> *Of human food*
> *So please to pass Olympian rosy*
> *We built up palaces*
> *Where ruins stood*
> *And find them much more snug and cosy.*

Stephen Foster coupled *rain/again* in "Old Uncle Ned." Even in the classic "After the Ball" we find consonance in the lines "after the break of *morn*/after the stars are *gone.*" In the last two decades near rhyme has been more the rule than the exception.

There are over a dozen vowel sounds in English, and therefore many possible groups of words in consonance with any given word. What if, for example, you want a fresher mate for *love,* rather than the hackneyed pairings: *of/above/dove/glove/shove?* And who wouldn't! Consonance offers these alternatives: *save/have/sleeve/nev(er)/arrive/sieve/grove/ carve/groove/nerve/you've.*

Another favorite end-line word of songwriters is *time;* its perfect mates are few, and not particularly useful—*lime, crime, dime.* Lyricists tend to match it with any other *i* sound; we therefore hear a great many lyrics with the overworked pairings of *time/wine, time/life, time/cried,* and so on. Consonance could offer such alternatives as: *aim, brim, cram, fame, tomb, and home.*

"It is always a fault," said Clement Wood in his classic, *Rhyming Dictionary,* "if a word chosen as a rhyme dictates a rhyming mate that is irrelevant, second rate, or not at all appropriate." Rather than settling for a stale rhyme, or one that doesn't truly reflect your idea, experiment with consonance.

PARA RHYME is a kind of consonance in which the initial and final consonant sounds are identical but the vowel sounds differ: *moan/ mourn, wild/world, laughed/left, nine/noon.* This form of rhyme was first labeled and used widely by the English poet Wilfred Owen to enrich his verse with "unexpectedness." Here's an example from the work of a class member whose inclination to overrhyme tended to render his lyrics predictable. He was encouraged to substitute forms of near rhyme; since experimenting with para rhyme, his lyrics have taken on a new freshness:

> *I'll wear my old sweat shirts from college,*
> *That sat in the bureau for years,*
> *I'll trade in my Dodge for a Rabbit,*
> *Get rid of that Porsche of yours.*

© 1983. Used with permission.

FEMININE PARA RHYME is two-syllable para rhyme in which the two final consonant groupings agree: *tutor/teeter, pilot/pellet, summer/simmer, winter/want her, relive/relieve.* It is also a minor accent rhyme. Substituting feminine para rhyme for feminine perfect rhyme eliminates the problem of that predictable pinging of "stalemates" like *never/ forever; stranger/danger; parted/brokenhearted,* and the ubiquitous *met you/forget you.*

Assonance

Assonance has already been discussed in Chapter 13 as a valuable device to link words by means of echoed vowels. It also has long been used as an end-rhyme substitute. Assonance—also called slant, oblique, or half rhyme—allows for a greater naturalness in sound—the hallmark of today's pop style.

It is the most commonly heard stand-in for perfect end rhyme in contemporary songs: *meet/seen/greed/dream; way/pace/trade/waste.* Rock writers especially are given to mating words solely by their inner vowels: In Rod Temperton's "Thriller" (made into an international hit by Michael Jackson), we hear these linkings: *dark/heart, scream/freeze, night/ strike, slam/hand, eyes/while, time/life, get/possess, time/night.* It might be that the naturalness of the unpolished rhyme worked well with the menacing thrust of the subject matter and thereby contributed to the record's phenomenal success.

Unstressed Rhyme

This is a pairing in which the final syllable of both words is unstressed, as in *given/heaven, hollow/willow, river/under.* In Leonard Cohen's "Suzanne" we hear the fresh combinations of *answer/lover, forever/mirror.* Unstressed rhyme is also a minor accent rhyme.

Augmented Rhyme

This is a term I've given to the pairing of like sounds where the rhyme mate is extended by an additional consonant, the most common of which are *d, g, s, t,* and *v.* For example: *rain/stained, plunder/wondered, pain/strange, rent/cents, harbor/starboard, mess/chest, play/crave, blue/gratitude.*

The rhyme agent (the first of the pair) sets up the expectation in the listener to hear a perfect mating of sounds. Augmented rhyme gives us what we expect to hear—and more. For that reason, I find it the most satisfying substitute for perfect rhyme. Its use greatly extends the possibilities of fresh sounds in end rhymes.

Diminished Rhyme

This is augmented rhyme in reverse, with the enriched rhyme sounding first. To me, diminished rhyme is less satisfying because it disappoints the ear. For example, if we hear the word *around* first, the expectation is to hear *found, ground,* and so on. If the sound of the rhyme mate is smaller, as in the word *down,* not only is the matching an unequal one, but more important, the hearer may be confused. While he is straining to distinguish exactly what word was sung (*downed? drowned?*), the song is moving forward and the plot unfolding. The listener has been put at a disadvantage by having to work to decipher the meaning.

Although diminished rhyme is prevalent in today's lyrics, its proliferation might be due more to ineptitude than to conscious design. In ballads, I find the sound offensive. On the other hand, in a lyric such as "Sniper" (page 160), diminished rhyme sounds natural because it is appropriate to the overwrought mental state of the singer: no one about to gun down dozens of people would be thinking in perfectly formed phrases; also, no end word is sustained on a long note, as is often the case in ballads. In a theater song, of course, the sound of *nights/light* or *found/town* would be about as welcome as a fingernail on a blackboard.

When a lyricist rejects true rhyme in favor of near rhyme for a specific purpose, that's one thing: a creative decision. But, to rhyme haphazardly for no specific purpose is something else: more likely, lack of skill. The tendency to shun perfect rhyme in favor of a looser sound coupling prevails in today's pop songs. Perhaps it's simply another manifestation of our generally relaxed standards of excellence. "The real thing" has been widely replaced by the synthetic: Tang for orange juice, dacron for cotton, plastic for leather. These may be equivalents in function, but certainly not in quality. If one can truly differentiate the mock from the real, the choice of the synthetic over the genuine should be made for a good reason.

SOME BASIC PRINCIPLES OF END RHYME

Rhyme is a verbal adhesive. It helps ideas to stick in the memory: *I like Ike*. The words you highlight by rhyming should embody the ideas you want to stress: *Right* makes *might*. By giving a word an echo, you are telling your audience: pay attention to this, it's important. If a word is insignificant to your overall meaning, don't rhyme it.

I remember a particular student lyric in which the singer was recalling the beginning of a romance: strolling hand in hand, stopping at a sidewalk cafe, sipping wine, and so on. The lyricist had begun to create a romantic atmosphere—then abruptly ruined it with a poorly chosen end rhyme: *trees/cheese*. After the lyric was read, the one word the class remembered most vividly was *cheese*—a word that suggests a strong (and sometimes unpleasant) smell. The word worked against the lyric by calling attention to itself. Had the writer chosen the word *wine* to rhyme—a word that can connote a romantic setting, or even intimacy—she would have maintained her desired effect and achieved her objective. The words you rhyme hang in your listeners' memory.

A good guideline: *Rhyme only those words that highlight the lyric's meaning, reinforce its emotion, and unify its atmosphere.*

Design a Rhyme Scheme That Surprises

A lyric, like a poem, has an overall end-rhyme pattern called a *rhyme scheme*. We indicate the pattern by assigning the same small letter of the alphabet to lines that rhyme with each other. To illustrate, here is the first verse and first chorus of Rupert Holmes's number one hit "Escape."

ESCAPE (The Piña Colada Song)

Verse:	*I was tired of my lady*	a
	We'd been together too long	b
	Like a worn-out recording	c
	Of a favorite song.	b
	So while she lay there sleeping	d
	I read the paper in bed	e
	And in the personal columns	f
	There was this letter I read:	e

Chorus: *"If you like piña colada*   a
    And getting caught in the rain   b
    If you're not into yoga   c
    If you have half a brain   b
    If you'd like making love at midnight   d
    In the dunes on the Cape   e
    Then I'm the love you've looked for   f
    Write to me and ESCAPE."   e

To ensure a framing unity to your lyric, each stanza—verse, climb, bridge, chorus—should maintain a clearly perceived and consistent end rhyme scheme. There are always exceptions, of course, but in principle you should decide upon it, and stay with it. In "Escape" Rupert Holmes used the same abcb pattern, rhyming every other line, for both verse and chorus. You can make the rhyme schemes of your verse, bridge, and chorus the same or different, whichever seems natural for the individual song. The verses and choruses of country songs are often identical in the number of lines, the rhythm, and the rhyme scheme; pop songs more frequently vary all three elements for contrast.

Try Not To "Telegraph"

A common goal of fine craftsmen is to surprise the listener with the rhyme. Yet it often happens that, on hearing a song for the first time, we can predict a rhyme a line or two before it arrives. That's called "telegraphing" a rhyme, and it has been traditionally considered hack writing. To make words sound inevitable and simultaneously sound fresh requires some effort.

In the following example, three separate elements conspire to produce predictable rhymes: feminine (two-syllable) rhymes, the abab pattern, and the length of the lines:

    I can't believe the many ways I miss you   a
    The morning smile that used to light your face   b
    And all the nights I'd wake and reach to kiss you   a
    Are memories that time just won't (daDUM)   b

We knew what we were going to hear: *erase*. Maybe *replace*. But what's the difference? It's boring with either word, because it was predictable. We heard it coming. We also hear *miss you* announce the imminent arrival of *kiss you*—for several reasons. First of all, the feminine rhyme problem arises. Feminine rhymes simply have a built-in tendency to telegraph their rhyme mates. To underscore the point, I picked the particularly overworked coupling *miss you/kiss you*. We've heard it in so many songs that by now it has as much ability to interest the ear as *one two/buckle my shoe*.

The second culprit is the rhyme scheme itself: the easiest way to avoid telegraphing is to avoid the abab pattern. Two sets of end rhymes per stanza are more than the ear requires to stay tuned to the story. The abcb, for example—rhyming only every *other* line—does the job just as effectively, as you saw in "Escape." Less frequent end chimes will tend to keep your listener's attention more on the meaning of the words and away from predicting what rhyme is coming next.

The third element that leads to telegraphing is unvaried line length. If, for example, the last line had been extended, it would have delayed the arrival of the chime—making it less predictable. The delay tactic forces the listener to be mindful of the words while waiting for the ultimate mating of sounds. Here's another treatment of the same idea, only this time we don't hear the rhymes coming:

I can't believe the many ways I miss you	a
The morning smile that used to light your face	b
Your sudden laugh, your solemn frown	c
Are sights I wish were still around this lonely place	b

The lyric is immediately improved by reducing the end rhymes to one set, *face/place*. Now the *miss you/kiss you* trap is avoided. By shortening the third line to provide an inner chime (*frown/around*), you keep the listener waiting for the sound of *place*. That's all there is to it. The important thing is to develop a feeling for the rhythm of words that will create unpredictable sound pairings.

As you have already seen, Rupert Holmes is a contemporary songwriter who artfully combines fresh subject matter, conversational language, and perfect rhyme. And his rhymes often surprise. Here is the first verse and first chorus of "The People that You Never Get to Love":

THE PEOPLE THAT YOU NEVER GET TO LOVE

Verse:	*You're browsing through a second-hand bookstore*	a
	And you see her in non-fiction V through Y.	b
	She looks up from World War II	c
	And then you catch her catching you catch her eye.	b
	And you quickly turn away your wishful stare	d
	And take a sudden interest in your shoes.	e
	If you only had the courage, but you don't	f
	She turns and leaves, and you both lose.	e
	And you think about	
Chorus:	*THE PEOPLE THAT YOU NEVER GET TO LOVE*	a
	It's not as if you even have the chance.	b
	So many worth a second life	c
	But rarely do you get a second glance	b
	Until fate cuts in on your dance.	b

In the verse, Holmes holds end rhyme to a minimum to keep the listener concentrating on the story. Extending the fourth line, "and then you catch her catching you catch her eye," prolongs the time of arrival of the Y/*eye* ping. This is an admired technique that has been called the "pleasurable frustration of delayed rhyme" (Donald Wesling). Holmes uses the same device in the eighth line with the phrase, "She turns and leaves," thereby lengthening the thought. It's an effective tactic which makes the sound of *lose* less predictable than if the line had been shorter. You'll notice that the rhyme scheme in "People," unlike that in "Escape," varies from verse to chorus.

"The People that You Never Get to Love" has a naturalness that conceals the work that went into it. Rupert Holmes, like all painstaking craftsmen, makes good writing sound effortless.

Vary the Color of Your Sounds

A varied mix of rhyme pleases the ear. When sameness is overdone, the result is usually tedious. Accomplished lyricists have a keen awareness of the color and weight of words, as a gifted cook considers the eye appeal and textural variety of food: the specter of a white platter offering filet of sole, creamed cauliflower and whipped potatoes could depress the heartiest appetite. With a broad spectrum of vowel colors to choose from, there is never a reason to write a monochromatic lyric—except purposefully, for effect, (more on that later).

Look back, for example, at "Marcie" (page 142) and read down the end-line words. Joni Mitchell treats her listener to a variety of sound effects: masculine rhyme, feminine, double mosaic, unstressed, assonance, consonance, diminished, and augmented. Her words produce sensual effects that are warm (*summer/sand/beaches*), or dank (*cold/river/cellars*); they make us see (*brown paper*) and feel (*snowing*). It is not surprising to learn that Mitchell is a "painter" in the literal as well as the figurative sense.

The kind of rhyme that earns the highest praise from rhyme theorists is the pairing of contrasting words. W.K. Wimsatt, renowned scholar and author, judges the best rhyme to be one that links different parts of speech or words that are semantically unlike. Here, for example, are what Wimsatt would term "minimum rhyme" because the words are all the same part of speech, verbs: *glows/shows/flows/blows/knows.* The sound is dull. What pricks the ear is the contrast of *different* parts of speech, such as a verb linked to a noun: *blows/toes,* or a name and a verb: *Joe's/snows.*

In "The People that We Never Get to Love" we heard fresh pairings: Y/*eye,* a letter of the alphabet with a part of the anatomy is a step up from the cliché coupling *why/I,* even though it's the same sound; (*World War)II/you,* a (Roman) number with a pronoun, somehow satisfies ear (and mind) more than the standard mating of *too/two/you;* so does *shoes/ lose,* the noun (an article of clothing) with a verb. We are simply more entertained with rhymes that contrast vividly yet sound unforced.

Rhyme for a Reason

Another guiding principle is: *Keep rhyme to a minimum.* When used excessively, rhyme can sound silly, especially those *ing* and other feminine rhymes: *singing/bringing, season/reason, kissing/missing.* If humor is the intention, multiple rhymes can be charming; if not, they can trivialize your thought. The point has already been made, but it bears emphasizing: excessive end-of-line chiming wrenches our attention away from the important thing—the song's meaning. The shorter the length of the lyric line, the more aware the listener becomes of the rhyme. Except when it is purposely overstated for comic effect—like makeup on a clown—a rhyme should never call attention to itself.

When Not to Rhyme: A Case History

When George Gershwin presented the melody of what would eventually become "I Got Rhythm" to his brother/collaborator Ira, the ideal lyric did not immediately occur to the lyricist. In fact, it took two weeks of struggle before Ira eventually discovered how to treat the incessantly repeated rhythmic figure of DUM DUM DUM da, DUM DUM DUM da, DUM DUM DUM da, etc.

In his memoir, *Lyrics on Several Occasions,* Ira lets us in on the genesis of the song. First read the lyric below, complete with its introductory verse. Then discover in Ira Gershwin's own words the kind of thought that went into the creative process.

I GOT RHYTHM

Verse: *Days can be sunny*
With never a sigh;
Don't need what money can buy
Birds in the tree sing
Their dayful of song
Why shouldn't we sing along?
I'm chipper all the day,
Happy with my lot
How do I get that way?
Look at what I've got:

A: *I GOT RHYTHM*
I got music,
I got my man
Who could ask for anything more?

A: *I got daisies*
In green pastures,
I got my man
Who could ask for anything more?

B: *Old Man Trouble*
I don't mind him
You won't find him
'Round my door.

A: *I got starlight*
I got sweet dreams
I got my man
Who could ask for anything more?
Who could ask for anything more?

Filling in the seventy-three syllables of the refrain wasn't as simple as it sounds. For over two weeks I kept fooling around with various titles and with sets of double rhymes for the trios of short two-foot lines. I'll ad lib a dummy to show what I was at: "Roly-Poly,/Eating solely/Ravioli/Better watch your diet or bust. Lunch or dinner,/You're a sinner./Please get thinner./Losing all that fat is a must." Yet, no matter what series of double rhymes—even pretty good ones—I tried, the results were not quite satisfactory; they seemed at best to give a pleasant and jingly Mother Goose quality to a tune which should throw its weight around more. Getting nowhere, I then found myself not bothering with the rhyme scheme I'd considered necessary (aaab, cccb) and experimenting with non-rhyming lines like (dummy) "Just go forward;/Don't look backward;/And you'll soon be/Winding up ahead of the game." This approach felt stronger, and finally I arrived at the present refrain (the rhymed verse came later), with only "More/door" and "mind him/find him" the rhymes. Though there is nothing remarkable about all this, it was a bit daring for me who usually depended on rhyme insurance.

But what is singular about this lyric is that the phrase "Who could ask for anything more?" occurs four times—which, ordinarily and unquestionably, should make that phrase the title. Somehow the first line of the refrain [the AABA section] sounded more arresting and provocative.*

You have probably identified the real dilemma Ira Gershwin faced: how to handle those three successive "feminine" melody notes. Certainly, three feminine rhymes was not the answer. At best, any three in a row would sound silly, even ludicrous. The lyricist's eventual treatment was the only way out: no end rhyme.

*Ira Gershwin, *Lyrics on Several Occasions* (New York: Alfred A. Knopf, Inc., 1959), p. 342. Used with permission.

To compensate for the lack of end rhyme, Gershwin provided other *figures of sound,* a term originated by Gerard Manley Hopkins to cover many kinds of rhyme substitutes. By now, you may recognize the device of anaphora: *I got/I got/I got.* That repetition of words at the start of a line gives the ear a kind of equivalence which diminishes the need for end-line word mating.

Gershwin found a way to reduce the potential sing-songy effect of the feminine word pattern even further: he varied the two-syllable words with two one-syllable words: *my man, mind him, sweet dreams.* It is the rhymed two-syllable words (*dinner/sinner*) that tend to sound the silliest in heavy repetition.

Given the tendency of today's lyricists to play down rhyme, this analysis may seem unwarranted fifty years after the fact. A contemporary pro might decide *instantly* not to rhyme George Gershwin's tune and not need two weeks of deliberation. Nevertheless, Ira Gershwin's ultimate treatment of "I Got Rhythm" illustrates a sound piece of lyric-writing theory put into practice by a master.

Keep Your Character "In Character"

Rhyme in general, and inner rhyme in particular, reflects an educated mind—not only the lyricist's but, by extension, that of the singer as well. In some cases, the singer is a character in a show. In others, the singer is an invented pop character who may be a lineman for the county or a jobless wanderer sittin' on the dock of the bay. In the majority of pop songs, the singer is simply speaking for himself or herself (and for us) in universal contexts such as "Time in a Bottle" or "I Get Along Without You Very Well." But whichever kind of lyric, it is critical to the integrity of the song—pop or theatre—that the kinds of rhyme and the amount of rhyme be appropriate to the song's "character"—in every sense of that word.

In "Ol' Man River," for example, Oscar Hammerstein carefully played down the use of the end rhyme for two reasons. The first reason was to fit the "character" in *Showboat,* an uneducated black dockhand on the Mississippi levee. The second reason was to play against the insistent and unvarying musical pattern given him by Jerome Kern's melody:

DUM DUM DUMda
daDUM DUM DUMda
daDUM DUM DUMda
daDUM DUM DUMda
daDUM DUM DUMda
daDUM DUM DUMda daDUM.

That rhythmic pattern reechoes in each bar of all three A sections without variation (not unlike the case with "I Got Rhythm"). Hammerstein's problem was twofold: not only to avoid the Mickey Mouse repetition of feminine rhymes that the final notes of the lines indicated (DUM-da), but even more important, to create a language style that accurately reflected the vocabulary of the singer. His solution was to avoid end rhyme completely in the first A section of the AABA chorus. Again, Hammerstein used the common rhyme substitute of anaphora (*He/He/He* at the start of lines) and immediately repeated the title line to achieve the necessary binding effect. We hear no rhyme at all until the twelfth bar of music (in the middle of the second verse) with the chime of *forgotten* paired with *cotton*. Hammerstein's mating of *un*repeated sounds to an incessantly repetitive musical motif accomplished two things: cued the listener into the seriousness of the content; and characterized the unschooled (*nothin'/sumpin'*) singer. His language style, of course, was appropriately ungrammatical and consistent: *He don'/He mus'/An' dem/*, and so on.

Discussing the lyric in an interview, Hammerstein said he kept the rhyme to a minimum because he didn't want his listener to become rhyme conscious; had he rhymed in the traditional way, he said, "It would have been a less effective song. It would have lost some of its primitive strength. The man on the Mississippi levee hasn't got many words, but he says exactly what he feels."

On occasion even a skilled craftsman such as Stephen Sondheim can lose sight of the relationship between a character's level of education and rhyme. Sondheim tells a story on himself of an inner rhyme in *West Side Story* that is still "embarrassing [him]." At an early runthrough of the show it was pointed out to Sondheim by his friend and fellow lyricist Sheldon Harnick that Maria was an uneducated Puerto Rican girl to whom language such as "It's alarming how charming I feel" would be unnatural. Sondheim quickly simplifed the line, but the rewrite was rejected by everyone connected with the show. The incongruity stayed.

In contrast to the uncultured Maria, Professor Henry Higgins of *My Fair Lady* is a philologist and phoneticist. It is appropriate for him to spout the multiple polysyllabic inner rhymes "exasperating," "vacillating," and "infuriating" given him by Alan Jay Lerner. In his mock exasperation with females in general, and Eliza Doolitle in particular, his emotion and rhymes were not incompatible.

Anger is a weightier matter. Mosaic rhymes, tricky inner rhymes, and multisyllabic rhymes are as incongruous for the angry singer as they are for the uneducated one. When we are upset, we spurt out words without thinking how graceful, clever, or syntactically correct they are. Rhyme is a matter of deliberate care, and therefore antithetical to the nature of anger. In *Gypsy,* when Stephen Sondheim designed Momma's final dramatic say in "Rose's Turn," he kept end rhyme to a minimum, with the first sound mate arriving in the thirteenth bar. Yet the audience was riveted by the intensity of the feeling produced by the repetitive figures of sound that Sondheim substituted for rhyme.

Make Your Words Sing

The words of your lyric not only should mean exactly what you intend them to mean, and ping in the right places, they should *sing*. What makes a word singable has to do with rather complex principles of phonetics. The reason that some words are easier to sing than others is a matter of how much work is required of the lips, tongue, and teeth, and how much the mouth must reshape itself to pronounce words in a sequence. Delving into phonetics is beyond the scope of this book, but a few pointers should keep you aware that you're writing words to be sung, not read.

The key ingredient is vowels. The basic principle is to try to use a lot of open-ended long vowel sounds, *a, e, i, o, oo.* The most singable consonants are the liquids *l* and *r,* and the nasals *m, n,* and *ng.* To illustrate the singability of such combinations, say this line aloud: "The rain is falling like a silver chain on the willow." Now sing it to a dummy tune. The line sings well because every word flows into the next one without causing the mouth to reshape itself. The string of sounds is made euphonious by the accented long *a* in *rain* and *chain,* combined with words featuring *l: line/like/ silver/willow.* The final word, *willow,* gives the singer an open vowel sound which can be sustained as long as the breath holds out.

Be mindful of the all-important word at the end of a line: can it be held? Again, think vowels. It's no mystery why, in ballads, we so often hear such words as these: *I/lie/try/sigh/cry/die; you/true/through/knew/blue; pay/play/day/say/way; be/me/free/see/agree.* A singer can hold on to these open vowels because they are not closed off by any plosive consonants—*p,b,t,d,k.* Words such as *talk/dump/ask/trade/snob/last* are impossible for a singer to hold. Consequently, they are a poor choice for the end of a line. They are also difficult to sing when they butt up against each other; for example, in order to clearly articulate *huge chest,* the mouth must perform some acrobatics or the words may come out sounding like *hugest.* Other tough combinations would be *pink crepe, love fun, crunch cherries;* a general rule would be to try to avoid placing words back to back where the identical consonant sound ends one word and starts another.

The simplest way to ensure that you write singable words is to sing them—really sing them out loud. If you're not writing to a melody, make up a dummy tune. That's the way many pros go about it. When every word feels good in your mouth, easily follows the next one, and sings exactly the way it's said, you know you did your job well.

GETTING INTO THE SUBTLETIES: THE FUSION OF SOUND, SENSE, AND EMOTION

The Bee Gees and Stevie Wonder are among the highly successful pop writers who admit to developing songs more from sound than sense. Wonder has said: "A lot of times when I start a song all I have is a melody or a basic idea for a lyric. I'll use . . . vowel sounds in place of lyrics. Then I'll make the lyrics fit the inflection of the sound." That's not an uncommon process. Craig La Drière, in his book *Structure, Sound, and Meaning,* has said "whether meanings or sound more often initiate the . . . process

. . . there is no theoretical reason to suppose the primacy of either."

Often it is the *sound* of words and not their sense that triggers the creative process—perhaps more often when a lyricist is setting words to music. Oscar Hammerstein told an interviewer the genesis of "Make Believe": "Jerome Kern played a melody for me; in the middle of it, I got some words to fit the middle part—the words were *couldn't you, couldn't I, couldn't we.* At the moment I thought of them, I had no idea what [it was] *you and I* couldn't do. It just seemed to sing. The music gave me those words."

Once the process has begun, first-rate lyricists, like first-rate poets, instinctively use the sound of words to reinforce meaning and intensify emotion. Linguists have noted that certain sounds seem to produce certain effects, and theories abound that sense and sound reflect each other.

Make Sound Reinforce Meaning

ONOMATOPOEIA, which means "name making," is a figure of speech in which the words that are used sound like the action described or the object named. In Gilbert and Sullivan's *Princess Ida* we hear the "rum tum tum of the military drum and the guns that go boom boom." "Blues in the Night" includes the "clickety clack" of the train and the "whooee" of its wail. In "The Trolley Song" we get treated to the range of its sounds: ". . . clang, clang . . . ding, ding . . . buzz, buzz . . . plop, plop . . ."

Onomatopoeia, in its narrowest application, (such as the example just cited), tends to sound trivial. Yet inventively applied, it can add significantly to a song, as in, for example, Stephen Sondheim's "Franklin Shepard, Inc." from *Merrily We Roll Along.* The lyric depicts a songwriting team in a creative session trying to sustain the muse through the incessant interruption of the phone: "humm humm humm . . . mutter mutter mutter . . . bzz! bzz! drrring!" Sheldon Harnick put the device to amusing use in "If I Were a Rich Man" by giving Tevye barnyard sounds to perform: the quack, cluck, gobble, and honk of his poultry. The Beatles in "Drive My Car" added a little innuendo to the sound effects: "beep beep mm, beep beep, yah!"

PHONETIC INTENSIVES function as a useful subcategory of onomatopoeia; they are words whose meaning is either suggested or intensified by their sound. Smallness, for example, seems to be suggested by the short *i* in such words as *midget, little, snip, trim, zip code, fidget, miniature, trip, itty bitty.* When Alan Jay Lerner wrote the lyric, "A Little Bit of Luck" for *My Fair Lady,* he chose sounds that supported his intended meaning; *little bit* is preferable to *tiny bit,* given that the short *i* has the power to reinforce the idea of smallness.

In "She's Leaving Home" (page 115), the daughter slips outside "*clutching* her handkerchief." Words ending and beginning with *ch* frequently convey the idea of sudden or violent action—*wrench, lurch, chop, pitch, belch, chase.* "Holding" her handkerchief would have provided empty alliteration; the sound of clutching subtly contributes to the listener's awareness of the nervousness felt by the runaway making her early morning escape.

Quick motion is also suggested in words beginning with *sc: scurry, scamper, scuttle, scan, scorch*. Another initial combination, *cr*, frequently introduces words that "alter structure," as in *crash, crumble, cream, crease*.

EUPHONY is a pleasant acoustic effect produced by a particular group of words. Because vowels produce musical overtones, a lyric line that contains a high percentage of long vowels and liquid consonants will tend to sound melodious. Long vowels such as in *rain, beer, lime, tote*, and *gloom* are richer and more resonant than the short vowels in *ran, bear, limb, tot*, and *glum*. Consonants, the framework of a word, make noises rather than music, although a few can sound fairly mellifluous: *m, n, l*, and *r*. In "Moonlight in Vermont" the "warbling of a meadowlark" is a euphonious line. John Hartford's closing refrain from "Gentle on My Mind" makes music with its interlacing *r, m, n*, and *l* with *oo, i, a, ee* vowels: "You're *m*oving o*n* the back *r*oads by the *r*ivers of *m*y *m*em'*r*y and for hou*r*s you're just ge*n*tle o*n* *m*y *m*i*n*d." (The lyric appears on page 238).

CACOPHONY or DISSONANCE (the opposite of euphony) is the clash of sounds intentionally placed side by side for effect. The "explosive" (or plosive) consonants *b,d, g, k, p*, and *t* create an especially harsh or sharp effect, as exemplified in phrases from "Sniper" (page 160): "s*t*a*ck*ed u*p* the car*t*ri*dg*es" and "we*dg*ed her agains*t* the *d*oor." When Stephen Sondheim was designing "Rose's Turn," he not only kept end rhyme to a minimum, he chose words whose plosive consonants affirm her disgust: scra*p*boo*k*s, *b*a*ckg*roun*d*, qui*ck* loo*k*, *g*ar*b*a*g*e.

NONSENSE SYLLABLES, ironically enough, can be extremely effective. The sound made by an open-ended vowel preceded by a consonant—such as *la la, dee dee, hey hey*—is inherently neither gleeful nor doleful, but produces different connotations depending on the context in which it's used. For example in "Heigh-Ho," the seven dwarfs' marching-to-work song from the film *Snow White*, the *heigh ho, heigh ho* resounds with cheeriness; the same two words in Noel Coward's classic "If Love Were All" (pronounced here as *hayho*) intensifies the sense of the singer's wistful resignation to the single state.

The use of the nonsense sound *daidle deedle daidle* in "If I Were a Rich Man" heightens Tevye's pleasure as he contemplates the multiple joys that money could bring. Conversely, in *Sweeney Todd*, when the giddily crazed Beggar Woman picks up an imaginary infant and rocks it wildly while muttering "deedle deedle," the effect is eerie and foreboding.

The ironies in Stephen Sondheim's sophisticated theater lyrics are frequently intensified by vowel syllables. In *A Little Night Music*, for example, as Desirée ticks off the cracks on the façade of the "glamorous life," she tosses off its flaws with "la la la." Sondheim uses the sounds of yawns to emphasize the *ennui* of *blasé* golf players who claim in "Pour Le Sport": "we're having *such* fun . . . aah ahh ahh."

Paul Simon's "Mrs. Robinson" is a lyric whose appeal was significantly increased by the mysterious connotations of "wo wo wo (did he mean "whoa" or "woe"?) . . . hey hey hey . . . coo coo ca choo . . . woo woo woo." In fact, the song is unthinkable, if not impossible, without them. Even the *wo wo wo* in "Feelings" (ridiculed as it has been) serves to confirm the misery of the singer.

Looking over the piano copy of Lennon and McCartney's classic "Yesterday" yields an interesting fact: the hummed final line on the original record's vocal arrangement was kept on the printed sheet music. In other words, the writers deliberately chose not to repeat the song's final phrase, "I believe in yesterday," but rather to hum it, "mm mm mm mm mm mm mm." I think that by so doing, they added to the wistfulness of the preceding line. Try it: first sing the final line of the song and repeat the phrase, then sing it again and replace humming for the echo. See if you don't agree that it's more effective.

Make End Rhyme Intensify Emotion

The standout song of 1983, "Every Breath You Take" by Sting of the Police, is notable for the manner in which sound supplements meaning. The rhyme scheme is as limited as the rejected lover's thoughts. In its narrow three-vowel pattern, the emotion rocks between the *As* of pain and *Es* of pleading, offset only by *oo* of the word *you: take/make/break/take/you; day/say/play/stay/you; see/me/aches/take/; make/break/take/stake/you,* and so on throughout the song. Here's the pattern made by each stanza with the capital letter representing the dominant sound: A/oo, A/oo, E/a, A/oo, A/e, E/a, A/oo, A/oo. (You'll find the complete lyric on page 240.) Sting validated a theory that poets back to Petrarch have believed: that vowel "pitch" can suggest emotional states. In theory, the narrower the range of sound, the more static the range of feeling. The obsession of the singer for the singee in "Every Breath You Take" would appear to bear out the concept. The potential for augmenting sense by sound is enormous and bears experimentation. The sole guideline: sound must never violate meaning.

A CLOSEUP OF AN UNRHYMED CLASSIC

A song usually has end rhymes, just as a clock face usually has numbers. Usually, but not always. If your watch had only small squares or dots spotted at regular intervals, you could still make a 5:49 train: the structure of the 24-hour circle of time is so familiar that a clock face needs only hands to do its job. A well-conceived lyric will also work without end rhymes—given sufficient rhyme substitutes. When the form of a melody is clearly defined and its rhythm is persistent, and when words and sounds reecho in minirepetitions, the binding effect of end rhyme usually isn't missed.

"Moonlight in Vermont" is an oldie (1945) that has had over two hundred different vocal recordings, from Margaret Whiting to Frank Sinatra. Working from the title and writing to Karl Suessdorf's melody, lyricist John Blackburn recalls the process of creativity: "After completing the first 12 bars of the lyric, I realized there was no rhyme and then said to Karl, 'Let's follow the pattern of no rhyme throughout the song.' It seemed right." Obviously it was right. The song is a standard. Read the lyric aloud and try to identify the alternative chiming devices Blackburn used in place of end rhyme.

MOONLIGHT IN VERMONT

A: *Pennies in a stream,*
    Falling leaves,
    A sycamore,
    MOONLIGHT IN VERMONT.

A: *Icy finger waves*
    Ski trails on a
    Mountain side
    SnowLIGHT IN VERMONT.

B: *Telegraph cables*
    They sing down the highway
    And travel each bend in the road
    People who meet
    In this romantic setting
    Are so hypnotized by the lovely

A: *Ev'ning summer breeze*
    Warbling of a meadowlark
    MOONLIGHT IN VERMONT,

Coda: *You and I and*
    MOONLIGHT IN VERMONT

The fullest verbal echo is the title itself placed strongly in the final line of all three A sections. In the second A there's a slight variation, and in the coda the title repeats for emphasis. Alliteration and assonance interplay on the first A: the *e* sound in *pennies, stream,* and *leaves* braids itself between the alliteration of *l*s in *falling, leaves,* and *moonlight.* The *i*s have it in stanza two with *ice, side,* and *moonlight,* which interlace with the alliterative *ss* of *ski, side,* and *snow.* End rhyme is not missed.

Throughout the bridge, repeated sounds link up words: the long *a*

in *cables* with *highway;* the *a* sound in *telegraph* and *travel* (which also al-
literate with *t*; the long *e* in *people/meet/lovely;*) the long *i* in *highway* echoes in *hypnotized,* and again they connect with the alliterated *h*. Then
there's the nature design with the seasons subtly changing from autumn to
winter, to spring, to summer. This motif, of course, also serves to tie the
stanzas together.

Another rhymeless wonder is John Denver's "Annie's Song." Denver proves what poets have known for centuries: effective repetition can
substitute for end rhyme. Denver designed his lyric on patterns of "equivalence," a term used by the renowned linguist Roman Jakobson to cover a
variety of balanced repetitions. For example, the classic AAA refrain outlines the end of each verse. Anaphora starts five consecutive lines: *like a .
/ like a . . ./like a . . . /*and so on. The ear grasps the pattern through repetition and is prepared to accept a series of unrhymed nature-linked words
at the end of successive lines: " . . . *forest/ . . .springtime/ . . . rain/ . . .
desert/ . . .ocean.*"Again, it works. In the second verse we hear the same
device in the repetition of *let me* at the start of five successive lines. The design of the lyric is strong, and the meaning is clear without benefit of
rhyme.

"Moonlight in Vermont" and "Annie's Song" are, of course, the
deviations from the norm that test the rule.

WHEN YOU'RE STUCK FOR A RHYME

One of the most frustrating times in the life of a lyric writer is
when a rhyme can't be found that suits the sense. Sometimes compromises
are necessary—assonance or consonance is preferable to a perfect rhyme
that either contorts natural speech or distorts your intended meaning.

Gus Kahn, legendary lyricist whose career was immortalized in
the film *I'll See You in My Dreams,* had a useful trick: Let's say, for example, that the line, "I want to hold you all night long" is giving you trouble because none of the available rhymes suits your thought. Get yourself a
new rhyme agent by rephrasing your idea: "I want to hold you all night
through" or "through the night." Two new sounds will now multiply your
potential rhyme mates by the dozens.

Stephen Sondheim says he finds it advantageous to "make a list of
useful rhymes related to the song's topic, sometimes useful phrases, a list of
ideas that pop into my head." Cole Porter, master of the slick multiple
rhyme, said, "I try to pick, for my rhyme, words of which there is a long list
with the same ending." Sound advice.

A WORD ON RHYMING DICTIONARIES

Your bookcase should certainly hold a rhyming dictionary, pref-
erably the Clement Wood; the preface alone is invaluable. Use it, however,
as a supplement to your own inventiveness, not as a crutch.

Ira Gershwin, who wrote such composite delights as *Da Vinci/pinchy,* told me, "I rarely used one for rhyme but to see what rhymes were *not* there." Irving Berlin claimed, "I never use a rhyming dictionary; I'm too impatient to look up the words." Mitchell ("Stardust") Parish told me, "I didn't use rhyming dictionaries. You've got to have it in you." And Oscar Hammerstein, who could match mosaics with the best of them, called a rhyming dictionary a "handicap" when one is writing a lyric that features rhyming. After all, intricate polysyllabic chimes, traditionally the hallmark of the best theater lyricists, are not listed in any book; they are the by-products of a fertile imagination. Irving Caesar, who penned such inventive mosaics as *conquistador/never missed a door, think a/Inca,* and the fresh three-line rhyme in the verse of *"Tea for Two" (place is/oasis/chase is),* confirmed my guess: "I don't think I've ever gone to a rhyming dictionary for a rhyme; it would inhibit me."

A rhyming dictionary is a bit like a food processor; it's a convenience that speeds up the process, but you can certainly obtain fine results without one.

WRAPUP

When you're writing the lyric first, think about a rhyme scheme that will permit you to surprise the listener. Vary masculine rhymes with some feminine ones. Shun cliché sound mates, like *wine/time* and *love/above,* which have lost all power to evoke anything but a ho-hum response. For freshness, try some of the minor accent rhymes.

If you're putting words to music, study the structure of the melody before you plunge in to write. Decide what kind of rhyme treatment would create the most effective total song—patterns of repetition, perfect rhyme, near rhyme, or a mix of all three. Remember how Hammerstein and Gershwin went about it.

Elegant ballads and film and theater songs virtually demand perfect rhymes. Considering the cost of Broadway tickets, the theater-goer is entitled to be delighted by insightful and sparkling lyrics studded with fresh, witty rhymes. One near rhyme in an otherwise perfect pattern would stick out like a paper napkin on a damask tablecloth.

If you hear that inner chime, write it, don't fight it—because that's your style; it simply means you gravitate more toward New York than Nashville.

The main questions are: Do your rhymes sound inevitable? Do they sound appropriate to the overall lyric style? Do they ring true to your character? Do they reinforce your meaning? Do they sing? If not, polish until they do.

"I got rhythm, who could ask for anything more."
Ira Gershwin

part five

FINDING
THE BEAT

chapter 18
Feeling the Rhythm

"We write . . . more than anything else . . . to rhythms . . .
[sometimes] sitting outside tapping out a beat hitting our hands
against our legs and working out a song with no instruments."
Barry and Robin Gibb (The Bee Gees)

In the fall of 1983 Carolyn Leigh gave a seminar at the New York 92nd Street Y on lyric writing for the theater. Leigh, lyricist of such Broadway scores as *Little Me, Peter Pan,* and *How Now Dow Jones,* and of such standards as "Young at Heart," "Witchcraft," and "The Best Is Yet to Come," discussed her collaborative relationship with Marvin Hamlisch on their theater project *Smiles:* "When I first met him, Marvin said to me: 'I don't want to write to your lyrics; I know they're lovely lyrics, but I don't want to write to them. I feel hemmed in.' Some lyric writers had probably gotten him into the Edgar Guest [a writer of light verse] kind of meter—da-dum dadum dadum dadum—and he was scared to death of that."

Many fine composers have felt "hemmed in" by four-square lyric meters: Jerome Kern, Harry Warren, Harold Arlen, Arthur Schwartz, Henry Mancini, and Michel Legrand, to name a few, have preferred free rein with their melodies rather than having to write music to words. Composer Jule Styne puts it this way: "When you give a lyric writer music, you've given him the best of you, and now he's going to give you back the best lyrics. If he gives you the lyrics [first], he'll never get the best from the composer. It's not a *fitting* business."

Lyric writers traditionally have been delighted to give the music man his way. It made the job that much easier for Hart, Harburg, Hammerstein, Fields, Dietz, Mercer, *et al.* Lyricist Otto Harbach, speaking of writing to Jerome Kern's music, said that it "was so simple in its construction and in its conversationlike rhythm that adapting words to it proved an elementary chore. A lyric like 'Smoke Gets in Your Eyes' took me no time at all." When you put words to a melody, the meter is all laid out with its strong and weak accents, its pauses, its peaks and valleys of emotion. A gifted writer simply fills in the blanks. Well, almost.

Many contemporary lyricists prefer to write to music—writers such as Carole Bayer Sager, Paul Williams, and Cynthia Weil. Though these fine craftsmen can capably shape a lyric without a rhythmic scaffolding (in addition to making words fit a melody like Saran Wrap), each admits to preferring the music-first process. They seem to consider a composer's sense of rhythmic possibilities superior to their own. Even many self-contained performers—those who write both words and music—prefer to make the rhythm of their tunes initiate the lyric writing process:

Randy Newman: "The music comes first . . . the words don't come first ever."

Paul Anka: "I start at the piano and get into a groove. I've never written a lyric . . . gone to the piano and put it to music."

Stevie Wonder: "For the most part, I come up with the music first."

Bob Dylan: "I usually know the melody before the song."

Billy Joel: "The music's usually the first thing I write."

Al Jarreau: "Ideally, the music comes first."

Paul Simon: "I write the music first."

It would appear that to start with a melody rather than a lyric is simply a more "musical" method of song writing. A lyric written from scratch can be *earthbound,* so to speak. Faced with a blank yellow pad and a silent room, a noncomposing lyricist can easily fall into one of two traps: wordiness or a monotonous meter. Words, instead of singing off the page, may sprawl across it more like a letter from camp. Or else the words may plink in a singsong rhythm. That's not surprising. Something is missing from the scene: a strumming guitar or pulsing left hand of the pianist creating a rhythmic undercurrent. A solo lyricist has only that internal metronome beating out an unvarying taTUM taTUM taTUM. So, it's totally understandable that the tendency is to fill in the silence with words, and words, and words.

Composers, on the other hand, instinctively think of held tones, and they tend to carve out melodies with some open spaces between the notes. Consider, for example, the opening of Jerome Kern's "All the Things You Are." The first bar has only one note (the word *you*) held for four beats of music. How many noncomposing lyricists writing without music would conceive of a lyric line of one lone word? Or in the case of Kern's "The Way You Look Tonight"—half a word: *some(day)!* If my students were given an assignment to write an opening verse to the title "All the Things You Are," a result might be something like this: "You're the first sign of spring/you're a song lovers sing/you're the flight of a midnight star/ and I love all the things you are." Twenty-eight words as compared to the eight that Oscar Hammerstein fit perfectly to Kern's four-bar melody. It would be a rare lyricist who, without music, would hear an internal rhythm that went: "You(pause) (pause) (pause)/Are(pause) (pause) the/. . . ."

It's highly unlikely, for example, that Yip Harburg, as great a lyric writer as he was, would ever have shaped such a sparsely worded lyric as "April in Paris" without Vernon Duke's economical melody as a framework. Harburg once said, "The tune inspires. It *must* come first." As we know, it usually did. So, in effect, the cadence of the words to most of the standards, (written from the thirties to the fifties), was initiated by the inherent rhythmic as well as melodic gifts of the composing half of such teams as—Rodgers and Hart, Gershwin and Gershwin, Kern and Hammerstein, Schwartz and Dietz, and Arlen and Mercer. One-man wonders like Irving Berlin and Cole Porter were successful at writing lyrics first because they shaped them with a composer's feel for rhythm.

It would appear that composers have the rhythmic edge. To state the obvious: they use notes for the musical framework of a song, whereas lyricists must struggle to make musical structures with mere words. But lyricists brimming with ideas to express certainly can't wait around for the ideal melody or the perfect collaborator to materialize. Realistically, there are projects and situations that require a lyric first. Also there are first-rate composers who like to work from a well-wrought lyric. So the question looms: How does a lyric writer close the creative gap? How does one avoid "the Edgar Guest syndrome" and learn to shape more "songlike" lyrics? The answer is by knowing enough about rhythm to use it as a tool.

RHYTHM: HOW TO THINK IT, FEEL IT, AND SEE IT

Rhythm refers to any steady movement distinguished by regular accents of strong and weak beats—the *tick* tock/*tick* tock of a clock. The lub *dub*/lub *dub*/lub *dub* of a heartbeat. There's a rhythm in the way we brush our teeth, or jog, or rake leaves. Conversational speech is rhythmic too. Our words tumble out in a stream of stressed and unstressed syllables: I BET you're SAG-i-TAR-i-us. TaTUM taTUM taTUM tata. WAN-na see a MOV-ie on SUN-DAY? TUMtatata TUMtata TUMTUM? Unstructured and unmeasured, yet rhythmic.

Feeling the Stresses and the Pauses

Meter, from the Greek word *metron,* is measured rhythm. Music, of course, is metered. Because a lyric is written to be sung to music, its words must be conceived in measured rhythm, a song beat. Most pop songs are written in 4/4 time, known as common time—four beats to a measure (or bar) of music. The first accented beat of the measure is the downbeat. "Over the Rainbow," for example, starts on the downbeat. Here's the rhythm of the opening two measures; each line represents one measure of 4/4 meter. To get the feeling of the rhythm of the song, snap your fingers, or tap your feet, or—as the Bee Gees do—beat your hand against your leg in a steady *one, two, three, four:*

Some- / (hold) / where / (hold) /
O-   / ver the / rain- / bow /

In effect, what you are doing is reading like this:

> SOME- *(pause)* WHERE *(pause)*
> O- VER the RAIN- BOW

Or:

> DUM / *(pause)* / DUM / *(pause)*
> DUM / DUMda / DUM / DUM

Now let's suppose Yip Harburg, instead of writing those words to Harold Arlen's melody, wrote the lyric first, without a melodic structure. It's quite possible that Harold Arlen, reading those same four words on a lyric sheet, might have heard them in a different rhythm. Again, pat your leg in a steady 4/4 beat:

> SOMEwhere / Over the / RAINbow / *(pause)* /
> DUMda / DUMdada / DUMda / *(pause)* /

The stresses on the words have changed, producing a different rhythm and a different effect. In the first example you can see how Harburg broke up the word *somewhere* into two parts, each sitting on two half notes. In the second example you can see how Arlen might have left some open space: there is no word in the fourth beat of the measure. When writing a "dry" lyric (as Stephen Sondheim calls it), it's important to think in terms of sustaining words and of leaving spaces. In other words, be conscious that you're writing words to be set to music. The objective is to feel the rhythm of your words the way you would imagine them sung. For instance, how do you hear the line, "Baby, I love you, I really do." Get your 4/4 rhythm going and try these two rhythmic treatments:

> BA- / *(hold)* / BY / I /
> LOVE / *(hold)* / YOU / I /
> REAL / *(hold)* / LY / *(hold)* /
> DO / *(pause)* / *(pause)* / *(pause)* /

Or:

> BAby I / LOVE you / *(pause)* / *(pause)* /
> BAby I / LOVE you / *(pause)* / *(pause)* /
> *(pause)* I / REALly do / *(pause)* / *(pause)* /
> *(pause)* I / REALly do / *(pause)* / *(pause)* /

The first version sounds plaintive because it's drawn out, with the word *baby* having three beats. The second treatment is clearly uptempo. So you can see that you have lots of rhythmic options with every line you write. The more you hear the rhythm of emotion you want to communicate, the more effective your lyric will be.

Making the Pattern

It's equally essential in writing a lyric from scratch to know how to create a pattern of stressed beats that scans the same from verse to verse, or bridge to bridge, or chorus to chorus. In an AAA song, for example, the same melody is sung to all the verses. In writing an AAA lyric, you must design verses whose stresses are consistent from verse to verse: the first verse is your pattern, and all subsequent verses should match its stressed beats line for line. This does not mean, however, that the number of *syllables* must be identical in each verse; what must be identical is the number of beats. To illustrate, let's take a second look at "By the Time I Get to Phoenix." This time we'll examine its rhythmic pattern.

"Phoenix," unlike "Over the Rainbow," starts on an upbeat—two pickup notes (and two pickup words) before the downbeat: *by the TIME*. To see how Jim Webb varied the syllable count yet maintained the beats from verse to verse, we'll look at the first lines of each of the three verses, vertically. Above them is the equivalent note value for the melody.

	1	2	3
1) By the	Time——— I Get to	Phoe-nix— she'll be	ris- in'. —
2) By the	Time I make Al-bu-	quer-que— she'll be	work- in'. —
3) By the	Time I make Ok-la-	ho- ma — she'll be	sleep- in'. —

	4	5	6
1)	She'll	find the note I left	hang-in'— on her
2)	She'll	pro- b'ly— stop at	lunch and give me a
3)	She'll turn	soft-ly ——— —and	call———my name out

© 1967, Charles Koppleman Music/Martin Bandier Music/Jonathan Three Music.
Used with permission.

In a measure of 4/4 time, a whole note (**O**) gets four counts, a half note (♩) gets two counts, a quarter note (♩) gets one count, and an eighth note (♪) gets a half count. Therefore, you would feel the third line like this:

By the/TIME/(hold)/I make/OK-la/ (or)
dada/DUM/(pause)/DUMda/DUMda/

Look at the first measure: line one has four syllables, and lines two and three both have five. A lesser writer than Jim Webb might have evened out the meter by saying: *THAT I/GET to* (DUMda/DUMda) in order to match *I make/ALbu* and *I make/OKla*. But regularizing the syllables can contribute to a singsong effect—exactly what a good lyricist wants to avoid. Now look at bars four, five, and six: no two lines match perfectly in their syllable count. But, they match exactly in *beats*, and that's the important thing. In "By the Time I Get to Phoenix," Jim Webb did what every good lyricist and composer does, consciously or unconsciously—he varied the unstressed syllables.

DEVELOPING THE KNACK OF VARIATION

All art is built upon an interplay of repetition and variation. Every great creative work—sonnet, sonata, pas de deux, or pop song—balances the familiar with the new. This principle has been applied earlier to both a lyric's structure and to its sound patterns. It applies equally, perhaps especially, to the rhythm of its words.

Perfect regularity of meter is not a measure of merit. On the contrary, it is a flaw. When meter alternates too precisely between light and heavy accents, it becomes mechanical. Like rhyme, meter can work for you if you know how to manipulate it, or against you if you are unaware of its potential either to enhance your words or to weaken their impact.

First rev up your motor—whether by snapping your fingers, clapping your hands, or using some kind of rhythmic physical movement. Walking is a wonderful way to get a beat going. (Huey Lewis says he writes songs while running.) When you get a strong rhythm going, say the lyric aloud, or hum to a dummy melody, to hear how the accents of the words fall. To make sure you've maintained a pattern of stressed beats from verse to verse, you might want to type up a rough draft of your lyric and put a diagonal mark (/) between the feet, as in the examples. That could be helpful if you feel that rhythm is the weakest of your lyric writing talents. If, on the other hand, you feel the beat right down to your toes, such a procedure is unnecessary.

In the lyric to "Phoenix" Jim Webb showed how the stressed beats must be consistent but the syllable count can vary from verse to verse. Not only does varying the accents prevent monotony, it enables the composer to write a more interesting melody. The AAA in particular, lacking the contrast of a bridge or chorus, needs all the help it can get to offset its inherent potential for boredom. Because AAA songs often lack sufficient rhythmic, melodic (and harmonic) contrast, they are seldom recorded without their words. "Phoenix" is one of the few in this form whose music has earned instrumental treatment.

Variations within a Verse

Any verse composed solely of lines written in a regular meter—for example, taTUM, taTUM, taTUM, taTUM, taTUM—requires manipulation of its rhythms to give the ear a change from the sameness. You can do the job three ways: vary the accents, vary the natural pause within a line, and vary the punctuation. Here's a rhythmic look at "Richard Cory," which is written in seven-beat lines:

> They say/that Rich/ard Cor/y owns/one half/of this/whole
>   town/,
> With polit/ical/connec/tions//to spread/his wealth/around/.
> Born/into/soci/ety//a bank/er's on/ly child/,
> He had ev/'ry thing/a man/could want//power,/grace,/and style.

© 1966, Paul Simon. Used by permission.

Basically, the meter is a rising rhythm (when the unaccented syllables come first) of taTUM, taTUM, taTUM, seven times. Without variation, the sound would be as annoying as a dripping faucet. The meter of "Richard Cory," however, doesn't bore because it never repeats the same accents in any two consecutive lines: For example, in the first line there is no pause until the comma at *town;* in the second line, there is a natural pause after *connections*—the word itself breaks the regularity of the meter. Imagine if Simon had chosen to mirror the meter of the first line with something like this: "he had/some pals/in pol/itics/who spread/his pow'r/around." Perfect, but singsong and trivial sounding. The third line—the only one of the four that starts on a stressed syllable—divides itself into a four-beat plus three-beat feel with a pause after the word *society*. The word *POWer* (TUMta) in the last line is a switch in rhythms (to falling rhythm), and as an added variant, there are three emphatic pauses after *want, power,* and *grace*.

THE RUN-ON LINE All the lines in "Richard Cory" are "end-stopped," meaning that the end of the thought and the end of the line coincide. In contrast, a "run-on" line continues the thought beyond the normal pause into the next line. This "wrapping a thought around a corner" is a useful technique to soften the strictness of the meter. Joni Mitchell used the device in "Marcie":

> Marcie's faucet needs a plumber;
> Marcie's sorrow needs a man.
> Red is autumn, green is summer—
> Greens are turning, and the sand
> All along the ocean beaches
> Stares up empty at the sky.

© 1968, Siquomb Publishing Corp. Used by permission. All rights reserved.

"Marcie" is in a four-beat falling rhythm—TUMta/TUMta/TUMta/TUM-ta—one of the most common in lyric writing because it matches the common time of music. Without any alteration, it would deaden the senses. In the fourth line Mitchell breaks up the tick/tock regularity of the middle and end pauses with a thought whose sense flows on until the end of the sixth line. Obviously no pause is intended after either *sand* or *beaches*. Unfortunately, even professional recording artists have been known to pause and let their voices drop at the end of a line (especially when there's a rhyme), even though it's not the end of a thought. A run-on line, therefore, is always a risk for that reason alone. Its occasional use has the potential of adding drama and elegance to a stanza, but, of course, only if the vocal performance is equal to the writing. As a general guideline, run-on lines should be used sparingly. Because they require a listener to work hard to follow the thought, several such lines in a row can be wearying.

Ac-cent-tchu-ate the Op-po-site

The importance of the principle of rhythmic repetition and variation is seen most dramatically in both the AABA and the verse/chorus forms.

It's for good reason that the denizens of Tin Pan Alley jokingly referred to the B section of the AABA as "the relief." That's just what it was designed to be—a musical contrast to the three verses. Good lyricists, taking a cue from the composer's shuffling of the rhythmic cards, also make contrast the operative word in developing the bridge: switching from the general to the particular, from the past to the present, from the first person to the second, and so on. Altering the previous musical statement, often by reversing it, is, of course, exactly what composers do so often with rhythm.

CONTRAST THE BRIDGE. Let's take a close look at the rhythmic contrast in "Over the Rainbow." The melody, one of Harold Arlen's most famous, came first. Here is the 8-bar A pattern and the 8-bar bridge pattern visualized both in syllables and in their note values:

OVER THE RAINBOW

A SECTION

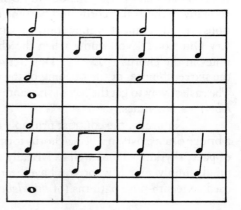

BRIDGE SECTION

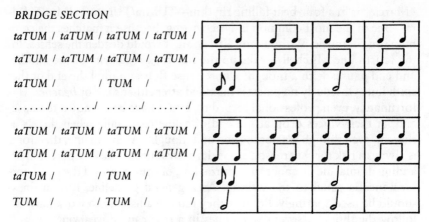

taTUM / taTUM / taTUM / taTUM /

taTUM / taTUM / taTUM / taTUM /

taTUM /   / TUM /

......./ ..../ ..../ ..../

taTUM / taTUM / taTUM / taTUM /

taTUM / taTUM / taTUM / taTUM /

taTUM /   / TUM /   /

TUM /   / TUM /   /

See how Arlen shuttled between one-, two-, and four-beat lines. Whole notes and half notes dominate the As, while eighths frame the bridge. Repetition and variation. The metric pattern alone pleases the ear. That's exactly what a lyricist should do with words when writing from scratch: shape an idea into a lyric that is rhythmically satisfying. All the verses of "Over the Rainbow" start on the downbeat, and in contrast, each measure of the bridge begins on a pickup note. Translating that into a lyricist's terms, we would say that the verses begin on stressed syllables (words that go TUM or TUMta) and the lines of the bridge begin on unstressed words (that go taTUM). To get rhythmic variety in your AABA lyrics, simply contrast the accents, pauses, and number of unstressed beats in the bridge with those in the verses.

VARYING THE VERSE/CHORUS. The principle of contrast that makes an AABA song interesting applies as well to the verse/chorus form. The entire point of writing a verse/chorus song is to sock home the chorus. Yet even many professional songwriters camouflage the chorus, treating it as if it were another verse. It seems to me that the chorus should shout: Here I am; listen to me. Contrasting the meter of your chorus with that of your verse will help to ensure that attention will be paid. One of the reasons that Peter Allen's melody to "Don't Cry Out Loud" has garnered so many orchestral records and become a standard on easy listening stations is the dynamic rhythmic contrast between the two sections. In "Don't Cry Out Loud," you know when the chorus has struck: those quarter notes in the chorus ♩♩ (Don't/cry/out/loud)—wonderfully set off the sixteenth notes at the opening of the verse— ♫♫ (baby cried the). The easiest way to get the feel of sixteenth notes is to repeat the word *huckleberry* a few times.

Naturally, the contrast principle extends to bridges too. After all, a bridge often exists in a verse/chorus form solely to give the song a change of pace, rhythmically as well as lyrically and melodically. Bearing that in mind, simply switch what you have been doing. If, for example, you've used sixteenth-note patterns (of *huckleberry* words), slow down to quarter-note words with lots of breathing space in between: for instance, "Don't cry out loud." It's as easy as that.

THINKING INSTRUMENTALLY. Because of their lack of rhythmic, melodic, and harmonic variety, country tunes are rarely heard without their words. Admittedly, many country writers lean toward folk-structured story songs with music written solely in service to the story; stripped of their meaty lyrics, the bare musical bones can't sustain listener interest. Even the trend toward the verse/chorus country crossover song hasn't produced many melodies that make it into the mainstream. As adept as country writers are at the nuances of wordplay, they seem, for the most part, either unaware of or uninterested in the significant contribution that variation in rhythm, melody, and harmony makes to extending the life of a song.

In an interview with a successful country lyricist/composer, I asked a question about his writing a particular hit song: Did you purposely choose to make the meter of your verse and chorus the same? The response was: "I never thought about it; I figured that I'd just try for the song—for the sake of the song, not the cover records."

The song never got cover records: not only did no other singer record it, but its melody was not sufficiently tuneful to stand on its own as an instrumental. Instrumental versions of songs—those played on easy listening radio stations and by Muzak (or other wire services supplying music to restaurants, factories, airplanes, and the like)—account for a significant percentage of a songwriter's performance income. It seems odd, then, that so many professional writers fail to consider that a little more rhythmic and melodic variation in their songs could substantially increase their royalties.

GETTING THE GROOVE

Record producers seek winning formats—not simply good songs, but ones whose "sound" exerts a broad appeal. For example, here's a list (from a music industry trade publication) of the kinds of songs being sought for recordings: "Uptempo dance, pop-techno-funk, R&B-dance, hi-energy rock, and synth-pop." Translation: Songs with a groove—a beat. (Slow ballads have been on a decline for years.)

Synthesizer wizardry has arrived. The good news for lyricists is that musical hi-tech products are not for the exclusive use of the musician. They're valuable new tools for lyric writers who have the basics under their belts and are ready to get commercial. Experiments with a continuing group of writers in my advanced class have convinced me that when lyricists are exposed to fresh rhythmic ways of thinking, their versatility improves dramatically.

Every lyricist labors, to some degree, under the tyranny of meter. As Arthur Miller said in another context, it comes with the territory. In some writers the beat is faint, and stanzas are shaped more like paragraphs; in others, a personal meter unconsciously takes over in jingling precision. These are varieties of meter hangup. Even the most successful professionals, composers and lyricists, acknowledge the problem: "Writing by myself," said Carly Simon, "I tend to get stuck in rhythms I've used before." Sheldon Harnick has echoed the sentiment: "Left to myself, I tend too often to fall into the same kind of forms, and I've had to watch that."

Every writer could use a rhythmic shot in the arm occasionally.

Working with Rhythm Tracks

Except for special assignments to set words to music, writers in class work from scratch, without a melodic framework to structure their rhythmic patterns. Guided by intuition alone, some students meet the challenge. On the other hand, the early efforts of others are often shaped with cookie-cutter monotony. But not for long.

My first rhythmic experiment was making "groove tapes," specially prepared three-minute tracks programmed on a Dr. Rhythm machine and then duplicated on cassettes. Each track replicates the bass figure and tempo of a popular groove, such as the ♫♫ (DUMdadada) undercurrent of "Maniac." In class sessions we play several hit records featuring one particular beat, and then we analyze the song's melody, lyric (content, style, and form), arrangement (including instrumental breaks), vocal, timing—everything. The assignment then is to use the corresponding groove track as the foundation for a "record," and to write a lyric that could be a follow-up single for one of those artists. The results are stunning in their divergence from the writer's usual style. Working from a rhythmic base serves to make lyricists dramatically aware that they are more versatile than they realize.

That's the icebreaker. After that, the creative process expands. The writers begin to internalize the process and consciously program their own inner rhythm machine. Some practice writing over the instrumental breaks of records. Many invest in a piece of rhythm equipment as a writing adjunct. How you achieve rhythmic adaptability is unimportant. Doing it is all.

WAYS AND MEANS. A large financial outlay is unnecessary. One inexpensive aid to writing rhythmically is a "Drum Drops" record (roughly ten dollars per LP). Each of the six LPs in this series features ten three-minute tracks offering a broad range of styles—bluegrass, swing, funk, rock. In addition to helping you get the groove, they can substitute for a live drummer on a home demo. These records, however, are fixed in length and tempo and therefore not as adaptable as a drum machine like the Dr. Rhythm (in the hundred-dollar price range).

For the cost, a Casio "electronic musical instrument" is a marvelous rhythmic tool for a lyricist. The portable twelve-inch VL-1 (under thirty dollars) contains a 29-note keyboard, ten different rhythms which are adjustable in tempo, and five simulated instrument sounds. This minisynthesizer can plug into a cassette so you can record a lyric right over the track. One student found the system worked successfully in her long-distance collaboration with a Canadian composer: the "lyric demo" gave him a precise idea of the groove she had in mind, and his tunes always hit the target.

More sophisticated (and much pricier) versions of the Casio feature an expanded keyboard, a greater groove potential, and more instrumental sounds. The features of expensive models can add impact to your demos, but they won't further enhance your writing ability. Using a simple Dr. Rhythm, for example, you can learn to match up the beat and tempo of the latest record that you admire, whether by Prince or Culture Club or the Eurythmics. Hearing that constant pulse as an undercurrent will free you to write words in a meter that would never have occurred to you without such an aid.

PROGRAMMING THE BEAT. In a newspaper interview, Annie Lennox of the Eurythmics stressed the importance of rhythm in their songs: "We like to have the sense of two things battling at once. You have something that sounds nice on the surface [the vocal], but underneath there's an ominous side [the rhythm]. It's a feeling of sweet decay. There's an element of danger, of roughness and crudeness that goes along with something very melodic. But underlying all that you have to have a fantastic rhythm." You too can create that kind of oxymoronic rhythmic figure of "sweet decay," if that's your style.

Or, you could design the beat for what Arista Records president Clive Davis terms a "power ballad"—a dramatic song that gives the artist a chance to get emotional with a melody that frequently contains sustained high notes. Under Davis's guidance, Arista artists have produced a string of power ballad hits: "Don't Cry Out Loud" (Melissa Manchester), "I'll Never Love This Way Again" (Dionne Warwick), "Mandy," "I Write the Songs," and "Weekend in New England" (Barry Manilow), "Come What May" (Air Supply). A power ballad groove is a strong 4/4 meter pulsing at a speed of approximately eighty-six beats per minute. (Such a tempo is indicated on sheet music by a quarter note showing the number of beats to the minute: $\quarternote = 86$.) You can create such a groove on a drum machine by using any of the power ballad hits just cited as a guide. Once you get the beat going, the words with the right feel will come.

Writing to a Rhythmic Outline

Another bit of rhythmic calisthenics used in class is writing from a preset rhythmic outline. Such an exercise yields three results: a lyricist will write in a more compressed manner and thereby eliminate the flabby adjectives and superfluous connectives with which so many amateur lyrics are afflicted; a writer will begin to break loose from any personal meter straitjacket and instinctively to alter the number of unstressed syllables in a line; the biggest bonus is that the lyric will be rhythmically "musical." Here, for example, is a verse/climb/chorus whose rhythmic patterns contrast sharply from section to section. A writer who follows the design automatically creates a lyric whose parts are well defined. First the form:

A RHYTHMIC OUTLINE

Verse:	*TUMtata*	*/TUMta*	*/TUMta*	*/TUM*	/
	TUMtata	*/TUMta*	*/TUM*	*/(Pause)*	/
	TUMtata	*/TUM*	*/TUMtata*	*/TUM*	/
	taTUM	*/(pause)*	*/taTUM*	*/(pause)*	/

Climb:	*TUM*	*/TUM*	*/TUM*	*/TUM*	/
	TUMta	*/TUMta*	*/TUM*	*/(pause)*	/
	TUM	*/TUM*	*/TUMta*	*/TUM*	/
	TUM	*/(pause)*	*/(pause)*	*/ta*	/

Chorus:	*TUM*	*/(hold)*	*/TUM*	*/(hold)*	/
	TUMta	*/TUMta*	*/TUM*	*/TUM*	/
	TUM	*(hold)*	*/TUM*	*(hold)*	/
	TUM	*/TUMta*	*/TUM*	*/(hold)*	/
	TUM	*/(hold)*	*/TUM*	*/(hold)*	/
	TUMta	*/TUMta*	*/TUM*	*/(hold)*	/
	TUMta	*/TUMta*	*/TUM*	*/ta*	/
	TUM	*/(hold)*	*/(hold)*	*/(hold)*	/

Verse:	*TUMtata*	*/TUMta*	*/TUMta*	*/TUM*	/
	TUMtata	*/TUMta*	*/TUM*	*/(Pause)*	/
	TUMtata	*/TUM*	*/TUMtata*	*/TUM*	/
	taTUM	*/(pause)*	*/taTUM*	*/(pause)*	/

Climb:	*TUM*	*/TUM*	*/TUM*	*/TUM*	/
	TUMta	*/TUMta*	*/TUM*	*/(pause)*	/
	TUM	*/TUM*	*/TUMta*	*/TUM*	/
	TUM	*/(pause)*	*/(pause)*	*/ta*	/

Chorus:	TUM	/(hold)	/TUM	/(hold)	/
	TUMta	/TUMta	/TUM	/TUM	/
	TUM	/(hold)	/TUM	/(hold)	/
	TUM	/TUMta	/TUM	/(hold)	/
	TUM	/(hold)	/TUM	/(hold)	/
	TUMta	/TUMta	/TUM	/(hold)	/
	TUMta	/TUMta	/TUM	/ta	/
	TUM	/(hold)	/(hold)	/(hold)	/

The assignment was to utilize the format "loosely," with the freedom to modify the rhythm and to add or drop pickup words as needed. Here is one result: the student followed the basic structure, with some slight variations, and added a bridge of his own design.

SOMEHOW

Verse: *I've lost at love so many times,*
More than I care to tell.
Singin' the blues each time I lose
I go
Through hell.

Climb: *Sighing, trying*
Getting through the day,
I just swallow and say, that

Chorus: *SOMEHOW*
I'll be back in business
SOMEHOW
I'll smile again.
Someday
Not too long from now
I'll be over love
SOMEHOW

Verse: *Somebody dimmed the stars again,*
Somebody stole the moon,
Somebody fled—somebody said
Goodbye
Too soon.

Climb: *Gray days, long nights,*
         Once again they start—
         Still I know in my heart, that

Chorus: SOMEHOW
         I'll be back in business
         SOMEHOW
         I'll smile again.
         Someday
         Not too long from now
         I'll be over love
         SOMEHOW

Bridge: *Love enough, lose enough,*
         Soon enough you find
         Another love comes along
         And leaves the old one behind.

Chorus: SOMEHOW
         I'll be back in business
         SOMEHOW
         I'll smile again.
         Someday
         Not too long from now
         I'll be over love
         SOMEHOW

The lyric produced a definite rhythmic pattern suggesting eighth notes (♪♪♪♪) in the verse, quarter notes in the climb (♩♩), and half notes in the chorus (♩ ♩). It's got space and pauses and variations of rhythm. Admittedly, I created the metric design with a composer's instinct. The point is, however, that the more a lyricist can think like a composer, the more inherently "musical" every lyric will become. In the absence of a melody to write to, even a noncomposing lyricist could design a rhythmic pattern such as this one ror "Somehow." Writing well-crafted lyrics is a matter of talent plus *technique,* and part of that technique is a matter of meter.

Think Record: Give Your Demo a Groove

A successful lyric today is more than merely written; it's orchestrated. Weekly music trade magazine charts verify that 85 percent of the

Hot-100 songs are created by self-contained writing/performing/producing teams. They think *record,* rather than song.

In order to turn out a competitive product, the nonperforming pop lyricist and composer should also think in terms of designing a song with a finished record in mind, building in contrasting shapes and meters which will allow an arranger to exploit every element to its utmost. Björn Ulvaeus, in discussing the philosophy behind the group Abba's international hits, put it this way: " . . . each part in a song is equally important, whether it's an instrumental interlude, a bridge, or a chorus."

THE INSTRUMENTAL BREAK. In our increasingly techno-pop music business, commercially minded writers often make an instrumental break as intrinsic an element in the concept of their songs as a climb or bridge.

To electronically sophisticated ears, the bridgeless verse/chorus song can sound mighty simplistic. But what if you don't *need* a bridge: what if you've said all you want to say without one? Consider (*before* you invest in your demo) an instrumental restatement of a fragment of the verse as a wordless musical bridge before introducing the final chorus. Or you might add a four- to eight-bar break for breathing space, especially if your lyric packs a high ratio of words per square inch. Many a record has been catapulted over the finish line with a virtuoso solo interlude by a guitar, piano, or horn. Synthesizer-based pop makes a feature of extended instrumental sections. Dance (and exercise) records, often lasting eight to ten minutes, are designed to keep the lyric to a minimum and emphasize the musical groove. Once, elements like the groove and instrumental breaks were the sole concern of composers, arrangers, and musicians—but no longer. To paraphrase Bob Dylan, the sounds they are a-changin', and every career-committed lyric writer is well advised to stay on top of the trends with both ears to the radio, and to contribute ideas to the general concept of the song, especially the all-important shaping of a demo. The demo is the matrix for the record to come, and many a record producer is guided by the suggested treatment given in a well-wrought one. The more rhythm-conscious you become, the better.

WRAPUP

As a method of getting a feel for accents and pauses, there is nothing that beats writing words to successful songs. You have your pick of "collaborators" from top-40 pros like Barry Mann and Tom Snow, to theater composers such as Charles Strouse and Andrew Lloyd Webber. Simply give yourself the assignment to write new words to the melodies of "Sometimes When We Touch," "Somewhere Down the Road," "Tomorrow," or "Memory."

Every lyric you write to a successful melody will teach you something new about song shaping. The process yields rich rewards; you'll not only absorb a sense of structure and of rhyme and rhythmic patterns, you'll also get a feeling for the all-important pause, the held note, the wordless measure. Cynthia Weil began her career by writing new verses to Cole Porter songs. Now novices are doing the same with hers.

chapter 19

Reinforcing Meaning and Emotion

"Rhythm is a matter dependent upon emotion." Bertrand Russell

"Meter is an emotional constituent of meaning." Paul Fussell, Jr.

It is a lyricist's attitude that inspires the choice of words. And it is the meter of those words that establishes the mood of the lyric—from the bouncy playfulness of a MAIRZ-y-DOATS and DOZ-y DOATS to the stately cadence of CLIMB EV-'ry MOUN-TAIN.

When a song rings true, every element in it—its language style, tone of voice, syntax, and last but assuredly not least, the meter of its words—substantiates its professed meaning. It's rather like a person in that regard: our rhythms match our moods. When we are happy, enthusiasm accelerates our footsteps and energizes our gestures; our speech often bounces with polysyllabic thoughts: *sensational . . . terrific . . . block-buster.* Sadness, on the other hand, winds us down. The joyful skip slows to a trudge. We slouch. We sigh. Our conversation sometimes moderates to monosyllables: *that's all . . . too bad . . . so long.*

Small gestures of a shaking hand, a shrug, a raised eyebrow—in effect, our rhythms—reflect our true feelings. When we don't feel what we profess to feel, an involuntary action can give us away. We may, for example, take pains to appear calm and in control, perhaps at a crucial business meeting, while under the conference table one foot swings in concealed anxiety. Our individual rhythms are controlled by our emotions. The same principle operates in a song.

If, for instance, a lyric is expressing, "I'M FED UP!" but the dominant rhythmic feeling those words beat out is, "I'm wistful," the song sends a mixed message. Here, for example, are two treatments of the same thought:

> *I don't/WANna/TALK to/YOU/*—four beats
> *Idonwanna/TALK to/YOU/(pause)/*—three beats

Same words, but both the accents of the words and number of beats are different, and so is the effect each creates. In the first setting the singer would sound more weary; in the second, more fed up. The real difference is one of speed: the first example is mainly eighth notes—DAda/DAda/DAda/DA. The second line starts out with sixteenths: DAdadada/Dada/DA/(rest). To produce the effect you're after, the rhythm of your words should coincide with their emotion.

Sometimes the sentiment that words profess conflicts with the feeling that their meter evokes: for example, if the beat of a line resonates with dignity while the words reflect banal concerns, a listener will be confused, not knowing whether to respond to the meaning of the words or to the emotion of the rhythm. That's the case with this odd fusion of thought and rhythm (beat a slow 4/4):

> Junk / food   / (pause)I am   / crazy for   /
> Junk / food   / (pause)I love / peanuts and   /
> Pop- / corn   / (pause)tho they/ stick in my   /
> Teeth / (pause)/ (pause)   / (pause)   /

The combination sounds foolish, rather than fun—for a reason which we shall soon explore.

USING A POET'S TOOLS

When lyricists write to music, they have a powerful partner to help them achieve varying effects: music can stress words, underplay them, stretch them, sustain them, even syncopate them. When working without music, a lyricist, like a poet, should know how to manipulate meter to achieve emotional effects. It is helpful to a lyric writer, therefore, to be familiar with some theory.

A Little Elementary Greek

So far, we've been using terms like taTUM, TUMta, and TUMtata to express different stresses on words. The Greeks identified the common rhythms of our speech, giving a name to each two- and three-stress group. As time is measured by the units of the second, the minute, and the hour, verse is measured by the units of the foot, the line, and the stanza. Before we discuss how meter can contribute to meaning and emotion, it will be useful to identify specific meters and their effects. Here are the commonly used meters in lyrics, as well as their equivalent in music:

FOOT NAME	ACCENT	EXAMPLES	MUSICAL NOTATION (in triple meter)
iamb	ta TUM	to-DAY, the SNOW	♪♩
trochee	TUM ta	AL-ways, TRY and	♩♪
spondee	TUM TUM	QUICK-SAND, TIN CUP	♩.♩.
dactyl	TUM ta ta	HEAV-en-ly, RAIN on the	♩.♪♩
anapest	ta ta TUM	in-ter-JECT, on a TRAIN	♪♩♩.

A verse or lyric line is measured by the number of feet (or beats, in music) it contains. For example, a line composed of three dactyls— HOPE you can/COME to our/BARbeque (TUMtata/TUMtata/TUMta-ta)—is called dactylic trimeter. A pattern of four trochees—WANna/ 'NOTHer/CUP of/COFfee? (TUMta/TUMta/TUMta/TUMta)—is trochaic tetrameter. Iambs (taTUM) and trochees (TUMta) are two-syllable feet known as double meters; dactyls (TUMtata) and anapests (tataTUM) are three-syllable feet called triple meters. Meters of fewer than five feet are considered more songlike than longer ones.

The "most important" meter in English poetry is iambic pentameter (pen-TAM-eter), so called because its stanzas are composed of lines of five feet of words that go taTUM (iambs). It is the meter that most closely resembles the rising and falling rhythms of everyday speech:

> *Ta TUM/ta TUM/ta TUM/ta TUM/ta TUM/*
> *I WON/der IF/you EV/er THINK/of ME/*
> *There's GOT/to BE/a REA/son FOR/it ALL/*
> *When I/conSID/er HOW/my LIGHT/is SPENT/*

With its five-foot line, iambic pentameter is ideally suited for serious themes, and great poets have consistently chosen it for their loftiest works: Shakespeare for his plays, Milton for *Paradise Lost,* Chaucer for *The Canterbury Tales.* Their verses, usually unrhymed, were designed, of course, to be read or acted, not sung.

Song Style and Meter Length

Oliver Wendell Holmes, a physician as well as a poet, suggested that both the accents and the length of a writer's meter are related to pulse beat. Perhaps that's true. My proposed theory (equally unprovable) is that the relationship between a lyricist and his or her meter has more to do with personality and outlook on life.

For example, long lines of five, six, or seven feet seem to be the instinctive choice of lyrical storytellers and philosophers. The extended rhythm of such lines fits the voices of loners in boxcars and losers in back rooms trying to make sense of the existential dilemma. The writings of both Jackson Brown (during his folk period) and Bob Dylan are dominated by seven-foot lines: "Stuck Inside of Mobile with the Memphis Blues Again." Dylan returned to that same loping gait (iambic heptameter) for more than twenty of his songs.

In contrast, sophisticated musical theater writers, who view life from canyons of steel, appear to match the city's syncopated rhythms with a clipped cadence. Cole Porter, a self-contained lyricist/composer, more often than not shaped his songs in three-foot lines. In fact, he wrote over a dozen whose opening line repeats the identical beat: Ta ta TUM/ta TUM/ ta TUM.

Stephen Sondheim, like his wittily cynical theatrical forebears

Porter and Noel Coward, picks predominately two- and three-foot lines for his characters' trenchant comments on society. His ironic "Send in the Clowns" is characteristically terse:

> *TUMta/taTUM*
> *TUMta/taTUM*
> *TUMtata/TUMtata/TUM*
> *TUMta/taTUM*

The identical rhythm also underpins "Children and Art" (TUMta/taTUM) from his musical *Sunday in the Park with George.*

Favoring a three-, five-, or seven-foot line is common among songwriters. Such a preference is not surprising considering we exhibit a characteristic rhythm in our walk and speech and gestures. A dominant meter is not in itself a problem. The best writers are versatile and blessed with an unfailing instinct for altering accents. However, with less flexible lyricists, a particular meter can prevail to the point of monotony. Almost everyone has listened to an album of ten songs written and performed by one singer/songwriter and ended up with the reaction: *Everything sounds the same!* The listener has suffered from meter fatigue caused by the writer's dominant line length.

In the preceding chapter we stressed the importance of varying the length of the lines—for example, from three-beat to four-beat—the way composers seem to do, and of breaking up the evenness of a regular meter within the line (as Paul Simon did in "Richard Cory"). In addition to using those devices to achieve variety, you can also learn to manipulate rhythm to create more subtle effects: to speed up a line, to slow it down, and either to add to or to subtract from its emotional weight.

Weighing Your Words

THE SLOW SPONDEE. One of the most useful substitutions in a regular iambic (taTUM, taTUM) or trochaic (TUMta, TUMta) meter is the spondee, that two-syllable foot of equal stresses (TUMTUM) as in *this time, sandbox, eggplant.* Because each syllable is stressed equally, a spondee *(RICH MAN)* takes more time to pronounce than either an iamb *(aLONE)* or a trochee *(SUMmer).* Because, in effect, a spondee is twice as slow, it is said to "stretch" time. In lines in which you deal with serious concerns—weariness or sadness or discouragement—spondees will help you create the desired effect. As the singer is forced to slow down to place equal stress on each syllable, the listener is alerted to respond seriously. Remember *West Side Story*'s lovers' plaintive "SOME-WHERE . . . SOME-HOW. . . ."

In "Memory" it is the introductory slow spondees of the title's dotted quarter notes that creates the stately quality of the melody. The weight of the words on the music matches the stressed notes: *MIDNIGHT, DAYLIGHT, TOUCH ME, PAVEMENT, LAMPLIGHT, OLD DAYS, NEW LIFE.*

"Climb Every Mountain" also illustrates the power of the spondaic foot. The throb of the meter in itself, featuring a terminal spondee [TUM/(hold)/TUM(hold) ta/TUM/TUM/(hold)/(hold)/], evokes from the listener a thoughtful response. Another technique that will underscore words you want emphasized is to butt consonants against each other. For example, in the line from "Send in the Clowns" "don't you *love farce,*" the last two words not only get the equal stress of spondees, they are exceptionally difficult to articulate: they require the tongue and lips to reform themselves after intoning the *v* in *love,* in order to shape the *f* in *farce.* The singer, in taking care to pronounce each syllable so the words will ring clear in the listener's mind, highlights their importance. As discussed in Chapter 17, the combining of sounds that are hard to pronounce is usually to be avoided. But the careful and judicious use of this technique can produce special emphasis.

THE SPEEDY ANAPEST. Just as the spondee adds weight, trisyllabic feet—dactyls (SUDdenly) and especially anapests (in the RAIN)—inject levity. Introducing a three-syllable foot into a dominantly iambic or trochaic meter (either taTUM taTUM taTUM or TUMta, TUMta, TUMta) speeds it up and consequently adds a breeziness to it. Think about "In Our Mountain Greenery" in terms of its meter: TUM/TUM/TUMta/TUMtata. It's that extra beat in TUMta*ta* that does it. In "Nearsighted" (page 55) Rupert Holmes added an extra unstressed accent into his regular iambic meter, making the line "undeNIably, certiFIably" bouncier.

Triple meters, consisting primarily of anapestic feet, seem to emit something joyous or even superficial. That is why they are so suitable for comedy. And what is more lighthearted than a limerick? The five-line (aabba) nonsense poem is the only fixed form with a built-in smile. Since its popularization by Edward Lear, its meter alone—independent of any words—has taken on a frivolous connotation:

> *There was a young lady named Harris*
> *Whom nothing could ever embarrass*
> *Till the bath salts one day*
> *In the tub where she lay*
> *Turned out to be plaster of Paris.*

Because our ears now associate anapestic trimeter with flippancy, it has become virtually impossible to say anything heartfelt in that meter. The rhythm announces, "Don't take me seriously."

THE LIGHTHEARTED THREE-FOOT LINE. Stephen Sondheim, whose ear for the cohesion of meaning and emotion appears flawless, used iambic trimeter for his classic and amusing "Gee Officer Krupke" from *West Side Story* (music by Leonard Bernstein). When the street gang lightheartedly begins its litany of complaints about the familial deadbeats who contributed to their "depraved" behavior (besotted grandpa, drug-dealing grandma, transvestite brother, and so on), the audience is ready to be amused: the rhythm alone radiates a gaiety.

> *TaTUM/TaTUM/TaTUMta*
> *TaTUM/taTUM/taTUM*
> *TaTUM/taTUM/taTUMta*
> *TaTUM/taTUM/taTUM/*
> *TaTUM/taTUM/taTUMta*
> *TaTUM/taTUM/taTUM*
> *TUMta/TUMta*
> *TUMta/TUMta/TUM*

Notice, too, how Sondheim varies the endings of first, third, and fifth lines and then reverses the rising iambic rhythm to trochaic to punch up the final line.

To "translate" Sondheim's lyric into, say, iambic tetrameter (taTUM, taTUM, taTUM, taTUM), would unquestionably drain off some of the amusement. A great deal of comedy resides in meter alone.

THE DRAMATIC DACTYL. Dionysius said that dactyls make for grandeur. They did in Greek poetry, and they do in pop songs—when the song's tempo is slow. Not many songs generate the drama of "The ImPOSsible DREAM." And what sounds more majestic than the duet ballad "Somewhere" from *West Side Story*" when the lovers claim: "WE'LL find a/NEW way of LIV ING/WE'LL find a/WAY of for/GIV ING." Each syllable of *giving* and *living* bears the equal stress of the spondee, thereby adding more weight to the line's emotion. The dominant meter of "She's Leaving Home" (page 115) is dactylic; the trenchant assessment of the generation gap plays against the cello: "SHE's leaving/HOME after/LIVING a-/LONE for so/MANy years." Once again we hear that meter is a primary component of meaning.

MAKING METER AND EMOTION COHERE

When the Meter Fights the Sense

Having been introduced to the spondee, you can now identify the problem in the "junk food" ditty (page 232) that makes it sound foolish instead of fun:

> *Junk/food/(pause)I am/crazy for/*
> *Junk/food/(pause)I love/peanuts and/*
> *Pop-/corn/(pause)tho they/stick in my/*
> *Teeth/(pause)/(pause)/(pause)/*

With equal stress being put on *junk food* and *popcorn*, the frivolous words have been given emotional weight by spondees: the result is incongruity, a primary component of *humor*. If humor was the intention, the combination might work. If, however, simple lightheartedness is the objective, a more appropriate mating would be something like: I am CRAZ/y 'bout POP/corn and PEA/nuts. Anapests reinforce the triviality of the sentiment.

Here is an example of a student lyric in which the intention is to move the listener with the seriousness of the theme: comforting the homeless. These are excerpted verses from a longer lyric:

I work a shelter for homeless New Yorkers,
In a church on the upper East Side;
From eight at night till six a.m.,
Twice a month I'm their host and their guide.

I make tea, get the towels and the blankets,
Set up rows of cots on the floor,
When the school bus pulls up out in front,
My guests are led up to the door.

Some look like they were found on the Bowery,
Others look like they drove from Cape Cod,
A few aren't more than twenty-one
And a few must be older than gawd.

They undress while I get milk and cookies,
Then they give me a taste of their lives,
Of the jobs that went, the lungs that failed,
Of those who lost husbands or wives.

They share their Luckies and photos and memories,
Clean their teeth, take their pills, say their prayers
They sleep till five, then I wake them up,
And their gratitude hangs in the air.

© 1984. Used with permission.

The lyric certainly does contain altered meters and a variety of accents, but somehow, in spite of substitutions, the overall effect is singsong. The main culprit is the sound of anapests: dadaDUM/dadaDUM/dadaDUM (in a CHURCH/on the UP/per East SIDE; Twice a MONTH/I'm their HOST/ and their GUIDE; Then they GIVE/me a TASTE/of their LIVES; Clean their TEETH/take their PILLS/say their PRAYERS). It's virtually impossible for a listener to feel concern for those who lack health and jobs and homes when their plight is set to a bouncing beat.

Anapests (dadaDUMs) have a breezy lilt, and to substitute one in a line of iambs (daDUM daDUM *dadaDUM* daDUM) makes the line move faster and breaks up an otherwise regular meter, as in "Nearsighted." But, when anapests are used three at a time, as they are here, they tend to trivialize the thought and thereby undermine the intended seriousness of the message.

When the Meter Fits the Sense

If, on the other hand, the thought *is* trivial, then anapestic meter will reinforce the feeling. Here's an exaggerated example of a jaunty attitude mated to the appropriate meter:

I don't care if you're bald
Or too fat, or too thin
Or what kind of shape
That your bankroll is in
You are all that I need
You've got all that I lack
Wontcha please come on home
Wontcha hurry on back
On a train, on a bus
In a trance, in a truss
Without fanfare or fuss
Come home.

THE MOTOR OF EMOTION. In "Gentle on My Mind" John Hartford wrote a paeon in both senses of the word. A paeon is two things: It's any song or hymn of joy, praise, or triumph, and it's also the name of a classic four-syllable foot composed of one long and three short syllables (TUMtatata).

GENTLE ON MY MIND

It's/know-ing that your/door is al-ways/o-pen and your/path is
free to/walk
That/makes me tend to/leave my sleep-ing/bag rolled up and/
stashed be-hind your/couch,
And it's/know-ing I'm not/shack-led by for-/got-ten words and/
bonds and the/ink stains that have/dried upon some/line
That/keeps you in the/back-roads by the/riv-ers of my/mem-'ry
that/keeps you ev-er/GEN-TLE ON MY/MIND.

It's not/cling-ing to the/rocks and/iv-y/plant-ed on their/col-
umns now that/binds me
Or/some-thing that some-/bod-y said be-/cause they thought
we/fit to-geth-er/walk-in'
It's just/know-ing that the/world will not be/curs-ing or for-/
giv-ing when I/walk a-long some/rail-road track and/find
That you're/mov-ing on the/back-roads by the/riv-ers of my/
mem-'ry and for/hou-rs you're just/GENT-LE ON MY
MIND.

Though the/wheat fields and the/clothes lines and/junk-yards
and the/high-ways come be-/tween us
And some/oth-er wo-man/cry-ing to her/moth-er 'cause she/
turned and I was/gone
I still run in/si-lence, tears of/joy might stain my/face—and/
sum-mer sun might/burn me 'til I'm/blind
But/not to where I/can-not see you/walk-in' on the/back-roads
by the/ri-vers flow-ing/GENT-LE ON MY MIND.

*I/dip my cup of/soup back from the/gurg-lin' cracklin'/caldron
    in some/train yard
My/beard a rough-'ning/coal pile and a/dir-ty hat pulled/low a-
    cross my/face
Through/cupped hands 'round/a tin can I pre-/tend I hold you/
    to my breast and/find
That you're/wav-ing from the/back-roads by the/riv-ers of my/
    mem-'ry ev-er/smil-in' ev-er/GENT-LE ON MY MIND.*

The lyric pulses like a chugging freight train. Its incessant TUM-ta-ta-ta, TUM-ta-ta-ta, TUM-ta-ta-ta carries us across the wheat fields and high- ways and rivers of a wanderer whose recurring vision of an ever-waiting lover gives him the only roots he knows. Hear how midline spondees work to stress the words he wants emphasized: *ink stains, back roads, cupped hands, tin can;* they break up the regularity of the paeon meter and under- score the earthy words.

John Hartford discussed with me some lyric-writing techniques that concerned him around the time "Gentle" was conceived. Among them was meter: "At that time I was very much intrigued with the fact that most songs did not run at the normal gait that speech runs at. Some songs are like listening to someone who talks real slow. I tend to want to say, 'Come on, come on, say it, say it, I ain't got all day.' That's what governed the speed of 'Gentle'; I wanted a lyric that went past your ear at a faster speed that was closer to speech.

"It came out more like prose—I wasn't really thinking lyrically—I was thinking more like writing a letter to somebody. I was in a mood, and I was just putting down the mood. It came out so fast it's hard to say, but I think the lyrics came first but the music was right there after I wrote it. It all took about fifteen or twenty minutes. I didn't have the title—I started writ- ing the lyrics and when I got down to that part of the song I just kind of came into it. So that's what I called it. In fact I almost changed that title line because I thought it was too commonplace.

"The song was written on the banjo, which has a lot to do with its harmonic construction. I had the melody and the chord progression in my mind, so I started singing it right off the page. Then I corrected a few things. At that time I was fascinated trying to write songs that didn't rhyme but sounded like they did. I think that sometimes rhyme can get in the way of meaning. 'Gentle' has very little rhyme."

When I asked if the song had some particular personal signifi- cance for him, Hartford responded: "Oh, definitely." His choice of the me- ter was instinctive, making it substantiate meaning, just as it should. The song rings true. Perhaps that's why "Gentle on My Mind" has earned a unique place in the annals of BMI, as the only song ever to be honored as the Most Performed Country Song of the Year for *three* consecutive years.

"The Gambler's" Last Ride

After his father's death, Don Schlitz admitted to being "so caught up in my own feelings . . . I had been blocked for about six months." Then one night, while he was experimenting with the open D tuning on the guitar, "The Gambler" poured out in twenty minutes. Later, in analyzing his own lyric, he concluded: "The song was about my father. I translated the meaning of his influence on me into the influence of the gambler upon the singer of the song."

A finely wrought song such as "The Gambler" (page 51) rings true in every detail, including its meter. Schlitz chose the rhythm of a three-foot line (one, two THREE [silent four]) for his gambler's last train ride. The butting of those midline stressed syllables—*warm/summer, train/bound for, took/turns a*—effectively slows down the words, adding weight to their meaning. His primary falling rhythm, DUM/DUM da/DUM da ("train bound for nowhere"), fittingly matches the somber cadence of Chopin's "Funeral March" from the B minor sonata: DUM/DUM da/ DUM/DUM da/DUM da/DUM da/DUM. The meter not only supports, but augments, the meaning.

A CASE IN POINT: "EVERY BREATH YOU TAKE." In discussing the qualities of a fine poem, critic John Crowe Ransom once commented: ". . . [it] approaches to merit—even to virtue—when its head, heart, and feet, are all cooperating." The remark might as easily have been made about the 1983 Grammy song of the year, "Every Breath You Take," written by Sting of The Police. Obsession is the theme, and every element of the song—its words, its rhyme scheme, its bass figure, and most of all its meter—not only support it but reinforce it. The incessant and unvarying rhythm, TUMta/TUM/taTUM, that frames its A sections contributes immeasurably to the song's total effect. But, with the instincts of a trained talent, Sting knew precisely when enough was enough and gave us a change of pace by augmenting this classic AABA with a C section that has a fresh accent.

EVERY BREATH YOU TAKE

A: *EVERY BREATH YOU TAKE*
Every move you make
Every bond you break
Every step you take
I'll be watching you.

A: *Every single day*
Every word you say
Every game you play
Every night you stay
I'll be watching you.

B: *Oh can't you see*
You belong to me
How my poor heart aches
With every step you take.

A: *Every move you make*
Every vow you break
Every smile you fake
Every claim you stake
I'll be watching you.

C: *Since you've been gone I been lost without a trace*
I dream at night I can only see your face
I look around but it's you I can't replace
I feel so cold and I long for your embrace
I keep crying baby, baby please.

B: *Oh can't you see*
You belong to me
How my poor heart aches
With every step you take.

A: *Every move you make*
Every vow you break
Every smile you fake
Every claim you stake
I'll be watching you.

Coda: *Every move you make*
Every step you take
I'll be watching you
I'll be watching you
I'll be watching you

In discussing the genesis of his international hit, Sting said: "I woke up in the middle of the night . . . and went straight to the piano, and the chords and song just came out within ten minutes. If there's a feeling of sadness . . . it's genuine." As if we couldn't tell! The song was obviously a spontaneous and deeply felt work, and that's why it evoked a worldwide response.

An Expert Creates the Beat

It would appear that meter is pretty much an instinctive matter. Certainly it was in "Gentle on My Mind," "The Gambler," and "Every Breath You Take." Those are close-to-the-bone songs: words and music fused in the heat of the writers' deep personal concerns. But what do you do when you're not bursting with an idea to express? When a song doesn't emerge in a twenty-minute miracle? When you have to write something—for a collaborator, or a singer, or a character in a show? That's when you need craft. Nothing illustrates the informed process better than the way Stephen Sondheim sets about writing theater songs.

The kind of detailed thought that precedes Sondheim's writing—the mental steps he takes to discover the authentic rhythm of a character's words in a particular scene—can serve as a navigational chart for every songwriter. In an interview with Samuel J. Freedman in the *New York Times Magazine*, Sondheim discussed the genesis of his most famous song, "Send in the Clowns." Once again, meter emanated from emotion—not the personal emotion of the writer this time, but the emotion of a character which the writer clearly understood. Sondheim first gave thought to what Desirée was feeling in a scene with her former lover: "wounded" is how he succinctly labeled it. The situation is ironic: just when she's decided, after all these years, that she wants him, he's unavailable. How would she react? He considered Desirée's unsentimental personality—someone "who doesn't want to give in to the depth of her feelings." Would she make statements? Would she ask questions? Questions, he decided. But not long ones: He thought that *"someone who was wounded wouldn't speak in long phrases"* (italics mine). Therefore, he narrowed it down to short questions. Ironic questions: the song should have a "light, dry quality about it, rather than a sweet quality."

Now, out come the Blackwing 602 soft lead pencils, a stack of yellow legal pads (one for every stanza in a song), and a thesaurus and rhyming dictionary. The actual writing process starts. What would she say? He begins to put down random thoughts: "We are a pair of fools, aren't we?" Then "It's really funny." And then, "Isn't it fun?" The words *bliss* and *farce* and *rich* appear on the pad. Finally, "Aren't we a pair?" A rhythm is emerging: TUMta/taTUM/TUMta/taTUM. The rhythm triggers a melody. A song is beginning, one with authenticity born of a combination of insight and craft: the magic fusion.

WRAPUP

If the choice of meter is as instinctive as it appears to be, how can a songwriter ensure that emotion, meaning, and meter coalesce? Certainly, part of the technique lies in an understanding of the ways in which stresses, pauses, and the length of lines work with words. As you listen to successful songs, analyze how rhythm contributes to their emotional effect. Also study your own lyrics to see if the rhythm of your words is doing the job you want done.

Every idea can be expressed hundreds of different ways. Now that you know what a spondee and an anapest can do, experiment. Try out different rhythmic versions of the same thought until one feels just right. Take your time. Not all successful songs were written in twenty minutes. Remember, it took Ira Gershwin two weeks to figure out how to handle DUM/DUM/DUMda.

chapter 20

Setting the Tune

"To simplify the task of writing a lyric to a melody . . . I suggest that finding a suitable title is half the battle." Arthur Schwartz

"A good lyric writer can put words to music and have it come out as though he'd put music to words." Howard Dietz

WHEN THE MUSIC COMES FIRST

Ideally, the listener shouldn't be able to answer the standard songwriter interview question: "Which came first, the lyric or the tune?" The fitting together of words and music should be seamless, sounding as though the whole song came from one mind and one heart. The best songs sound that way, even when they didn't. It takes a lot of craftsmanship on the part of the lyricist to make it appear that the composer wrote it all.

What constitutes the perfect wedding of words to music? In essence, the words should sound inevitable. They should be so fused to the tune that they leave a verbal afterimage whenever the music alone is played. Every word should *sing,* with no word warped out of its natural shape to accommodate the meter of the melody. The rhymes should surprise us, or at the very least, please us—but never telegraph themselves. The emotional peak of the lyric and the emotional peak of the music should coincide. Those are the qualities of a perfect marriage. Ideally, the lyric says something fresh that no one has ever said quite that way before.

Identify the Mood of the Tune

Although the purpose for which you set words to a melody will vary—the finished song may be targeted for a pop artist, a scene in a musical, a children's album, a movie or TV theme, or a supper club act—the fundamental guidelines remain the same: the words must support the emotional statement of the music. Identifying the mood will help put you on the right emotional track.

What is the feeling of the melody? Is it posing a question? Is it making an assertion? Is it celebratory, lighthearted, ruminative? Is it wistful like "Autumn Leaves"? Introspective like "If You Go Away"? Optimistic like "Great Day"? Buoyant like "Lullaby of Birdland"? Or jaunty like "Fascinating Rhythm"? In each of these songs a lyricist reinforced the mood of the melody so artfully that the words and music sound as if they were written simultaneously. That is the art of writing words to music.

DON'T CONTRADICT THE TUNE'S EMOTIONS. Not only must the words match the accents of the music, and the emotion of the melodic peaks and valleys and harmonic nuances, but the combined effect of the component parts must make a unified statement. Certain combinations don't work. If, for example, the music is a melancholy melody sounding as though its heart is broken because love is over, like "Summer Knows" (from the film *Summer of '42*), the lyric certainly can't celebrate the start of a relationship, sighing "hip, hip, hurray, hip, hip, hurray, hip, hip, hurray" over a wistful closing A minor melody. A student actually made such a misalliance: the rhythm of the words fit, but their sentiment contradicted that of the melody. Such a mispairing dooms a song to oblivion because the music makes a liar of the words. The lyricist, instead of trying to discover what the tune was saying, superimposed his idea on top of it. The *unintentional* effect was ironic, resulting from the incongruity of the conflicting statements: the music said "how sad," while the lyric was saying "how marvelous!"

Musicologist Alec Wilder, in his classic *American Popular Song,* cited the bewildering mismatch of a Yip Harburg lyric, "This Is Only the Beginning," whose sentiment belies "the somber, almost tragic" flavor of its Harold Arlen melody. The song, composed for the 1933 film *Let's Fall in Love,* possesses one of Arlen's most beautiful, but unrecorded, melodies. Because of a tune's marriage to an unsuitable lyric, the song is virtually unknown.

DON'T TRIVIALIZE THE TUNE'S EMOTION. Another kind of mismatch is a trivial or lighthearted idea wedded to a melody of some substance. As a case in point: Burton Lane once played me one of his characteristically elegant melodies—a slow, wistful waltz built on the rhythmic motif: TUM ta ta/TUM TUM. The rhythm, melody, harmony, and tempo combined to suggest a thought of some weight—for example, "once in my lifetime" or "you'll be my last love." But not "pancakes for breakfast," "love on a ski lift." What Lane's lyricist wrote is more like the latter pair than the former. The syllables fit the melody, but the idea was too lightweight. The character of the music called for a lyric that would match the weight of its emotion. What it got was a lyric that trivialized it. Consequently, another beautiful melody has never been recorded.

Once in a great while, an incompatible pairing slips through the editorial talents of composer, lyricist, producer, and artist and makes it to vinyl: an infrequently programmed album cut of Frank Sinatra's extolls the pleasures of leisurely Sunday morning lovemaking—surely one of life's delights. The odd alliance of its jaunty brunch-in-bed words teamed with a plaintive melody makes the romp sound about as much fun as reading the obits. On occasion, the ears of even top professionals can be out to brunch.

Thus, words cannot violate the inherent sentiment in the music either by contradicting or trivializing it. What they *can* do is artfully play against a melody, understate or overstate it for effect, and, of course, duplicate its expressed emotion.

ALWAYS CONSIDER THE TEMPO. Irving Berlin's uptempo "Blue Skies" proves that minor is not always sad. The apparent dichotomy between the minor melody and the sunny outlook of its lyric has had song analysts wagging their heads for decades. Its affirmative lyric would seem to contradict what's just been said about mismatching the emotion expressed by the tune. But the lively tempo is the key, modifying the wistfulness. The tune as an instrumental simply does not *sound* sad—minor mode notwithstanding. Tempo is always a significant factor.

Beginning writers confronted with a slow ballad in the minor frequently match it identically in mood, thereby reinforcing its sadness to such a degree that it blankets the audience with melancholy. The object is to touch, not oppress. The amateur often etches misery in stone: "I'll always feel the pain/every time I hear your name." "I'll long for you to the day I die." Such overstatement evokes as much genuine feeling in the audience as a silent film villain tying the heroine to the railroad tracks.

A pensive tune does not automatically require a sad lyric. A positive romantic sentiment works well with a thoughtful melody; the pairing serves to reinforce the genuineness of the emotion in "Always" (Berlin), "More Than You Know" (Eliscu/Rose/Youmans), and the Youmans/ Edward Heyman classic, "Through the Years": the lyrics are saying you'll be the only one for me forever—and they ring true.

LEAVE A LITTLE HOPE. William Butler Yeats's contention— that we love "what vanishes"—may account for the perennial appeal of the breakup song. Audiences, as we know, like to relive peak emotional experiences through songs. It seems that the most affecting (and enduring) breakup songs acknowledge present sadness, without predictions of lifetime despondency, as in such ballads as "I'll Remember April," "I'll Never Love This Way Again," and "I Wouldn't Have Missed It for the World." The secret of such successes may be that they leave listeners with an expectation that time heals all things: "I'll remember April, and I'll smile," "I'll stand here and remember just how good it's been . . .," "I'm glad for all the good times. . . ."

An unleavened sad lyric teamed with a melancholy tune produced those three-minute sagas of female despondency known in the twenties and thirties as torch songs: "Can't Help Lovin' Dat Man" and "Stormy Weather." But torch songs, like art deco, are relics of the past—collector's items, not contemporary designs. Today's emphasis on emotional well-being frowns on the lyrical wimp.

Try Emotional Counterpoint

Many times words and music make surprising bedfellows. Think, for example, about "They Can't Take That Away from Me." Ira Gershwin was presented with a finger-snapping tune, and he chose to use it as the framework for a blithe (Fred Astaire to Ginger Rogers) breakup song: It's over, but I'll be all right—I'll remember the best of you and me. Kay Swift's lilting melody to "Can't We Be Friends" was similarly teamed to a lyric by Paul James declaring that once again love was a letdown. The continued popularity of these songs both written over a half-century ago lies in their genial acceptance that all good things must end, and life goes on. The audience is both entertained and touched.

Larry Hart played against the romantic lilt of a Richard Rodgers melody to memorialize the self-mocking saga of an older woman's fatal attraction to a young gigolo in "Bewitched." The combination resulted in a classic and enduring "charm song."

THE UPTEMPO/DOWNBEAT COMBO. As odd as it may seem at first, a downbeat idea can work with a bright lively tune—if the attitude is lighthearted. Hal David's sound instinct for lyrically playing against a carefree melody has resulted in some memorable songs: "There's Always Something There to Remind Me," "Raindrops Keep Falling on My Head," and "I'll Never Fall in Love Again." In "Raindrops," everything in the singer's world is going wrong, but instead of feeling dejected or self-pitying, he's smilingly philosophical.

Hal David reinforces the breezy tone of "I'll Never Fall in Love Again" with rhymes like *phone ya/pneumonia*. The song's conclusion confirms what we knew all along: that the singer has been complaining tongue-in-cheek and can't wait for the next romantic adventure.

The uptempo lament hits the top of the charts time and again. Our fingers snap and our feet tap while we complain "It's too late, baby, it's too late," "I can't smile without you," "Nothing but a heartache," "It never rains in California, it just pours," "I'm alone again, naturally," or "Why did you have to be a heartbreaker?" The listener sings along, acknowledging life's bad luck, breakups, hard times—even death—but the lilting optimism of the music tells us to try to shrug off depression. The downbeat/uptempo song works as catharsis to get us through life's low spots.

INTENTIONAL IRONY. What if irony is your intention? What if you wish to tell the audience: don't be fooled by the singer's stiff-upper-lip attitude, the doleful emotion of the *melody* is what she's actually feeling? That's *purposefully* playing against the message of the music. You'll remember how Barbra Streisand first burst upon the scene with her uniquely downbeat treatment of "Happy Days Are Here Again"; by slowing the tempo and reinterpreting the spirit (without changing a word or a chord), she told us that *un*happy days were here again for her.

Stephen Sondheim counterpointed the cynical outlook of "(ah well) Every Day a Little Death" against a bouncy waltz. How else could "death" in a song's title have been made acceptable! In "She Knows" (page 57) I intentionally mated the word "hooray" with a diminished chord to underscore the discrepancy between the singer's claim and her true feelings. In spite of her gutsy goodbye ("I say hooray for what's been"), as she sends her lover back to his wife, it's perfectly clear to the audience, hearing that harmonic shift, that the moment he walks out the door she'll cry. The song always works its desired effect upon an audience; *they* cry because the lyric didn't. Treating important things casually engenders poignancy whereas treating them flippantly is likely to render them trivial and therefore humorous. (As in "Lizzie Borden" on page 182).

SOME GUIDELINES TO FITTING THE WORDS TO THE MUSIC

Listen to What the Music Is Saying

A lyricist needs to be a kind of tune sleuth, searching for clues to solve the mystery contained in the melody. "Every piece of music says something," says Hal David. "When you write to a melody, you're trying to find what the melody is saying." Most fine lyricists start with the premise that the words must be pulled from within the tune, not be superimposed from without. In theory, any number of serviceable lyrics can be written to a wonderful melody, but I believe that only one perfect one can.

The first lyric a tune gets isn't always the ideal mate. Nor is the last. Sometimes the right lyricist, the one who will hear what the tune is really saying, isn't around when the melody needs words. Vernon Duke had a melody languishing in obscurity mated to a lyric, "Face the Music with Me," until Ira Gershwin got the chance to discover that the tune actually was saying, "I Can't Get Started with You." A charming summer camp song by Larry Hart and Arthur Schwartz, "I Love to Lie Awake in Bed," found its ultimate lyric when the music spoke to Howard Dietz: "I Guess I'll Have to Change My Plan." The melody of Peabo Bryson's 1984 chart hit "If Ever You're In My Arms Again" (Michael Masser/Tom Snow) came alive only with its second lyric, when Cynthia Weil discovered what the tune seemed to be saying.

Internalize the Tune

After you have identified the mood of the music and considered all the potential treatments, the next step is to memorize the melody. Play it over and over and over, however many times it takes to program your psyche with it. Once you know it by heart, it will begin to speak to you. From all that playing of the melody and asking yourself, "What is the music saying?" words will start popping into your head. Let the stream of consciousness flow. Honor those random words or lines; write them down, however seemingly disconnected. One will be the open sesame to the lyric.

My own favorite procedure, after internalizing the melody, is to test dummy vowel sounds that seem to be suggested by the tune. The process tends to "magnetize" a tentative sound pattern, not specific rhymes, necessarily, but a sonic palette of *-ay-, -ee-, -i-, -o-, -oo-* sounds which respond to both the melodic and harmonic texture of the music. Often the sound leads to the sense, and the sense to the title.

Find the Title Spot

One of the most practical and widely used techniques is to spot the title line and work from there. All strong AAA, AABA, and verse/chorus melodies assert at least one title placement, sometimes two. The accomplished word writer chooses the music's most dominant and memorable strain. As Irving Berlin put it ". . . if the title and tune are tied together . . . [it] enables the listener to remember the song."

As you know from the chapters on structure, there is an ideal place for the title in each of the three forms. As strongly as I believe in the usefulness of the "title first" procedure, I recognize that creativity dictates no immutable methods. Unquestionably, there are times when a writer discovers what he or she has to say only in the process of saying it. Every song has a life of its own. Sometimes an idea takes over that vetoes all the "rules." Don't fight it; there's a method in every *genuine* emotion. The wise lyricist will follow the pull of the idea, letting the first draft pour out and polishing from there. The one right title will eventually emerge.

To Make the Words Sing, Sing Them

Because every word must sing, the lyricist must sing. Many of the most successful writers of words to music—Hart, Caesar, Mercer, Gershwin, Fields, and so on—claimed they sang as they wrote, as a test of the sense, the sound, and the singability. The best contemporary writers continue the technique. Cynthia Weil told me, "I learn the music until it's organic, so that when I'm in the car I can be singing, because a lot of my work goes on while I'm driving." Dean Pitchford, lyricist of the score of the film *Footloose,* has said: "I always write a lyric thinking about how it would feel to sing. Would the sentiments feel good in the mouth?" To which I would add, "And do the syllables sound right to the ear?"

Don't Warp the Words

There is no art at all in merely putting words to notes. It's *what* words with *which* notes. No serious craftsman will distort a word's pronunciation to accommodate a music's rhythmic pattern—except for humorous effect. "Good prosody" means that all words are sung the way we speak them. It may take a lot of floor pacing and erasures to eliminate the offenders, but writers who aspire to quality lyrics always seek to pass the ultimate test: When you read the words, the music plays.

Sad to say, many a beautiful tune has been saddled with a second-rate lyric and, as a consequence, the song is heard primarily in instrumental records. Discriminating singers will simply pass over songs whose words either are inept or have been contorted to accommodate the melody. Recording artists like Linda Ronstadt and Willie Nelson, not finding compelling contemporary songs, have sought out the classics.

Poor prosody frequently results from a particular melodic pattern that snares the unskillful: If the tune you're setting ends with a phrase of three sustained notes, beware. That slow TUM TUM TUM is the trap. The inept (or lazy) lyricist looking for a quick rhyme, picks a three-syllable word instead of three one-syllable ones whereby the stress would automatically be even and, consequently, perfect. Hence we hear many lyrics with words mis-stressed into *rev-er-IE, ten-der-LY,* and *fan-ta-SY.* It's worth restating a point already made in the rhyme chapter: try a three-word combination such as *home to me/glad to see/when you're free,* and so on. Three-syllable words work best where they can be sung the way they're spoken: Paul McCartney made the perfect marriage when he placed *YES-ter-day* squarely on his melodic DUM da da.

Make Your Emphasis Match Your Meaning

In poetry, ambiguity not only is permissible, often it's desirable. Not in lyrics. A well-written song communicates instantly and clearly. Clarity is achieved partly through syntax—the arrangement of the words in a logical order—and partly through the rhythmic emphasis given key words. *Emphasis changes meaning.* If emphasis is carelessly placed where it wasn't intended, meaning will be obscure or distorted.

A simple five-word phrase will illustrate the danger of ambiguity: "You don't want me anymore." Isolated from a context or a musical underpinning, it is wide open to interpretation. Meaning alters with each shift in emphasis:

> *You* don't want me anymore (but *he* wants me)
> You *don't* want me anymore (you just *say* you do)
> You don't *want* me anymore (but you *need* me)
> You don't want *me* anymore (you want *her*)
> You don't want me *anymore* (though you *used* to want me)

To ensure that your listener perceives your intended meaning, you must place the word you want stressed on a stressed note. In other words, if the music is going *DA*da dada dada da, and you want to say, "*YOU* don't want me anymore," you've done it; the accents match, and your meaning is clear. *However,* if you wish to say "You DON'T want me anymore!" you flunked. The music italicized the *first* note, not the second, so you did not say what you intended to say. The right words alone are inadequate; they need to fall on the right accents. Meter and meaning must coalesce.

As a general rule, words or lines denoting rising or falling emotions or actions should coincide with similar movement in the melody. For example, ideas like "high on a hill," "reaching for a star," "up in the clouds" tend to sound incongruous paired with a descending melodic phrase; similarly, "down in the dumps" or "I'm feelin' so low" would be less effective linked to a rising one.

THE ANATOMY OF A FILM SONG

When the wedding of words and music is perfect, the lyricist makes it sound as though there had been no struggle, no floor pacing, no anguished decisions over *buts* and *ands,* that it had simply flowed out in a moment's inspiration. "The Shadow of Your Smile" is such a marriage. For the film *The Sandpiper,* Johnny Mandel composed a haunting melody in the ABAC form. The studio then assigned Johnny Mercer to write the lyric. Mercer—certainly a distinguished lyricist of hundreds of hits—was, as it turned out, not the one born to hear what that tune was saying. His lyric was rejected. It was Paul Francis Webster to whom the music spoke.

The first duty of a film lyricist is to capsulize the movie's plot (or a particular scene) in seventy-five words or less—and make it sing. If the sentiment expressed can be made both broadly appealing and timeless, so much the better. Then the life of the song will extend far beyond its function in the film. Here is the lyric complete with the introductory verse:

THE SHADOW OF YOUR SMILE

Verse: *One day we walked along the sand*
One day in early spring.
You held a piper in your hand
To mend its broken wing,
Now I'll remember many a day
And many a lonely mile.
The echo of a piper's song
The shadow of a smile.

A: *THE SHADOW OF YOUR SMILE*
When you are gone
Will color all my dreams
And light the dawn.

B: *Look into my eyes,*
My love, and see
All the lovely things
You are to me.

A: *Our wistful little star*
Was far too high
A teardrop kissed your lips
And so did I.

C: *Now when I remember spring*
All the joys that love can bring
I will be remembering
THE SHADOW OF YOUR SMILE.

"The Shadow of Your Smile" meets every criterion for a well-wrought lyric and passes the ultimate test: when you think of the words, you hear the music. That's doing the job. Webster outlined the song, top and bottom, with the title. With only one hearing, we all knew what to ask for in the record store.

The rhyme scheme is ideal: he wisely chose to treat each four-bar musical phrase (in the ABAC section) as a whole thought, without breaking it in two with a rhyme. Amateurs sometimes think that rhyming in itself is an indicator of talent, or that the more rhymes, the more Brownie points. Given the melody's short phrases, rhyming every line would have produced a jingle-jangle sound devoid of feeling. A nonpro might have come up with something like "The shadow of your smile/when you are gone/is something I know I'll/miss night and dawn." In the melody's final C section, the descending melodic sequence virtually demanded a triple rhyme scheme—which a pro instinctively delivered. It's evident that Paul Francis Webster *sang* as he wrote this lyric. The words feel good in the mouth and sound good to the ear. On every important note we hear a one-syllable word: *smile, gone, dreams, dawn, eyes, things, me, star, high, lips, I.* Also the words are singable, long vowels (*day, see, me*) and diphthongs (*high, I*) that allow the mouth to be open wide.

Reading the lyric aloud will help you hear a subtle tonal design: the final words in each *non*rhyming line of the AB section—*smile/dreams/eyes/things*—make a pattern of alternating assonance, -i-/-e-/-i-/-e-. There's nothing remarkable about that, other than the fact that it reflects the ear of a lyricist who delights in making vowel music.

Now here's something only the top-notch craftsmen demand of themselves: each line's final word flows smoothly into the opening word of the next line. This is a hallmark of an eminently singable song: on one breath a singer can meld one word into another: *gone* pours into *will, dawn* into *look, see* into *all, me* into *our,* and on throughout the lyric. Nowhere at the end of a line does a closed consonant (*b, p, k, t*) inhibit the singer's phrasing. Such back-to-back pairings as *look kind* or *can't part,* for example, require the mouth to reform before pronouncing the second word. The sole instance of a butting of closed consonants is *teardrop kissed,* which comes in a melodic spot where the singer can pause a millisecond to get ready for the -k-.

"The Shadow of Your Smile" is a lyric that is easy to remember. This is so not solely because of its brevity (many short lyrics defy memorization), but because of a number of devices Webster used that make for memorability: for example, the parallelism of *your hand* and *my dreams;* the repetition of my eyes/my love; the alliteration of the liquid -l- threaded throughout the lyric subtly linking *will, color, all, light, look, love, all, lovely, little, lips, love, will,* the inner rhyme *star* and *far;* and the (augmented) repetition of *love/lovely remember/remembering.* All this is aided, of course, by full end rhyme. The melody of "The Shadow of Your Smile," independent of words, would rate recordings, but paired to a lesser lyric, it might never have earned, as it did, both the 1965 Grammy and Oscar awards.

Good writing sometimes appears deceptively easy. Ironically, it is from bad writing that we can often learn the most. To illustrate what *not* to do, I've purposely mutilated Paul Francis Webster's lyric concept and violated virtually every tenet of good prosody:

THE ECHO OF YOUR LAUGHTER

THE ECHO OF YOUR LAUGH-
TER *in the rain*
Is bound to cheer me up
And ease my pain

Won't you look into
my eyes and see
That I love you oh
so ten-der-ly

Our wistful little can-
dle burned too fast
I should have seen that it
could never last

Though I know it sounds absurd
Yet each time I'll hear a bird
I will think of when I heard
THE ECHO OF YOUR LAUGH.

For starters, a song's title should rest squarely on the melody's dominant strain. In this case, the opening five-note pickup phrase (anacrusis), culminating on the downbeat, lala lala laLA, is clearly the title spot. When you merely think the words "The Shadow of Your Smile," you hear Johnny Mandel's melody. "The Echo of Your Laugh*ter*" overlaps the melodic phrase instead of sitting firmly on it. So the lyric is off to a poor start.

The opening line compounds the error. End-of-line notes, where the music comes to a natural pause, should be mated with significant—and whole—words, not with a meaningless syllable: *up, (in)-to, oh, -ly, can-(dle), it,* signify nothing. Compare those *sounds* to the specificity of *smile, dreams, eyes, things, star, lips!*

Here's another common blunder: a trivial word is stressed. In the second line the preposition *in* has been highlighted by being placed on a sustained dotted half note. Webster, of course, gave the emphasis to an important word, *you.* Such fragmented thoughts as "Won't you look into," "our wistful little can-," and "I should have seen that it" underscore the importance of mating a complete thought to a musical phrase. As we know, even the best of run-on lines are a risk. They should at least end on a full word, not a syllable which, by breaking the phrase in two parts, makes the listener wait three beats for the end of the idea.

Here's a double whammy: the word *up* simultaneously breaks two precepts of good writing; in addition to hampering the singer with a closed *-p-* on a sustained note, it also contradicts the direction of the melody. Now we come to word warping, that esthetic offense against the ear. *Ly,* a meaningless syllable, does not warrant the emphasis of being held for a full measure. My campaign against splitting a trisyllabic word into three stretched-out parts may achieve no more results than Edwin Newman's crusade against the widespread misuse of *hopefully,* but I'd like to think it might. A lyric writer who is constantly singing while writing will easily spot the hiss of "sound*s* absur*d*" and the thud of three deadly *d*s in *absurd, bird,* and *heard.*

In the preface to his book *Lyrics,* Oscar Hammerstein tells a story about a failed calculated risk he made. In writing the lyric to "What's the Use of Wond'rin'?" a charming song from *Carousel* he knowingly violated a cardinal law of lyric writing: always end a song with an open-vowel word. He very much wanted to say, ". . . and all the rest is talk"—and he did. The song was never a success beyond the show, and Hammerstein attributed its failure to his flouting a fundamental principle of lyric writing. He said he would never take such a risk again.

WRAPUP

You learn how to write words to music, of course, by writing words to music. No one is excused from practice on the plea, "I don't have a collaborator." You do. You have your pick of composers, past and present—from Bach to Bacharach. To start off, you could challenge yourself to reset Johnny Mandel's melody for "The Shadow of Your Smile." Or you could turn a public-domain (free from copyright restrictions) classical theme from Tchaikovsky, Chopin, Dvorak, Rachmaninoff—to name a few who have been raided—into a pop song. Plunge in. Get a first draft down. Check it against professional criteria outlined in this chapter. Then eliminate the flab, and polish until every word sings.

chapter 21

Putting It Together: Styles of Collaboration

"Part of this awful process is finding a wonderful composer. The ideal situation is to write both. There is no substitute for a single mind attempting to achieve a work of art." Carolyn Leigh

"A collaborator . . . must be somebody compatible, somebody whom—in the broadest sense of the word—you can trust."
Dorothy Fields

You don't need all ten fingers to count the truly outstanding, prolific, enduring words and music collaborations: Gershwin and Gershwin, Rodgers and Hart, Rodgers and Hammerstein, Lerner and Loewe, Schwartz and Dietz, Kander and Ebb, Bacharach and David, Mann and Weil.

Collaboration appears to be a short-term affair, even for its enthusiastic advocates; sometimes it's only a one-song stand. An ongoing songwriting partnership is one of the most intimate of relationships. In order to survive, it has to be founded on mutual trust and respect, each teammate manifesting flexibility and an honesty tempered by tact. That's a tall order to fill, much less sustain.

For noncomposing lyricists, collaboration is a necessity, but for the twice blessed it's an option many frequently decline. Rupert Holmes summed up his attitude toward collaboration this way: "I don't like it. I think of it as one bolt of cloth. I can't separate the music from the lyrics. One spawns the other; it's a hand-over-hand process." Randy Goodrum seconds the emotion: "I've tried co-writing, but I enjoy writing by myself. It's like co-painting a picture. You get more enjoyment if you paint it yourself." At a Songwriters Guild seminar on theater writing Stephen Sondheim was asked, "Do you miss having a composer to argue with?" He quickly replied, "The answer is no."

From the lyricists' point of view, the process, of necessity, gets mostly positive reviews. Yip Harburg relished the variety in partnerships: ". . . each elicits a different style or mood from you . . . a different psychological experience." The hit country team of Kye Fleming and Dennis Morgan votes in favor: "Co-writing is better because you can bounce things off each other. If you're going out on a limb, you can bring each other back. We feed off each other all the time." Carole Sager told me: "I feel much better when somebody is there as a sounding board. I love the feedback of somebody else who can say, 'I love that—I hate that—give it to me another way.' "

DEALING WITH POTENTIAL PROBLEMS

Be Sure You're Working From the Same Script

That's the plus side, but there are pitfalls too, especially when two heads are trying to fashion one lyric. Carole Sager told me about a particular incident: "Collaborating can run into trouble when one says, 'I don't want to say that, that's not how I feel it,' and the other says, 'But that's how *I* feel it.' It happened on a song with Peter Allen. To me the final lyric didn't make any sense. It was recorded in fact by Helen Reddy as an album cut, but I don't think it could ever be a hit song. It was called, 'Ah My Sister.' I had one distinct idea in mind and Peter had another. I was talking about a kind of sisterhood of women and Peter was talking about his actual familial sister, and we fought each other on it in terms of what we would be contributing and what we would end up with. It was a total mixture of thought which sounded to me schizophrenic." (Carole Sager's experience is not uncommon: I found that when two lyricists collaborate on the same song an unfocused lyric often results.)

Honesty Versus Diplomacy

Collaboration can be a difficult process. How does one reject a lyrical phrase or melodic line without rejecting the writer? How can one be candid without being hurtful? There are no pat answers. Veteran composer Burton Lane told me his credo: "I believe in total honesty. The first thing I say to every lyric writer who works with me for the first time is, 'I never want you to write a lyric to a melody you don't love. Forget it! And I want the exact same treatment from you—that you never try to force an idea on me that isn't right.' The only way two people with talent can come up with something they like is if they are honest." Richard Kerr echoes Lane's demand for candor: "You have to be able to say whatever you feel; if you don't like a line of lyric, for example, you can't hold back your feelings, you have to say so."

A musician tends to feel more secure in verbalizing a criticism of a lyric than a nonmusical wordsmith usually is in voicing dissatisfaction with a melody, so it's not surprising that lyricists can be reticent with their composers. Johnny Mercer, for example, said he would "clam up" and sit in a corner a while to wait out the storm: "After all," he confided to author Max Wilk, "how the hell are you going to tell Jerome Kern, 'I don't like that middle, why don't you do it this way?' " Mercer couldn't do that. His criticism would extend only to casual remarks like, "Don't you think it's a little slow (or short, or long)?" Sammy Cahn has a diplomatic way of dealing with his collaborators: "I never tell a composer I don't like his melody. That's a thing that anyone who deals with creativity knows—you never say, 'I don't like that.' There's a gentler, kinder, more graceful way. I say, 'Look, we have this, let's try for something else.' "

Take Responsibility for the Tune

At a seminar for aspiring theater lyricists, Carolyn Leigh summed up her philosophy: "You are responsible for the quality of [your collaborator's] music, and never forget it, because if you let him get away with less than wonderful, you're guilty." Her point was that a composer's best possible melody isn't necessarily his first inspiration. She illustrated with an anecdote on the genesis of "The Best Is Yet to Come":

"In the case of 'The Best Is Yet to Come' I wrote from a title. I had had this idea burning to write. Cy Coleman came over and began playing one of the more banal melodies of the century (forgive me, Cy) and I couldn't get into it. I felt, at best, it was a modest effort, and not worth the energy. So we sat there glaring at each other for a while, and finally I said, 'I can't write a lyric to that. What about the release [the bridge of an AABA]?' And he played [she hums what was to become the opening phrase of the song] and I said, 'You know, *that* I could do!' And he said, 'What would you say, smartie?' I replied, 'Out of the tree of life I just picked me a pl-um.' He said, 'That's ridiculous, that's the release of the song.' I said, 'That's what I hear.' Cy is a brilliant musician and he's smart enough to know when to change his mind; so should we all be! So he took that pattern and then began to paraphrase it melodically. We stayed up all night and finished the song."

That's what good collaborating is all about. Successful teamwork requires both individual self-confidence and mutual trust in the other's talent. Because each knows the partner's potential, either can reject the mediocre and demand the other's best efforts. But the insight required to recognize when a song needs to be better as well as the diplomacy to request changes from a collaborator are the by-products of experience.

Every successful songwriter has a few "if-I'd-only" stories. Carole Sager told me about her early tentativeness with composers: "There're a couple of songs that I would rather I hadn't called completed. I wish I had just put them aside and thought, 'That's not it yet.' Once I used to concentrate just on my lyrics. Now I'm more critical of [my collaborator's] melody—and of the whole. There are a few melodies I set lyrics to in the past that, because my lyrics worked well, I considered that the songs were fine. But in fact, the melodies weren't strong enough for those songs to come out to be hits. So I'm more prone now to stand up and exert my feelings with a composer if I don't think their melody is strong enough. I would be as hard on the composer as I am on myself. I used to be seduced by the fact that the singer was usually the songwriter, right next to me, and it all sounded so compact that I never really listened carefully enough to know that—wait a minute—this may not be a hit melody. Therefore, some very fine lyrics have gone by the wayside, because a great lyric won't do it alone."

Unfortunately, it simply won't, and that's why it's vital that a lyricist make sure every tune passes the "whistle test." My theory is, if you can't hum the main strain of a collaborator's melody after hearing it once, "pass," as the expression goes. It's a safe bet that if you can't remember the

music, neither will the public. To spend time putting words to a tune that you don't hear as a potential success is simply a waste of creative energy.

PROFILES OF WINNING TEAMWORK

The Pop Team: Mann and Weil

The ability to "hear" a hit tune is one of the hallmarks of a successful lyricist. It is a talent that Cynthia Weil has displayed for more than twenty years.

Since 1961, when Barry Mann and Cynthia Weil began their dual partnership in marriage and songwriting, it's been a rare month when either her words or his music has not been on the charts—from the classics "On Broadway" and "You've Lost That Lovin' Feelin'," to such contemporary hits as "Sometimes When We Touch," "Just Once," "Somewhere Down the Road," "If Ever You're in My Arms Again," and "All of You." Their combined hits in every genre from country to R&B have sold over 145 million records.

They learned their craft at what Cynthia calls "The Aldon School"—the New York Brill Building publishing company of fabled record producer Don Kirschner, where they were staff writers in the early sixties. In addition to working together, they have always maintained outside collaborations which serve to revitalize their own. Cynthia, who teams up with such composers as Tom Snow, Michael Masser, and Julio Iglesias, likes to write to a tune: "I feel that if it sounds like a hit before I do anything, then I'm halfway home. Also I find it very hard to criticize melody writers. I'd rather be the one on the line than put someone else on the line." She generally takes home a cassette, plays it enough so that the tune becomes "organic," and works until the right idea starts coming—a process that takes anywhere from a few days to a few weeks. While writing, she self-edits to such a degree that rewriting is virtually unnecessary. Yet, even after her years of sustained success, each time at bat can produce a certain amount of anxiety. She told me, for example, of her first work session with Tom Snow at his house: "We were both scared to death. He said, 'I have a tune, and maybe you'll like it,' and he played it for me. I said it sounded like a hit. Then I got the feeling, Oh God! I hope I can do something." (She turned the tune into "Holding Out for Love," which has had four recordings so far.) Weil admitted that the day Tom Snow played her the melody that eventually became "Somewhere Down the Road" she again "had great feelings of anxiety. Because I loved it so much, and I wanted to do right by it." Cynthia Weil does right by so many melodies that she is one of the most sought-after lyricists in Hollywood. Her songs often express personal feelings ("Come What May," for example), and sometimes those of people in her life, such as "Here You Come Again," which mirrored an experience of a close friend. She sums up the result she tries to achieve in a song: "It should sound as if it's always been."

Barry Mann's composing track record spanning over two decades is, to say the least, impressive. His ongoing success results from keeping his ears on the evolution of musical styles and adapting his talents to the marketplace. Mann, an accomplished pianist who has studied theory at New York's Juilliard School, has also been produced as an artist on Arista records. Says Mann: "Music is not as simple as it was fifteen years ago. Melodic styles have changed incredibly. The Dionne Warwick record ['Never Gonna Let You Go'] took me about a month to write. It's harder for a melody writer to keep up with the times than for a lyricist. I listen a lot. Sometimes I try to analyze. But it's mainly by listening." While writing a tune—even before there's a lyric—Mann is thinking ahead to the record: "We're thinking who it could be for. And how should I approach the song in the demo: Will I need a guitar? Or should I use a Rhodes? Or a piano? Or a synthesizer? What kind of singer should I get? If you're going to write an R&B song, for example, the groove is very important. I have a Roland drum machine that'll do different drum grooves—a rock and roll groove, a rock waltz groove, and you can speed it up or slow it down. I'm now looking to expand my equipment."

Creative growth through experimentation is important to both writers. Accustomed as Barry is to writing a whole melody first and as Cynthia is to setting a lyric to a completed tune, they are seeking new ways to write. Intrigued by the creative methods of award-winning writer/arranger/producer Quincy Jones (who produced "Just Once"), Mann and Weil would like to find a more spontaneous approach to songwriting—maybe from the stimulation of rhythmic grooves and chord changes. Whatever the change in their creative process, it's likely that the future songs of Barry Mann and Cynthia Weil will continue to feature strong melodies and universally appealing lyrics.

Committee-Style Collaboration

The collaborative style of today's pop groups is frequently rap-session writing—simultaneous shaping of words and music with all the partners (sometimes a half dozen) tossing ideas into the musical pot. More often than not, *hit records,* rather than songs, are the objective, and for self-contained groups that dominate the top 40, the "sound" is all. With the Bee Gees, for example, it's always a committee affair. As Barry Gibb put it in an interview in *Songwriter* magazine, "We find that bashing it between each other is the best way." Using their voices as almost another instrument, they "sit and strum until something happens." The Bee Gees don't plan songs, nor do they write them down until they've got the structure pretty well set. When the song is at the point where they can hear the finished record in their heads, they go into the studio. "The matter of production becomes easy because we can hear all the things we want on the record."

With the internationally successful group Abba, the music comes first, because the *sound* is the thing. Lead writer Björn Ulvaeus says:

"Once we have the melody ready, we go into the studio with a phony lyric. Then we record the backtrack and do a few overdubs, and after that the lyric is written."

The touring lifestyle of the top contemporary pop group Huey Lewis and the News is fairly typical: six months a year on the road. Lewis and guitarists Chris Hayes and Johnny Colla write the songs for the group; generally Huey writes the words and Chris and/or Johnny write the music. Their songs represent the point of view of all six band members, who grew up together in the same town in the San Francisco Bay area. A lot of writing goes on in the back lounge of their tour bus, where they "hash around ideas" and put them down on a four-track cassette recorder. When they're home, the scene shifts to a rented rehearsal studio, actually a garage, where another four-track serves to record the spontaneous flow of ideas. Ideally, songs get tested on a live audience in a club before a master is laid down in a 24-track studio. Lewis says that from the live performance he can tell instantly how the song is "wearing . . . if a verse is too long, if the chorus is too short. . . ." The committee work continues right into the studio, where the group produces its own records.

Theatrical Teamwork

Theater songs, written as they are for a particular character in a specific situation, usually require lengthy discussions before the songwriting process begins. The writers must determine what the character is feeling, the motivation for the song, and how it serves the theatrical moment.

Many Broadway teams really do shape their songs in that and-then-I-wrote movie cliché—the composer at the piano (with an overflowing ashtray), his wordsmith pacing the floor, pencil behind the ear. In his biography Alan Jay Lerner confirmed the tableau: when Fritz Loewe improvised at the piano, Lerner stayed unobtrusively in the room throughout the germinating process. As the melody unconsciously took shape, Loewe would "almost go into a trance" until Lerner would suddenly cry out: "Wait, that's it."

In the book *Musical Stages* Richard Rodgers recalled his collaboration with Larry Hart, which had a similar pattern. Although on occasion Hart would hand the composer lyrical fragments—a verse, the start of a chorus, or an inspiring title—"most of the time" Rodgers would play a finished tune and "we'd sit around tossing titles and lyric ideas at each other."

John Kander of Kander and Ebb, a successful team that dates back to 1962, stresses the enjoyment their partnership provides. They work daily together from ten to four, even when they're not working on a specific project: "We're very secure with each other, open and free. We have a very good time writing. And fun is important."

Charles Strouse continues the melody-first tradition: "With everyone I've worked with I just play the melody incessantly and sometimes contribute lyric ideas, and sometimes they have musical ideas. When Lee Adams really liked a tune, he might say, 'Put it down on a cassette and let me work on it over the weekend.' "

Sheldon Harnick enjoys either writing to melodies or constructing lyrics first. He discussed the creative process at an Ask-a-Pro session: "When Jerry Bock and I were working together, it was a wonderful way to work—the way I like best. While I was preparing words, he was preparing music, so that he would give me tapes on which there might be two music ideas. And it's wonderful 'cause I find an idea by virtue of its rhythms—its emotional content—or sometimes just the sheer catchiness of it may suggest lyrics I never would have thought of. In listening and listening and listening, and letting the music sink in, thinking, 'What does it do to me,' lyrics will occur to me and I think, 'Oh boy, bless you for that!' Also I love having music because it solves that very difficult problem—the form." Harnick shifted creative gears working with Joe Raposo on a musicalization of the film, *It's a Wonderful Life*. This time it was lyrics first: "When I write lyrics I always have some kind of a rhythmic scheme in mind. And I try not to write dummy melodies because I may get attached to a dummy melody and then be terribly disappointed when my composer does it his way. So when I sing it out loud to myself, I do it in a rather toneless way, but with a very definite rhythmic scheme. As a matter of fact, I asked Joe if it would be okay if I did something. 'Tell me if you don't want me to do this, and I won't: Is it okay for me to give you a rhythmic lead sheet so that you'll know exactly what I have in mind? Feel free not to use that, but there are passages (which happens) where you can't see any form to what I've given you—it all looks like rambling. At least this way, you'll see what I had in mind and that there's a rhythmic structure to it.' So I've done that a couple of times."

TO SET THE RHYTHM OR NOT. Sheldon Harnick's rhythmic lead sheet concept would be received with delight by some composers and with dread by others. Harnick said he mentioned his experiment to John Kander, who was aghast: "John said, 'Oh my God, if Fred Ebb gave me that, it would handcuff me; I wouldn't be able to feel free in writing my music.' " Thus there are no hard and fast methods, no "best way." Different techniques work with different collaborators. Some lyricists whose sense of rhythmic structure is strong use an "aural" demo for collaborators: they recite into a cassette in a clipped rhythm. Others lay down a rhythm track and read over it in a strict meter. If your collaborator is happy about being directed by your rhythmic concept of the music, fine. A guiding rule of thumb would be: ask first.

POINTING THE DIRECTION WITH YOUR LYRIC SHEET. Even if you don't want to suggest a rhythmic treatment to your composer, it's a good idea to indicate the song's form on your typed lyric sheet; there is always the possibility that your collaborator may know less than you do about structure. As a case in point, I recall the first collaboration of a student who handed his lyric sheet to a pop composer without any discussion of either the form or groove of the song. The musician took the lyric home and, assuming that the third stanza (after the first two verses) was a chorus, treated the lyric musically as a verse/chorus song—despite the fact that the song's title came at the end of each verse and not in the bridge—making it clearly an AABA song. The first time the lyricist heard the melody was when his collaborator played him a studio-made demo; hearing the words of his bridge emphasized musically as if they were the lyric's main statement (and repeated at the conclusion of the song) confused the writer, but being less experienced than his professional composer, he said nothing.

To insure that your lyric gets the right musical form, type AAA, or AABA, or verse/chorus at the top of your lyric sheet; also label each stanza as verse, chorus, or bridge, and clearly indicate your title by either full caps, italics, or underlining. If you are not going to sit down in a room together and kick around musical ideas until your composer comes up with a treatment you both like, at least read the lyric to your collaborator and offer whatever musical thoughts you may have. Before any demo is made, arrange to hear and approve the melody.

It is a collaborating convention that the writer who initiates the song is the one who has to be satisfied by the partner; in other words, if you give a lyric to a composer, he or she must please you. If a composer gives you a melody, you have to turn in a satisfactory lyric. Should the originating writer be totally dissatisfied with the treatment—when the words or the music simply sound all wrong, and there's nothing to salvage—the partner has to be told, as gently as possible. The usual solution is for each to take back the respective words or music, with no hard feelings. The objective in collaborating is to write a song you are *both* enthusiastic about.

WRAPUP

It has been my observation that lyric writers often feel inferior to their collaborators. It's particularly true of lyricists who don't play an instrument, or if they do, are not knowledgeable about music theory. It's not unusual to hear a lyricist say, "I write just the words." I have yet to hear a composer say, "I write just the music."

As already noted, even some of the most successful lyricists tend to have difficulty expressing a negative reaction to a partner's tune. A lyricist may instinctively feel that the chorus should sound more important, or that the chords should sound more varied, but—not knowing how to put such thoughts into musical terms—says nothing. The song and the collaboration are hurt by such silences.

It's important to be articulate about how you want a tune to sound or not sound—to be able to say where it is not working, and to suggest what kind of change might make a stronger melody.

Lyricists should be able to communicate with their collaborators on equal terms. By "equal," I mean by using a musician's own terms, even if that means taking an elementary theory course. The more musically competent the lyricist, the better the collaboration, and of course, the better the song.

"I work damn hard—I edit, I struggle, I throw away, and I resurrect."
Harry Chapin

part six

TAKING IT TO THE LIMIT

chapter 22

Avoiding Common Pitfalls

"Go in fear of abstractions." Ezra Pound

"Most bad writing is the result of ignoring one's own experiences and contriving spurious emotions for spurious characters."
Oscar Hammerstein

A song is an entertainment. All successful lyricists are accomplished entertainers who can provide an audience with an emotionally satisfying experience. All successful songs say something that makes millions of people want to listen, not just once, but over and over again.

What makes us stay tuned? A lyric that presents identifiable characters, understandable situations, and universal emotions. What makes us tune out? A lyric that confuses, bores, or annoys.

No one will remain attentive to a plot that's hard to follow, a situation that's unrecognizable, or a character who is unsympathetic. And no one wants to be preached to or scolded. What the novice needs to learn, in order to graduate to a professional, is the knack of talking to the world so that it will keep listening.

Lyrical faults break down into two main categories: treatable and terminal. A multitude of minor blunders come under the heading of treatable errors; for example, mixed metaphors, ambiguous lines, poor sequence of events, or inconsistent tone. These can be fixed—once the writer recognizes the problem and knows how to deal with it.

A terminal error, on the other hand, is one that disregards the keystone of lyric writing: universality. The most fatal mistake a writer can make is to presume that the world wants to listen to his or her private problem or idiosyncratic attitude. Equally deadly are the sounds of anger and sarcasm.

Often, a poorly written lyric suffers from a number of ailments; in pinpointing the flaws in the following student examples, we'll limit the discussion to those that are central to the lyric's downfall. Here are the most common problems in descending order of seriousness.

The Hidden Scenario

To enjoy a song, the audience must first understand it. The writer's prime objective, therefore, is to transfer the details of the script in his or her head into words on paper. Here's a lyric that resulted from an assignment to write to a given title and chorus, "We Gotta Start Meetin' Like This." It required the lyricist to create, in two verses, a credible situation in which two people accidentally meet and, with a love-at-first-sight feeling, plan to meet again.

WE GOTTA START MEETIN' LIKE THIS

Sparky baby, you're here again
You never miss a time.
The hood is clean, alive with sheen
While I'm still here on line.

The spring brought showers
With lots of flowers
And May just slipped away
Your 'vette is bright, boy, what a sight,
Today's my lucky day.

WE GOTTA START MEETIN' LIKE THIS
WE GOTTA START MEETIN' LIKE THIS
I never had a feelin' that felt so right
So I never wanna letcha get outta my sight
WE GOTTA START MEETIN' LIKE THIS

I pulled in just next to him
With towels, sponge and hustle
Start my routine, while in between
My eyes drink in his muscle.

If only I could interest him
In sharing my clean towels
Oh, Sparky, please, please look my way
Behind your car, I'll follow.

(CHORUS)

A well-written first verse should establish who, when, and where. In this lyric the *when* is clearly now (from the present tense verbs), but the *who* and *where* are a mystery. The word *here* appears twice, but without any clues to where "here" is. The singer is female (the writer told the class) and is addressing a singee named Sparky who owns a clean, shiny hood. The hoods of parkas don't usually shine, so maybe it's a car hood. (We'll stay tuned for clues.)

The second verse spends three lines on irrelevant seasonal musings. Then we hear that Sparky has a "bright *vet*" (I say "hear," because it's a class policy to distribute lyric sheets only *after* the lyric is read in order to smoke out aural ambiguities.) "Vet" could mean a friend who's a smart veteran, or a reference to an intelligent veterinarian. A sharp listener—assuming anyone is still paying attention—might link *hood* from verse one with *vet* and come up with a Corvette. But that sleuthing doesn't help much. Even after we hear the first chorus (half the song is now over), some critical questions remain unanswered: Who is the singer to the singee? Where are they? On what kind of line? Maybe for gas? What does "you never miss a time" mean? Why are there references to April showers and May flowers? Where's the payoff? What is the lyric *about?*

The last two verses, which include mention of towels and a sponge, suggest a car wash. But we're still confused: some lines make us think that she's a customer and others that she's an employee. We ultimately have no plot we can synopsize and no characters we can identify. That's because the scenario is all in the writer's head instead of in the lyric. The critique session pried these facts from the lyricist: At seventeen she had a crush on a garage attendant, and as a ruse to see him, she would go to have her car washed every week.

Drawing on an autobiographical incident is a good start, and the theme of a one-sided attraction certainly has universal appeal. Unfortunately, this lyricist (unlike Alan Jay Lerner in "On the Street Where You Live") failed to get the details of the script out of her imagination and into her lyric. That's an example of a hidden scenario: a listener can only know what's actually written in the lyric.

The Personal Problem

I'M SHORT
(Excerpt)

My last lover was six foot three
In his stocking feet
When he bent to kiss me
Our lips would never meet
And when we stepped out to dance
I wore heels four inches high
But my platforms never helped me
I reached the bottom of his tie, oh my.

I'M SHORT, yes I'M SHORT
Not yet five feet tall
I'M SHORT, so short
But my life is still a ball.

© 1983. Used with permission.

The last verse tells of acquiring a new seven-foot lover, and it ends, "So I'll gladly give my little hand/To become big Billy's wife." This lyric asks us to identify with one short woman who doesn't mind being short because she has lots of Goliath-sized lovers. On what common ground can the audience meet the singer? Why should we listen? Once again, the song doesn't speak for us, but only for the writer.

On the other hand, the Randy Newman hit "Short People" sent a global message. The lyric was not a personal statement about the singer's being short; nor was it actually about short people in general. Its obvious tongue-in-cheek putdown of "short" people was an amusing statement about mindless prejudice, and reached millions.

The Judgmental Attitude

When Lennon and McCartney portrayed two of the world's solitary people—Eleanor Rigby and Father McKenzie—they never placed blame or passed judgment. Rather, they gave us glimpses of a woman who attended strangers' weddings and waited by a window for life to start, and they gave us a closeup of a priest writing his sermons and darning his socks. We drew our own conclusions. Knowing that the world is filled with Eleanor Rigbys and Father McKenzies, we sing along with the compassionate narrator: all the lonely people, where do they all come from? Now meet "Elizabeth Grey."

ELIZABETH GREY

Elizabeth,
Some fine spark ignites your eyes
And you're laughing
And while I wish I had your gift
There's that other look that says
Life's rushed right past you.

ELIZABETH GREY
How can you flit your days away
Watching other people live
Their lives, their way.

And Elizabeth,
I've seen your face light up enough to know
Your impish mind turns somersaults in glee
Only at the thought of someone's stupidity.

ELIZABETH GREY
How can you flit your days away
Watching other people live
Their lives, their way.

But Elizabeth
In spite of all the times
Your sharp tongue's made me cry
I still say this with as much love as anger

ELIZABETH GREY
How can you flit your days away
Watching other people live
Watching other people live
Watching other people live
Their lives, their way.

© 1982. Used with permission.

Every performer tacitly extends the audience an invitation: "Let us live this song together," as concert artist Lotte Lehman put it. Successful songs merge us with the singer and make us want to sing along, as in "all the lonely people. . . ." But how can we identify with "Elizabeth Grey"? The singer, apparently an intimate friend of the singee, characterizes her as disdainful of others' frailties, critical of others' lifestyles, yet seemingly unfulfilled herself. In other words, what the writer has done is make the singer sit in judgment of a "friend," and, by extension, asks both a potential performer of these words and the audience to do the same. While a judgmental attitude is the most obvious flaw of "Elizabeth Grey," it is not its sole one; for example, instead of unifying one clear and consistent emotion, it projects several: admiration, envy, pity, disdain, and love—enough for a novel.

The writer, tapping autobiographical material, lacked the technique to translate the private into the universal. Instead of talking to the world, she is talking only to her diary.

The Angry Tone

Though anger is a universal emotion, it is one for which we often feel both regret and shame. Lyrics that seethe with rage and characterize the singer as ill-humored, churlish, petulant, resentful, peevish, belligerent, bitter, shrewish—in short, unappealing—seldom get set to music. The rare times they do, the verbal abuse has been tempered by charm, or treated with a light touch such as "You Irritate Me So," and "You're No Good," or—as we've pointed out earlier—they've been written by the recording artist.

Here's unmitigated anger without a redeeming feature:

ANGRY
(Excerpt)

I'm so damn ANGRY, just sittin' here thinkin' about you
And thinkin' about you is bad
ANGRY, just sittin' here wonderin' about you
And why you wanna make me so mad.

ANGRY, just sittin' here wonderin' where you are
And thinkin' 'bout what I should do

I'm ANGRY, thinkin' well, you did it again,
Oh I wish I could find someone new.

ANGRY ANGRY ANGRY ANGRY
I'm so ANGRY—can't you see
Just what you're doin' to me.

© 1983. Used with permission.

The lyric offers no specific justification for the anger, such as the singee's lying or cheating; we get the impression that he simply does not care for her. As a consequence, the singer appears both lacking in pride and self-pitying—someone with whom few would want to identify. On the other hand, we readily identify with songs that portray the more benign (and nonhostile) negative emotions—loneliness, regret, longing, bewilderment, anxiety, discontent, even hopelessness. Anger directed at a particular person (rather than at the ills of society) makes a poor candidate for the topic of a successful lyric.

The Unsympathetic Singer

Nonperforming lyricists must continually remind themselves that they are writing words for a professional performer to sing. Remembering that the singer becomes the song should help to shortstop lyrics like this excerpt:

VICTIM

VICTIM, I'm a VICTIM of the street
But you know I can make a VICTIM
Of anyone I meet.
The city—it taught me to be tough,
Even when I was a kid I
Learned to look both ways at once
Always someone ready to take what they want.

My daddy, you know he never gave me time
He spent it all nursing a habit
He wasn't pretty when he died.

My mother she said, "Boy, work for honest pay,"
But with the thrills I'm used to buyin'
Ain't gonna make enough that way
Got to keep my head above the street every day.

© 1981. Used with permission.

It was the writer's obvious intent to make the statement that criminals are shaped by society. Fine—as far as the subject matter goes. It's the first-person singular treatment that does the lyric in. Who wants to identify with the threats of a potential criminal: "I can make a victim of anyone I meet"? And what vocalist would be willing to "merge" with a victimizer!

By way of contrast, Mac Davis's "In the Ghetto" made his social statement successfully by putting it in the third person. With Chicago's inner city as the backdrop, we're told of the vicious circle of poverty and crime. Elvis Presley took the song to the top of the charts, because it neither scolded nor threatened the listener. We weren't asked to identify with a complaining victim or an angry victimizer, but with a narrator who observes the scene like a camera.

Sarcasm

"Wonderful weather we're having" can mean either exactly that or, if it's said sarcastically, the opposite. A speaker's voice will make the intended meaning clear; sarcasm generally requires the use of vocal inflection to produce its effect. For that reason, an isolated caustic line is difficult to hear when it's sung; a singer can't introduce a song by saying to the audience, "When I come to the part that says 'forgive you? Of course, I forgive you!' I'm being sarcastic." It's virtually impossible in a lyric to say one thing while meaning another. And it's foolish to try. Sarcasm rates right up there with a judgmental attitude in terms of lyrical appeal. Here's a lyric structured entirely on a sneer.

PERFECT TIMING
(Excerpt)

Machine voice told me
You can't come to the phone
But I know that voice is lyin'
I know you're still at home
So I'm standin' right behind your door
Turnin' the key you gave to me
I hear a lady laughin'
And she doesn't sound like me

I've got PERFECT TIMING
Yeah, I've got PERFECT TIMING
Each time you try to cheat
I've got PERFECT TIMING

Don't you two look cute
Wrapped up in that satin sheet
Let me throw you this warm blanket
Cover up your frozen feet
I guess I'm an unexpected guest
Caught your hands as they turn red
Just stopped by to pack my things
Please don't get outta bed.

© 1983. Used with permission.

With all the potential positive treatments of the title "Perfect Timing," what a waste to throw it away on sarcasm.

Misleading the Listener

A failed lyric is sometimes the result of the misconception that good writing is about cleverness. The common defense of an author of a convoluted plot is the response, "I didn't want to say the *obvious* thing." So instead of being direct and clear, the writer misleads the listener, as in this deceptive introduction.

> *Always thought that I was all alone*
> *Then one night I called you on the telephone*
> *'Cause I had the urge to start cheating*
> *And I guess you know that you were grea⁺*
> *Helping me get over being overweight*
> *You have made me want to stop eating*
>
> *I was never good at setting goals*
> *All I ever thought about were buttered rolls*
> *Now I think of you with gratitude*
> *All my days are bright, my nights are bliss*
> *Thanks to Overeaters Anonymous*
> *You always take my mind off food.*
>
> *Now I know up from down*
> *Now I know north from south*
> *Now I'm no longer living*
> *Hand to mouth . . .*
> © 1983. Used with permission.

Had the writer started the lyric with the *second* verse, she would have set the authentic tone for the song and thereby properly prepared her listener for an amusing idea. What she did instead was throw us off balance with a false lead: we expected to hear a serious song about sexual cheating, not a funny song about a food junkie. When the word *overweight* clunked at the end of the fifth line, our train of thought jumped the track; we then had to reprocess the four previous lines and start from there to enjoy the real story. Tricking the audience isn't cricket.

Here's another example of the wrong way to go about not being "obvious."

> *I see you standing far away*
> *I know you're coming here today*
> *So HELLO, GOODBYE BLUES*
> *I know you're on your way.*
>
> *Now you're standing at the door*
> *Your bags are sitting on the floor*
> *So HELLO, GOODBYE BLUES*
> *Come in and close the door.*

> *Ever since she left me,*
> *I knew you weren't too far away*
> *I watched my dreams all disappear*
> *That's when I felt you coming near*
> *And now you're here to stay.*
>
> *I see you've made yourself at'home*
> *I guess you're glad you're not alone*
> *So HELLO, GOODBYE BLUES*
> *My heart is now your home.*

© 1984. Used with permission.

Misleading the listener in "Hello, Goodbye Blues" is just one of the lyric's two big problems. First, why are we confused? Because the listener naturally assumes "you" is a person: we've been led to believe someone is on the way, and we are trying to picture the singer looking out a window watching the singee approach from a distance. Time moves (unaccountably) in the second verse and the singee mysteriously appears inside the front door with suitcases parked on the floor. With the shift of pronoun from *you* to *she* in the third verse, we're beginning to get the idea—aha, the writer is using personification! The *you* isn't a person at all, but an emotion the singer is feeling. Unfortunately, we've made the connection too late to understand, and thereby enjoy, the lyric: it's more than half over.

Personification certainly works as the basis for a song, but it must be instantly clear, as, for example, in Barbara Mandrell's 1984 hit record, "Happy Birthday, Dear Heartache (you're one year old today)" by Mack David and Archie Jordan. We know from the song's opening line that the singer was addressing her misery, and we are entertained by the charm of her ironically playful attitude. "Hello, Goodbye Blues," on the other hand, neglected to clue us in. We needed to be prepared for the title by a line such as "When she said goodbye, the blues said hello." Then we would at least have been pointed in the right direction.

Part of the lyric's lack of clarity stems from the title itself. The ear can't hear the punctuation; is it "hello, goodbye blues," or hello-goodby blues"? An untricky title such as "I've Got the Goodbye Blues" would have helped. But even if we'd understood the lyric from its opening line, we would have been turned off eventually by the overkill: an "emotion" standing at the door with suitcases puts too much strain on our credulity, and we tune out.

The Failed Double Entendre

One ill-conceived double entendre in an otherwise well-written lyric can be corrected or removed so that the lyric stands. If the entire song rests upon a faulty double entendre, however, the lyric automatically crumbles. That's what happened to this one.

COME AND GET IT WHILE IT'S HOT
(Excerpt)

I'm cooking the spaghetti
I'm simmering the sauce
Late night dinner's almost ready
I'll give the salad one last toss
Sneak a peek in my compact mirror
Check and see how the table is set
Then walk over to you and whisper
COME AND GET IT.

COME AND GET IT WHILE IT'S HOT
Come and let it hit the spot
If you want it, just get on it
And COME AND GET IT WHILE IT'S HOT.

I don't cook like this for everyone
Only guys I like a lot
So now baby don't you waste it
Come and taste it while it's hot.

The lyricist thought she was writing double entendre. She unintentionally wrote single entendre: a lyric about a dinner menu. A double entendre suggests two things simultaneously, one of which has a risqué meaning. The writer had hoped to make a cooking metaphor work for serving up a sexual delight, but when she specified spaghetti sauce and salad, she blew it. Spaghetti sauce is spaghetti sauce; it suggests nothing other than food. The trick is to make one word or idea suggest another, for example, lines like "Am I *cooking* up a *feast* for you!. . . My *oven* is hot tonight . . . You're gonna love the *buns* . . . Wait till you taste my *dessert* . . . I hope you come good and *hungry* . . ." and so on. The object is to let the listener's imagination make the connection.

The Mixed Metaphor and the Synthetic Simile

Some metaphors don't work. Depending upon their weight in the song, they range from merely silly to fatal. In a generally well-conceived lyric an occasional inept comparison—one that is vague, forced, or foolish—can get by. For example, here are two *mixed metaphors* from recent records by major artists: In one, a tenuous romantic relationship was compared to living in a "house of cards." The singer hoped the "thread" could be "saved." Cards don't have threads; fabrics have threads. What's more, it would be the *fabric* that one would want to save, not merely a *thread* of it. In another song, life in an inner-city neighborhood was likened to living in a jungle, with the constant fear that one will "go under." One wouldn't "go under" in a jungle, but in quicksand or a whirlpool. In these instances, the songs were stronger than the misbegotten metaphors.

A song built entirely upon an artificial analogy has no reality to stand on—like this chorus:

> WE STILL MAKE LOVE LIKE THUNDER,
> Like a flood that drowns the hills.
> Yes, we still make love like thunder,
> With a force that burns and chills.
>
> WE STILL MAKE LOVE LIKE THUNDER,
> Like a sudden storm.
> But after thunder comes the lightning
> And lightning can harm.
>
> © 1983. Used with permission.

How does thunder apply to lovemaking? Their passion is vehement? Or they moan a lot? One counterfeit comparison can slip by in a lyric that is essentially well conceived, but here the problem is at the essence of the song—its chorus. Consequently, the lyric can't support such a faulty construction. The incongruous coupling of *drowns, burns,* and *chills* with thunder—none of which is an attribute of a noise—renders the metaphor synthetic. And even poetic license doesn't allow for making thunder *precede* lightning. Most important, though, a contrived linking of ideas is incapable of engendering any emotion.

Overextended and Multiple Metaphors

A little figurative language goes a long way. The trick is in knowing when enough is enough.

HEART ON HOLD

> You were the princess
> That phoned by mistake
> A wrong number put us in touch.
> It didn't take three minutes to tell
> I liked what I heard very much.
> We went out that night
> And to my delight
> Your touch was as nice as your tone
> I had my head set for a great romance
> But now I sit by my phone alone.
>
> You put my HEART ON HOLD
> You put my HEART ON HOLD
> I thought we had a good connection
> I'm hung up on you, but you hung up on me
> And put my HEART ON HOLD.

What went wrong
That put such a long
Distance between us today?
Now you're in Idaho
And how was I to know
You'd operate in this way?
If I could trace the line
That didn't make you mine
I would make a quick repair,
But my directory is no assist to me
And I'm ready for dial-a-prayer.

(CHORUS)

Please reverse the charges
You've condemned me to
Accept my message that I love you still
Call collect and I'll accept you back again.
I promise you I'll even pay my bill.

Please take my heart off hold
Take my HEART OFF HOLD
Let's reestablish our connection
You can make a wrong number right again
Please take my HEART OFF HOLD.

The lyric boasts many good points: It's simple, direct, and clear; its breezy tone is totally consistent; and the linear plot progresses from something, through something, to something—with a neat wrapup. And it's fun. Once. Before the first stanza of "Heart On Hold" is over we're on to the writer's game, so it remains only a matter of curiosity to see how far he can milk the conceit; it was too far. The excessive and strained telephone allusions become wearying and render the plot so artificial that the lyric can't work; a *popular* song is something we want to hear over and over.

Actually, any overextended metaphor puts a strain on the listener because it's unreal. Consider this one.

THE BRIDGE IS BREAKING
Too much strain
Feel it shaking
From the pain
Now it's swaying
Hear it creak
The link between us
Way too weak.

THE BRIDGE IS BREAKING
Far too frail
The love we're faking's
Bound to fail
We make the motions
Live the lie
Know it's over
Doomed to die.

So I'm gonna change my direction
Before I fall down the abyss
Find me a better connection
Look for the love that we missed.

A BRIDGE WAS BREAKING
Done is done
Now I'm making
Stronger ones
Now I know that
To succeed
Love's the strength
Two lovers need.

© 1981. Used with permission.

The writer's intention here, unlike "Heart on Hold," was clearly to evoke real emotion in the listener, but how can an audience respond to the emotional distress of two people when they hear only about a creaking, swaying, shaking bridge?

When Paul Simon conceived of a singer being a "Bridge Over Troubled Water" to a friend, he instinctively knew when to drop the metaphor and pick up on real life—those dark and down-and-out times when one feels weary, and small, and in need of comfort. Real lyrics evolve from the real feelings of real people.

Here is a lyric whose sincerity collapsed under a barrage of relentless and unrelated allusions:

WANNA SHED THIS SKIN

Volcanoes shoot lava boiling inside.
Caterpillars turn into butterflies.
One tiny seed grows into a redwood tree.
Oh, where is the power to set me free?

The past is a drug imprisoning my soul.
Regret is a shovel digging a hole.
Fear is a master standing over me.
Oh, where is the power to set me free?

Wanna leave this rut, wanna learn to strut,
Wanna stand up tall, tired of feeling small.
I'm eager to begin, let the me within
See the light of day, find a brand new way

WANNA SHED THIS SKIN, WANNA SHED THIS SKIN,
WANNA SHED THIS SKIN, WANNA SHED THIS SKIN,

Man conquers outer space, walks the moon.
Woman creates new life inside her womb.
Stevie Wonder's music makes us see.
Oh, where is the power to set me free?

Wanna leave this rut, wanna learn to strut,
Wanna stand up tall, tired of feeling small.
I'm eager to begin, let the me within
See the light of day, find a brand new way

WANNA SHED THIS SKIN, WANNA SHED THIS SKIN,
WANNA SHED THIS SKIN, WANNA SHED THIS SKIN,

Someday I'll find the key to me,
And when I do then I'll be free

And I'll leave this rut, show the world my strut,
Pull myself up tall, no more feeling small.
I'm eager to begin, let the me within
See the light of day, find a brand new way

(repeat chorus)

© 1984. Used with permission.

The spunky chant is compelling: "wanna leave this rut, wanna learn to strut . . . see the light of day, find a brand new way"; but the number of disparate allusions (volcanoes/caterpillars, moon/womb/Stevie Wonder, rut/skin/key) distract our attention from the essence of the lyric's theme—wanting to move on in life. Metaphoric overkill is often the result of a writer's misinterpretation of "show, don't tell." Multiple word pictures, in themselves, don't create a superior lyric. Figurative language is a writer's spice rack: A little seasoning with the right imagery can enhance the theme; too much of one kind or too many different kinds can overpower it.

The Contrived Situation

The best lyrics are grounded in the writer's reality—something the lyricist has personally experienced, or thought, or observed, or imagined. Many failed lyrics are the result of contrivance—a concocted plot that a writer hopes is realistic but has not thought through enough to make ring true. Like this one—an assignment to write a country song.

YOUR FLIRTIN' IS A-HURTIN' ME

Let's have one more beer before we go,
Wanna have a talk with you.
There's somethin' wrong between us,
And I don't know what to do.
Tonight ev'ry place we visit
You play your little game—
And if I don't stop you now,
I may be the one to blame.

Cause YOUR FLIRTIN' IS A-HURTIN' ME.
I look away but, baby, I still see
The eyes that once loved me alone
Are wand'rin' far away from home.
YOUR FLIRTIN' IS A-HURTIN' ME.

Last night I felt you driftin'
You slept on your side of the bed.
And this morning when I went to kiss you,
You turned away instead.
Now tonight you turn to others;
You nod, they answer silently—
With a little wink, a little smile—
And you think you're foolin' me.

But YOUR FLIRTIN' IS A-HURTIN' ME.
I look away but, baby, I still see—
The eyes that once loved me alone
Are wand'rin' far away from home.
YOUR FLIRTIN' IS A-HURTIN' ME.
Just wanna clear the air
And make this old romance brand new.
Can't we lock eyes again
Just like we used to do.

(CHORUS)

In the second verse we are told the singer and singee live together. Learning that fact makes us question the plausibility of the lyric's premises, because it is totally unbelievable that: (1) an evening out for a couple living together consists of hopping, apparently unaccompanied, from one drinking place to another; (2) the singer would suggest remaining in a public place like a bar (or wherever they're having the beer) to discuss a highly emotional matter; (3) she *just discovered* he is a flirt (flirting being a characteristic way of behaving), as opposed to noticing he's become attracted to a particular woman; and (4) his ignoring of her in bed and at breakfast is symptomatic of a flirt.

If the lyricist wants to write what the title declares, "Your Flirtin' Is A-Hurtin' Me," then the song should be a complaint against the singer's bad luck in falling for a flirt, telling how disturbed she is by his behavior. But we've been given overtones of something more serious. If the singer suspects he has found someone new, that's a whole other story—about suspicion. This lyric is split between two plots. In other words, it's contrived and, consequently, without genuine feeling.

When you are writing about something you have not directly experienced, it's important to create believable people in genuine situations. To help root your lyric in reality and develop true-to-life characters, ask yourself focusing questions like: Who is this man? This woman? Are they single, married, living together? Where are they? What are they doing there? What are they feeling?

Audiences respond to a song when they believe what a singer is thinking, or feeling, or doing. Before the audience can believe it, the writer must believe it.

Semantic Blunders

Sometimes an inventive lyricist will alter a common expression for comic effect; for example, in the song "He Had Refinement" from the musical *A Tree Grows in Brooklyn*, Dorothy Fields had Aunt Cissy brag about her well-bred lover: "a gentlemen to his finger*nails* was he." That, of course, was purposeful for characterization. An *unintentional* contortion of proper usage in a lyric is of course not a plus, but a potential pitfall. The extent of the damage depends upon the size of the faux pas; some are easily cut and others may send a lyric into oblivion.

On occasion a misused expression imbedded in an otherwise strong lyric defies detection, and the song makes it to the charts. A little background on a case in point: "Comin' In On a Wing and a Prayer," a 1943 hit by Harold Adamson and Jimmy McHugh, immortalized the confident response of the pilot of a disabled World War II fighter plane to a ground control station, as he maneuvered his aircraft to a safe landing. The expression "on a wing and a prayer" has consequently come to mean "I'm in bad shape, but with the help of heaven, I'll make it." Four decades later, a top-40 ballad, celebrating the heights of new love, applied the expression as if it meant soaring carefree through the sky. The misused phrase didn't keep the song from success, because the lyric was basically well-conceived. But a chorus constructed on such a misuse is likely to render a lyric fatally flawed.

For example, a dismembered axiom can't be expected to work very well. The adage "the proof of the pudding is in the eating" refers to a test or trial of the truth. A student accidentally abbreviated the axiom in a lyric based on the title, "The Proof is in the Pudding." The elliptical phrase, leaving out the crucial step of "eating," has no meaning.

"Waterloo" was the result of a one-word title assignment. It's a memorable title and rich in potential. At least, it would have been, had it been used correctly. The lyric told of a long-term loser who decided he was ready to fight the battle of life again, and this time to win. The trouble was, the lyricist wrote the opposite of what he meant; the chorus said, in effect, "I'm ready for another Waterloo"—using the word as if its definition were "a battle." *Waterloo* stands for a downfall, not a fight. Webster makes it official: any disastrous or decisive defeat. The lyricist, unfortunately, was enamored of what he had written and became convinced (after some affirmative feedback from nonprofessional friends) that the song would find its audience. The lyric—which had genuine potential—remains an unrevised (and unrecorded) Waterloo.

The plot line of another student lyric entitled "The Eye of the Hurricane" centered upon a couple surviving a particularly stormy time, with the expression used as a metaphor for the crux of the crisis. The eye of a hurricane, however, is the small, *calm* center of the storm, not its most violent area.

On occasion, even a kindergarten word or everyday expression trips up a lyricist. For example, in a treatment of the title "Meanwhile," the lyricist used the word to mean "at the same time" (while) instead of its real meaning, "during the *intervening* time": "Everyone else has a lover; meanwhile I've got no one." What she meant was more like, "Someday I'll meet Mr. Right, but meanwhile I'm spending a lot of nights alone." In another lyric, the expression "on my own" was used as though it meant "alone" instead of "by my own effort." For example, "I'm going to get to be president of the company on my own—without your help" uses the phrase properly. But "He went to a business meeting and left me to watch TV on my own' does not. Some novice writers have a tendency to defend lyrics featuring such semantic errors; they naively believe that the song will make it in spite of its misuse of words, that in fact their skewed perception of a term's meaning will some day supplant the current dictionary definition.

The best way to avoid an error in usage is to check key words or expressions in either a dictionary or a phrase book. The proper use of a maxim or adage is especially critical when it's to be the title of a song. (A useful resource is the *Handbook of Commonly Used American Idioms;* not only is it fun to read, it's a good source of new titles.)

The Idiosyncratic Negative

A negative title works well when it represents commonly felt emotions: "You're No Good," "Goin' Out of My Head," or "I Can't Smile Without You." But not:

I DON'T WANT TO GROW OLD IN MANHATTAN
Don't want to turn grey in this town.

How many singers will relate to that idiosyncratic sentiment? A simple reversal from the negative to the positive would save the song. The story line can still revolve around the singer's disenchantment with Manhattan, but if the chorus stated that he *wants to go somewhere,* rather than that he *doesn't want to stay somewhere,* there would be a lot more listener identification. Think of all the hits: "Alabamy Bound," "Carry Me Back to Old Virginny," "Wabash Blues," "Tulsa Time," and so on.

Here's another chorus that's done in by the negative:

I CAN'T MAKE IT SINGLE NO MORE.
When you held me near
Through the deep satin night
You melted my fear
And you made love feel so right
That I CAN'T MAKE IT SINGLE NO MORE.

© 1981. Used with permission.

Stating the same idea in an affirmative way would immediately attract a broad sing-along audience; for example, "I Want to Move in with You" or "I'm Ready to Fall in Love Forever" or "I Could Go the Distance with You." "Can't Make It Single" makes the singer sound ineffectual and clinging, whereas any of the suggested affirmative titles would make the singer sound strong and loving. Positive titles that represent universal emotions bear the weight both of repetition within the lyric and of repeated hearings by the public.

The Nonpop Subject

Here is an excerpt (the first two verses) from a lyric that concerns itself with kinky sex:

TEA FOR THREE

My momma told me tea for two
Was the right and proper thing to do
For every girl there's just one boy
To break your heart or bring you joy
But now I know it just ain't true
I want more than tea for two.

TEA FOR THREE
Cause two just ain't enough for me.
TEA FOR THREE
I take it strong as you can make it.
Can't you see
It's much more fun for ev'ryone
Let's have TEA FOR THREE.

© 1981. Used with permission.

The title is both fresh and fun. Although the *ménage à trois* certainly exists, it's not exactly a universal situation. And that's what *pop* songs are all about: common denominator subjects. "Tea for Three" might make it in a supper club or revue, but not on a top-40 radio station. It's important to learn to discriminate between pop lyric subject matter and the "special material song" so that you can aim your darts at the right target.

Beware of Bluntness

Blunt can be defined as tactless at worst, plain-spoken at best. Here are some snippets from student lyrics that win no prizes for subtlety:

> *Sometimes we had the makings of the best.*
> *You made me cry and thought it was great.*
> *What began as* **love turned to hate.**

> *You give me just what I've needed*
> *Make me young and alive*
> *Can this feeling last for a lifetime?*
> **I'm forty, you're just twenty-five.**

> *He didn't tell me he was* **gay** *right away.*
> *I don't know what the hell he was waiting for.*

> © 1982. Used with permission.

In a lyric, to label hate as hate, identify characters by age and sexual preference—in other words, to be blunt—is usually to be boring. Bluntness is for sandwich signs. Though directness is unquestionably a top-ten principle of lyric writing, there are times when it can be suitably softened for good effect. In each of the foregoing excerpts, obliqueness would have been decidedly more artful. If we look beyond the bluntness of these lyrics to their central ideas, we'll find workable universal themes: it's over between us; we're worlds apart but right for each other; I picked the wrong one to love. The lyricists could have treated the subjects in ways that would have enabled us to sing along; instead they made the situations so explicit that the listener is shut out.

Mixing Figurative with Literal Language

When you write a series of ideas, make sure they truly work together. For example: "I love the look in your eyes, the sound of your laughter, the touch of your hand, the feel of your lips." That series works convincingly because the grouping is composed of items of like kind, each expressed in a literal way. Just as important, the thoughts are presented in ascending order of emotional sequence—see/hear/touch/feel. Any rearrangement would render the series less effective. Here's another grouping: "I promise you we'll ride on a rainbow, dance on the moon, and sleep on a pillow of clouds." This time the grouping is romantically figurative, yet, a convincing impossibility, as Aristotle put it. To create convincing impossibilities, unify both the lyric's language style and tone.

Both examples maintain their integrity by being consistently literal or consistently figurative. They are consequently believable statements.

By contrast, here's an ineffective sequence of ideas from a student lyric: "I want to smell your hair, feel your soul, touch your sighs, hear your heart." It's synthetic. Mixing the figurative (touch your soul) with the literal (smell your hair), and putting them in a hodgepodge order, sounds both pretentious and hollow.

When you're going for genuine feeling, it's important to be consistent in your style. Remember that incongruity is the hallmark of comedy. When it comes to literal and figurative language, determine the effect you're after—then match for the sigh, and mix for the laugh.

Aural Ambiguity

If you want your meaning to be clear, make sure your words can be understood on the first hearing. No explanations allowed. Songs built on homonyms, for example (see page 134) require careful preparation. The student title "Reel to Real" stemmed from a woman's feeling that films mirrored her life. When the lyric was read in class the audience pretty much got the idea, but couldn't pinpoint which reel came first. On the other hand, "Solo," a lyric structured on a pun, didn't fare as well. The repeated line, "I'm solo when you're away." was perceived as *so low*.

Ira Gershwin tells a story of some homonym confusion in a line from "My Ship." During a *Lady in the Dark* rehearsal, Gertrude Lawrence suddenly stopped singing midline and called out to Gershwin, who was monitoring from the orchestra, "Why does she say 'I could wait *four* years'—why not five, or six?" Of course, the line was "I could wait *for* years." The painstaking lyricist immediately substituted *the* to clarify the aural ambiguity.

Fusion, the melding of two adjacent sounds into each other to form a third, results in *con*fusion if you're not careful. The long-running Archie Bunker theme song (Strouse/Adams) contained a line that confounded listeners for years; no amount of concentrated attention could decipher what sounded like "geearole lasalren grate." In response to listener requests to clarify the line, the theme was rerecorded. This time the singers were instructed to articulate each word with great care. The mystery was then solved: we could finally hear "Gee, our old La Salle ran great!" (La Salle being a 1930s automobile). The *L* in *La* following the terminal *d* from *old* requires the mouth to reform. Separating two butting consonants necessitates more effort from singers than they may be willing to expend, so they often drop the final letter, causing words to fuse.

Record dealers have reported being perplexed by requests for the songs "Disguise in Love" (This Guy's), "Your Kiss Is on My Lips" (List), and "Totally Clips of the Heart" (Total Eclipse). I remember a particular word combination in the bridge of a student lyric that muddied an otherwise "demo-ready" song:

> *This time there's give and take*
> *This time there are chips at stake*
> *For two—for two.*

The last three words in the second line were heard by some as "ships of state" and others as "chips and steak." Another class lyric confused us with the line: "I don't wanna lover." The intention was: "I don't wanna love her." Keep in mind the potential ambiguity of sounds. The best safeguard against losing your audience by confusing them is to read a lyric aloud to someone, asking if every word is clear. Then have your listener check the lyric sheet to verify what was heard against what was written.

Bodily Gaucheries

Some unintentionally funny things happen when writers get figurative with parts of the body, as in these contorted one-liners:

> *"I want to nest inside your gentle brown eyes."*
> *"You knew how to open my heart without tearing it apart."*
> *"My eyes are empty, I've got no time for tears."*
> *"I'll thank you not to wipe your feet of clay on me."*
> *"No one else could set a foot in the door of my heart."*
> *"Can't we lock eyes again?"*
> *"You give me goose pimples big as dimples."*
> *"I used to fall all over every pretty face."*
> *"All I got was a chewed-up heart."*

Obviously, being figurative with the eyes and the heart is the trickiest. The best policy would seem to be to avoid attempts at cleverness when parts of the body are concerned.

WRAPUP

Those are the commonest detours and dead ends on the lyric writer's road to success. An occasional review of this chapter will keep you in the express lane.

chapter 23

First-Draft Pointers

*"In constructing plots and completing the effect,
a writer must keep the scene before his eyes. Only thus,
by getting the picture as clear as if he were present at the actual event,
will he find what is fitting and detect contradictions."* Aristotle

There's a widely held belief that the best songs come fast. Noel Coward, for example, said "It is as though they've been set out in advance for use, and at that proper moment we just reap them in." Billy Joel agrees that "The best songs are the ones you write quickly. You're just sitting there and it comes out." It would appear that every professional songwriter, at least once, has experienced that marvel of marvels when—like shaving cream out of an aerosol can—a song comes out in a whoosh, as though it had simply been waiting for that button to be pushed.

If only the process were always that easy! More often than not the struggle can go on for days or weeks—even months. Some songs have given their authors long labor pains: Oscar Hammerstein said that it frequently took him as much as three weeks to write a lyric; Norman Gimbel "spent practically an entire summer writing 'Live for Life,' trying to make the song work"; Janis Ian admitted that her Grammy Award-winning "At Seventeen" took about three months to complete.

What counts, of course, is not how long it takes, but how good it is. A song that instantly ejects itself is not necessarily a superior one. In the hands of a professional, it sometimes is, but in the hands of an amateur, often it isn't. Among beginning writers there's an unfortunate tendency to confuse speed with quality. The novice often falsely anoints a ten-minute wonder "inspired" and, consequently, above criticism. It is not written that speed confers superiority; on the contrary, fast may only mean facile.

I suspect that the reason some successful works are created so seemingly fast is that the artist has been "assembling" that song or novel or play in the unconscious over an extended period of time. The apparently effortless realization is the result of a long gestation period culminating in one intensely focused eruption. The key word is *focused*.

For reasons both varied and complex, many lyrics take a long time to cohere. When so-called inspiration doesn't come, writers need the support system of craft to fall back on. One thing is certain: the more a lyricist can learn to focus on the lyric idea before writing, the better the first draft will be.

Think Before You Write

A first-rate lyric is an organic whole: all sections are related, each being indispensable to the central purpose of the song. The words evolve in the right order. They mean to the listener what they meant to the writer.

A lyric presented in class is initially judged by how fully it achieves its objective. Whether the target is a country duet, a synthesizer dance record, or an off-Broadway revue, the ultimate question is: Do the words work? Do they accomplish the writer's intention? More often than not, and in varying degrees, they don't. The most common flaw is vagueness. If a lyric is muddled, then the writer's thinking is muddled. As Cleanth Brooks so neatly put it, "A thought vaguely expressed is a vague thought." Many first-draft flaws can be avoided if you think ahead, focusing on every detail of what the lyric is about.

Some student first drafts mystify the listener. After considerable probing, it turns out that the writer had a mental plot which never got transferred to paper: a hidden scenario. The detailed critique which every assignment undergoes sometimes requires a lyrical third degree to uncover what the student had assumed he or she had written: "Where is your lyric taking place? On the dance floor? In bed? Is the singer *thinking*? Or *talking* to someone? Is the action of the song still going on? Or is it all over?"

The usual response from beginning writers to such questions is, "I don't know," or "I never thought about it," or "What difference does it make?" Or worse, "Why do I have to know these things?" The answer is: You have to know them so that the listener will understand your lyric.

Some lyricists are blessed with a natural ability to picture their characters and settings—to see the frizzy blonde hair, the red leather miniskirt, the spike, Lucite heels cruising the corner of Broad and Forty-third— and they don't need Aristotle's timeless advice: keep the scene before your eyes. They do it automatically. Those who don't—and they're in the majority—need help focusing. One advantage of collaborating is the process of batting an idea back and forth to clarify the lyric's objective. The writer without a partner must acquire the knack of playing a kind of internal verbal ping-pong to sort out all the creative options. All accomplished writers have worked out a personal system for staying on the subject, such as Stephen Sondheim's practice of outlining his lyric idea at the top of the page.

To help students in my Basic Course acquire the habit of defining the geography of their lyric *prior* to writing, I give them a focusing sheet with their first writing assignment. It's a questionnaire covering various treatment options. The object of the exercise is to reinforce the importance of clarifying the concept of the lyric.

If you know the answers to all these questions *before* you begin to write, you will certainly produce a clearer first draft than if you don't.

FOCUSING QUIZ

WHO IS SINGING?

1. _____ male _____ female _____ either _____ potential duet

2. What is the relationship of the singer to the singee? _____

3. Is the singer addressing _____ a particular "you"? _____ a universal "you"?

4. Is the singer __ thinking the lyric? __ talking to someone?
   __ works as either an interior monologue or one side of a conversation.

WHAT WILL BE THE SINGER'S ONE CONSISTENT EMOTION OR ATTITUDE TOWARD THE SUBJECT MATTER? For example:

1. _____ self-assertive (I Will Survive)
2. _____ puzzled (What Are We Doin' in Love?)
3. _____ grateful (Come What May)
4. _____ ironic (I'm Not in Love)
5. _____ pleading (Help Me Make It Through the Night)
6. _____ resentful (What About Me?)
7. _____ resigned (Just One of Those Things)
8. _____ confused (Your Love Is Driving Me Crazy)
9. _____ tongue-in-cheek (Nobody)
10. _____ self-pitying (Cryin')
11. _____ wistful (Can't Smile Without You)
12. _____ inspirational (You'll Never Walk Alone)
13. _____ apologetic (I've Been a Bad Boy)
14. _____ lighthearted (Let's Go Dancing)
15. _____ affirmative (It's My Turn)
16. _____ thoughtful (Imagine)
17. _____ romantic (Endless Love)
18. _____ proud (I Am What I Am)
19. _____ hopeful (I Just Can't Help Believin')
20. _____ (other)

WHAT OTHER ELEMENT DO YOU PLAN TO PARTICULARIZE?

1. _____ The circumstances. What are they? _____
2. _____ The setting. Where is it? _____
3. _____ The singer. Who is it? _____
4. _____ The singee. Who is it? _____
5. _____ A story or vignettes. Briefly sum up. _____

WHAT IS THE SETTING?

1. Is there a specific setting? _____ yes _____ no Where? _____
2. If there is more than one, how will you make the transition clear? _____

WHAT IS THE TIME FRAME?

1. Is the action taking place now? (Come In from the Rain) _____ yes _____ no
2. Is the action over? (Mandy) _____ yes _____ no
3. Is the clock moving? (By the Time I Get to Phoenix) _____ yes _____ no
4. Is there a flashback? (When Sunny Gets Blue) _____ yes _____ no
    A flashforward? (Over the Rainbow) _____ yes _____ no

IN WHAT SONG FORM WILL YOU WRITE?

_____ AAA _____ AABA _____ Verse/Chorus

CAN YOU SUMMARIZE THE IDEA YOUR LYRIC EXPRESSES IN A SHORT PROSE SENTENCE? _____
_____

WITH WHAT UNIVERSAL ELEMENT DO YOU EXPECT YOUR AUDIENCE TO IDENTIFY? _____
_____

Before you write a word of the lyric, make it a practice to go over these focusing questions. Write your answers on a clean notebook page; a handy place is directly opposite where you'll be starting your first draft. Outlining a lyric gives you a "song map" to keep you on the right road. Pretty soon you'll internalize the questions, and the process. Being focused will become second nature. The ultimate objective, of course, is to master the technical aspects of lyric writing so that your ideas are free to flow.

How the Process Works

Let's say you're a member of the Basics Course at The Songwriters Guild in New York and you've gotten the assignment to write a lyric to the title "Anchor Man." It's what is known in the music business as a strong hook title: a fresh and universally recognized expression, which (at least at this writing) hasn't been plucked out of the air and put on the charts.

Probably the instant you read the words "Anchor Man," they triggered ideas for several potential treatments. For example: (1) an interior monologue in which the singer wishes she had someone steady in her life—an anchor man who would keep her on an even keel in rough times—leading to a chorus that would make the statement, "I wish I had an anchor man. . . ." or (2) a one-sided dialogue with her lover in which she tells him how good he is for her, how he gives her life stability: "You're my anchor man. . . ." or (3) maybe the singer is one of those luckless country women cursed by a fatal attraction for rolling stones, and she moans, "What I need is an anchor man, someone who won't drift away. . . ." or (4) you could treat the title playfully, and chronicle the plight of a TV news fan who falls for a Dan Rather type. That's how one student handled the title:

ANCHOR MAN

I never cared about world affairs
But I've changed my point of view
It happened when I fell in love
With the man on the network news
Every night at seven, I'm in heaven
When I turn on my TV.
If I sit real close it feels
Like he's talking right to me.

ANCHOR MAN, ANCHOR MAN
How about a lead on how you need
Some love in your life
ANCHOR MAN, ANCHOR MAN
How about a feature
On where I can meet you tonight.

He's got warm brown eyes and designer ties
His voice has a soothing sound
He's got style like a movie star
And the whitest smile around
He knows the score on the latest war
He can even tell the sides apart
But there's a crisis here at home
And it's burning in my heart.

(CHORUS)

I'd love to go to the studio
And see him face to face
Catch him when he's concentrating
On a strike or Senate race
Over to the right, near the TV lights,
He'd see me standing there
Then with everybody watching
I'd sweep him off the air.

ANCHOR MAN, ANCHOR MAN
How about a lead on how you need
Some love in your life
ANCHOR MAN, ANCHOR MAN
How about a feature
On where I can meet you tonight.

After the First Draft

So you've done it. You've written a real lyric. You're thrilled. And you should be. It's one of the greatest feelings in the world—the first of many that may be in store: when you get your first listener's applause; when the words get set to music; when you hear them performed on a demo; when a publisher says, "I want your song"; when you sign your name on the contract; when you get the call that it's been recorded; when you catch it for the first time on the radio; when you read the title on the charts; when you hear the grocery clerk singing your words; when the first royalty check arrives; and that moment next April when a tuxedoed figure rips open the envelope and announces: "The winner is. . . . 'Anchor Man!' " You've lived it all in a flash.

Of course you're dying to read your first draft to a friend, a lover, a neighbor, the mailman—anyone who will stand still for ninety seconds. Probably no amount of sensible advice will convince you to put it away for a day or so—even a few hours—to let it jell. You're too excited. I'm going to try to convince you anyway. It's what professionals do.

If you take a tip from Oscar Hammerstein, you won't show it off quite yet. Hammerstein made it a practice never to show a lyric to a soul until he felt every single word was in the right place. That's the kind of attitude that separates the professional from the amateur. Norman Gimbel once said, "You can always write a better song than the one you've done. If you think you've written the best one, it's because you're exhausted. There's a better one."

Here's a post first-draft checklist to help you smoke out the imperfections and determine whether you've done the job as well as you can. Be ruthlessly honest. It will pay off. Being tough on yourself now will make your song more viable in the marketplace later. Put your lyric to the test of professional standards: remember that every lyric you write is vying for that record cut against songs by pros like Rod Temperton, Dean Pitchford, Tom T. Hall, and Jim Steinman.

After you've given yourself some time to cool down from all the creative heat, pick up your lyric with the dispassionate eye of a critic, and ask yourself:

FORM:

1. Have I grabbed my listener on the first line and interested him or her enough to want to hear more?
2. Have I chosen the most appropriate song form to develop my idea: AAA, AABA, or verse/chorus?
3. Does the story progress logically?
4. Does the bridge (if any) add a new dimension to the plot?
5. In a verse/chorus song, is the chorus a reasonable outcome of the verses?
6. Is the title a synopsis of the chorus?
7. Did I repeat the title enough so that the listener—without needing to be told—would know it after one hearing?
8. Have I varied the meter enough from verse to chorus to bridge to enable a composer to write an interesting melody?

BACKDROP:

1. Is the setting of the story clearly indicated—barroom, bedroom, or boardroom?
2. If I changed locales or time zones, did I include a well-defined transition?

PLOT LINE:

1. Does the plot move forward in each verse, or did I merely repeat the same thoughts in different words?
2. Midway through the song, can the lyric pass the who, what, where, when, and why test?
3. Have I maintained a consistent interior monologue, or a definite dialogue? (Don't let the lyric slip in and out of both.)
4. Have I cluttered the story with subplots? (Remember one idea is enough.)
5. Is every aspect of my plot spelled out in the lyric, or are some essential details still in my head? (The audience can only know what the lyric *states*.)
6. Did I consider doubling my recording potential by adjusting a specifically female or male lyric to a unisex one?

EMOTIONAL CONTENT:

1. Have I maintained a consistent tone and language style throughout?
2. Did I fall in love with a clever line that calls too much attention to itself?
3. Does an unappealing tone—anger, sarcasm, self-pity—put the singer in a poor light?
4. Did I preach or moralize concerning the rightness or wrongness of anyone's personal conduct?
5. Have I built to a satisfactory emotional payoff?
6. Does my lyric express a universally understood meaning?
7. Can I imagine several important recording artists singing these words?

SYNTAX:

1. Are the tenses of my verbs consistent?
2. Is the language conversational?
3. Are my pronouns in place to show who is doing the thinking or feeling?
4. Did I clearly indicate when someone is speaking, by including such expressions as "I said," "He told me," or "She whispered"?
5. Did I use any homonyms that have to be read to be understood: "chairman of the *bored*" or "*thyme* on my hands"?
6. Did I reverse the natural order of words: "Upon your smile I still depend"?

7. Did I make sure every quote is clear? (You can't hand out explanations.)
8. Did I eliminate clutter: *very, a little, sort of,* and so on?
9. Did I delete trendy expressions that obsolesce quickly and will date my lyric, such as: *outasight, get down, uptight, go for it, where's the beef?*

RHYMING:

1. Did I maintain the rhyme scheme I established in the first verse throughout subsequent verses?
2. Is my rhyme style consistent? (If you've set up a perfect rhyme pattern, stick to it, especially in theater songs.)
3. Did I succumb to a tricky rhyme at the expense of naturalness?
4. Are the sounds of the rhymes varied enough, or are there too many of one kind that would bore the listener?

PROSODY (when you've written to a melody):

1. Are the accents stressed the same way they are when the words are spoken: *e-TER-nal-ly,* not *e-ter-nal-LY?*
2. Do the important words fall on the important notes? (Don't give *it* and *but* to sustained notes.)
3. Did I give the singer too many *s* sounds in a row?
4. Is there space for the singer to breathe? To phrase?
5. Did I give the singer an open vowel to sing on the sustained words at the ends of phrases? (Open *i, a,* and *o* vowels are easier to sing than *e.)*
6. Do the words and music feel married to each other?

WRAPUP

Unless your lyric passes this screening with a 100 percent score, it's revision time. Before a publisher, producer, or artist finds inconsistencies or other flaws in your words, find them first yourself. And fix them. Never let a lyric leave the launching pad until it's in the best possible condition. When you've made it as good as it can be, you'll be armed with the confidence it takes to beat down the doors of the music business.

chapter 24
Review—Revise— Fine Tune

"Once the words are down, the idea expressed, then, of course, must come the fixing, the revising, the polishing, the never-being-satisfied until you feel it is as perfect as you can make it." Dorothy Fields

Good writers are generally good editors. Any serious writer will tell you that plays, novels, and poems aren't just written—they're *re*written.

The long-range objective for the lyricist is to develop that third eye of self-criticism, that inner flaw-detector that buzzes: *bad line, bad line, bad line.* You will often have to throw out a clever rhyme or line, or even a whole verse that you love. It's hard to believe sometimes that the words you like best are working against the lyric instead of for it. And it's common to look for someone who will tell you what you want to hear: that the lyric is fine just the way it is. Becoming a successful writer in any field, however, is a process of learning to let go of the mediocre, with the implicit belief that you will replace it with something much better. And you will— once you understand *what* doesn't work and *why*, as well as *how* to go about fixing it.

So far you've seen some of the potential pitfalls and gotten some guidelines on how to avoid them. Now here is a closeup of the editing process in action, illustrated by class writing assignments: the first draft, the analysis, and then the rewrites.

PROBLEM: CONTRADICTORY TONE AND LACK OF FOCUS

Back in Chapter 9 you learned why consistency is a requisite for tone. Here is a case of unintentional mixed emotions and a shifting viewpoint.

DOUBLETALK
(First Draft)

Verse: *When I called to say, Honey, I'm on my way home,*
Do you want anything from the store?
I could tell by her laugh she was not home alone,
And my stomach felt tight, like before.

Verse: *When I asked her, Honey, just what's goin' on? she said*
Maureen had come by for a chat.
I'd like to believe you but this time I can't,
Cause I saw Maureen down by the laundromat.

Chorus: *DOUBLETALK, DOUBLETALK*
I can't take these lies,
DOUBLETALK, DOUBLETALK
I see our love dying away.

Verse: *She said, Wait just a minute, darlin'*
Just who do you think was here?
Well Maureen doesn't smoke and Maureen doesn't joke
And Maureen doesn't drink my beer.

Verse: *She said, You must have seen her sister,*
She has a twin you know.
Yeah, but her twin sister lives on the coast
So you better try harder to show, that this ain't

Chorus: *DOUBLETALK, DOUBLETALK*
I can't take these lies,
Stop your DOUBLETALK, DOUBLETALK
Our love is dying, I know.

Verse: *Maureen told me her twin sister*
Was visiting for a week. Yeah, but
Your friend Maureen had her hair dyed green
So how could I make a mistake, You're talkin'

Chorus: *DOUBLETALK, DOUBLETALK*
I can't take these lies,
DOUBLETALK, DOUBLETALK
I see our love dying away.

© 1982, Jim Payne. Used with permission.

Analysis:

We can readily understand the story line of "Doubletalk": a husband thinks his wife is cheating. But we don't know how to react because the tone switches from serious ("my stomach felt tight") to silly ("hair dyed green") back to serious ("I see our love dying away"). We are further confused by the shift from "her" and "she" in the first four verses to "your" and "you're" in the last verse: is the husband telling the incident to a friend, addressing the audience, having an internal monologue, or talking to his wife? Because the writer failed to develop a consistent attitude toward the story, the lyric was unfocused and, consequently, it lacked impact.

The critique made the lyricist understand the duality of feeling and perspective in his first draft. He realized that he had to decide on his own attitude toward the plot: it turned out to be empathy for the fellow being cuckolded. Here's the rewrite, which successfully implements two of Aristotle's precepts: The writer must keep his eyes on the scene, and characters should be true to life and internally consistent.

DOUBLETALK
(Second Draft)

When I called to say, Honey, I'm on my way home,
Do you want anything from the store?
I could tell by your laugh you were not home alone,
And my stomach felt tight like before.

You told me, Relax, please don't get upset, dear,
It's Maureen, she's come by for a chat,
But on my way home when I stopped for some beer,
I saw Maureen by the laundromat . . .

DOUBLETALK, DOUBLETALK
I can't take these lies, I'm leavin'
DOUBLETALK, DOUBLETALK
Your alibis are driving me away.

Now you're standing in front of me smilin',
The place is a mess and I'm sore,
I can tell by your smile you been cheatin',
And you think I'll stay here for more.

If this was the first time, I'd take it in stride,
But I know that he's been here before,
There's no use pretending there's nothing to hide,
Cause I saw him leave by my own back door. . . .

DOUBLETALK, DOUBLETALK
I can't take these lies, I'm leavin'
DOUBLETALK, DOUBLETALK
Your alibis are driving me away.

I'm leavin' tonight and I'm takin' the car,
I'm takin' myself somewhere new.
I can tell by your eyes that you really don't care,
And I don't care what you do, with all your

DOUBLETALK, DOUBLETALK
I can't take these lies, I'm leavin'
DOUBLETALK, DOUBLETALK
Your alibis are driving me away.

The lyric starts off strong. Throwing out *her* and sticking with *you* throughout simplifies the story and unifies the focus. Also, treating the phone call as a flashback serves to clarify the singer's whereabouts and enable the plot to progress with a new unity and clarity. Now the chorus sounds like a logical outcome of the first two verses. In the third verse we follow the singer inside his front door, where he is physically confronting the evidence of his suspicions. There are no jokes this time to confuse us. The second draft works because it maintains a steady tone that builds from irritation and frustration to the next step: action.

PROBLEM: UNSPECIFIED CHANGE IN SETTING AND TIME FRAME

When the clock moves, and the scene changes, and the singer shifts from thinking to speaking, the listener needs to know.

ONE HIT SONG
(First Draft)

A: *It's time to get another plane*
Time to play another town
Three week gigs—yeah it's a pain;
Don't you let it get you down.
'Cause all I need is ONE HIT SONG
To make our dreams come true,
I'll settle down and quit the road
And make it up to you.

A: *For eight long years I played saloons*
Sang them all my country tunes
Now I'm playing better rooms
To tourist folks on honeymoons
And all I need is ONE HIT SONG
To make our dreams come true.
I'll settle down and quit the road
And make it up to you.

B: *Oh, the towns I've played*
And the fans I've made
With my razzle-dazzle style
Will take me far
Make me a star
And in a little while
Telegrams from Nashville
And guest shots on TV
And Hollywood producers
Fighting over me.

A: *Hi Hon, I'm calling from L.A.*
My tour was really out of sight
Don't cry, hon, I'm on my way
I'll fly the "red-eye" back tonight.

> Yeah, all I need is ONE HIT SONG
> To make our dreams come true.
> I'll settle down and quit the road
> And make it up to you.

Coda:
> Yeah, all I need is ONE HIT SONG
> To make our dreams come true.
> I'll settle down and quit the road
> And make it up to you.

Analysis:

For two A sections of the lyric we can imagine the singer at home saying goodbye to his wife (or whomever) as he's about to leave for the airport on a three-week road tour. The bridge loses the conversational quality and sounds introspective. In the last verse we are confused as the singer pulls a superman trick and magically materializes in a phone booth. Now we are forced to reassess the first part of the lyric (while the song is moving forward): Have three weeks passed? Was he at home in the first two verses? Was he only thinking, until the last A section?

The most effective approach to the story would be to make the whole song a phone call and to let the listener know in the very first line. The lyric, with its repeated long refrain at the end of each verse, sounds like a chorus being straitjacketed by an AABA structure. Opening up the song to a turnaround chorus (one that can bear immediate repetition) would give it a much stronger commercial flavor. The writer mulled over the critique and came up with this rewrite:

ONE HIT SONG
(Second Draft)

Verse:
> Hi, hon, I'm calling from L.A.
> My gigs are really outta sight
> They all say my songs are great
> Wish I were with you tonight
> But I gotta catch another plane
> It's time to play another town
> Three-month tours—yeah, it's a pain,
> But don't let it get you down.

Chorus:
> All I need is ONE HIT SONG
> To make our dreams come true.
> ONE HIT SONG, I'll quit the road
> And make it up to you.

Verse: *How are the kids—don't wake 'em*
I miss you all a lot
I know it's tough, but I can't give up
I worked too hard for all we've got.
Eight long years, I've played saloons
Sung 'em all my country tunes—
At least I'm playing better rooms.
Cheer up hon, it's comin' soon.

(Chorus)

Bridge: *There'll be telegrams from Nashville,*
Guest shots on TV
Hollywood producers
Fighting over me—

Chorus: *All I need is ONE HIT SONG*
To make our dreams come true.
ONE HIT SONG, I'll quit the road
And make it up to you.

© 1981, Locke Wallace. Used with permission.

That's a well-conceived revision. The writer, by setting up the phone call at the start of the song, tells us immediately where the singer is and what he is doing there. Reshaping the stanzas into the verse/chorus mold and shortening the bridge makes the entire lyric cohere (even though we lost the charm of the singer's self-proclaimed "razzle dazzle" in the pruning process). The touch about not waking the children verifies his family-man status and validates the reason his wife misses him over the long stretches. "One Hit Song" is a success metaphor which works for any listener who is hanging on to a dream.

PROBLEM: MINOR INCONSISTENCIES

"I Just Didn't Know It at the Time" is the result of an assignment to write in the AAA form. The lyric reflects a total grasp of the structure. The student emphasized the AAA design at both the beginning and end of each verse with opening line echoes of "The . . . she left reminds me," plus a repeated closing line ironic refrain. It's a model of "Show, don't tell." In three vignettes the writer paints a picture of a thoroughly charming singee—calm, understanding, and supportive—counterpointed against the short fuse of the impatient and bungling singer. The lyric is fresh, and it rings true. Almost. A fine first draft was marred by two small blunders in the last stanza. Here's the original, including the four-line blemish; its revision is to the right:

I JUST DIDN'T KNOW IT AT THE TIME

A: *The string she left reminds me*
Of the day we flew the kite
How I couldn't get it right
How she hid her laughter
And helped me make it climb.
She was all I needed
I JUST DIDN'T KNOW IT
　　AT THE TIME
I JUST DIDN'T KNOW IT
　　AT THE TIME.

A: *The glass she left reminds me*
Of the night the lights went out
How I stormed about
How she found the candles,
Tequila, salt, and lime.
She was all I needed
I JUST DIDN'T KNOW IT
　　AT THE TIME
I JUST DIDN'T KNOW IT
　　AT THE TIME.

A: *The pen she left reminds me*
Of that silly song I wrote　　*Of that song I tried to write*
How I couldn't play a note　　*How I stayed up half the night*
How she sat for hours　　*How she poured the coffee*
And helped me make it rhyme.　*And found the perfect rhyme.*
She was all I needed
When I failed, we succeeded
I just couldn't show it
I JUST DIDN'T KNOW IT
　　AT THE TIME
I JUST DIDN'T KNOW IT
　　AT THE TIME.

Analysis:

The hyperbole of "I couldn't play a note" is inconsistent with a lyric notable for its emotional low-key profile and genuine feeling. The line sticks out because it rings false. (It also sounds as if he were playing notes with a pen instead of his fingers.) But mainly, "play a note" and "make it rhyme" are a jumble: was she helping him write a melody on a piano or write a lyric on a piece of paper? (Or maybe the writer was using the word *rhyme* in the metaphoric sense.) Anyway, the revision eliminates the confusion. The student let go of his *wrote/note* rhyme and started fresh: ". . . the song I tried to write" is an appealingly understated line in contrast to the synthetic self-deprecation of the original. The lines "How I stayed up half the night/How she poured the coffee" create an intimate picture of the couple—rather like a Taster's Choice TV commercial.

"I Just Didn't Know It at the Time" has both a conversational style and real feeling. It also rhymes perfectly. Many successful contemporary lyricists contend that because rhyme sounds "polished," it lacks the ability to sound conversational, and therefore rhyme is antithetical to genuine emotion. Naturalness and perfect rhyme don't have to be mutually exclusive. Not, at least, in the hands of a writer whose talent is supported by technique and motivated by high standards. "I Just Didn't Know It at the Time" demonstrates that rhyme and feeling can coexist.

PROBLEM:
IDIOSYNCRATIC CHARACTERIZATION
AND PATNESS

The lyric "A Little Rearranging" went through a lot of rearranging—of its tone and its characterization. The three drafts printed here serve to illustrate the value of rewriting skills.

A LITTLE REARRANGING
(First Draft)

Verse: *I just bought some blue towels at Macy's,*
Because I was sick of the green,
Tonight I won't listen to Callas,
Or tune in to Channel Thirteen.

Verse: *Next winter I'll fly to St. Thomas,*
'Stead of freezing my butt off at Stowe
My phone bill is sure to get smaller,
My booze bill is likely to grow.

Chorus: *A LITTLE REARRANGING is all it's going to take*
A small amount of changing to get me back in shape
A LITTLE REARRANGING, I know will do me good,
From now on I'll do what I want
And not just what I should.

Verse: *I'll wear my old sweaters from college,*
That hung in the closet for years,
I'll trade in my Ford for a Porsche,
Get rid of that Rabbit of yours.

Verse: *There'll be a new name on the mailbox,*
Just one where there used to be two
I won't have to think about Christmas
I won't have to think about you.

Chorus: *A LITTLE REARRANGING is what I'm going to need,*
A small amount of changing, to get me back to speed
A LITTLE REARRANGING to straighten out my head,
I'll have a lot more closet space, a lot more room in bed.

Verse: *I won't have to put down the john seat,*
Or listen to jokes from your dad,
The joint account changes to single,
The living room changes to plaid.

Verse: *I'll still spend my days at the office,*
I guess I'll spend nights here at home,
I know I can boil ravioli,
I think I can make it alone.

Chorus: *A LITTLE REARRANGING that goes from A to Z,*
Just a small amount of changing, in every part of me,
A LITTLE REARRANGING, since you walked out as my
wife,
What am I rearranging? Just my whole god-damn life!

© 1983, Eben W. Keyes. Used with permission.

Analysis:

It's not until the end of the third verse (when the song is almost half over) that we get the first hint—with the word *yours*—of the reason behind all these changes: it's a breakup song. Though a lyric's plot should inch along, slowly letting the listener in on the facts as the story develops, that doesn't mean to withhold the theme from the audience until midway through the song. Successful lyrics start their story at the first line, then take us *from* something, *through* something, *to* something. The first recommendation to the writer was to let us know at the outset why the singer is making all these changes.

Next, the patness problem. When we're told that the singer bought *blue* towels because he was sick of the *green* ones, we've learned nothing other than that he now owns blue towels. Similarly, hearing that next winter he's going to fly to St. Thomas rather than ski at Stowe can only elicit a reaction of: So? What does the change in resort *mean?* And what are we to make of the fact that tonight he's not going to listen to opera records or view the public broadcasting channel? Why not? And what's the implication of the three different makes of cars? We're getting specificity without significance.

Then there's the tone. In some parts of the lyric, it sounds petulant, rather like a child who when left by a parent plans to misbehave by eating a quart of ice cream before dinner. In some sections the tone is ironically wistful: "I'll have a lot more closet space, a lot more room in bed . . . I think I can make it alone." In other places it's bitter: "I won't have to think about you." And finally angry: "Just my whole god-damn life!"

The writer thought over the critique and came up with this second draft:

A LITTLE REARRANGING
(Second Draft)

Chorus: *A LITTLE REARRANGING is all it's gonna take,*
Just a small amount of changing, that's what I have to make,
A LITTLE REARRANGING to straighten out my head,
To handle all that closet room, all that extra space in bed.

Verse: *I just bought some red towels at K-Mart,*
I never thought much of your beige,
Tonight I won't listen to Callas
I'll put on some old Patti Page.

Verse: *No more flights on the Concorde to Paris,*
I'll work on my slalom at Stowe,
My phone bill is sure to get smaller,
My squash bill is likely to grow.

Chorus: *A LITTLE REARRANGING is what I'm going to need,*
Just a small amount of changing, to get me back to speed,
A LITTLE REARRANGING I know will do me good,
To help me do the things I want, and not the things I should.

Verse: *I'll wear my old sweat shirts from college,*
That sat in the bureau for years,
I'll pick up a second-hand Rabbit,
Get rid of that Porsche of yours.

Verse: *Have to put a new card on the mailbox,*
One name where there used to be two,
Won't plan for our next anniversary . . .
Remembering the last one will do.

Chorus: *A LITTLE REARRANGING is all it's gonna take,*
Just a small amount of changing, that's what I have to make,
A LITTLE REARRANGING to straighten out my head,
To handle all that closet room, all that extra space in bed.

Verse: *I won't have to put down the john seat,*
Or refight World War II with your dad.
Now the joint account changes to single,
Now the living room changes to plaid.

Verse: *That blonde actress who does our commercials,*
        In time I'll invite her back home
        I know how to heat ravioli,
        I don't plan to eat it alone.

Chorus: *A LITTLE REARRANGING that goes from A to Z,*
         Just a small amount of changing, in every part of me,
         A LITTLE REARRANGING, since you walked out as my
             wife,
         What am I rearranging? Just my life.

© 1983, Eben W. Keyes. Used with permission.

Opening the lyric on the chorus has the virtue of showing us, with the extra closet and bed space, that he's been left. That's a major improvement over the initial draft.

The changes in the first verse now characterize the singee as a conservative (beige towels) opera buff (Callas), contrasted with the singer—a lover of 40s pop whose taste in decor runs to upbeat colors. The references to college sweat shirts, Rabbit, and Porsche now take on some significance: the singee is being painted as a well-heeled woman very concerned with outward show who, it appears, called the shots in the relationship. The mixed tone has narrowed down to one: bitter ("remembering the last one will do . . . I don't plan to eat it alone").

The bottom-line question is: Has this rewrite become a potentially recordable lyric? Well, the theme is certainly universal—a breakup based upon incompatibility. However, the second draft etches the couple in idiosyncratic fashion: he is a "suddenly single" man semi-celebrating his unexpected (and unsought) freedom; she is a rather stuffy jet setter who apparently dominated every aspect of the singer's life. That, in essence, is the situation with which we, as audience, are asked to "merge" (in a first-person song). It's hard to find the universal in that script. Fortunately, the lyricist is blessed with the attitude: "as many rewrites as it takes to get it right."

A LITTLE REARRANGING
(Third Draft)

Verse: *You took off one spring day in the Mustang,*
        Left a note and your ring on the porch;
        I had eight years of living a marriage
        Got a lifetime to live ⌐ divorce.

Verse: *When I was one half of a couple,*
        Never dreamt I'd be solo again,
        Without rules for the suddenly single—
        Have to work out my own master plan.

Chorus: *A LITTLE REARRANGING is what it's gonna take,*
A fair amount of changing, that I am gonna make,
A LITTLE REARRANGING to realign my head.
To handle all that closet room—that extra space in bed.

Verse: *I just bought maroon towels at Macy's,*
Cause I never cared much for your beige,
And tonight I won't listen to Callas
I'll play some old Patti Page.

Verse: *I've recycled a sweater from college,*
That you said was too shabby to wear;
And replaced your Bordeaux and your brandy
With some sour mash bourbon and beer.

Chorus: *A LITTLE REARRANGING is what I'm gonna need,*
A fair amount of changing, to get me back to speed.
A LITTLE REARRANGING I know will do me good,
I'll start to see more friends I like, not merely those I should.

Verse: *I don't have to put down the john seat, or*
Go outdoors when I want a cigar
Gonna work on improving my backhand
Try something I've not done before.

Verse: *That new neighbor whose dog bit the mailman,*
Gonna see if she'll come for a meal;
Getting sick of my soup-for-one diet,
Gonna cook up some mushrooms and veal.

Chorus: *A LITTLE REARRANGING that goes from A to Z,*
A fair amount of changing, in every part of me,
A LITTLE REARRANGING, since you walked out as my
*   wife,*
What am I rearranging? . . . just my life.

© 1984, Eben W. Keyes (words) and Ronald Gold (music). Used with permission.

Now the emphasis is on a concept we can all relate to more easily: surviving change. The singee's overly particularized monied background—Concorde flights, Porsche (and in an interim rewrite, a mink)—has been replaced with the more universal *difference in tastes*. It's stronger. The tendency toward pluralization (towels, sweat shirts), the sweeping predictions ("the living room changes to plaid"), and improbable events (entertaining a TV actress) have all been excised. The result: a lyric more about one human being's struggle to rally from the blow of a failed relationship and become his own person.

A footnote: Even after these fine rewrites of "A Little Rearranging," which have obviously resulted in a much more workable lyric, I must admit to still having a serious reservation about the choice of meter: tata-TUM tataTUM tataTUMta/tataTUM tataTUM tataTUM (You took OFF one spring DAY in the MUStang/Left a NOTE and your RING on the PORCH). To my ear, the singsong rhythm violates the emotion of the words. It has the echo of a limerick and seems to me to work against the genuineness of the expressed feeling. The writer warrants that his choice was deliberate: to make the lyric "optimistic." It remains to be seen (or rather, *heard*), if a collaborator's musical setting can manage to offset the superficiality inherent in the short anapestic lines.

PROBLEM: LOVE AS EUPHEMISM

"Love," in addition to making the world go round, predominates as the subject matter of pop songs. The results of a ten-year study published in *Popular Music and Society* (1983) showed that 73 percent of the songs surveyed dealt with "love"—of one kind or another. Actually, the word *love* in lyrics has been appearing under false pretenses for so long we don't even notice. Only sociologists, whose studies probe society's prevailing attitudes as manifested in pop lyrics, have caught the euphemism. What we're really singing about, more often than not, is sex. Or dependence. Or obsession. The word *love* is made to stand for all of them.

An authentic *love* song, such as "Just the Way You Are," is a rare commodity. But whether the actual subject of a song is "getting it on," ("Afternoon Delight") or dependence ("Can't Smile Without You") or obsession ("Every Breath You Take") is immaterial. What is important for the integrity of the lyric is that the writer discern which aspect of the umbrella term *love* he or she wants to write about. Pick one, and then stay on the subject. A stunning example of differentiating between love and lust is "What's Love Got to Do with It?"—a number-one record for Tina Turner in 1984: physical attraction is the lyric's sole subject. Such emotional honesty—rare in a lyric—unquestionably contributed to the song's success.

A lyricist who treats the words *sex* and *love* as though they were synonymous trivializes the emotion of loving (with its multitude of caring, thoughtful, and generous acts) by interchanging it with the singular act of lovemaking. If, within the same lyric, the word *love* alternates between signifying the deep emotion and the sexual act, the meaning of the song is diffused and, as a result, so is its power to affect. Such blurring of ideas prevents a lyric from becoming a strong song on either subject. For example, this first draft:

TELL ME IN THE MORNING
IF YOU'RE LEAVING

Verse: *How did she steal your heart?*
Did I make it that easy?

And what makes you so sure
That my love's gone completely?
With so many years behind us
How could you walk out the door
If you stay with me tonight
We'll see who loves you more.

Chorus: TELL ME IN THE MORNING IF YOU'RE LEAVING
Give me one more night to prove my love to you
Baby it's the least that you could do
YOU CAN TELL ME IN THE MORNING IF YOU'RE
      LEAVING
Let me love you like I should have all along
Don't walk out if you doubt my love is gone.

Verse: *I won't scream and I won't cry*
There's just one thing I want to do
Let me love you through the night
It's the only way I'm gonna fight for you
And maybe in the morning's light you'll see things differently
But tomorrow if you still want to go, you're free.

(Chorus)

© 1984, Eda Galeno. Used with permission.

Analysis:

By pop music business standards, it's close to a recordable lyric—producers not being notable as seekers of semantic accuracy. In fact, if the lyric were mated to a strong dramatic melody, the first draft might even get by. So, you ask, where's the problem? The answer is: it's synthetic.

The opening lines grab our attention and capsulize the situation: a woman (wife or co-vivant) has been told by her mate that he's found someone new. The line "Did I make it that easy?" is suffused with wistful self-recrimination and sets the serious tone of the song. We're hooked by genuine feeling, and our expectation is to hear a song that's going to touch us. And what do we get? Contrivance: "If you stay with me tonight, we'll see who *loves* you more." The singer is now challenging her rival to a competition: any way she can please, I can please better. What? You mean a relationship of "many years" will either stand or fall on how she performs in bed tonight? Nonsense. You may argue, "But that ploy worked in the song 'Nobody' with a similar plot" (see page 177). It certainly did, but remember, "Nobody" was built on a pun: Its one *consistent* tone was *playful*. That makes a big difference. Given the emotional attitude of this lyric's opening, what the singer would want to do, after recovering from the shock of his announcement, would be to talk. She'd want to find out how it happened, to listen to how he's feeling, to learn what's been missing for him and figure out what she can do about it. It was pointed out to the writer in the critique that she could treat the song from the I-want-to-save-our-relationship angle or from the attitude of am-I-gonna-make-love-to-you! but not both simultaneously. She realized the split feeling in the first draft and chose to stay with the initial tone she had set:

TELL ME IN THE MORNING
IF YOU'RE LEAVING
(Second Draft)

Verse: *How did she steal your heart, did I make it that easy?*
When did you turn to her for love you couldn't find in me?
I can't believe I didn't feel you slippin' away
For all the years behind us, I'm askin' you to stay . . .

Chorus: *TELL ME IN THE MORNING IF YOU'RE LEAVING*
Just give me one more night so we can talk it through
I'm not ready to give up on me and you. You can

TELL ME IN THE MORNING IF YOU'RE LEAVING
Just give me one more chance to try and change your mind
From leaving me and my love far behind.

Verse: *Is it too late to apologize for times I took more than I gave*
If a little spark is still alive, then there's something we can
    save
And maybe in the morning's light you'll see things differently.
But tomorrow if you still want to go, you're free.

(CHORUS)

© 1984, Eda Galeno. Used with permission.

The second draft eliminates the duality. The writer has made the singer believable. Now another question arises: Is the song's title what the song is all about? Clearly, it isn't. If you saw that title on the charts you would expect to hear a song that says, in effect, don't tell me tonight that you're leaving me, wait until morning to tell me. The problem is that the title itself, in spite of the word *if*, connotes a foregone conclusion that he's leaving (rather like "Touch Me in the Morning"). But that is not the writer's intention. What she means to say is: Give me one more night to try to hold on to you. Here's the fifth draft:

ONE MORE NIGHT
(Fifth Draft)

Verse: *How did she steal your heart?*
Did I make it that easy?

> *When did you turn to her*
> *For love you couldn't find in me*
> *I can't believe I didn't feel you slippin' away*
> *For all the years behind us*
> *I'm asking you to stay, and give me*

Chorus: ONE MORE NIGHT
> *So we can talk it over*
> *One more chance to try and change your mind*
> ONE MORE NIGHT
> *To say the things I should have said*
> *I'm not ready to give up on us yet.*

Verse: *Is it too late to apologize*
> *For times I took more than I gave?*
> *If a spark is still alive*
> *Then there's something we can save*
> *Maybe in the morning's light*
> *You'll see things differently*
> *And tomorrow if you still want to go, you're free,*
>   *Just give me*

Chorus: ONE MORE NIGHT
> *So we can talk it over*
> *One more chance to try to change your mind*
> ONE MORE NIGHT
> *To say the things I should have said*
> *I'm not ready to give up on us yet,*
>   *Please give me*

Chorus: ONE MORE NIGHT
> *Don't leave before the morning, give me*
> ONE MORE NIGHT
> *And we can pull love through*
> ONE MORE NIGHT
> *Cause I know my love can hold you*
> *Won't you give me ONE MORE NIGHT with you?*

A major improvement. "One More Night" has the makings of a pop ballad hit, one of those biggies like "Somewhere Down the Road" and "Just Once." The lyricist still needs to polish some rough edges, such as using the word *love* twice in the last chorus, but the lyric is on its way.

PROBLEM: WEAK METER AND UNEVEN SCANSION

The first draft of "Wrong Number" showed immediate promise. The theme—the ending of a relationship—is timeless and universal. The tone is breezily self-assertive. The form—verse/chorus/bridge—fits the "hooky" title perfectly:

WRONG NUMBER
(First Draft)

Verse: *I used to spend my evenings waiting*
To hear your voice on the telephone.
But you didn't take the time to call,
You were busy making time on your own.
When you do get around to dialing
Apologetic and sincere
Mr. Big Time Operator,
This is the message you'll hear:

Chorus: *You got the WRONG NUMBER*
So you've been disconnected.
WRONG NUMBER
Too late to correct it.
But it should be explained
You got the WRONG NUMBER
'Cause this number has changed.

Verse: *I found myself somebody new*
Who doesn't have a party line
And when he feels like talking
The only number he calls is mine.
So erase my name from your little black book
It was much too crowded in there
And if you decide to call again,
This is what you'll hear:

(Chorus)

Bridge: *Once I thought our names could be*
Side by side in the directory
But, we were never right for each other
'Cause I wanted love
And you just wanted a lover.
(Chorus)

Analysis:

The recommendations were to shorten the line "so erase my name from your little black book" to conform to the pattern of the corresponding line in the first verse, to augment the meaning of "and when he feels like *talking,*" to condense the chorus, and to abbreviate the bridge—the couplet, "I always thought that we would be/side by side in the directory" sounds like something out of *H.M.S. Pinafore*. Here is the solid rewrite, which fixed the main flaws.

WRONG NUMBER
(Final Draft)

Verse: *Used to spend my evenings waiting*
To hear your voice on the telephone.
But you didn't take the time to call
You were busy making time on your own
And when you get around to dialing—
Apologetic and so sincere,
Mr. Big Time Operator
The next time you're gonna hear:

Chorus: *You got the WRONG NUMBER*
You've been disconnected
It's the WRONG NUMBER
You're too late to correct it
It's the WRONG NUMBER
This number is not your number anymore.

Verse: *Found myself somebody better*
Who doesn't use a party line
And when he feels like making love
The number he calls is always mine
So forget you ever knew me
And I'll forget I used to care
And when you feel like talking to me
The next time you're gonna hear:

(Chorus)

Bridge: *Once I thought we could be*
Right for each other
But I wanted love
And all you wanted was a lover

(Chorus)

© 1984, Arline Udis (words) and Hec Stevens (music).

The final rewrite of "Wrong Number" earned for the lyricist (who had been writing just one year) her first publishing contract.

PROBLEM: A LETDOWN ENDING

The assignment was to write a lyric about a place. "Queens" is not a contender for the top 40, nor was it meant to be. What it is is a lyric with charm, wit, and freshness:

QUEENS
(First Draft)

Across the East River lies New York, New York
Fabled in song and story
A fine domestic champagne with a stubborn cork
And I'm waiting to taste its glory.
And I go to work there five days a week
And I roam through postcard scenes
What I just can't bear, five nights a week
I take the train home to QUEENS.

QUEENS! What can you say about QUEENS?
I don't have a day without QUEENS.
QUEENS, somehow hasn't my loyalty
QUEENS, It's just nothing like royalty
QUEENS seems to rhyme with Heinz baked beans.

QUEENS—I ask you, what is it?
QUEENS—no one comes here to visit
QUEENS—has the sound of finality
QUEENS—it has no personality
QUEENS—where they all wear Bonjour jeans.

Brooklyn has memories of the Bums
The Bronx has very dramatic slums
In Staten Island, the ferry comes
But what can you say about QUEENS?

QUEENS. You get tuna au gratin from QUEENS
You get to look at Manhattan from QUEENS
In QUEENS little leaguers are hardier
QUEENS is the way to La Guardia
QUEENS—they don't put in magazines.

On the Island, neat little houses
Westchester, neat little blouses
Connecticut, neat little trousers
But what is so neat about QUEENS?

QUEENS, I bet everyone knows I'm from QUEENS.
I hate that it shows I'm from QUEENS
QUEENS. It is not quite suburbia

It's a cross between Yonkers and Serbia
It's where size nines become size eighteens.

Someday I'll meet a man
Who'll sweep me off my feet
To the Top of the Sixes, the Rainbow Room and posh Broad-
*   way mezzanines*
We'll live and love on East 83rd
We'll have one or two kids, but comes the third
I bet we'll pack and all move back to QUEENS.

© 1983, Francesca Blumenthal. Used with permission.

Analysis:

That's a lyric with an original voice! The fine first draft has, how-ever, one central flaw—a downbeat ending. Not only downbeat, but unbe-lievable. Given *that* woman's feelings, if she ever moved to Manhattan, there's only one way you could ever get her near Queens: in a cab to Kenne-dy Airport *en route* to Paris!

The other flaws are minor matters: too many Queenses; "little" as the repeated adjective for *blouses* and *trousers* is meaningless; the stanzas need tightening; and some of the rhymes don't ping in the right places, or they sound inept where a slight shift in pronunciation (and spelling) would make them sound clever. Here's the rewrite:

QUEENS
(Second Draft)

Across the river lies New York, New York
Like a fine champagne with a stubborn cork
Like caviar on someone else's fork
What a shame to waste it
I long to taste it.
I go to work there five days a week
When the rush hour crowds are at their peak
We swing and sway, all cheek to cheek
And each night what I must do
Is take a train and bus to

QUEENS!
What can you say about QUEENS?
There's a wide choice of fine gasolines.
QUEENS hasn't captured my loyalty,
QUEENS, it is nothing like royalty
QUEENS, it's where potholes turn into ravines.

QUEENS. I ask you what is it?
QUEENS—no one comes here to visit.

QUEENS—*has a ring of banality,*
QUEENS—*is no principality*
QUEENS—*where they all wear Vanderbilt jeans.*

Now Brooklyn has memories of dem Bums
The Bronx has such dramatic slums
In Staten Island, the ferry comes
But who beats a drum about QUEENS?

Still there's the view—
You can look at Manhattan from QUEENS.
You get tuna au gratin from QUEENS
Few little leaguers are "hardia"
True, it's the way to La Guardia.
But who wants to go to a party in QUEENS?

On the Island, neat little houses,
Westchester, neat flannel "trouses"
Connecticut, neat preppy blouses
But what's so neat about QUEENS?

Fate—thumbed its nose when it chose to make QUEENS.
I hate—everyone knows I'm from QUEENS.
QUEENS—*it is not quite suburbia.*
Lost between Yonkers and Serbia
QUEENS—*it's where size nines become size eighteens.*

Someday I'll meet up with a super man
Who'll sweep me up, up and away
To the Top of the Sixes, the Rainbow Room
Like King Kong with Fay Wray.
From our apartment on FDR Drive
We'll gaze on those dull, distant scenes
And they'll never ever take me alive
Back to QUEENS.

That's an authentic ending! In the rewrite the dull thud of the identity *finality/personality* is upscaled to the ping of perfect rhyme *banality/principality,* and the other nonrhyme—*East 83rd/third* was eliminated. (Spelling doesn't count.) The lyric sounds better after the deletion of five mentions of Queens. Also it's more insightful to characterize Westchester execs as dressed in *flannel* trousers and Connecticut matrons in *preppy* blouses, than to repeat *little.* The added length of the introductory verse permits the switch in rhyme scheme from ababcdcd to aaabbcccdd, adding to rhyming fun. It's a good example of how triple-line rhymes and inner rhyming enhance a comedy song. "Queens" was set with a melody it deserved, and at this writing it has been accepted for an off-Broadway revue.

WRAPUP

What separates the amateur from the professional is not so much degree of talent as it is difference in attitude. A professional looks upon a newborn lyric as a first draft, a work in progress to be put aside to jell and later examined dispassionately for flaws—ultimately to be polished to a fine luster.

The amateur views an initial outpouring of words as if it were cemented in place. The very idea of rewriting is emotionally rejected. Because it is frightening, rewriting sometimes becomes impossible; the amateur generally finds it difficult to write on demand—in a given form, on a particular theme, to a specific title, and within a limited time. The amateur clings to the myth that writing is a matter of inspiration. As a result, frequently nothing comes: there's no technique to draw upon. So for many, "amateur" becomes a lifetime status.

The promising preprofessional, on the other hand, seeks appraisal rather than praise. He or she can discern that rejection of the writing is not a rejection of the writer. Assignments are viewed as a challenge instead of a threat, and rewriting is accepted as inevitable.

A song is a process of evolution, and revising is simply a part of the process. Understanding that fact is a requisite for success. The simple secret is to think of your lyric-writing talent as a wellspring of words that—with skill, patience, and perseverance—you can shape into a lifetime of songs.

Coda

"If what you're saying is sincere and honest, the audience is going to feel that honesty. If it is real to you, it will be real to others. If not, why bother. Nobody's gonna care." Irene Cara

Now you have an idea of how to go about putting a song together: the basic song forms, the principles of good writing, some theory of rhythm and rhyme, and guidelines to help you avoid the most common pitfalls. You have everything you need to write a lyric—except one. It's something that cannot be taught—something no assignment can generate and no exercise can develop. When it exists in a song, an audience responds. When it's missing, nothing offsets the lack. It is, of course, genuine feeling—something every great song has.

The music business's emphasis on "hits" and "hooks" and "grooves" is spawning a generation of songwriters who design *successful records,* yes. But *enduring songs?* Rarely. Small wonder that among the hundreds of gold and platinum successes of the last twenty years, the number of new standards—songs performed and recorded by artists other than the original one—has been relatively small.

Everywhere aspiring songwriters turn—to books, workshops, seminars, publishers—they hear the same thing: go home and write a hit. If many preprofessionals seek success by looking for a formula, they can hardly be blamed. They've been brainwashed—told, in effect, to clone what's on radio and MTV. Rarely are they encouraged to write about the things that are important to them, or to mean every word they say.

It's ironic that the finest songwriters, past and present, creators of our long-term superhits, when asked if they tried to write a hit, unanimously affirmed they hadn't the foggiest idea how to go about it. For these writers who have turned out our most original and enduring songs, producing a hit had never been an objective, but rather a result:

HAL DAVID: "Unless I can create an emotion to which I can respond, I throw it away. I try to write good songs instead of hit songs."

ALAN JAY LERNER: "I like to write stories that move me, with the implicit hope that they will move others too."

OSCAR HAMMERSTEIN: "Technique and professional polish do not make a song . . . there is an element much less tangible: sincerity."

HAROLD ARLEN: "Nobody can sit down to write a hit."

DOROTHY FIELDS: "You write what you feel. You write because of that need for expression. But you don't write with the specific purpose of trying to create a hit."

STEPHEN SONDHEIM: "The business of writing songs to become hits has never bothered me because I don't know what makes a hit and it's a great relief not to worry about it."

COLE PORTER: "I haven't the faintest notion of how anyone writes hits, except for Irving Berlin, who can't help writing them."

IRVING BERLIN: "You have to know and feel what you are writing about."

There is no substitute for sincerity. Cleverness and contrivance may get published. Imitativeness and shallowness may make it to the charts. All these elements can even produce a number-one record, but never a great song.

Appendix

FOR THE LYRICIST'S BOOKSHELF

Every budding lyricist should be on intimate terms with the best work of the past. One can aspire to the heights only if one knows what the heights are. The books listed here contain the lyrics and theories and describe the creative processes of our finest practitioners of popular and theater songs. Find your mentors and study their writings; absorb their theories; analyze their techniques.

Many of the biographies and lyric collections listed, unfortunately, may be difficult to find; they may even be out of print. Nevertheless, if you know of their existence, you can search libraries and prowl secondhand bookstores. And badger publishers to reprint!

For Study

The Annotated Gilbert & Sullivan
Penguin Books
Middlesex, England (1982)

Thou Swell, Thou Witty
The Life and Lyrics of Lorenz Hart
By Dorothy Hart
Harper & Row, New York (1976)

The Lyrics of Noel Coward
The Overlook Press,
Woodstock, New York (1975)

Lyrics
By Oscar Hammerstein II
Simon & Schuster, New York (1949)

Lyrics on Several Occasions
By Ira Gershwin
Alfred A. Knopf, New York (1959)

The Gershwins
By Robert Kimball and Alfred Simon
(Lyrics, photographs, letters, etc.)
Atheneum, New York (1973)

Dancing in the Dark
Words by Howard Dietz
An autobiography
Quadrangle/New York Times Book Co.
(1974)

The Complete Lyrics of Cole Porter
Edited by Robert Kimball
Alfred Knopf, New York (1983)

American Popular Song
The Great Innovators 1900-1950
(Analysis of the music of Kern/
Gershwin/Rodgers/Porter/Arlen etc.)
By Alec Wilder
Oxford University Press, New York
(1970)

They're Playing Our Song
By Max Wilk
(Interviews with Dorothy Fields,
Johnny Mercer, and others)
Atheneum, New York (1973)

How to Write a Song
As told to Henry Kane
(Interviews with Hoagy Carmichael,
Dorothy Fields, Noel Coward, and others)
The Macmillan Company, New York
(1962)

I Should Care (An Autobiography)
By Sammy Cahn
Arbor House, New York (1974)

Harold Arlen: Happy with the Blues
The Life and Times of the Composer
of "Stormy Weather"
By Edward Jablonski
Doubleday & Co., New York (1961)

Our Huckleberry Friend
Life, Times, and Lyrics of
Johnny Mercer
Lyle Stuart, Secaucus, NJ (1982)

Their Words Are Music
The Great Theatre Lyricists
and Their Lyrics
By Lehman Engel
(Includes among others: Sheldon
Harnick, Alan Jay Lerner, E.Y. Harburg,
Comden and Green, and Frank Loesser)
Crown Publishing, New York (1975)

*Great Musicals of the American Theatre,
Volume One*
Edited by Stanley Richards
(The book and lyrics to ten musicals
including *Brigadoon, West Side Story,
Gypsy,* and *Fiddler on the Roof.*)
Chilton Book Company, Radnor, PA
(1973)

*Great Musicals of the American Theatre,
Volume Two*
Edited by Stanley Richards
(The book and lyrics to ten musicals
including *Lady in the Dark, Cabaret,
Fiorello!,* and *A Little Night Music.*)
Chilton Book Company, Radnor, PA
(1976)

Musical Stages
(An Autobiography)
By Richard Rodgers
Random House, New York (1975)

The Street Where You Live
(An Autobiography)
By Alan Jay Lerner
W.W. Norton, New York (1978)

The Stephen Sondheim Songbook
Introduction by Sheridan Morley
Chappell & Co. Ltd., London (1979)

*Playwrights, Lyricists, Composers
on Theater*
Edited by Otis L. Guernsey, Jr.
(Articles by Sheldon Harnick, Jerry
Herman, Stephen Sondheim, others)
Dodd, Mead & Company, New York
(1974)

What the World Needs Now
(The lyrics of Hal David)
Simon & Schuster, New York (1970)

The Poetry of Rock
Edited by Richard Goldstein
(Collection of lyrics includes: Chuck
Berry, Paul Simon, Peter Townshend)
Bantam Books, New York (1968)

Baby, That Was Rock and Roll
The Legendary Leiber and Stoller
Text by Robert Palmer
Harcourt Brace Jovanovich, New York
(1978)

Great Rock Musicals
Edited by Stanley Richards (The book
and lyrics to eight musicals including *Hair,
The Wiz,* and *Tommy.*)
Stein and Day, Briar Cliff Manor,
New York (1979)

The Beatles Illustrated Lyrics
Edited by Alan Aldridge
Delacorte Press, New York (1969)

How to Be A Successful Songwriter
As told to Kent McNeel and Mark Luther
(Interviews with, among others:
Jeff Barry, Barry Mann, and Cynthia Weil)
St. Martin's Press, New York (1978)

*Nowhere to Run
The Story of Soul Music*
By Gerri Hirshey
Times Books, New York (1984)

In Their Own Words
As told to Bruce Pollak
(Interviews with, among others: Randy
Newman, Frank Zappa, and Harry
Chapin)
Collier Macmillan Publishing Co.,
New York (1975)

Writings and Drawings
By Bob Dylan
Alfred A. Knopf, Inc., New York (1973)

For Writing Skills

*Writing the Natural Way:
Using Right-Brain Techniques to Release
Your Expressive Powers*
Gabriele Lusser Rico
J.P. Tarcher, Inc., Los Angeles, CA (1983)

Elements of Style
William Strunk Jr. and E.B. White
The Macmillan Company, New York
(1959)

The Complete Rhyming Dictionary
Edited by Clement Wood
Doubleday Publishing Co., New York
(1943)

The Songwriter's Rhyming Dictionary
By Sammy Cahn
Facts on File, Inc.
New York, NY (1983)

Webster's New World Dictionary
The World Publishing Co.
New York and Cleveland

Roget's International Thesaurus
Thomas Y. Crowell Co., New York

*The Second Barnhart Dictionary
of New English*
Harper & Row, New York (1980)

Dictionary of Modern English Usage
By H. W. Fowler
Oxford University Press, New York
(1965)

*A Short Etymological Dictionary
of Modern English*
by Eric Partridge
The MacMillan Company, New York
(1959)

A Dictionary of Clichés
By Eric Partridge
E. P. Dutton, New York (1940)

Dictionary of American Slang
Wentworth and Flexner
T. Y. Crowell, New York (1975)

The Word Finder
By Rodale Press
Emmaus, PA (1947)

*Morris Dictionary of Word
and Phrase Origins*
By William and Mary Morris
Harper & Row, New York (1962)

Reverse Dictionary
By Theodore M. Bernstein
Quadrangle/The New York Times Book
Co. (1975)

The Garden of Eloquence
A Rhetorical Bestiary
By Willard R. Espy
Harper & Row, New York (1983)

Familiar Quotations
By John Bartlett
Little, Brown & Co., Boston

*Handbook of Commonly Used American
Idioms*
Edited by Adam Makkai, Ph.D.
Barron's Educational Series
Woodbury, NY (1984)

For the History

*An Introduction to Popular Music
Publishing in America*
By Leonard Feist
National Music Publishers Association,
New York (1980)

All the Years of American Popular Music
By David Ewen
Prentice-Hall, Englewood Cliffs, NJ
(1977)

Yesterdays
Popular Song in America
By Charles Hamm
W.W. Norton, New York (1979)

American Musical Theatre, A Chronicle
By Gerald Bordman
Oxford University Press, New York
(1978)

*The Rolling Stone History
of Rock and Roll*
Edited by Jim Miller
Random House/Rolling Stone Press
(1980)

For the Business

Breakin' in to the Music Business
By Alan H. Siegel
Cherry Lane Books
Portchester, NY (1983)

This Business of Music
(A Practical Guide to the Music Industry
for Publishers, Writers, Record
Companies, Producers, Artists, Agents)
By Sidney Shemel and
M. William Krasilowsky
Billboard Publishers, Inc., New York
(1979)

Making Money Making Music
(No Matter Where You Live)
By James W. Dearing
Writer's Digest Books, Cincinnati, Ohio
(1982)

The Platinum Rainbow
(How to succeed in the music business
without selling your soul)
By Bob Monaco & James Riordan
Swordsman Press, Sherman Oaks,
California (1980)

Songwriter's Market (An Annual)
(Where to Sell Your Songs)
Edited by Rand Ruggeberg
Writer's Digest Books, Cincinnati

The Music Connection
(Biweekly magazine)
6640 Sunset Boulevard, Suite 201
Hollywood, CA 90028

American Songwriter
(Bimonthly magazine)
1300 Division Street
Nashville, Tennessee 37203

SONGWRITER ORGANIZATIONS

Along with acquiring the craft, of equal importance is surrounding yourself with people of like interest—other lyricists, composers, musicians, artists, producers. It is also essential to learn about the business side of your business. There are many national and regional organizations whose function is to protect, educate, and generally serve the songwriter.

The three performing rights societies—ASCAP, BMI, and SESAC—collect royalties due their members (or affiliates) from radio, TV, and concert performances. Every professional writer belongs to one of the three organizations. The ASCAP Foundation, the educational arm of AS-CAP, conducts annual pop and theater workshops at its New York headquarters, as well as periodic regional workshops. BMI's esteemed Lehman Engel Theatre Workshop and Librettists' Courses have helped nurture budding Broadway writers for over two decades. Each of the societies welcomes associate members.

The Songwriters Guild, formerly known as the American Guild of Authors and Composers (AGAC), for over fifty years has championed and protected the rights of the songwriter. Its songwriter/publisher contract is considered the industry's finest. Each of its offices in New York (the national headquarters), Nashville, and Hollywood presents regularly scheduled Ask-a-Pro rap sessions that feature notable industry professionals as well as songwriting workshops which are open to all. For members only there are a collaborating service, free contract review, and royalty collection plan.

The Nashville Songwriters Association International (NSAI) is another important organization whose membership spans the country. In addition to conducting local workshops and seminars, NSAI travels with weekend miniseminars to regional vest-pocket branches in forty cities from Maine to Florida. These locations can be found by calling Nashville headquarters' phone number.

The National Academy of Recording Arts and Sciences (NARAS) is the nonprofit membership organization that presents the annual Grammy Awards. In addition, it engages in professional educational activities such as seminars, provides scholarships, and has established a Hall of Fame to recognize and house significant historical recordings. Like The Songwriters Guild and the performing rights societies, NARAS offers an associate membership.

The Dramatists Guild, founded in 1920, is a professional association of playwrights, composers, and lyricists. Its services include use of the Guild's seven contracts, counseling on all theatrical contracts, advice on dealings with producers, and an annual marketing directory. Headquartered in New York, the Guild maintains an 800 number to inform its national membership of the many symposia and weekend workshops held in major cities across the country. (For anyone with theatrical interests, its renowned publication *The Dramatists Guild Quarterly* alone makes an associate membership worth the fee.)

The Musical Theater Works, Inc., is a new not-for-profit membership organization in New York City dedicated to the development of original theater music. MTW encourages the growth and development of new librettists and introduces the work of new composers and lyricists. The organization programs include a librettist's workshop, a lecture series, a works-in-progress reading program, a Meet the Composer series, and production showcases of new musical works.

In 1984, the Hollywood-based SRS (Songwriters Resources & Services) changed its name to the National Academy of Songwriters (NAS). The 2,000-member Academy has established a new professional division which will implement its "strong commitment to the developing writer through workshops, counseling, and information services."

The Los Angeles Songwriters Showcase (LASS) is a nonprofit service organization for songwriters sponsored by BMI and founded by Len Chandler and John Braheny in 1971. The resource and informational center presents a weekly interview/showcase/critique session to bring songwriters and their songs to the attention of the music industry, offers career counseling, and holds seminars. LASS is the producer of Songwriters Expo, an annual two-day series of panels and classes on all aspects of the craft and business of songwriting held in Los Angeles in November.

In addition to these organizations, a number of local and regional associations dedicated to educating and supporting the aspiring songwriter have sprung up during the last decade. The following list makes no claims to be inclusive (nor 100 percent up-to-date on addresses and phone numbers) but I hope it will serve to open a door or two for you into the music *business*.

ALABAMA

Muscle Shoals Music Association
P.O. Box 2009
Muscle Shoals, AL 35662
(205)381-1442

ARIZONA

ASCAP
9200 North Central Avenue
Phoenix, AZ 85020
(602)861-2128

Arizona Songwriters Association
P.O. Box 678
Phoenix, AZ 85001
(602)841-6397

Tucson Songwriters Association
620 North 6th Avenue
Tucson, AZ 85705
(602)624-8276

ARKANSAS

Arkansas Songwriters Associaton
P.O. Box 55128
Little Rock, AR 72205
(No listing)

CALIFORNIA

The Songwriters Guild
6430 Sunset Boulevard
Hollywood, CA 90028
(213)462-1108

National Academy of Songwriters (NAS)
6772 Hollywood Boulevard
Hollywood, CA 90028
(213)463-7178

The Los Angeles Songwriters Showcase
(LASS)
6772 Hollywood Boulevard
Hollywood, CA 90028
(213)462-1382

ASCAP
6430 Sunset Boulevard
Hollywood, CA 90028
(213)466-7681

BMI
6255 Sunset Boulevard
Hollywood, CA 90028
(213)465-2111

SESAC
9000 Sunset Boulevard
Hollywood, CA 90069
(213)274-6814

Santa Barbara Songwriters Guild
P.O. Box 2238
Santa Barbara, CA 93120
(805)962-9333

California Copyright Conference
P.O. Box 145
North Hollywood, CA 91603
(213)980-3357

NARAS (National Office)
303 Glenoaks Boulevard
Burbank, CA 91502
(213)849-1313

NARAS
2731 Franklin Street
San Francisco, CA 94123
(415)777-4633

NARAS
4444 Riverside Drive
Burbank, CA 91505
(213)843-8253

Musicians Contact Service
6605 Sunset Boulevard
Hollywood, CA 90028
(213)467-2191

South Bay Songwriters Association
407 California Avenue
Palo Alto, CA 94306
(415)327-8296

California Country Music Association
721 Cipriano Place
Monterey Park, CA 91754
(213)289-4204

Songwriters of San Diego
7972 Mission Center Court
San Diego, CA 92108
(No listing)

Orange Entertainment Songwriter Services Division
421 North Tustin Avenue
Orange, CA 92667
(714)633-8200

The Songwriters Stage
P.O. Box 809
Half Moon Bay, CA 94019
(No listing)

San Gabriel Valley Music
Box 396
West Covina, CA 91709
(No listing)

Santa Cruz Songwriters Guild
P.O. Box 76
Ben Lomond, CA 95005
(408)338-2891

San Francisco Folk Music Center
885 Clayton Street
San Francisco, CA 94117
(415)441-8910

Southern California Songwriters Guild
P.O. Box 723
Cypress, CA 90630
(No listing)

North Bay Songwriters Association
P.O. Box 6023
Santa Rosa, CA 95406
(707)887-1445

Sacramento Songwriters Showcase
4632 U Street
Sacramento, CA 95817
(916)456-3911

North County Songwriters Guild
13828 Tobiasson Road
Poway, CA 92064
(619)748-5138

COLORADO

ASCAP
3090 South Jamaica Court
Aurora, CO 80014
(303)695-6754

Country Music Foundation
Box 19435
Denver, CO 80219
(No listing)

Colorado Songwriters Association
3050 South Xeric Court
Denver, CO 80231
(303)755-2223

CONNECTICUT

Connecticut Songwriters Association
P.O. Box 115
Torrington, CT 06790
(203)489-4403

DISTRICT OF COLUMBIA

Songwriters Association of Washington
(SAW)
1377 K St. N.W.
Washington, D.C. 20005
(202)682-7361

Black Music Association (BMA)
P.O. Box 68683
Washington, DC 20019
(No listing)

FLORIDA

ASCAP
1065 N.E. 125th Street
North Miami, FL 33161
(305)895-6390

Central Florida Music Association
P.O. Box 5102
Winter Park, FL 32793
(305)896-5601

GEORGIA

ASCAP
One Georgia Way, N.W.
Atlanta, GA 30339
(404)952-8843

Atlanta Songwriters
P.O. Box 52540
Atlanta, GA 30355
(404)922-2272

NARAS
c/o Master Sound
1227 Spring Street Northwest
Atlanta, GA 30309
(404)876-1644

Friends of Georgia Music Festival
West Georgia College
Div. of Con. Ed./Pub. Services
Adamson Hall
Carollton, GA 30118

ILLINOIS

ASCAP
999 East Touhy
Des Plaines, IL 60018
(312)827-6810

NARAS
P.O. Box 11614
Chicago, IL 60611
(312)269-0393

American Music Conference
1000 Stokie Boulevard
Wilmette, IL 60091
(312)266-7200

INDIANA

Indianapolis Songwriters
Box 176
McCordsville, IN 46055
(No listing)

Whitewater Valley Songwriters
and Musicians
RR #4 Box 12
Liberty, IN 47353
(317)477-3665

KANSAS

Composers, Arrangers & Songwriters
of Kansas
117 West 8th Street
Hays, KS 67601
(913)625-9634

LOUISIANA

ASCAP
3340 Severn Avenue
Metairie, LA 70002
(504)889-0278

New Orleans Songwriters
2643 De Soto Street
New Orleans, LA 70119
(No listing)

Louisiana Songwriters
4775 Arrowhead Street
Baton Rouge, LA 70808
(No listing)

MARYLAND

ASCAP
One Parkway Drive Building
7258 Parkway Drive
Hanover, MD 21076
(301)796-5222

Baltimore/Washington Songwriters
5507 Stuart Avenue
Baltimore, MD 21215
(No listing)

MASSACHUSETTS

ASCAP
Ten Speen Street
Framingham, MA 01701
(617)875-3515

New England Songwriters
141 Danforth Street
Framingham, MA 01701
(No listing)

Massachusetts Songwriters
c/o Sparkie Allison
P.O. Box 211
Westfield, MA 01086
(No listing)

MICHIGAN

ASCAP
755 West Big Beaver Road
Troy, MI 48084
(313)362-2444

Detroit Songwriters
2310 Highland
Detroit, MI 48206
(No listing)

MINNESOTA

ASCAP
7851 Metro Parkway
Bloomington, MN 55420
(612)854-0763

Minnesota Songwriters Association
13 West 26th Street
Minneapolis, MN 55404
(612)872-1229

MISSOURI

ASCAP
Trade Center Building
300 Brookes Drive
Hazelwood, MO 63042
(314)895-1830

Missouri Songwriters Association, Inc.
3711 Andora Place
St. Louis, MO 63125
(314)894-3354

NEW YORK

The Songwriters Guild
276 Fifth Avenue
New York, NY 10001
(212)686-6820

ASCAP
One Lincoln Plaza
New York, NY 10023
(212)595-3050

BMI
320 West 57th Street
New York, NY 10019
(212)586-2000

SESAC
10 Columbus Circle
New York, NY 10019
(212)586-1708

The Dramatists Guild
234 West 44th Street
New York, NY 10036
(212)398-9366

Musical Theatre Works
133 Second Avenue
New York, NY 10003
(212)677-0040

Hudson Valley Songwriters
P.O. Box 176
Goshen, NY 10924
(914)294-5756

The Songwriters Advocate (TSA)
47 Maplehurst Road
Rochester, NY 14617
(716)266-0679

Westchester Songwriter's Guild
P.O. Box 1256
White Plains, NY 10602
(914)965-1867

NORTH CAROLINA

Middle Atlantic Songwriters, Inc.
444 Rocky Run Road
Midway Park, NC 28544
(918)353-2872

OHIO

ASCAP
3550 Curtis Boulevard
Eastlake, OH 44094
(216)946-8828

Columbus Songwriters
3312 Petzinger Road
Columbus, OH 43227
(No listing)

PENNSYLVANIA

ASCAP
Benjamin Fox Pavilion
Old York Road
Jenkinstown, PA 19046
(215)885-2510

ASCAP
North Point Building
9800 McKnight Road
Pittsburgh, PA 15237
(412)366-2345

Pennsylvania Association of Songwriters,
Composers and Lyricists (P.A.S.C.A.L.)
P.O. Box 4311
Allentown, PA 18105
(No listing)

Black Music Association (BMA)
1500 Locust Street
Philadelphia, PA 19102
(No listing)

TENNESSEE

The Songwriters Guild
50 Music Square West
Nashville, TN 37203
(615)329-1782

ASCAP
2 Music Square West
Nashville, TN 37203
(615)244-3936

BMI
10 Music Square East
Nashville, TN 37203
(615)259-3625

SESAC
11 Music Square South
Nashville, TN 37203
(615)244-1992

Nashville Songwriters Association
International (NSAI)
803 18th Avenue South
Nashville, TN 37203
(615)321-5004

Memphis Songwriters
1922 Jermyn Court
Memphis, TN 38119
(No listing)

NARAS
7 Music Circle North
Nashville, TN 37203
(615)244-1992

NARAS
66 S. Front Street
Memphis, TN 38103
(901)525-0621

TEXAS

ASCAP
16990 Dallas Parkway
Dallas, TX 75248
(214)248-8022

East Texas Songwriters
408 Haden Street
Tyler, TX
(214)597-0416

VIRGINIA

Southwest Virginia Songwriters
Association
P.O. Box 689
Salem, VA 24153
(703)380-2921

WASHINGTON

ASCAP
10740 Meridian Avenue North
Seattle, WA 98133
(206)367-8316

Pacific Northwest Songwriters
P.O. Box 98324
Seattle, WA 98188
(206)824-1568

CANADA

Canadian Songwriters Association
135 York Street
Ottawa, Ontario, Canada K1N 5T4

Indices

SONGS

Lyrics, which appear either in their entirety or in extensive excerpts, are indicated by boldface type

PEOPLE

Names and page numbers printed in boldface italic type denote quotations

TOPICS

Process. *See* Lyric writing process
Pronouns, 9, 22, 125, 128, 133, 161; in bridges, 65-67; in first lines, 22
Proportion, 120-23
Prose synopsis. *See* Plot development
Prosody, 248-50, 251, 252-53, 292. *See also* Warping, word
Public Domain (PD), 10, 253
Pulitzer Prize, 173
Pun, 177, 179, 182, 186
Purple prose, 169

Question plot, 23

Redundancy, 129-31, 151
Refrain, 30, 32, 37, 40; "outside," in AAA form, 40-44; question, 151
Release (bridge), 31
Repetition, 71, 74, 140-51, 210, 211, 252
Return, the, 141
Rewriting, 90-91, 101, 114, 119-20, 129, 136-37, 293-314
Rhyme, 185-212, 292; apocopated, 191-94; assonance, 145, 210, 211; augmented, 197; broken, 191; cliché, 195; comedy songs and, 188; consonance, 145, 195-96, 211; contiguous, 192; couplets, 55; dictionaries, 212; diminished, 197; dissonance, 208; echo, 192; emotion and, 43, 145, 196, 205, 299-300; euphony, 206, 208; eye, 186; feminine (double) 186, 199, 204, 212; humor and, 188, 192, 202; identities, 185; influence of W.S. Gilbert, 186-87; internal, 190, 193-94, 204; light, 191; linked, 192; masculine (single), 186; mosaic (composite), 186, 212; near, kinds of, 195-98; nonsense syllables, 208; onomatopoeia, 207; para, 196; perfect, 185, 194, 212, 299, 313; phonetic intensives, 207-08; pop songs and, 193, 196, 197, 204; reason to, 198, 202; schemes (patterns), 198-201, 313; sense and, 206-09; singability of, 206; theater songs and, 186, 193, 212; theories of, 198-206; trailing, 191; tricks, 187-88; trisyllabic

(triple), 186, 312; unstressed, 197; warping words to, 188, 191; when not to, 43, 202-03, 204, 210
Rhythm, 214-42; demo grooves, 229; emotion and, 234-42; equipment, 226; falling, defined, 220-21; humor and, 235, 236, 237; outline, 226-27; rising, defined, 219; "rhythmic" leadsheet, 260; tracks, 225; varying the, 218-24. *See also* End-stopped line; Run-on line
Rhythm and Blues (R&B) 79, 223, 258
Run-on line, 220-21, 253

Sally, 187
Sandpiper, The, 250
Sarcasm, 170, 270
Satire, 173
Scansion, 216, 217, 308
Scene, the, 21, 22, 113-16
"Scratch" (dry) lyric, 26, 193, 217-29, 222, 224
Script, the, 156
Self-contained writer/performers. *See* Singer/songwriter
Semantic blunders, 279-80
Sequence, 144
SESAC, 319
Setting, the. *See* Scene, the
Setting the tune, 19, 62, 128, 132, 207, 212, 214, 215, 243-53
Shoestring Revue, The, 173
Showboat, 204
Show, don't tell, 43, 154-62, 277. *See also* Specificity
Simile, 167, 273
Simplicity, 125-28, 176
Singee, 23, 51, 89, 101, 107-09, 118; addressing the, 89, 118; definition of, 89; over-particularizing the, 107-09; -singer connection, 101
Singer, listener identification with, 2; put in attractive light, 86, 109, 110, 130, 137; -song fusion, 3, 4-5, 87
Singer/songwriter, 15, 74, 228; broader subject matter of, 108-09; novelty songs and, 13; taboo subjects and, 176; topical subjects and, 12-13

Singsong (rhythm). *See* Meter

Situation (plot), 21, 106-07, 109, 155-56, 172. *See also* Plot development

Slang, 148

Smiles, 214

Snow White, 208

Song sharks, 10

Songs. *See* Circular lyrics; Collaboration; Country songs; Duets; Film songs; Forms; Gospel songs; Ideas for lyrics; Linear lyrics; List songs; Modes of lyrics; Novelty songs; Pitfalls; Plot development; Pop songs; Principles of good writing; Rhythm & Blues; Setting the tune; Story songs; Techno-pop; Theater songs; Themes in songs; Universality; Uptempo/downbeat combo

Songwriters Guild, The, 13, 159, 173, 254, 288, 319

Sorcerer, The, 186

Specificity, 152-62; overdoing, 107-08; show, don't tell, 43, 155-62. *See also* Bluntness; Imagery; Verbs

Spondee, 234, 236, 239

Standards, 4, 30, 315

Stanza (verse), 35

Story songs (examples), 38-40, 51-53, 122-24, 157-62

Strophic form, 32

Structure Sound and Meaning (La Driere), 206

Sunday in the Park With George, A, 92, 182, 234

Structures. *See* Forms

Suspense plot, 25

Suspension of disbelief, 84, 86

Sweeney Todd, 208

Symbol, 40, 156

Symbolism, 169

Synchronicity, 72

Synecdoche, 168, 169

Syntax, 291

Taboo words, 174-76

Techno-pop records, 30, 223-30

"Telegraphing" (rhyme), 199-200. *See also* Rhyme schemes

Tension, 24

Theater songs, 23, 38, 72, 88, 93, 170, 172, 173, 177, 184, 193, 212. *See also* Lyricists; Rhyme

Theme words, 154

Themes in songs: breakup, 87, 171, 245; cheating, 177; dependence, 305; inspirational, 3, 88; love, 3, 305; obsession, 305; patriotic, 3; seasonal, 3; sex, 305; social, 90, 99, 105; torch songs, 245; x-rated, 15

Thespis, 195

Time frame, 11-16, 21, 112-13, 127, 161. *See also* Pitfalls

Tin Pan Alley, 10, 194, 221

Titles, 15-20, 122; copyright and, 17; framing of, 40; "Hook," 19, 49; one-word, 18, 56, 75; placement of, in AAA, 34; placement of, in AABA, 63; placement of, in Verse/chorus, 48; poor, example of, 307; previewing the, 50; repetition of, 20, 49, 63; reserving the, 50, 56; spotting the, in a tune, 63, 248

Tone of voice, 94-98. *See also* Pitfalls

Tony Award, 10, 170, 178

Trochee, 233

Turnaround plot, 24

Twist plot, 24

Understatement, 171-72, 180, 247; in comedy, 180, 184, 247; poignant effects through, 92, 171, 172, 300. *See also* Bluntness; Directness; Irony; Overstatement

Unity, 82, 112, 124, 158. *See also* Consistency; Proportion

Universality, 2-5, 86, 99-109, 137, 204; attaining, 99, 102-104; roadblocks to, 104-10, 266-70, 280-82, 303-05

Uptempo/downbeat combo, 246

Verbs, 98, 134, 153; active, 134; specific, 153, 154, 158, 161; tense of, 113-15, 125

Verse/chorus form, 26, 30, 31, 45-60, 140; diagrams of, 47, 52, 55, 59-60

Verses, 30, 31, 35, 53, 60; in AAA form, 35; in AABA form, 30; introductory in AABA songs, 61; in Verse/chorus form, 53, 60